Analyzing the Curriculum

Analyzing the Curriculum

THIRD EDITION

George J. Posner
Cornell University

Boston   Burr Ridge, IL   Dubuque, IA   Madison, WI   New York
San Francisco   St. Louis   Bangkok   Bogotá   Caracas   Kuala Lumpur
Lisbon   London   Madrid   Mexico City   Milan   Montreal   New Delhi
Santiago   Seoul   Singapore   Sydney   Taipei   Toronto

Higher Education

ANALYZING THE CURRICULUM THIRD EDITION

Published by McGraw-Hill, a business unit of The McGraw-Hill Companies, Inc., 1221 Avenue of the Americas, New York, NY 10020. Copyright © 2004, 1995, 1992 by The McGraw-Hill Companies, Inc. All rights reserved. No part of this publication may be reproduced or distributed in any form or by any means, or stored in a database or retrieval system, without the prior written consent of The McGraw-Hill Companies, Inc., including, but not limited to, in any network or other electronic storage or transmission, or broadcast for distance learning.

Some ancillaries, including electronic and print components, may not be available to customers outside the United States.

This book is printed on acid-free paper..

6 7 8 9 0 DOC/DOC 0 9 8 7

ISBN-13: 978-0-07-282327-1
ISBN-10: 0-07-282327-5

Vice president and editor-in-chief: *Thalia Dorwick*
Publisher: *Jane E. Karpacz*
Developmental editor: *Cara Harvey*
Senior marketing manager: *Pamela S. Cooper*
Senior project manager: *Marilyn Rothenberger*
Production supervisor: *Enboge Chong*
Manager, Design: *Laurie Entninger*
Associate designer: *George Kokkonas*
Cover/interior designer: George Kokkonas
Cover image: ***Clear Connection*** by Wassily Kandinsky, *Corbis images*
Director, Art : *Jeanne M. Schreiber*
Manager, Art: *Robin Mouat*
Photo research coordinator: *Alexandra Ambose*
Senior supplement producer: *David A. Welsh*
Compositor: *Thompson Type*
Typeface: 10/12 *Palatino*
Printer: *R. R. Donnelley/Crawfordsville, IN*

The credits section for this book begins on page C-1 and is considered an extension of the copyright page.

Library of Congress Cataloging-in-Publication Data
Posner, George J.
    Analyzing the curriculum / Georger J. Posner. —3rd ed.
        p. cm.
    ISBN 0-07-282327-5
1. Education—United States—Curricula. 2. Curriculum evaluation—United States. I. Title

LB1570.P643 2004
375′.00973—dc21

2003050986

www.mhhe.com

About the Author

DR. GEORGE J. POSNER is Professor Emeritus at Cornell University. He has a B.S. in psychology (Union College, 1965), a masters degree in physics teaching (Union College, 1970), and a doctorate in curriculum (University at Albany, 1972). For more than thirty-five years he has been teaching and advising youth and has been active as a teacher educator. For thirty-one years, as a faculty member at Cornell, he served as both Coordinator of Undergraduate Studies in Education and Coordinator of the Graduate Program in Curriculum and Instruction and received awards for his teaching. He was alos the principal author of more than thirty articles on teaching and curriculum and a consultant to schools, universities, foundations, and states throughout the country and in several countries abroad on matters of curriculum, teaching, and teacher education. He is also the author of *Course Design: A Guide to Curriculum Development for Teachers* (Addison Wesley Longman), now in its sixth edition, and *Field Experience: A Guide to Reflective Teaching* (Addison Wesley Longman), now in its fifth edition. In addition, Dr. Posner has served as a member of the Board of Education, Ithaca City School District (Ithaca, New York) and as a teacher at The Albany Academy. Since his retirement from Cornell, Dr. Posner has become a Certified Educational Planner and founded Educational Consulting Services *(www.gposner.com)*, helping families with private educational placements. He is married to his wife, Adrienne, and has two married daughters, one a veterinarian in Rochester, NY, the other, a special education teacher in New York City.

Contents in Brief

Part III
THE CURRICULUM IN USE

Part IV
CURRICULUM CRITIQUE

Contents

Part I
CURRICULUM DOCUMENTATION AND ORIGINS

Part II
THE CURRICULUM PROPER

Part III
THE CURRICULUM IN USE

Part IV
CURRICULUM CRITIQUE

List of Figures

List of Tables

Preface

An Introduction to the Text

Analyzing the Curriculum grew out of a series of attempts to offer a basic course in curriculum for undergraduate and graduate students who were either preparing for teaching and administrative positions or seeking to build on previous professional experiences. These professionals and preprofessionals had a reasonable set of expectations. They all wanted a course that not only would give them a solid theoretical introduction to curriculum but also would show them how they could use that knowledge. Many existing texts either failed to provide the kind of introduction to the foundational aspects of the curriculum literature that was needed, or failed to show the practical application of those valuable ideas. Therefore, I found myself in the position of gradually developing materials for the course. Over a twelve-year period, these course materials matured to the point that they seemed to have the potential for a text in their own right. Four additional years of writing finally produced this text.

As a primary text, *Analyzing the Curriculum* can provide the backbone for a basic curriculum course. In such a case, the selection of readings that augment the text could determine the level of the course—that is, whether it is intended primarily for undergraduate or for graduate students. I use the book this way with beginning graduate students. As a supplemental text, *Analyzing the Curriculum* could be used alongside a more comprehensive text as a means of helping students apply their knowledge to a particular case study. Lately, I have also been using the book in a required seminar in our teacher education program either during or immediately following student teaching. The purpose of this seminar is to encourage our students to reflect on their student teaching by examining their experience in the context of the curriculum they were teaching.

The book offers students many benefits. They learn how the parts of a curriculum fit together and how to identify assumptions underlying curricula. In so doing, they develop the ability to determine why a curriculum proves better for some students than for others; what approaches to teaching are compatible with a particular curriculum; what difficulties a curriculum is likely to encounter during implementation; and what kinds of changes in the curriculum parents, students, and administrators are likely to demand. These are valuable skills for evaluating, selecting, and adapting existing programs to suit particular situations.

Coverage and Organization

Discussion of five theoretical perspectives is woven throughout the book. An understanding of the conceptual underpinnings of these five perspectives, each of which has influenced a great deal of curriculum development in the United States and other countries, is conceived of as a set of lenses for viewing a set of mainstream curriculum topics: curriculum purpose and content, curriculum organization, curriculum implementation, and evaluation. The perspectives allow students to examine each of these from divergent viewpoints in order to expose the assumptions that underlie decisions in each area.

The book is organized into four parts. Part I provides the foundation for the book and for the curriculum analysis project to which students apply what they learn. It presents definitions of basic terminology, key concepts, basic elements of a curriculum document, and the general parameters of curriculum analysis. Then Part I helps the student unravel the story behind the development of a curriculum and presents five contrasting theoretical perspectives on curriculum. Part II concerns curriculum purposes, content, and organization. It includes a discussion of educational aims, goals, and objectives, and a comparison of behavioral and constructivist approaches to objectives. It also discusses curriculum organization: basic concepts are introduced, and a comparison of three conflicting perspectives is offered—in this case, a top-down, a bottom-up, and a project-centered approach to curriculum organization. Part III concerns the curriculum as it is actually used. The first half of this part considers the topic of curriculum implementation as a process of curriculum change. It describes the various physical, organizational, political-legal, personal, cultural, and economic resources and constraints within which any curriculum must function. Then it presents two alternative approaches to curriculum change, the research, development, and dissemination (RD&D) and the collaborative approach. The second half of Part III focuses on curriculum evaluation, presenting basic concepts and then contrasting a measurement-based with an integrated approach. Part IV looks back at the analysis of the previous three parts and asks the student to assess the strengths and limitations of the particular curriculum under examination.

Each of these parts provides concepts and perspectives that you can employ to analyze a curriculum of your own choosing. In order to help you learn to apply these ideas to a specific curriculum, the book uses two features. First, each chapter concludes with a set of curriculum analysis questions. Second each part provides examples and case studies to illustrate how the concepts and perspectives are manifested in actual curricula. This feature also has the benefit of exposing you to several noteworthy nationally known curricula, including Whole Language, the Individually Prescribed Instruction curriculum for elementary mathematics, Man: A Course of Study, Reading Recovery, PSSC Physics, Foxfire, Science: A Process Approach, ChemCom, and Distar.

One of the problems in writing a curriculum text is the almost unlimited scope of the field. Special care has been taken not to omit significant topics not directly related to curriculum analysis. Some important aspects of curriculum study that would otherwise be omitted are infused into other chapters. For example, although no chapter is devoted solely to the history of the field, nearly every chapter provides historical background for its major topics. Similarly, although no chapter is devoted solely to a critical perspective, each part of the book considers the topics under study from a critical viewpoint.

The second edition expanded and updated the first edition in several significant ways. A separate section on authentic assessment was added to Chapter 11. Current trends in curriculum, such as curriculum alignment, outcomes based education (OBE), and constructivism were made more explicit. A discussion of curricula for youth at-risk was added to Chapter 7.

New Coverage

The third edition substantially updates and expands previous editions in several important ways. First, as the standards movement has gained momentum, its influence on curriculum content and evaluation has significantly increased. Similarly, technology (especially electronic technology) has also affected what is taught, how it is taught, and how students are tested. This edition includes special sections describing these two movements and helps the reader examine their impacts on curriculum. Second, issues of diversity, including multicultural curriculum; tracking; and gender and racial equity are treated more explicitly with separate sections throughout the book. Third, although constructivism was discussed in the second edition, the third edition goes much further, including constructivism as one of the five basic perspectives, replacing the nearly identical cognitive perspective. Finally, the work of Howard Gardner and several newer influential curricula, including Saxon math, Success for All, and Everyday Math are discussed. Of course, the references have been updated accordingly.

Acknowledgments

The writer of a text such as this owes a debt of gratitude to many people. There were those colleagues who graciously contributed to the work by writing pieces for it or by critiquing it and offering valuable suggestions. These colleagues include William Schubert, George Willis, Margaret McCasland, Pamela Moss, Helena Spring, Decker Walker, Ed Short, Gerry Ponder, Ken Strike, and Phil Smith. This third edition has also benefited from the work of Don Duggan-Haas on both standards and technology and the work of Nancy Zimmet on multicultural education, tracking, and issues of equity in testing. Colleagues who unknowingly but substantially contributed to the work through the ideas I found in their published writings include Peter Johnston, Ernest House, J. Myron Atkin, Michael

Apple, Mauritz Johnston, Bernard Baars, Robert Zais, Dorothy Nelkin, and Lawrence Cremin. Students who took my basic curriculum course, Curriculum Theory and Analysis, over the past twenty-six years have supplied more ideas than they will ever know. More important, they taught me that I can only write when I teach and only teach when I write. Thank you to the professors who provided feedback on the revision plan for the third edition: Eugene Bartoo, University of Tennessee, Chattanooga; W. F. Benjamin, University of South Florida; Anne Cox-Petersen, California State University, Fullerton; Charles W. Elliott, Jr., Bridgewater State University; Jill Beloff Farrell, Barry University; Stacey E. Marlow, University of Hawaii at Manoa; Judith Harmon Miller, Castleton State College; Angela Spaulding, West Texas A&M University; Dorothy E. Williams, Our Lady of the Lake University. Lane Akers, my friend and former publisher believed in this work from the outset, took risks with it, and was a constant source of encouragement and professional guidance whenever the project seemed impossible. I wish to thank my former secretary, Berni Oltz, for her patience and editorial help. Last, and most of all, I wish to express my gratitude to my wife, Adrienne, who read virtually every line of this book and offered the kind of criticism only an artist can offer. In spite of these many contributions, I accept responsibility for any shortcomings of this work.

George J. Posner

Analyzing the Curriculum

Curriculum Documentation and Origins

Part One of this text explores the many important reasons for curriculum study, and proposes the analysis of a particular curriculum as an effective way to direct this study. The term "curriculum" means many different things to different people, and curricula take many different forms. We attempt to sort out all these diverse elements so that you know what kinds of documentation to expect when choosing a curriculum for analysis. We begin the actual analysis of a particular curriculum by examining the curriculum's origins and the reasons behind its development. Finally, we explore five theoretical perspectives on curriculum that have influenced educational practice during the past century and continue to dominate debate on the subject.

CHAPTER I

Concepts of Curriculum and Purposes of Curriculum Study

Why engage in curriculum study? What good does it do?
What is a curriculum? For example, is a textbook or a syllabus a curriculum?
What should a curriculum include?

As you begin curriculum study, these questions are important to answer. It is important to know what the benefits of curriculum study are and to recognize a curriculum when you see one. These questions are especially important to address at the beginning of this book because of one major assumption on which this book is based: that the study of curriculum in general ultimately requires an in-depth examination of a particular curriculum. Therefore, the book takes you through one approach to the study of curriculum: the process of curriculum analysis. In this chapter, you will learn what curriculum analysis is, why it is important to do, and how to go about it.

Before we can get to questions about curriculum analysis, we have to address questions about the purpose of curriculum study and what a curriculum is.

CURRICULUM STUDY

I make every effort to teach my courses on curriculum in a nondoctrinaire manner, believing that students should be exposed to various perspectives on education. This approach has always seemed the fairest and most exciting way to teach about a topic with a diverse body of literature like curriculum. Recently, a graduate student named Peter came to my class, told me he was very frustrated, and then said this to me: "I'm totally confused! I came to Cornell to find out how to make curriculum decisions, and all I am learning is that different experts have different answers to basic questions. Now I have more problems than when I started. What are we supposed to do when the so-called experts disagree?"

My initial response to Peter was that he was discovering something inherent in the field of curriculum—and something inescapable about education, for that matter—that others share his frustration, and that he would have to learn to deal with this lack of absolute certainty if he planned to continue with his graduate studies. I then pointed out to Peter that in certain, limited ways, the development of standards represents a movement toward consensus about what it is that students should learn. The development of standards in each subject required a range of experts—academic specialists (i.e., historians), educational researchers (generally also academics), and teachers in the respective disciplines. The writers of the standards tended to agree that curriculum as commonly configured in American schools is "an inch deep and a mile wide." This phrase is the drumbeat of the Third International Mathematics and Science Study (Schmidt, 2001; Schmidt, McKnight, & Raizen, 1997), and this idea and the closely related idea that "less is more" (Sizer, 1982) is a common theme in standards across many subjects. I asked Peter if the standards movement satisfied him. He correctly pointed out that agreement on what students need to learn is not necessarily the same as agreement on curriculum, and even this agreement is woefully incomplete.

After reflecting on Peter's question and my answer at some length, I began to realize how important his question is and how inadequate my response was. What should we do once we realize that the experts in our field are in fundamental disagreement? It seems to me that, faced with this realization, many students in the field choose from three options:

1. Ignore all experts and just use one's own common sense.
2. Follow one authority's ideas.
3. Borrow from all experts as long as their ideas "work."

As reasonable as each of these options appears, each is fraught with danger. Ignoring all experts, one runs the risk of seat-of-the-pants decision making. If one follows only one expert, the risks are cultism and "tunnel vision" (Schwab, 1969). Borrowing uncritically from all experts can lead to "garbage-can" eclecticism, in which practices based on contradictory or invalid assumptions are collected into a "bag of tricks."

I decided that in my answer to Peter's question I must avoid all these dangers, but still express a posture that can lead to decisive action. The only viable answer I could find is one that includes the idea of reflective eclecticism.

Reflective eclecticism is based on the assumption that, much as we would like to deny it, there is no panacea in education. People who are looking for "the answer" to our educational problems are looking in vain. Different situations require different practices. The curriculum "cultists" make a fundamental error in assuming that they have the answer to any problem, regardless of the particulars of the situation. What curriculum decision makers need is an understanding of the myriad curriculum alternatives. But to avoid the trap of garbage-can eclecticism, they should understand the dilemmas that underlie each curriculum decision and be able to unpack the tacit assumptions behind each alternative. When they can do this, they will have gained the ability to assess critically the alternatives and the claims their proponents make (Schwab, 1971). It is reflective eclecticism that is at the heart of curriculum study, as I conceive it, and therefore at the heart of this book. Shortly, we will address the ways in which curriculum analysis contributes to the development of reflective eclecticism. But first we need to clarify a key concept: curriculum.

THE MEANING OF "CURRICULUM"

Since the purpose of this book is to enable you to analyze a curriculum, we will need to be as clear as possible about what a curriculum is. As we will see, this is no simple matter.

Definitions of "Curriculum"

What do people mean when they use the term "curriculum"? Some claim that a curriculum is the content, standards, or objectives for which schools hold students accountable. Others claim that a curriculum is the set of instructional strategies teachers plan to use. These conceptual differences are based on a distinction between a curriculum as the expected *ends* of education, e.g., the intended learning outcomes, and curriculum as the expected *means* of education, i.e., instructional plans.[1] Others argue that plans, whether for ends or means, are insignificant when compared with actual learnings and actual instructional methods. Curriculum for these people is most productively conceived as the students' actual rather than planned opportunities, experiences, or learnings. Thus, there are fundamental differences between people's conceptions of curriculum, focusing on curriculum as means or ends and curriculum as a plan for or a report of actual educational events.

Why not just stipulate a definition and then adhere to it? The problem with this common approach to the definition of this central concept is that definitions are not philosophically or politically neutral. A clear conceptual distinction between the ends and the means of education leads to consequences with political and ethical implications. For example, this distinction supports the view that certain kinds of decisions—e.g., about ends—require certain kinds of expertise and authority in contrast to other kinds of decisions—i.e., about means—and that some people—e.g., teachers—have one kind of expertise but not another.

The distinction between ends and means is also a matter of dispute for pragmatic philosophers, among others. They argue that it is impossible to decide on ends independently of means and that intended outcomes are fully understood only in retrospect or as teaching unfolds: How does a teacher really know what she is trying to achieve except as she actually teaches?

Similarly, when we focus our concept of curriculum on educational plans, standards, and intended outcomes, we are taking a political stand. While this focus does not require that we take a hard line on holding teachers accountable, it does support efforts of this sort by administrators. Once we legitimize the idea of formulating plans for teaching and for students' learning outcomes, we have also established the rationale for holding teachers accountable both for the effectiveness of their plans and for the implementation of curricula in a predetermined manner.

With these thoughts in mind we examine some common concepts of curriculum.

1. *Scope and sequence* A school's or department's *scope and sequence* typically embodies a concept of curriculum as a set or series of intended learning outcomes. A scope and sequence document is a document listing the intended learning outcomes in each grade level, thereby giving the sequence of the curriculum; the outcomes are grouped according to topic, theme, or dimension, thereby giving the scope of the curriculum. (See Figure 1.1.) This concept assumes that there is a clear distinction between educational ends and means, restricting the concept of curriculum to educational plans rather than including actualities. By distinguishing curriculum from instruction, this concept places curriculum in the role of guiding both instructional and evaluation decisions.

2. *Syllabus* The *syllabus* is a plan for an entire course. The plan typically includes the goals and/or rationale for the course, topics covered, resources used, assignments given, and evaluation strategies recommended. Occasionally syllabi might also include learning objectives, learning activities, and study questions. Thus, the syllabus represents the plan for a course, elements of both the ends and the means of the course. (See Figure 1.2.)

3. *Content outline* Equating curriculum with a *content outline* assumes that the content of instruction is equivalent to a curriculum plan. When the sole purpose of education is to transmit information and teaching consists of covering content, such a definition may suffice. However, when education and teaching have other purposes, then the content outline leaves unanswered questions of objectives, not to mention instructional method. Nevertheless, many people, when asked for their curriculum, provide a content outline. (See Figure 1.3.)

4. *Standards* The authors of standards note that a set of standards, like a content outline, is not a curriculum. Standards, however, are also more than a content outline and different from a scope and sequence. Standards often describe what students should be able to do and, in some cases, describe processes towards achieving the learning outcomes. Unlike a scope and sequence, however, standards do not prescribe specific teaching activities. Standards do prioritize what ideas are fundamental to the discipline and how key ideas are interconnected. They also cover the grades from kindergarten through twelfth grade and thus can lay the groundwork for a course of study or a scope and sequence. Standards include more about the nature of the discipline and how both specialists and laypeople (often alluding to citizenship duties) use the discipline than other concepts of curriculum typically do, and they include themes that cut across the topics of a curriculum. Further, standards are uniformly addressed to *all* students. (See Figure 1.4.)

5. *Textbooks* The ubiquitous textbook, for teachers who teach "by the book," functions as a day-to-day guide, that is, as a guide to both the ends and the means of instruction. Traditional texts present the content, without much guidance as to what is important to learn or on how to teach. Contemporary

Grade/Strand	1	2	3	4	5
	Physical Health, Nutrition, and Disease Prevention	Sociological Health Problems	Family Life and Emotional Health	Environmental, Community, and Consumer Health	Education for Survival
K	Health habits; Food variety; Senses; Care of teeth–Personal; Feelings–well/sick	Uniqueness of self/Choices; Safe and unsafe substances; Smoking effects on self; Kinds of alcohol	Feeling special/Friends; Family lifestyles; Living and nonliving things; Body parts/Parent communication; Privacy/touch; Trusting feelings/Saying no	Self environment; School health and safety helpers; Personal health products and services	Fire drill (home and school); Safety rules (swimming and boating); Pedestrian rules; Bus safety rules; Bicycle safety rules; Safe habits and behaviors/Address and phone number; Playground and classroom rules; Appropriate clothing; Wounds (clean and cover)/Seeking help
1	Growth; Four basic food groups; Body parts; Primary and secondary teeth; Cause and spread of disease	Variety of feelings/Decisions and consequences; Proper use of drugs; Smoking effects on senses; Effects of alcohol	Expressing feelings/Handicaps; Family members; Functions of living things; Questions about sexuality; Victim/Offender; Confusing touch/Support systems	Community environment; Community health and safety helpers; Factors that influence choices	Fire drill (home and school); Safety rules (swimming and boating); Safety problems; Bus safety rules; Bicycle safety rules; Safe habits and behaviors/Address, phone number, parents' place of employment; Playground and classroom rules; Appropriate shelter.

FIGURE 1.1 The K-1 portion of a scope and sequence chart for a health curriculum.

UNIT 3 A Nation Is Created

UNIT GOALS <u>By the end of this unit, the student will be able to:</u>

1. describe and analyze major historical factors in the early development of the United States

2. demonstrate an understanding of the historic, economic, social, and political roots of American culture

3. discuss the nature and effects of change on societies and individuals

I. BACKGROUND CAUSES OF THE AMERICAN REVOLUTION

<u>Objective:</u>

To understand the economic, political, and social causes of the American Revolution

Content Outline:	Major Ideas:	Model Activities:
A. Economic Factors 1. Growth of mercantilism 2. Rise of an influential business community in the colonies 3. Cost of colonial wars against the French	Many colonial business people resented the lack of opportunity to compete fairly with their British counterparts.	European economic, political, and social structures were shaken up frequently from the mid-1600s to mid-1700s. The teacher should review some of these events with students, pointing out that the strategies these countries developed to cope with internal and international problems directly affected their American colonies.
B. Political Factors 1. The role of the British Civil War 2. Periods of political freedom in the colonies 3. Impact of the French and Indian War: Albany Plan of Union 4. Political thought of the Enlightenment influenced prominent colonial leaders	Ongoing changes affected the relationship between the British government and its American colonies. Political participation Political choices helped many individuals to form an identity.	Several topics that could be examined include: – The role of the Netherlands as an international trader; the impact of its war with Britain. – France's role in European affairs; how that role helped keep alive its conflict with Britain; how that conflict periodically spilled over into the American colonies. – Reasons why Britain had a civil war and how that war led it to pay less attention to its American colonies.
C. New Social Relationships between European Powers and the American Colonies: Development of a New Colonial Identity		– Spain's political problems and the effect those problems had on that country's ability to maintain its American empire.

Unit 3

FIGURE 1.2 A page from a syllabus.
(*From* Social Studies 7-8: United States and New York State History, *The State Education Department, Bureau of Curriculum Development, Albany, NY, 1987*).

I. Cultural, Aesthetic, and Historical
   Aspects of Clothing and Textiles

   A. Culture, history, and fashion cycles
      1. Theories of dress
      2. Origins of clothing
   B. Agents of fashion change
      1. Historical events
      2. Cultural events
   C. Relationships of fashion to
      art movements
      1. Art movements
         (1700–1850)
         a. Romanticism
         b. Neoclassicism
         c. Eclecticism
      2. Art movements
         (1850–1960)
         a. Functionalism
         b. Art nouveau
         c. Pop art

II. Clothing Decisions, Values, and
    Personal Appearance

    A. Clothing symbolism
       1. Clothing as a form of
          nonverbal communication
       2. Clothing and self-concept
    B. Clothing as an expression of values
       1. Decision making
       2. Personal values
       3. Self-expression
       4. Prestige, peer pressure,
          and economy

III. Clothing Design

     A. Elements of design
        1. Line
        2. Space
        3. Form
        4. Color
        5. Texture
     B. Principles of design
        1. Rhythm
        2. Balance
        3. Emphasis
        4. Proportion

IV. Fibers and Fabrics: Wearable Art

    A. Fiber types
    B. Fabrics—yarn and weaves
       1. Classification of weaves
       2. Methods of coloring
          a. Dyeing
          b. Printing
          c. Applied surface design
       3. Finishes
          a. Aesthetic
          b. Functional

V. Basic Clothing Construction

   A. Equipment and fabric selection
   B. Pattern selection and use
   C. Construction skills
   D. Evaluating ready-made
      garments

VI. Functioning Clothing and Clothing
    for Special Needs

    A. Functional limitations
       1. Physical conditions
       2. Environmental conditions
    B. Clothing for special activities
       1. Industry, careers, space travel
       2. Sports

VII. Selection, Care, Repair, and Redesign
     of Clothing

     A. Selection, care, and repair of
        clothing
     B. Redesigning clothing
        1. Painting and dyeing
        2. Stitching

VIII. Careers in Clothing and Textiles

      A. Career exploration
      B. Student career suitability

FIGURE 1.3 A content outline for a course in clothing and textiles.

The vision guiding these standards is that all students must have the opportunities and resources to develop the language skills they need to pursue life's goals and to participate fully as informed, productive members of society. These standards assume that literacy growth begins before children enter school as they experience and experiment with literacy activities—reading and writing, and associating spoken words with their graphic representations. Recognizing this fact, these standards encourage the development of curriculum and instruction that make productive use of the emerging literacy abilities that children bring to school. Furthermore, the standards provide ample room for the innovation and creativity essential to teaching and learning. They are not prescriptions for particular curriculum or instruction. Although we present these standards as a list, we want to emphasize that they are not distinct and separable; they are, in fact, interrelated and should be considered as a whole.

1. Students read a wide range of print and non-print texts to build an understanding of texts, of themselves, and of the cultures of the United States and the world; to acquire new information; to respond to the needs and demands of society and the workplace; and for personal fulfillment. Among these texts are fiction and nonfiction, classic and contemporary works.

2. Students read a wide range of literature from many periods in many genres to build an understanding of the many dimensions (e.g., philosophical, ethical, aesthetic) of human experience

3. Students apply a wide range of strategies to comprehend, interpret, evaluate, and appreciate texts. They draw on their prior experience, their interactions with other readers and writers, their knowledge of word meaning and of other texts, their word identification strategies, and their understanding of textual features (e.g., sound-letter correspondence, sentence structure, context, graphics).

4. Students adjust their use of spoken, written, and visual language (e.g., conventions, style, vocabulary) to communicate effectively with a variety of audiences and for different purposes.

5. Students employ a wide range of strategies as they write and use different writing process elements appropriately to communicate with different audiences for a variety of purposes.

6. Students apply knowledge of language structure, language conventions (e.g., spelling and punctuation), media techniques, figurative language, and genre to create, critique, and discuss print and non-print texts.

7. Students conduct research on issues and interests by generating ideas and questions, and by posing problems. They gather, evaluate, and synthesize data from a variety of sources (e.g., print and non-print texts, artifacts, people) to communicate their discoveries in ways that suit their purpose and audience.

8. Students use a variety of technological and information resources (e.g., libraries, databases, computer networks, video) to gather and synthesize information and to create and communicate knowledge.

9. Students develop an understanding of and respect for diversity in language use, patterns, and dialects across cultures, ethnic groups, geographic regions, and social roles.

10. Students whose first language is not English make use of their first language to develop competency in the English language arts and to develop understanding of content across the curriculum.

11. Students participate as knowledgeable, reflective, creative, and critical members of a variety of literacy communities.

12. Students use spoken, written, and visual language to accomplish their own purposes (e.g., for learning, enjoyment, persuasion, and the exchange of information).

FIGURE 1.4 Standards for the English Language Arts
(National Council of Teachers of English & the International Reading Association, 1996)

FIGURE 1.5 An instructional system.

texts are more appropriately described as instructional systems. They include teacher guides, student study guides or workbooks, tests, overhead projection masters, laboratory kits, and supplementary instructional materials. (See Figure 1.5.)

6. *Course of study* Both the derivation (from the Latin *currere*, meaning "the running") and the typical dictionary definition of the word "curriculum," "a course of study" or "set of courses," lead to a view of curriculum as a series of courses that the student must get through. This view provides a basis for one of the major metaphors that dominate thought in this field: the travel metaphor. According to this metaphor, education is a journey with an intended destination. We will discuss this and other metaphors shortly.

7. *Planned experiences* Many progressive educators[2] contend that the curriculum is more than a set of documents. These educators argue that rather than being a description of student learning, whether intended or unintended, or content covered—whether decided by the state, district, textbook, or teacher—curriculum comprises all the experiences of the students planned by the school. In other words, the experiences that coaches, yearbook advisors, drama teachers, band leaders, study hall teachers, assembly speakers, school nurses, and disciplinarians plan for students are as much

TABLE 1.1. Seven Common Concepts of Curriculum

1. *Scope and sequence* The depiction of curriculum as a matrix of objectives assigned to successive grade levels (i.e., sequence) and grouped according to a common theme (i.e., scope).

2. *Syllabus* A plan for an entire course, typically including rationale, topics, resources, and evaluation.

3. *Content outline* A list of topics covered organized in outline form.

4. *Standards* A list of knowledge and skills required by all students upon completion.

5. *Textbooks* Instructional materials used as the guide for classroom instruction.

6. *Course of study* A series of courses that the student must complete.

7. *Planned experiences* All experiences students have that are planned by the school, whether academic, athletic, emotional, or social.

a part of the curriculum as science, math, social studies, and English classes. Those who favor this concept reject the distinction between curricular and extracurricular activities discussed later in this chapter.

Each of these seven definitions (see Table 1.1) has different consequences in terms of accountability. When a school board states that a school district's curriculum consists of a particular set of standards, it is saying that the school board expects teachers in that district to teach in such a way as to achieve those standards. The board then is holding teachers accountable for outcomes but not for methods. When a board specifies a particular textbook or textbook series, the board is expressing an expectation that teachers will follow that text. Thus, the more specific the definition of curriculum, the more control the definition implies. Of course, when we define curriculum as a report of actual experiences or learnings rather than as plans, intentions, or expectations, we entirely eliminate the controlling function of the curriculum. We cannot hold teachers or students accountable for undetermined and unspecified notions of educational quality. As we noted earlier, no definition of curriculum is ethically or politically neutral. Different definitions lead to different conclusions about who should prescribe and control various aspects of education.

The Five Concurrent Curricula

Until now we have talked about the term "curriculum" as though it were possible to get at its real meaning, as though there is one thing we can consider to be the curriculum. Actually, we have not one but five concurrent curricula to consider: the official, the operational, the hidden, the null, and the extra curriculum.

The *official curriculum*, or written curriculum, is documented in scope and sequence charts, syllabi, curriculum guides, course outlines, standards, and lists of objectives. Its purpose is to give teachers a basis for planning lessons and evaluating students, and administrators a basis for supervising teachers and holding them accountable for their practices and results.

The *operational curriculum* consists of what is actually taught by the teacher and how its importance is communicated to the student—i.e., how students know that it "counts." That is, operational curriculum has two aspects: (1) the content included and emphasized by the teacher in class, i.e., what the teacher teaches, and (2) the learning outcomes or standards for which students are actually held responsible, i.e., what counts. The former is indicated by time allocated to different topics and types of learning by teachers, i.e., the taught curriculum; the latter is indicated by the tests given to students, i.e., the tested curriculum. Both the taught and the tested curricula are aspects of the operational curriculum, irrespective of their consistency with the official curriculum. As a matter of fact, there is typically little consistency between the official, the taught, and the tested curricula of a school. Management specialists in curriculum consider this situation to be a problem of "curriculum alignment" and tend to deal with the problem administratively (see, for example, Glatthorn, 1987, chap. 11). The operational curriculum may differ sharply from the official curriculum because teachers tend to interpret it in the light of their own knowledge, beliefs, and attitudes. Furthermore, as Powell, Farrar, and Cohen (1985) and Sedlak, Wheeler, Pullin, and Cusick (1986) argue, students strongly influence the operational curriculum. For example, students make informal agreements with teachers not to cause them trouble if they do not cause the students trouble. By making such agreements, these researchers claim, the teachers bargain away the substance of the official curriculum. They transform meaningful, challenging tasks into routine, risk-free tasks and turn the learning of critical thinking into the memorization of facts and the performance of mindless skills.

The *hidden curriculum* is not generally acknowledged by school officials but may have a deeper and more durable impact on students than either the official or the operational curriculum. Schools are institutions and as such embody a set of norms and values.[3] The messages of the hidden curriculum concern issues of gender, class and race, authority, and school knowledge, among others. The lessons that the hidden curriculum teaches include lessons about sex roles, "appropriate" behavior for young people, the distinction between work and play, which children can succeed at various kinds of tasks, who has the right to make decisions for whom, and what kinds of knowledge are considered legitimate (Giroux & Purpel, 1983).

The *null curriculum* (Eisner, 1994) consists of those subject matters *not* taught, and any consideration of it must focus on *why* these subjects are ignored. Why is it the case, for example, that psychology, dance, law, and parenting are typically not taught and certainly could not compete with the "big four"—that is, with English, social studies, math, and science? Cross-cultural differences in the null curriculum are useful for helping us become aware of the assumptions underlying the curriculum of U.S. schools.

The *extra curriculum* comprises all those planned experiences outside of the school subjects. It contrasts with the official curriculum by virtue of its voluntary nature and its responsiveness to student interests. It is not hidden, but an openly acknowledged dimension of the school experience. Although seemingly less important than the official curriculum, in many ways it is more significant. Consider the lessons about competition, "good sportsmanship," and team play learned on the playing field. Also consider the power and influence of most schools' athletic directors. Significant issues illustrating the political dimension of the extra curriculum include the way the opportunities of the extra curriculum are distributed among students (i.e., which segments of the school population participate) and the extent to which the extra curriculum supports and competes for time with the official curriculum—for example, does the drama teacher have to schedule rehearsals around basketball practice or vice versa?

All five curricula (see Table 1.2) contribute significantly to the education of students. However, what is most important for you to realize now is that as you analyze an official curriculum document, you will need to continually ask yourself how the other four curricula affect this piece of the official curriculum. What is likely to happen to it when it is implemented in schools with powerful hidden and extra curricula? Will it capture the attention of teachers and administrators as a regular part of the official curriculum, or will they push it aside along with other parts of the null curriculum? How vulnerable is it likely to be once teachers and students begin negotiating the operational curriculum? Will its essence be lost as a consequence of the bargains that are struck?

A CURRICULUM FRAMEWORK

A curriculum analysis is an attempt to tease a curriculum apart into its component parts, to examine those parts and the way they fit together to make a whole, to identify the beliefs and ideas to which the developers were committed and which either explicitly or implicitly shaped the curriculum, and to examine the implications of these commitments and beliefs for the quality of the educational experience. For the purposes of this book, a curriculum analysis takes the form of a set of answers to questions designed to help the reader identify these commitments and their implications. In order to analyze a curriculum we will need a framework for the analysis. Such a framework identifies a set of categories useful for sorting out curriculum decisions, documents, and assumptions.

One framework has, to date, dominated curriculum work. Let us now examine it closely in order to explore its use for curriculum analysis, and, at the same time, understand its underlying assumptions. In this way we will develop a tool but not allow the tool to limit our ability to reflect critically on our work.

TABLE 1.2. Five Concurrent Curricula

1. *Official curriculum* The curriculum described in formal documents.
2. *Operational curriculum* The curriculum embodied in actual teaching practices and tests.
3. *Hidden curriculum* Institutional norms and values not openly acknowledged by teachers or school officials.
4. *Null curriculum* The subject matters *not* taught.
5. *Extra curriculum* The planned experiences outside the formal curriculum.

The dominant framework is best represented in the work of Ralph Tyler. What has come to be called the Tyler Rationale for curriculum planning has been a major influence on curriculum thought since its publication in 1949. It has been interpreted by most educators as a procedure to follow when planning a curriculum; that is, it is an answer to the *procedural* question "What steps does one follow in planning a curriculum?"[4]

Tyler suggests that, when planning a curriculum for a school, four questions need to be answered (see Table 1.3). First, planners need to decide what educational purposes the school should seek to attain. These "objectives" should be derived from systematic studies of the *learners,* from studies of contemporary life in *society,* and from analyses of the *subject matter* by specialists. These three "sources" of objectives are then "screened" through the school's *philosophy* and through knowledge available about the *psychology of learning.* The objectives derived in this way should be specified as precisely and unambiguously as possible, so that evaluation efforts can be undertaken to determine the extent to which the objectives have been attained.

Second, planners need to determine what educational experiences can be provided that are likely to attain these purposes. Possible experiences are checked for consistency with objectives and for economy.

Third, the planner must find ways to effectively organize these educational experiences. The planner attempts to provide experiences that have a cumulative effect on students. Tyler recommends that experiences build on one another and enable learners to understand the relationships between what they learn in various fields. In so doing, attention should be given to the *sequence* of experiences within each field (e.g., mathematics) and to *integration* of knowledge across fields. Certain concepts, skills, and values are sufficiently complex to require repeated study in increasing degrees of sophistication and breadth of application, and sufficiently pervasive to help the student relate one field to another. The planner uses these *organizing elements* to provide the sequence and integration the curriculum requires.

Fourth, the planner needs to determine whether the educational purposes are being attained. Objective evaluation instruments—e.g., tests, work samples, questionnaires, and school records—are developed to check the effectiveness of the curriculum. The criterion for success is behavioral evidence that the objectives of the curriculum have been attained.

The Tyler Rationale, and in particular his four questions regarding the selection of educational purposes, the determination of experiences, the organi-

TABLE 1.3. Tyler's Four Questions

1. What educational purposes should the school seek to attain?
2. What educational experiences can be provided that are likely to attain these purposes?
3. How can these experiences be effectively organized?
4. How can we determine whether these purposes are being attained?

zation of experiences, and the provision for evaluation, has dominated thought on curriculum planning for approximately forty years. Moreover, the publication of the Tyler Rationale represents not the beginning of its influence but, instead, a distillation of ideas derived from the founders of the curriculum field in the first quarter of this century. In fact, Bobbitt's seminal books on curriculum (Bobbitt, 1918, 1924), and in particular their focus on the development of specific objectives based on "scientific" methods, established the basic approach to curriculum planning continued by Tyler.

Since its publication in 1949, educators representing a wide range of orientations have turned to the Tyler Rationale to answer procedural questions of curriculum. Test-oriented behaviorists such as James Popham use it explicitly for the selection of objectives (Popham & Baker, 1970). Course-planning guides, such as those by Posner and Rudnitsky (1994) and by Barnes (1982), use elaborations of the Tyler Rationale as the basis for their handbooks. Even humanistic educators such as Elliot Eisner (1994), who have spent considerable effort criticizing Tyleresque objectives and evaluation approaches, when it comes time to discuss procedure, revert, perhaps unknowingly, to a step-by-step approach that differs only slightly from the Tyler Rationale.

Perhaps the major reason for the Tyler Rationale's dominance is its congruence with our assumptions about both schooling and curriculum planning. Unquestioned acceptance of these assumptions even makes it impossible to conceive of an alternative to this basic approach. Schooling is assumed to be a process whose main purpose is to promote or produce learning. Students are termed "learners"; objectives are conceived in terms of desirable learning; evaluation of the school's success is targeted almost exclusively at achievement test scores; "educational" goals are distinguished from "noneducational" goals by determining if they can be attributed to learning;[5] "curriculum" is defined (not by Tyler but by his followers, such as Goodlad) in terms of "intended learning outcomes" (Goodlad & Richter, 1966). Thus, schooling is conceived as a *production system*, in which individual learning outcomes are the primary product. After all, if learning is not what schooling is for, then what could be its purpose?

Further, curriculum planning is assumed to be an enterprise in which the planner objectively and, if possible, scientifically develops the means necessary to produce the desired learning outcomes. There is no place for personal biases and values in selecting the means; effectiveness and efficiency in accomplishing the ends are primary. This *means-ends reasoning process* serves as the logic underlying all rational decision making. Educational experiences are justified by the objectives that they serve.

The means-ends basis for rationality is taken a step farther when ends serve not only as the primary justification for means but also as the starting point in planning. After all, as this framework rhetorically asks, how can one decide on educational means except by referring to educational ends? The use of a travel metaphor convinces planners that they must determine the destination before deciding on the route they should take and thus causes them to take a *linear* view of means and ends.

Means-ends rationality leads to the assumption that decisions on such issues as instructional method and content are technical ones. Technical decisions are concerned with technique, the how-to aspects of getting a job done. Decisions are considered technical if they appear to be value-free, appropriate for an expert with specialized knowledge to make in an objective manner. According to this view, curriculum decisions are best reserved for people with technical expertise about the methods and content optimally suited for particular objectives. Technical experts are responsible for making certain that their own values do not cloud their objectivity, that is, they try to keep their work value-free. Even decisions about purpose are conceived as technical decisions based on specialized knowledge that experts develop, either from studies of learners and contemporary society or by virtue of their subject matter expertise. After all, who is better equipped to make these decisions than the people with the most knowledge relevant to the decisions? Table 1.4 summarizes these points.

In reality no curriculum decision can be completely technical, completely value-free, since it inevitably concerns an intervention in people's lives. In other words, curriculum decisions are never limited to questions of how to do something; they always involve questions of why to do it and who should do it to whom. A decision to teach certain content, to approach a topic in a certain way, or to have certain teachers teach certain students using certain methods is more than a technical matter. This is because the decision always implies that certain other content, other approaches to the topic, and other ways of treating these students are less desirable, fair, or legitimate. Deciding about the desirability, fairness, or legitimacy of content, of an approach to topics, or of a way to treat students has historical, social, political, moral, cultural, and economic implications.

TABLE 1.4. Technical Production Frameworks

General Features	Meaning of Features	Application to Curriculum and Instruction
Production-oriented	Focus is on products.	Learning outcomes are emphasized.
Means-ends reasoning	Means are justified on the basis of ends to be achieved.	Instruction is justified according to desired learning outcomes.
Technical basis	Determination is made by experts.	Curriculum and instructional experts develop curricula.
Linearity	Ends are determined before means.	Planning begins with the ultimate educational purposes, or aims, using them as a basis for determining educational goals, learning objectives, and instruction, in that order.
Objectivity	Decisions can and should be made on a scientific basis without the influence of personal values and biases.	Instructional methods and objectives are selected on the basis of effectiveness and efficiency.

When these other aspects of a decision are obscured by considering only the technical aspects, we might say that the decision has been "technicized," and any approach which turns curriculum decisions into purely technical decisions we might call "technicist." A technicist approach to a decision doesn't even recognize that the decision has moral, political, cultural, social, and economic dimensions, much less address these dimensions.

We will refer to views on curriculum planning as based on a *technical production* framework if the proponents of these views consider educational decisions to be made objectively primarily by experts with specialized knowledge (i.e., the decisions are considered technical) and if they view schooling as a process whose main purpose is to produce learning, a process for which the logic of decision making should be based on means-ends reasoning (i.e., the framework is production-oriented). Further, they are *linear* technical production models if they require the determination of ends before deciding on means.

The technical production framework has, particularly when complemented by the assumption of linearity, served as a basis for a variety of models intended to guide thought about the curriculum. The current emphasis on "outcome-based education" (OBE) derives from this framework (see Brandt, 1994).

FRAMEWORKS FOR CURRICULUM ANALYSIS

Technical production frameworks of curriculum have dominated the curriculum field for most of this century. They have influenced the way people think about the curriculum development process, the components every curriculum should contain, the way these components should relate to one another, the basis for evaluating a curriculum, and the kinds of topics that a course or textbook on curriculum should discuss. Tyler suggested a set of inescapable questions that must be asked of any curriculum. The Tyler rationale is particularly well suited to help the curriculum analyst tease a curriculum apart into its component parts or, as Zais (1976) puts it, to understand the "anatomy of a curriculum."

But, so as not to become captive to this framework, we also employ other frameworks for curriculum analysis. First, there is a prior set of questions pertaining to the way the curriculum development process itself was framed. It examines the problems to which the curriculum responded and the theoretical perspectives it employed. Then, there is a set of questions about the implementation of the curriculum, the factors that it should have taken, or in fact did take, into account. In addition, throughout the book we attempt to make assumptions explicit and to take a critical look at the perspectives we employ. By working through this book and taking a critical look at our own perspectives on curriculum, we begin to address political and ideological questions, such as the following: Does the curriculum have a hidden agenda? Whose interests does the curriculum serve? Whose knowledge gets included in the curriculum?

Figure 1.6 provides an overview of the process of curriculum analysis, and the questions in Table 1.5 comprise the curriculum analysis presented by this book.

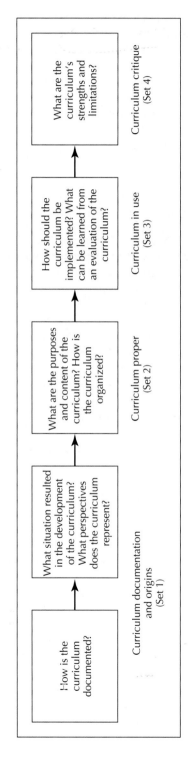

FIGURE 1.6 The process of curriculum analysis.

TABLE 1.5 Curriculum Analysis Questions

First Set: Curriculum Documentation and Origins

I. How is the curriculum documented? (Chapter One)
1. On what curriculum and standards documents and other resources will you base your analysis? Which state and national standards are relevant to the curriculum you have chosen?
2. On what aspects of the analysis do the curriculum and standards documents focus?
3. What limitations in documentation do you find?

II. What situation resulted in the development of the curriculum? (Chapter Two)
1. If you can find out, who made up the cast of characters in the development of the curriculum? What were their names, with what institution were they affiliated, and what were their respective roles in the project? Within the project team, who represented the learners, the teachers, the subject matter, and the milieu? Was there an obvious blind spot on the team?
2. To what social, economic, political, or educational problem was the curriculum attempting to respond?
3. What planning elements dominated the curriculum development process?

III. What perspective, if any, does the curriculum represent? (Chapter Three)

Second Set: The Curriculum Proper

IV. What are the purposes and content of the curriculum? (Chapter Four)
1. What aspects of the curriculum are intended for training, and what aspects are intended for educational contexts?
2. At what level, if at all, does the curriculum express its purposes?
3. What educational goals and educational aims are emphasized, and what are their relative priorities?
4. What types of learning objectives are included and emphasized in the curriculum?
5. What are the primary ways in which the curriculum represents the subject matter to students?
6. Does your curriculum have a view of multicultural education in its content? Would you consider it an assimilationist, multiethnic, or social reconstructionist view?
7. How is it determined if students have met the standards? What are the consequences for students, teachers and schools, if it is determined that students have not met standards? Does it matter if you adhere to the standards?
8. Is the curriculum aligned with the standards? Does the curriculum facilitate student understanding of the content and processes espoused by the standards? Are portrayals of the nature/structure of the discipline congruent between the curriculum and standards? Are the balances of depth and breadth of the curriculum and the standards congruent? Are the standards cited for each topic/activity?
9. How does technology affect the content of the curriculum?

V. What assumptions underlie the curriculum's approach to purpose or content? (Chapter Five)
  1. What conceptions of learning, objectives, curriculum, and teaching underlie the materials you are analyzing?
  2. What aspects of a hidden curriculum are likely to accompany the conceptions and perspectives underlying the curriculum?
  3. To what extent is the curriculum likely to play a hegemonic role in its purposes or content?

VI. How is the curriculum organized? (Chapter Six)
  1. What provision, if any, is made for macro-level vertical and/or horizontal organization?
  2. What basic configurations of content are found at a more micro level?
  3. How are various media and technologies employed to deliver the curriculum?
  4. What organizational principles does the curriculum employ? Does or can technology play a role in the curriculum organization?
  5. What are the social and political implications of technology in curriculum organization?
  6. Does the curriculum organization increase or decrease the likelihood that tracking will be used?

VII. What assumptions underlie the curriculum's organization? (Chapter Seven)
  1. What epistemological assumptions, if any, underlie the curriculum's organization?
  2. What psychological assumptions, if any, underlie the curriculum's organization?
  3. What other assumptions, if any, related to your curriculum's organization underlie the curriculum?

Third Set: The Curriculum In Use

VIII. How should the curriculum be implemented? (Chapters Eight and Nine)[1]
  1. What are the temporal, physical, organizational, and political-legal requirements of the curriculum?
  2. What are the probable costs and benefits associated with the curriculum change?
  3. To what extent will the curriculum be consistent with and appropriate for the teachers' attitudes, beliefs, and competencies?
  4. What values are embedded in the curriculum, and how well are these values likely to be suited to the community?
  5. To what extent is the curriculum aligned to the standards?
  6. What technologies are required for implementation of the curriculum?
  7. To what extent does the curriculum take into account the students' cultural, ethnic, or social backgrounds? To what extent does it accommodate gender differences?
  8. What approaches to curriculum change seem to be consistent with the curriculum?
  9. If your curriculum has already been implemented, what approaches characterized the change efforts?

(continued)

TABLE 1.5. Curriculum Analysis Questions *(continued)*

  IX. What can you learn about the curriculum from an evaluation point of view? (Chapters Ten and Eleven)
1. What, if any, available data does the curriculum provide? What conclusions about the curriculum seem warranted based on the data provided?
2. What standardized tests are relevant to this curriculum? How well is the curriculum aligned with the relevant standardized test?
3. What instruments or suggestions for collecting data does the curriculum provide? Are these tools equally fair for all social, economic, cultural, and ethnic groups?
4. What are your concerns about the curriculum that could be clarified by evaluation data? Consider short-term outcomes, long-term outcomes, antecedents, and transactions.
5. Does the approach to student evaluation in the curriculum manifest a measurement-based or an integrated approach, or both?
6. What would a non-conservative (or radical) evaluation of the curriculum look like?

Fourth Set: Critique

  X. What is your judgment about the curriculum? (Chapter Twelve)
1. What are its strengths and weaknesses?
2. Of what dangers would you want to be careful if you implemented it?
3. How would you adapt it to maximize its benefits and strengths and to minimize its limitations and risks?

---

[1]Note that these analysis questions for Chapter 8 are consistent with those provided at the end of that chapter but represent a condensed version. Check with your instructor for the version you should address.

The questions are organized into sets so that you can organize your work in a manageable and coherent fashion. Each set can be seen as constituting a unit of a course on curriculum study.

A complete and detailed curriculum analysis addressing all five sets of questions is rarely required in practice. More typically teachers and administrators may be called upon to make particular kinds of analysis on a moment's notice. Therefore, they must have the ability to carry out all kinds of analysis with rigor and thoroughness, even though they may never need to carry out all kinds of analysis for any one issue. Vignettes at the beginning of Chapters Four through Eleven depict some of these issues and the kinds of analysis required.

Answering these five sets of questions requires both that you apply the knowledge gained as you progress in your curriculum study and that you probe beneath the surface of the curriculum document in order to identify its meanings. If curriculum analysis were a straightforward process of document analysis, requiring simply that you find statements expressing the curriculum's explicit commitments, analysis would not be a significant part of curriculum study. In fact, most curriculum documents do not explicitly state their theoretical commitments, and even when they do, it is dangerous to take them at face value. It is not that curriculum developers are trying to hide something. They usually are simply unaware of the assumptions that influence their work.

WHY DO A CURRICULUM ANALYSIS?

Curriculum analysis is necessary by virtue of its centrality to two important tasks performed by teachers and administrators: curriculum selection and curriculum adaptation. When selecting or adapting a curriculum for use in a particular classroom, school, or school district, it is important to determine whether or not it is appropriate for the situation. This determination is not limited to an analysis of such matters as the reading difficulty, the quality of the graphics, the factual accuracy of the content, and the amount of math required. This examination also requires the ability to determine the extent to which the assumptions underlying the curriculum are valid for the particular class, school, or district. These assumptions consist of tacit beliefs about the central purposes of education, about the intended audience and the way people learn, about teachers and the best ways to teach, about the subject matter and how it should be organized, and about the community and what it values. An understanding of these sorts of beliefs is at the heart of reflective eclecticism. Uncovering these sorts of beliefs requires probing beneath the surface of the document, reading between the lines and making inferences on the basis of scattered evidence. Thus, curriculum analysis is more like detective work than clerical work, more like literary analysis than taking stock inventory. Further, if you believe the standards for your discipline are a reasonable description of what students should know and be able to do, your analysis should investigate how well the curriculum is aligned with those standards. Once you learn how to do a thorough and complete analysis, you will find that you have internalized a basic sense of the enterprise and even some of the steps. Once the process becomes second nature to you, you will be able to perform an adequate informal analysis in an hour or less.

OVERVIEW OF A CURRICULUM ANALYSIS— THE CASE OF MAN: A COURSE OF STUDY

In order to give you a clearer idea of what a curriculum analysis is and how this book will help you do one, we now examine a particular curriculum in some depth. The curriculum selected is worth some scrutiny, even though it is more than thirty years old. As you read about it, try to figure out why it is regarded on the one hand as one of the most elegant, scholarly, and ingenious curricula ever produced and on the other hand as one of the most disastrous attempts by the federal government to get involved in curriculum development. Chapters Four to Seven will help you understand the former aspect of this curriculum, titled *Man: A Course of Study* (M:ACOS). Chapters Eight and Nine will help you understand the latter.

M:ACOS—A Description

M:ACOS (CDA, 1972) was intended as a fifth- or sixth-grade social studies curriculum with a social science emphasis. It was developed and tested between 1963 and 1970 under the leadership of the cognitive psychologist Jerome Bruner (see Figure 1.7), together with the social scientists Irven DeVore, Nikolaas Tinbergen, and Asen Balikci. One way to describe M:ACOS is to say that it addresses three key questions:

What is human about human beings?

How did they get that way?

How can they be made more so?

The first of the three questions focuses on the characteristics of human beings. Answering this question first entails study of other species in order to provide a comparison and contrast with the many behaviors of human beings. Later in the curriculum a study of another human culture, the Netsilik Eskimos, applies these principles to a specific human setting.

The second question requires study of the distinctive features of human beings' adaptation to the world, achieved to a large extent through the vehicle of culture. Studies of acquired and innate behavior, natural selection, and adaptation are also included to help children understand some of the forces influencing human behavior and human society.

The third question is posed as a challenge to the children. This question is related to the study of values, of self, and of humanity. The open-endedness of the question allows children to engage in inquiry processes that are an integral part of the curriculum. Like the other two questions, this third question enables children to state their own views and subject them to the challenge of an open forum in the classroom for the purpose of establishing their own contact points with reality.

The three questions are studied by means of five fundamental themes or concepts, which are expanded throughout the course: toolmaking, language, social organization, child-rearing practices, and world view. These concepts are revisited in greater depth throughout the year at increasing levels of sophistication. This so-called spiral curriculum attempts to explore the concepts in greater depth with each topic, rather than cover them once and for all. These five concepts define the distinctiveness of human beings and their potential for even greater humanity.

Toolmaking is studied in a broad sense, as a means by which human beings amplify their capacities and implement their activities. This concept is studied particularly in the Netsilik Eskimo units to show how tools affect life, culture, and social organization. For example, students see how the Eskimos make various ingenious tools in order to survive in their harsh environment. In this way,

FIGURE 1.7 Jerome Bruner.

students develop a cross-cultural reference point. Netsilik are not studied to see "primitive" or uncivilized people, but to see how humanity meets and adapts to the adversity of a particular time and environment.

Study of the concept of language includes consideration of what communication is, and the concept is developed by contrasting how humans and animals manage to send and receive messages. Not all communication is written or oral. The kinds of communication range from the tactile contacts of bees to facial mannerisms to literature. For example, one unit in the animal section deals with baboon communication. Warning cries and even emotions are communicated. The students learn why DeVore, as a result of his study of baboon behavior, believes that grooming is a form of communication and mutual respect. The students compare and contrast the needs for baboon communication with the way the Eskimos' harsh environment requires the transmission of a great store of survival information from generation to generation.

Students learn that social organization is an important feature of both animal and human life. They realize that there is a structure to society and that the structure is not fixed once and for all time. It is an integrated pattern, and a change in one part of the pattern affects other parts—in fact, affects the whole of society. This social pattern establishes values and attitudes. The method of comparison and contrast is used again to help the child understand these ideas in new settings (baboons and Eskimos), where the children's own involvement will not lead them to accept views uncritically.

The general purpose for examining child-rearing practices is to examine the extent to which, and the way in which, offspring learn from their parents. Salmon, whose parents die before they are born, are contrasted with human beings, who have a long period of dependency. Students also study the mechanisms by which baboons learn behaviors necessary to become good members of a troop and to keep their positions in this survival group. Likewise, through the use of authentic ethnographic films utilizing only natural sounds, students observe the behavior of children in the Netsilik household. Through this comparison students learn the methods and procedures whereby children become acculturated.

The concept of cosmology or world view is used in M:ACOS to account for the human drive to explain the human condition and the world, and to devise ways to represent the world. M:ACOS looks at art, myth, legend, and how cultures attempt to account for those elements of the world that people cannot control or explain. The curriculum teaches that one kind of explanation is not more human than another.

Thus, M:ACOS is concerned with the nature of humanness and of human behavior. The specific content was selected based on the availability of usable materials from social science research, with heavy reliance on DeVore's study of baboons, Balikci's study of the Netsilik Eskimos, and Dr. Nikolaas Tinbergen's study of herring gulls, among others. These eminent scientists contributed directly to the development of the curriculum.

The year's course is roughly divided into two equal segments, the Man and Animal units (items 1 through 4 below) and the Netsilik Eskimo units (items 5 and 6).

1. Man
2. Salmon
3. Herring gulls and natural selection
4. Baboons
5. The Netsilik Eskimos at the Inland Camp
6. The Netsilik Eskimos on the Sea Ice

These topics are the instrumental content that serves as the vehicle for studying and for reexamining the curricular content made up of the five recurrent concepts.

M:ACOS has a rich, varied, and powerful array of instructional materials employed to implement the instructional plan. For instance, students do not passively watch movies, but are actively engaged in observation, inferring and hypothesizing from the primary data presented in unnarrated ethnographic films. In a sense, students have the opportunity to engage in inquiry similar to that of the social scientist in the field. The nature of the materials, and especially the absence of a textbook per se, allows the students to discover for themselves generalizations about human behavior.

Curriculum Analysis of M:ACOS

Suppose that you are analyzing this social studies curriculum using the four sets of analysis questions in Table 1.5: documentation and framing; purposes, content, and organization; implementation; and evaluation. Let's examine what each set of questions tells us about M:ACOS and preview what subsequent chapters of this book will contribute to the analysis.

1. The first set of questions concerns the way the curriculum is documented and framed. As this chapter comes to a conclusion, we will apply what we have learned about curriculum frameworks to the specification of the documentation necessary for a curriculum analysis. Then in Chapter Two we will consider the story behind the production of curriculum documents and how the situation leading to the development of curricula shaped M:ACOS. We will see in the next chapter that the approach used can best be understood as a response to a political situation in the United States during the 1960s. The way the problem was formulated led to a decision to organize the curriculum around a small set of fundamental ideas from the social sciences, in particular anthropology and social psychology. This decision meant that social studies would need to be conceived as social science and led to the curriculum development effort being dominated by social scientists. The developers of M:ACOS decided that the focus for the curriculum would be human beings, and that the overarching questions would be these: "What is human about human beings?" "How did they get that way?" "How can they be made more so?"

In Chapter Three you will find out that the development of M:ACOS was driven by two particular theoretical perspectives, namely, a structure-of-the-disciplines perspective and a cognitive psychological perspective, and that these perspectives each have an important history and intellectual tradition. More generally, you will learn about the kinds of theoretical perspectives that have influenced curriculum development in this country, the way a theoretical perspective represents a coherent set of assumptions underlying a curriculum, and how you can use this knowledge in curriculum analysis.

2. The second set of questions concerns the curriculum proper, its purposes, its content, and its organization. M:ACOS not only did not begin planning with a set of objectives but also never provided specific objectives for the teacher to use in teaching the units and lessons. Rather, there are five concepts toward which all the units are directed. These five fundamental concepts—toolmaking, language and communication, child rearing, social organization, and cosmology or world view—were presumed to be learned by comparison and contrast provided by the examination of other species and other cultures.

Chapter Four will help you decide if teaching of these five concepts constitutes the only purposes behind M:ACOS or whether there were other, more general or more specific ones. It will also help you see what these purposes imply about the overall priorities of any curriculum and its conception of the subject matter.

Chapter Five takes this analysis a step further by showing how the purposes and content of a curriculum reflect underlying psychological assumptions about how people learn. You will see why we can say that M:ACOS is based on a cognitive psychological perspective and how the assumptions of cognitive psychology produce distinctive concepts of learning, objectives, instruction, and content. You will also see that these cognitive assumptions lead to a curriculum that contrasts sharply with behaviorally oriented curricula. More generally, these chapters will help you unpack any curriculum's purposes and content, exposing its assumptions and implications.

With regard to the organization of the curriculum, one way to describe the organization of M:ACOS is to say that it is organized into six units, one on salmon, another on herring gulls and natural selection, and so on. Another way to describe its organization is to say that it is organized around the five fundamental ideas, which Bruner called "themes." Still another way to describe its organization would be to depict how it employs the various media to accomplish its purposes. Chapter Six will help you sort out the various types and levels of organization any curriculum embodies.

Chapter Seven, by examining conflicting perspectives on curriculum organization, will help you see that M:ACOS represents an attempt to provide a curriculum reflecting the structure of knowledge, in particular, academic disciplines. The curriculum regards fifth- or sixth-graders as novice social scientists engaged in a social science inquiry analogous to the research efforts of leading anthropologists and social psychologists. Like these social scientists, students engage in inquiry with a set of fundamental ideas to guide them and from which more specific facts and concepts derive. You will see that this view of curriculum can be considered "top-down," in terms of the relation between the overarching, fundamental ideas and the more specific facts and concepts that can be derived from them. You will also see how this particular perspective contrasts with other perspectives, embodying different assumptions about the integration of learning and the structure of knowledge. More important, you will see how any curriculum's organization reflects underlying assumptions, and you will learn how to identify them.

3. The third set of questions concerns the curriculum in use, both its implementation and its evaluation. M:ACOS has been one of the most controversial curricula ever developed. It was the focus of congressional hearings in Washington, D.C., and it has been the target of well-organized campaigns by the political right to remove it from the schools. In fact the vocal opposition to M:ACOS was one of the major reasons that the federal government and associated quasigovernmental agencies such as the National Science Foundation (NSF) backed away from curriculum development and dissemination for several years.

The major reason for the implementation problems with M:ACOS was conflicts in values between the developers and conservative members of the community. In Chapters Eight and Nine you will learn to identify potential value conflicts, as well as myriad other factors that strongly affect curriculum implementation.

With regard to the evaluation of a curriculum, M:ACOS was evaluated using various instruments, and it was found that students did, in fact, learn the fundamental ideas to a certain extent. Does this mean that the curriculum was successful? Chapter Ten will help you to answer this question and to decide what other information you would need to answer it.

Could the evaluation of M:ACOS have been carried out in entirely different ways, and would these other ways have been better? Chapter Eleven will help you answer these questions, to understand the particular approach to evaluation M:ACOS employed.

4. The fourth set of questions reexamines all previous question sets and attempts to develop an overall critique of the curriculum.

In Chapter Twelve you will see that the perspectives underlying M:ACOS place emphasis on the subject matter and the way children learn while ignoring, or at least subordinating to those concerns, issues related to the teachers and to the social context of schools. Through this discussion, you will begin to learn to identify any curriculum's blind spots. You will also be asked to use your analysis to determine how a curriculum like M:ACOS should be modified for purposes of improving it.

HOW TO CHOOSE A CURRICULUM FOR ANALYSIS

The first issue you will address as you get ready for your curriculum analysis is the choice of a curriculum for the project. Let's try to put the definitional points about curriculum discussed earlier in this chapter to work by helping us answer very practical questions that students raise as they begin curriculum analysis, questions like the following:

What should you look for when you search for a curriculum to analyze?

Will a textbook be suitable?

What about a state syllabus or a district scope and sequence chart?

The best way to answer these questions is by suggesting the kinds of information needed for a curriculum analysis. Ideally, the curriculum documents you will analyze should provide you with the six kinds of information listed in Table 1.6.

Clearly, most curriculum documents do not include all of these kinds of information. Figure 1.8 presents a sample format for a page of a locally developed curriculum guide. Notice that this format does not include items 1, 3, or 6 in Table 1.6. Often, curriculum documents contain only information about objectives, content, and sequence (item 2 in Table 1.6). Some textbooks do not even include objectives, much less information about the curriculum's history (items

TABLE 1.6. Information Provided by Ideal Curriculum Documents

1. Some clues about the *problem* to which the curriculum was responding and the kinds of *experts* included in the development process.

2. A clear idea of *what* students are supposed to learn, i.e., learning objectives; what teachers are supposed to teach, i.e., content; and *in what order* it should taught and learned, i.e., sequence.

3. A clear idea about *why* these learning objectives and content are important: i.e., *rationale,* sometimes called the *philosophy.*

4. Some guidance, whether in the form of suggestions or prescriptions, as to *how* to teach the objectives and content, i.e., teaching strategies.

5. An indication of *how* the curriculum and the students should be or have been *evaluated* and what the results were.

6. An indication of whether the curriculum has been *implemented;* if not yet implemented, for *what situations* it would be appropriate; if already implemented, *what happened* when it was.

1 and 5). Obviously, you will probably have to settle for less than the ideal. But as unattainable as the ideal is, it is useful to keep these six kinds of information in mind as you prepare for your analysis. As you select the curriculum for your analysis, one criterion (but only one of several) to use is the amount of information available. The following questions are intended to help you decide whether there is enough documentation regarding a particular curriculum:

1. Do the curriculum documents include learning objectives? Philosophy statements? Sample test items or evaluation strategies? Suggested teaching strategies? If the document is missing no more than one or two of these items, it is usable.

2. Can you find published articles or other materials that describe the curriculum's story? The curriculum's track record? Can you contact people involved in its genesis? Would it be possible to interview them about the planning process? If you can answer yes to one of these questions, the curriculum is usable.

In other words, curriculum analysis can range from an analysis of a single curriculum document—for example, a teacher guide—to a research project, including library searches and extensive interviews with curriculum project leaders. Your analysis is likely to fall somewhere between these two extremes. How extensive your analysis will be will depend on the availability of information and your interest in pursuing it.

Curriculum Analysis Questions

1. On what curriculum and standards documents and other resources will you base your analysis? Which state and national standards are relevant to the curriculum you have chosen?

UNIT: I. Life Science — Plants

GRADE: Three

CONTENT UNDERSTANDING: _____

SUBJECT: Science

PACING: 3 days

CONCEPT: (NYS 1.2) The flower is the structure in mature flowering plants that

enables offspring to be produced in the form of seeds.

INTEGRATION: _____

OBJECTIVES	LEARNING ACTIVITIES	EVALUATION
A. The student will identify the flower as the part of the plant that produces seeds for the next generation.	A. Dissect a flower (daffodil, tulip). (Use worksheet similar to this, depending on what kind of flowers are being used. Sample worksheet included.) Check each number after you do it. 1. How many different parts of the flower can you see? 2. Is there an odd or even number of petals? 3. Does every (daffodil) have the same number of petals? 4. Carefully take your daffodil apart and see if you can find the parts labeled on the diagram above. 5. Can you find the pollen inside? 6. How does it feel? 7. Look at it with a magnifying glass. 8. Why are the petals bright yellow? Teacher explains that the pollen must get on the stigma for seeds to form in the ovary. (Skills/Processes: Develop vocabulary, manipulate materials)	A. Given a flowering plant (or picture of one), the student will identify the flower as the "seed factory" for the plant. Resources: Addison-Wesley Science Level 3 Blackline master p. 11 "Where is pollen made in a flower?" Bud's World, NY: Agriculture in the classroom, pp. 3–67 "Parts of a Flower" "Parts of a Flower Vocabulary" "Making a Model of a Flower"

FIGURE 1.8 A page from a locally developed curriculum guide.

2. On what aspects of the analysis do the standards documents focus? On what aspects do the curriculum documents focus? (See Table 1.6.)
3. What limitations in documentation do you find?

Notes

1. See, for example, Johnson (1967).
2. See Chapter Three.
3. School subjects, as institutionalized versions of bodies of knowledge, owe their character more to the institution than to the discipline from which they derive. This fact explains the otherwise inexplicable similarities in the way very different subjects, for example, English and math, are taught and evaluated.
4. It should be noted, however, that Tyler (1949) himself disagrees with this interpretation. I will discuss this matter further in a subsequent section.
5. This distinction is attributable to Mauritz Johnson, not Tyler, who avoided definitions in his book. See Johnson (1977, pp. 47–48).

CHAPTER 2

Situating the Curriculum

Where does a curriculum come from?
Who develops curricula?
Why do people develop curricula?
How are curricula affected by social, political, economic, or cultural situations?

A curriculum, particularly one immortalized by a textbook or textbook series, appears timeless, objective, and absolute, handed down from the authorities as the official word on what to teach. However, curricula are constructed by groups of people confronted with situations that demand action on their part. A curriculum is part of an ongoing dialogue between people with differing beliefs about and commitments to education and, in particular, different beliefs about what people should learn to do in school. To view a curriculum as the product of a group of people faced with a series of technical, economic, and political decisions, guided and constrained by their own personal belief systems, is the first step toward a deeper understanding. In order to analyze a curriculum we need to determine what motivated and guided its developers.

Curricula, like constitutions, treaties, and laws, must be understood in terms of their historical context. Who were the architects of the curriculum, and what were their guiding principles? What existing educational situation—including current curricula—or set of problems was the curriculum addressing? To what social or political pressures was the curriculum responding? What was the focus of the curriculum development effort?

The purpose of answering these questions is to gain an understanding of your curriculum's historical context. We want to understand the way the curriculum's developers viewed their work. This chapter helps you understand the thinking behind a curriculum by considering the situation leading up to its formulation. In a sense this chapter helps you tell the story that provides the background for understanding the curriculum documents. In the next chapter we extend this study by analyzing the theoretical perspectives that shaped the curriculum.

THE CAST OF CHARACTERS

A logical place to start uncovering the story behind a curriculum is with the people who were involved in developing it. However, identifying the people behind the typical curriculum and their respective roles in its development can be challenging. Most textbook series list the authors and their institutional affiliations but provide little additional information about their respective roles or about other people involved in the development process. As FitzGerald (1979) points out, many textbooks are written by ghostwriters hired by publishers, while the listed authors serve merely as figureheads.

Products of national curriculum development projects usually provide more information. Often there are project newsletters or journal articles written about the project by its developers. The following books and reports represent a sample of information available from libraries. This list does not include journal articles.

American Institutes for Research in the Behavioral Sciences. 1972. *Product Development Reports* 1–21. Palo Alto, CA: American Institutes for Research in the Behavioral Sciences. Descriptions of 21 projects, including Science Curriculum Improvement Study (SCIS), Sesame Street, Taba Social Studies, Holt Social Studies, Distar, Frostig Program of Perceptual-Motor Development, IPI mathematics, among others.

Grobman, Hulda. 1970. Development Curriculum Projects. Itasca, IL: F. E. Peacock. Descriptions of BSCS biology, DEEP economics projects, among others.

Schaffarzick, Jon, and Hampson, David (Eds.). 1975. *Strategies for Curriculum Development*. Berkeley, CA: McCutchan. Stories behind the Kettering Art Project, IPI mathematics, SCIS, Career Education, Elementary Science Study, among others, written by the project directors.

Heath, Robert W. (Ed.). 1964. *The New Curricula*. New York: Harper & Row.

State curricula, on the other hand, typically provide little information about their development. However, by merely identifying the bureau or department that issued the curriculum and then finding out the name of the bureau or department head, one can identify a person to call or write for background information.

Locally developed curricula typically identify their developers (with some degree of pride). If these people are still in the area, they can be a valuable source of information about the development process.

At any rate, with some initial research, the names and respective roles of some of the developers can usually be discovered. If this information is not available, then the rest of this section should be read but cannot be employed in this analysis project.

Schwab (1971) contends that five sorts of people should be involved in curriculum deliberations. According to Schwab, there should be at least one representative for each of what he calls the *four commonplaces* of education, namely, the learners, the teachers, the subject matter, and the milieu. In addition, there should be someone to coordinate the deliberations, i.e., a curriculum specialist. Each commonplace should be represented because each one constitutes a significant aspect of education in its own right, not to be subordinated to another commonplace.

It would be instructive at this point to determine which of the four commonplaces were over- and underrepresented on the curriculum development team. Was there someone on the team—e.g., someone with a background in psychology—who understood the students, how they learn, and what their needs are? Was there someone on the team who understood the subject matter; understood how people generate new knowledge and theories in that discipline; what criteria of excellence apply; what the key concepts, knowledge claims, and telling questions are; what counts as evidence; and what values are implicit in the subject matter? Was there someone who understood teachers and the complexities of classrooms, the demands teachers face, and the constraints under which the curriculum was to be implemented? Was there someone who understood the economic and political realities of the community and the social problems related to these realities?

While examining the participants in terms of the four commonplaces, consider the role of experts and who counts as an expert. For example, the needs of the students can be addressed by psychologists, social workers, or students themselves. The context in which the curriculum is implemented can be addressed by consulting sociologists; elected officials; international, national, state, or local community groups; employers; parent groups; or individual community members. Teachers' concerns can be addressed by consulting individual teachers, teachers' unions, or education professors. Subject matter can be represented by teachers; university researchers, i.e., knowledge producers; practitioners, i.e., people who use the knowledge; or philosophers. The choice of representative for a particular commonplace reflects a view of both that commonplace and the role of expert knowledge in curriculum development.

Clearly, no curriculum is fortunate enough to find full representation of all four commonplaces on its development team. The point here is not to criticize curricula, but to identify potential blind spots.

Chapter Twelve will extend this idea of blind spots in a more explication of Schwab's work. For the time being, the point is simply to realize that the composition of a curriculum development team frames a curriculum, and that interpreting it requires knowing who was and who was not involved in developing it.

THE STORY BEHIND THE CURRICULUM: PROBLEM FORMULATION

The developers of a curriculum can be a valuable resource to you as you attempt to piece together the series of events leading up to the decision to develop the curriculum. If they are accessible, perhaps you can telephone them to find out their understanding of the situation. Another approach is to use the library to research any articles written either about the curriculum or by one of the curriculum developers. What you are looking for are the situational factors that caused the developers to become involved with the project and led the project team to approach the task in a particular way.

One way to portray a curriculum's story is to focus on the curriculum's formulation of a problem. Any new curriculum can be thought of as an attempt to respond to a problem. For example, current attempts to develop curricula in "thinking skills" are responding to a public consensus that students leave school unable to assess arguments critically. Multicultural education responds to concerns that school curricula do not represent the plurality of cultures that provides the unique strength of our country. Computer education curricula are responding to a growing sense that computers are becoming an important part of our everyday life and that computer literacy is part of what it now means to be well educated.

Often, curricula respond not only to problems commanding educators' attention but also to situations so urgent that they might be called crises. AIDS education, sex education, peace education, drug education, career education, driver education, nutrition education, and environmental education can all be seen as responses to problems so critical that they threaten the well-being of each of us personally or the well-being of our nation or planet. As one pundit said, "When the French have a crisis, they mount a general strike; when Americans have a crisis, they create a new course." We tend to look to schools, and to their curricula in particular, to help us solve the vast array of problems that confront us.

Although using education to solve problems may seem reasonable, it can create its own set of problems. Not all problems can be productively viewed as educational, much less curricular, problems. Appropriate formulation of the problem determines, in part, the effectiveness of the recommended solution. Consider, for example, drug education. Drug abuse has been called a national, if not an international, crisis. By formulating the problem as being, in part, an educational problem with a curricular solution, educators have assumed that what teachers teach and what students learn can reduce or even solve the problem. This assumption, in turn, rests on the premise that we will solve the problem by persuading individuals to stop using, or, at least, abusing, drugs ("Just say no!"), and that the necessary persuasion includes giving students information about drugs and their effects.

The issue here is not whether substance abuse is an educational problem. It may be an educational problem while simultaneously being a law enforcement, social, economic, medical, jurisprudential, political, and psychological problem, among others. The issue is whether formulating it as an educational problem is productive or counterproductive. Advocates of drug education programs have struggled to show that such programs can reduce the amount of drug use and abuse. Critics have even claimed that these programs lead to increases in drug use, that drug education courses function as consumer guides to drug experimentation. If this criticism is valid, it suggests one potential danger in assuming uncritically that a new curriculum is the means for solving our problems. A new curriculum may be just what we need, but it may also create its own set of problems. The correct formulation of problems is an essential part of educational and social progress.

The kinds of solutions we propose to problems often depend on unexamined assumptions. When we decide that a particular set of events is indicative of an educational problem, we are assuming connections between indicators and problems. The very act of deciding that we have a problem is based on certain assumptions.

Let us consider an example of the relation between problem formulation and underlying assumptions.

An Example of Problem Formulation: A Nation at Risk

In April 1983, the 18-member National Commission on Excellence in Education (NCEE) released its report, entitled *A Nation at Risk: The Imperative for Educational Reform*. The Commission had been formed by Education Secretary Terrel Bell in August 1981 to provide a report to the American people on the quality of American education. It was created to address the Secretary's concern about "the widespread public perception that something is seriously remiss in our educational system." The report began with an ominous warning: "Our nation is at risk. Our once unchallenged preeminence in commerce, industry, science, and technological innovation is being overtaken by competitors throughout the world" (NCEE, 1983, p. 5). Thus, the basic problem was delineated as one of international economic and technological competition, particularly from the Japanese.

The report continued with its analysis of the problem. It claimed that it would deal with "only one of the many causes and dimensions of the problem" (NCEE, 1983, p. 5), that is, education. It attempted to awaken the American people to the dangerous erosion of "the educational foundations of our society . . . by a rising tide of mediocrity that threatens our very future as a nation and a people" (p. 5). The very metaphorical language of the report reveals its formulation of the problem: "If an unfriendly foreign power had attempted to impose on America the mediocre performance that exists today, we might well have viewed it as an act of war. . . . We have, in effect, been committing an act of unthinking, unilateral educational disarmament" (p. 5).

In other words, the report argued that a lack of vigilance and determination on the part of all Americans, but particularly educators, had brought about a national crisis that posed an imminent threat to our economic well-being. According to the Commission, Americans were engaged in a bitter economic competition with foreign countries, and education was the key to success in that competition. What was needed, therefore, was to bear down by increasing standards, requirements, and state-level control of education; to focus on the basics in the curriculum; to increase funding for education; and to demand "tangible results." In general the report argued that the whole educational system needed to be tightened up and made more efficient.

FIGURE 2.1 The NCEE report *A Nation at Risk*.

Notice that several assumptions underlie this formulation of the problem:

1. The major threat to America was an external, economic threat.
2. Education was one of the causes of this problem.
3. Indicators of the problem included test scores that had declined or were poor in comparison with those in other countries. Other indicators were over-looked, for example, the increasing number of dropouts and the sense of alienation and despair that pervades the nation's poor and minority students. In other words, the problem formulation focused on excellence, rather than on equity in education.
4. One of the reasons for the loss of excellence had been the school's attempt to take on too much responsibility, thereby losing its sense of purpose and diluting its efforts.
5. Reform would come when educators improved the effectiveness and efficiency of the educational system, through attention to issues like graduation standards, amount of instructional time, and teacher qualifications. The report did not question the basic organization of schools, of the teaching profession, and of the basic subjects of the curriculum, with the exception of

the new basic subject, computer science. Educators were simply to take what they already had and just do more of it and more with it.

These assumptions remained unexamined by the report. Nevertheless, they framed the problem formulation and the kinds of solutions offered. It is in this sense that the NCEE report was like a new curriculum. It was a proposal for educational change, a proposal intended to respond to a particular formulation of a problem, whose solution had to be consistent with the assumptions on which the problem formulation rested.

A Curriculum as a Response to a Problem—The Story of M:ACOS

By viewing a particular curriculum as a response to a formulated problem, the curriculum analyst can make sense of the particular curriculum approach employed. An analysis of the problem to which M:ACOS responded will show how the points made above about the *Nation at Risk* report apply to curricula. M:ACOS is chosen because of its pivotal role in U.S. curriculum development. This role will become clearer as we examine it in this and subsequent chapters.[1]

As we will see in Chapters Three and Seven, the period during which this curriculum was developed was marked by many of the same concerns reflected in the NCEE report. Beginning around 1951, mathematicians had been working on curriculum revisions intended to reduce the gap between school and college mathematics teaching. Their efforts were joined by physicists in the mid-1950s working on the high school physics curriculum. But it was not until 1957, when the Soviet Union launched the first satellite into orbit around the Earth, that this early curriculum work assumed its eventual significance. The Soviets' technological achievement confirmed the warnings of educational critics, like Admiral Hyman Rickover (1959) and Arthur Bestor (1953), that America's military superiority was at risk and that the schools' intellectual "flabbiness" was to blame. What was needed was to bring the academic disciplines and the university professors to the country's rescue. The federal government considered the reform of school curriculum to be a matter of national defense. The similarities to the NCEE response to America's perceived economic and technological competition with Japan are striking.

The formulation of the national defense problem, and assignment of its cause to a failure of our schools, created the environment for the intervention of the federal government in the reform of the school curriculum. The problem became one of figuring out how to replace the traditional curriculum with one derived from the academic disciplines. Curriculum reform in social studies thus became a problem of reconceptualizing this subject matter as social science, history, or one of the other disciplines. One such curriculum effort was M:ACOS, drawing principally on the disciplines of anthropology, ethnography, and social psychology. The problem for M:ACOS became one of bringing the products of social science research, e.g., ethnographic films and field studies, to the elementary school in order to explore "the forces that shaped and continue to shape man's humanity" (CDA, 1972, p. 1). It is impossible to understand why this particular approach to curriculum reform was adopted without understanding it as a response to a particular problem formulation that conceived academic disciplines to be of primary significance to the country's well-being and assumed that the ever widening gap between school subject matter and the university-level academic disciplines was at the heart of the country's defense problem.

In this context, it is not surprising that the cast of characters in the development of this curriculum included only university scholars.

THE STORY BEHIND THE CURRICULUM: PLANNING FOCI

The background of a curriculum includes not only the story leading up to its development and the main characters but also the story of the curriculum development process itself. Except in rare cases, the story of the project available in the literature usually describes the situation surrounding the decision to develop a curriculum, names the cast of characters, then stops when the project begins and resumes again when the project releases its materials to the public. Little is usually known about the actual deliberations of the team that develops the curriculum.[2]

Nevertheless, much can be inferred from the curriculum materials themselves. Of particular interest is the relative attention paid to various elements. The elements to which we might expect some attention are listed in Table 2.1 together with the question each element suggests to the developer (adapted from Purves, 1975, and Smith & Sendelbach, 1982).

Even without historical data about the curriculum development process, you may be able to infer the priorities of the developers with regard to the above elements of planning. The format of the curriculum and the emphasis given to each of the format categories in the curriculum documents reflect, to some extent, the planning elements to which the developers attended. According to Smith and Sendelbach (1982), each of the elements listed above can function as a focus for planning.[3] At the extreme, each element can constitute a preoccupation, to the exclusion of other important planning elements. For example, if the curriculum materials seem to devote an inordinate amount of space to activities, you might infer that the planners considered activities highly important, that for these developers teaching primarily involves planning and managing activities, and that these developers believe that well-planned activities necessarily lead students to learn significant things. If, on the other hand, the materials seem to devote an inordinate amount of space to content, then you might infer that the planners regarded covering content as the teacher's major responsibility. Or, if the curriculum documents seem preoccupied with the philosophy supporting the curriculum, then you might infer that little consensus exists

TABLE 2.1. Planning Elements

1. *Objectives* What knowledge, skills, or attitudes should students acquire?
2. *Rationale or educational philosophy behind the curriculum* Why should they learn this? What is the value of this?
3. *Content* What content, i.e., what topics, concepts, skills, etc., should be covered?
4. *Characteristics of target audience* Who is this for? (Consider interests, abilities, background knowledge.)
5. *Activities* What should they do?
6. *Materials* What resources will they need?
7. *Sequencing principles* In what order should this be done?
8. *Schedule* How long will each part take?
9. *Teacher training and attitudes* What do the teachers need to know, be able to do, and be committed to?
10. *Evaluation* How will success be determined? What will count as success?
11. *Administrative structure, school facilities, and financial constraints* How will it be implemented in a school?
12. *Other parts of curriculum* How will it relate to other subjects?

in the field and that developing a rationale to justify a set of activities was the primary concern.

Occasionally, some limited aspect of curriculum, such as sequencing principles, has preoccupied developers, particularly in highly structured subject matters such as mathematics.[4] Some developers have even focused almost exclusively on elements that, however great their influence on the curriculum, are not, strictly speaking, elements of the curriculum: for example, teacher training;[5] school facilities, e.g., a computer lab; or administrative structures, e.g., team teaching.

You might be able to infer the primary planning foci by searching through the curriculum documents for evidence that the planners were preoccupied with one or more of the twelve questions listed in Table 2.1. By noting which of the planning foci received the greatest and least attention, you might also be able to predict potential problems arising from neglected planning elements—i.e., neglected questions.

Curriculum Analysis Questions

1. Who made up the cast of characters for the development of the curriculum? What were their names, with what institution were they affiliated, and what were their respective roles in the project? Within the project team, who represented the learners, the teachers, the subject matter, and the milieu? Was there an obvious blind spot on the team?

2. To what social, economic, political, or educational problem was the curriculum attempting to respond?
3. What planning elements dominated the curriculum development process?

Notes

1. See especially Chapter Nine.
2. For some notable exceptions, refer to Walker (1971) and Grobman (1970).
3. Smith and Sendelbach (1982, p. 101) use the term "frame" instead of my term "focus." They define "frame" as a "functional unit" of the planner's knowledge, "which had certain 'slots' for information to be filled in during the planning process."
4. See Chapter Seven.
5. See Chapter Nine.

CHAPTER 3

Theoretical Perspectives on Curriculum

What have been the most significant perspectives on curriculum development in the United States?
What would proponents of each perspective propose for the reform of today's curriculum?

Every curriculum represents a choice as to how to approach the education of students. As we discussed in Chapter Two, the particular approach chosen by the developers of a curriculum stems in part from how they formulate the problem to which they are responding. For example, if the problem were formulated as "cultural illiteracy," then the curriculum would likely emphasize those aspects of our culture about which people are presumed to be ignorant.1 If the problem were formulated as the school's lack of relevance to children's lives, then the curriculum would likely emphasize activities or content that students can relate to everyday living. If the problem were formulated as a lack of educational equality for students of different backgrounds and capabilities, then the curriculum would likely emphasize ways to remedy or compensate for perceived disadvantages.

The problem formulation influences but does not determine the curriculum. Cultural illiteracy can be solved by having students read the "Great Books," learn the basic concepts of each discipline of knowledge, or develop a critical awareness of the contradictions of daily life in Western culture. Education for relevance might mean learning marketable skills, studying pop culture, or becoming social activists. Educational equality might be achieved by establishing a "core curriculum" for all students but providing special classes that allow for differences in pace, e.g., accelerated and basic classes; native language, e.g., bilingual education; and disabling conditions, i.e., self-contained classes. Or it might be achieved by requiring all students not only to study the same core program, but also to do so in heterogeneous and mainstreamed classes. Educational problems can be responded to with various curricula. The approach chosen depends on the beliefs and assumptions (often termed "philosophies" or "perspectives") of the people who develop the curriculum.

In this chapter we introduce five different, coherent, but not mutually exclusive perspectives on curriculum. I call them "perspectives" because I want to think about the view of education each of them permits, what features of the educational landscape each allows us to see, and what each obscures from our view. Each perspective represents a particular, coherent set of assumptions about education. These assumptions can be considered distinctive answers to questions like the following:

How does learning occur, and how is it facilitated?

What objectives are worthwhile, and how should they be expressed?

What kinds of content are most important, and how should the content be organized for instruction?

How should educational progress be evaluated?

What is and should be the relationship between schools and the society at large?

Each perspective chooses which of these questions it will address. Some perspectives are more comprehensive than others and thus address a broader set of questions.

The five perspectives are named as follows: traditional, experiential, structure of the disciplines (or disciplines, for short), behavioral, and constructivist. In subsequent chapters we select from these five perspectives ones representing conflicting views about particular curriculum components. By contrasting divergent perspectives, we will be able to bring the assumptions associated with each component into sharper relief.

Although this chapter is primarily intended as an introduction to the five theoretical perspectives, it does lead to curriculum analysis questions in its own right. Some curricula have been strongly influenced by one or more theoretical perspectives. M:ACOS, for example, was dominated by both the structure-of-the-disciplines and constructivist perspectives. As you begin your curriculum analysis, you should ask yourself whether your curriculum was strongly influenced by, and thus reflects, a particular theoretical perspective—and if so, which one. For now you can only form hypotheses. The perspectives are described in this chapter in only introductory fashion, emphasizing their historical and intellectual roots. Subsequent chapters will provide more detail about each perspective and will help you identify specific ways in which these perspectives influenced various components of your curriculum, even though the curriculum as a whole may not reflect a pure case.

At the end of the book's final chapter you will ask yourself whether your curriculum, as a consequence of a particular theoretical perspective, evidences any significant blind spots. In that chapter we consider the limitations of theoretical perspectives and the ways in which an eclectic approach addresses these limitations.

Before presenting the five theoretical perspectives, a few caveats are necessary.

1. These perspectives summarize many, but certainly not all, approaches that curricula take. That is, they are representative, but not exhaustive. They are

TABLE 3.1 The Five Perspectives: Central Questions

1. *Traditional* What are the most important aspects of our *cultural heritage* that should be preserved?

2. *Experiential* What *experiences* will lead to the healthy growth of the individual?

3. *Structure of the disciplines* What is the *structure of the disciplines* of knowledge?

4. *Behavioral* At the completion of the curriculum, what should the learners *be able to do?*

5. *Constructivist* How can people learn to *make sense* of the world and to *think* more productively and creatively?

---

    not the only perspectives possible, but they are important ones. However, it is entirely possible that you may find a curriculum that has no elements of any of these five perspectives, but instead represents an entirely different one.

2. Each perspective may be regarded as a "family" of approaches to curriculum. Although there may be disputes within families, i.e., family squabbles, each family represents a coherent set of assumptions underlying a curriculum's emphasis.

3. Many actual curricula cannot be neatly categorized as belonging to only one of these perspectives. The five families represent analytic and pedagogical tools rather than actual curricula. You will need to use them in subsequent chapters to help you analyze your curriculum.

4. Presentation of the perspectives here is somewhat oversimplified in order to avoid technical jargon.

With these caveats in mind, we will now examine the five theoretical perspectives. Note that each perspective can be summarized by an overarching question directing our attention to its central focus, as depicted in Table 3.1.

TRADITIONAL

What is now called "traditional" education by many writers was, at an earlier period in history, actually a response to a contemporary problem. The problem in the United States during the late nineteenth century was "the seemingly intractable problem of universal schooling in an increasingly urban society" (Cremin, 1975, p. 20). William Torrey Harris, then superintendent of the St. Louis school system and a learned philosopher in his own right, believed that education needed to focus on transmitting the cultural heritage of Western civilization. (See Figure 3.1.) For Harris, education was the process "by which the individual is elevated into the species" (Harris, 1897, p. 813). Therefore, the curriculum, according to Harris, should make the accumulated wisdom of "the race" available to all children. The textbook would make a common body of facts equally accessible to the children, thereby serving as an antidote for the opinion-dominated newspapers of the day. The teacher, using the lecture-recitation

FIGURE 3.1 William Torrey Harris.

method, would be the driving force in the process and would be responsible for getting students to think about what they read. Examinations would monitor and classify the students as they progressed through a graded educational system. As Cremin points out, "all the pieces were present for the game of curriculum making that would be played over the next half-century only the particular combinations and the players would change" (Cremin, 1975, p. 22). I might add that the game remains the same to this day.

One of its leading critics, John Dewey, describes traditional education as follows: "The subject matter of education consists of bodies of information and skills that have been worked out in the past; therefore the chief business of the school is to transmit them to the new generation . . ." (Dewey, 1938, pp. 17–18). One of the leading contemporary *proponents* of the traditional perspective, humanities professor E. D. Hirsch, Jr. (see Figure 3.2), says essentially the same thing in somewhat different terms: ". . . the basic goal of education in a human community is acculturation, the transmission to children of the specific information shared by the adults of the group or polis" (Hirsch, 1987, p. xvi).

Perhaps because they dominated educational practice, traditional educators after Harris did not need to make their underlying assumptions explicit.

FIGURE 3.2 E. D. Hirsch, Jr.

That is, until recently they did not have to explicate their theories of learning, of motivation, of knowledge, or of school and society.

Today, the traditional perspective is promoted by writers such as political scientist Allan Bloom (1987); historian Diane Ravitch (1985); Hirsch (1987); and former Secretary of Education and chairman of the National Endowment for the Humanities William Bennett, most recently head of former President George Bush's antidrug campaign (1984, 1988). Hirsch and Bennett, because they have deliberately and eloquently expressed this perspective and wish to apply it to the curriculum of both elementary and secondary public education, will serve as our modern-day traditionalists in this book.

In his widely read 1983 article "Cultural Literacy," and his 1987 book of the same title, Hirsch argues that "to be culturally literate is to possess the basic information needed to thrive in the modern world" (1987, p. xiii). That basic information is composed of the facts that "literate" Americans possess— not what they should but what they do in fact possess. Literacy requires more than learning skills; it requires "the early and continued transmission of specific information" (p. xvii). Without this information, people are unable to communicate with one another: "Only by piling up specific, communally shared information can children learn to participate in complex cooperative activities with other members of their community" (p. xv).

Although Bennett appears to agree with Hirsch's emphasis on specific information, he represents the more generally accepted traditional view, which includes not only "worthwhile knowledge" but also "important skills and sound ideals" as educational goals (Bennett, 1988, p. 6). Like Hirsch and other traditionalists, Bennett believes that there should exist a core curriculum, a curriculum with an "irreducible essence . . . of common substance" (p. 6).

Although the traditionalists lost ground to progressive educators during the first half of this century, the current wave of popularity of traditional views demonstrates the resilience of this perspective. We will see that most other curriculum perspectives can be understood, in part, as responses to traditional education. Because these other emphases represent insurgent points of view, they have been much more deliberate in explicating their underlying theories.

EXPERIENTIAL[2]

Beginning toward the end of the nineteenth century, the traditional perspective exemplified by the views of Harris came under attack. Its critics claimed that its authoritarian posture was in conflict with the nature of a democracy, that its view of children as passive recipients of information was inconsistent with the growing body of psychological knowledge, and that its approach to school knowledge as compartmentalized, isolated from everyday living, static, and absolute made schools increasingly irrelevant to life in a rapidly changing and complex world. A new perspective was emerging that placed at its focal point the experience of the child.

The view that curriculum can be considered in terms of the experiences of students is essentially a twentieth-century development. Simply stated, an experiential view is based on the assumption that everything that happens to students influences their lives, and that, therefore, the curriculum must be considered extremely broadly, not only in terms of what can be planned for students in schools and even outside them, but also in terms of all the unanticipated consequences of each new situation that individuals encounter. The consequences of any situation include not only what is learned in a formal sense, but also all the thoughts, feelings, and tendencies to action that the situation engenders in those individuals experiencing it. But since each individual differs in at least some small ways from all others, no two individuals can experience the same situation in precisely the same way. Thus the experiential view of education makes enormous demands on anyone who attempts to make practical curriculum decisions, for it assumes that the curriculum is more or less the same as the very process of living and that no two individuals can or should live precisely the same lives. The twentieth-century development of experiential education revolves around efforts, first, to understand how curriculum can be considered in this broadest possible way, and second, to develop clear and workable principles to guide practical decisions about such curricula.

The historical roots of experiential education can be traced to the Enlightenment in Europe during the seventeenth and eighteenth centuries. During that time, philosophers such as Hobbes (1962) and Descartes (1931) emphasized the importance of both mind and sense impressions, thus laying a basis for the development of modern psychology and an emphasis in modern education on both reasoning and empiricism. Locke (1913) argued that learning arises directly from experience, from how sense impressions of the external world "write" on the mind, which he likened to a *tabula rasa,* or blank slate. Rousseau (1962) added to such ideas his notions about the primacy of the individual, arguing that by nature individuals are pure until corrupted by the influence of society, and advocating a pedagogy that protected the experiences and spontaneous development of children. During the nineteenth century, other child-centered pedagogies that were advanced by such European educational pioneers as Pestolozzi and Froebel, and that further emphasized the needs, interests, and experiences of developing children, gained increasing prominence in Europe and gradually began to come to the attention of American educators.

The results of these new influences were soon to be felt. In the United States at the beginning of the nineteenth century almost all formal education was based on the training of the mind. Formal education was limited to a small proportion of the population, however, and training in the practical skills needed by the masses to get along in American society went on primarily through apprenticeships and the activities of daily living. During the nineteenth century, major sociological changes in the United States gradually caused the curriculum of many schools to become increasingly oriented toward practical subjects and social utility. This change occurred as the nation became increasingly urbanized and industrialized, and as compulsory school attendance laws were passed. Given these internal changes and the emergence of child-centered pedagogy in Europe, the United States at the end of the nineteenth century was poised on the brink of an immense educational revolution.

The catalyst for this revolution was the development around the turn of the century of pragmatic philosophy and the progressive educational movement. John Dewey's ideas were the principal basis for both. Dewey (see Figure 3.3) believed that traditional philosophies were inadequate largely because they viewed reality as external to the individual. Such philosophies emphasized either thinking or sensing as the best way of knowing reality, but not both. Education based on traditional philosophies therefore emphasized as the best criterion of curriculum choice either training of the mind (reasoning) or training of the senses (empiricism). Dewey contended that under the former criterion curricula became unduly academic and intellectual, while under the latter they became unduly vocational and social. Neither criterion alone could emphasize properly balanced individual development. In contrast, Dewey believed that reality is not external to the individual; it is found within the experience of the individual, the composite of both the individual's internal reactions, such as thoughts and feelings, and external reactions, such as actions, to the influences of the external world. Reality itself is in constant flux as both individuals and their world constantly change. For Dewey, therefore, the only

FIGURE 3.3 John Dewey.

way of knowing if a belief is true is to weigh the consequences of testing it in action. True beliefs are those that have good consequences for the further development of the experience of the individual. These and similar ideas advanced by other American philosophers coalesced into pragmatic philosophy, the basis for experiential education, in which the curriculum is based on the needs and interests of students and is subject to constant change and reorganization in order to foster the best possible consequences for the further development of each student's experiences.

Any form of experiential education that is consistent with Dewey's ideas therefore rejects neither reasoning nor empiricism as a criterion of curriculum choice, but it does combine them in a way that at the beginning of the twentieth century was new. To the two older criteria for curriculum choice in American schools, the development of reasoning, then associated with academic subjects believed useful in the training of mind, and the development of empiricism, then associated with practical subjects believed to lead to socially useful skills, Dewey added a new criterion: the development or healthy growth of individual experience. The addition of this third criterion brought the first two into balance. In order to lead to healthy growth, no longer could a curriculum be justified as solely academic and intellectual or as solely vocational and social. Any subject or activity chosen for or recommended to individual students should contribute to both their intellectual and social development, and to their personal development as well. Dewey believed that, as individuals thus developed in healthy ways, so, too, would American society develop and progressively change in healthy ways.

The immediate challenge for the newly formed progressive education movement was, of course, to develop principles and forms of education that would be based on personal experience and promote the development in the individual of both intelligence and socially useful skills; however, in the early decades of the century progressive education was part of the wider progressive social reform movement. It was part of a response to a whole host of ills brought on by major changes in national life. Educators and the public alike increasingly believed that American schools should contribute directly to the solution of the nation's most intractable problems. When in 1918 the National Education Association (NEA) issued the famous *Cardinal Principles of Secondary Education,* which exemplified the national mood, the organization was suggesting that curricula be nearly as broad as life itself in order to deal with seven aims: health, command of fundamental processes, worthy home membership, vocational preparation, citizenship, worthy use of leisure time, and development of ethical character (NEA, 1918).

The magnitude of these demands on the progressive educational movement brought both the opportunity on a broad scale to reconstruct the curricula of American schools and disagreement about how curricula should be organized. Despite Dewey's explanations, many progressives did not keep the three basic criteria of curriculum choice in reasonable balance. Some emphasized what they considered a scientific study of individuals and society in order to create curricula that would efficiently fit individuals into prevailing social structures. Others emphasized curricula that would protect the free and spontaneous development of children. Still others emphasized curricula intended directly to reconstruct society itself.[3] Although during the 1920s and 1930s the traditional academic curriculum that American schools had inherited as a legacy of the nineteenth century gradually incorporated different progressive emphases, there were few real experiments in genuinely experiential education, and most of these were of small scale and short duration.

The major exception was the Eight-Year Study, possibly the most important and most successful experiment ever undertaken in American schools.[4] It compared nearly 1,500 students who attended 30 progressive, experimental secondary schools with an equal number of students from traditional schools, following all students through their eight high school and college years, mostly during the middle and late 1930s. No two experimental schools were alike. Each freely developed its own curriculum; however, almost all these curricula were developed directly and cooperatively by the students and teachers of the schools in accordance with their own perceived needs and interests. Furthermore, comparisons between experimental and traditional students were made in terms of the development of individual experience, including academic, vocational, social, and personal considerations. Thus the study was clearly an experiment designed to measure the success of curricula developed in general accordance with Dewey's basic principles. Comparisons seemed to indicate that students from the experimental schools, which emphasized experiential education, did slightly better academically in college than did students from the traditional schools, but were decidedly better off in terms of their overall development in a whole host of things such as thinking, taking initiative for their own lives, and social adjustment.

Even while the Eight-Year Study was still in progress, Dewey had issued a warning and a clarification in *Experience and Education* (1938) to those progressive educators who were still confused about experiential education and how to properly balance the three basic criteria of curriculum choice: that is, how to promote the development of intelligence, the development of socially useful skills, and the healthy growth of individual experience. Dewey pointed out that all education, like all living, is a process of experiencing, but not all experiences are equally or genuinely educative. Experience must be judged by its quality. High-quality, or educative, experiences are those that contribute to the healthy growth of further experience; low-quality, or "miseducative," experiences are those that distort or arrest the healthy growth of experience. The problem for the educator is to make suggestions to individual students about subject matter, materials, and activities that will contribute to educative experiences. In general, the highest-quality experiences are those that help individuals become increasingly autonomous and intelligent in guiding their own future educative experiences. The quality of the personal experiences that the curriculum contributes to is more important than how it is organized or whether it is primarily academic, vocational, or social.

Unfortunately, both the example of the Eight-Year Study and the significance of Dewey's message were obscured by World War II, and after the war ended, the national mood turned increasingly conservative. Progressive education was increasingly viewed by the general public as something whose time had come and gone, even as something that was now largely responsible for the same ills in American schools that the progressives themselves had identified and denounced earlier in the century. The general public, of course, made no distinctions between forms of progressive education that were consistent with Dewey's views of experience and forms that were inconsistent. As we shall shortly see, the national debate about education in the late 1940s and the 1950s—very much like the national debate of the 1980s—became a call for more emphasis on traditional forms of academic education, and by the time that call was answered by the nationally sponsored, academically oriented curricula, the Progressive Educational Association itself had quietly faded out of existence. Except for a brief period during the late 1960s and early 1970s of national attention to free schools and open classrooms, some of which were genuinely devoted to experiential education and some of which were merely reactions to the academic emphases of the time, the national mood has remained unreceptive to progressive education, the fundamental experiment in modern education begun at the start of the century.

So that part of the experiment devoted to experiential education remains incomplete. Experiential education has been talked about a great deal, it has been tried out on a small scale, a few of its tenets have even seeped into typical American classrooms, but the challenge remains largely the same at the end of this century as it did at the beginning: to understand how curriculum can be considered in the broadest possible way, as whatever experience fosters the healthy growth of further experience, and to develop clear and workable principles to guide practical decisions about such curricula. Good experiential education is consistent with Dewey's views about fostering the intelligent autonomy of individual students.

Although Dewey's views were criticized during the 1950s, they were rediscovered by reformers in the late 1960s, forming the basis for the "alternative schools" movement. More recently, Eliot Wigginton (1985), through his widely publicized Foxfire program, has given Deweyan ideas a rebirth in a modern form. We will examine this modern expression of a Deweyan experiential perspective in more detail in Chapter Seven.

STRUCTURE OF THE DISCIPLINES

Abuses and distortions of Deweyan ideas provided educational critics of the 1950s, like Arthur Bestor and Admiral Hyman Rickover, a scapegoat for America's inability to gain a decisive competitive edge over the Russians in the Cold War that followed World War II. Books such as *Educational Wastelands* (Bestor, 1953), accusing American education of being intellectually "flabby," turned the questions of what schools should teach and who should decide this matter into issues of national concern. These critics laid the groundwork for a perspective that returned the focus of the curriculum to subject matter, and in particular to the disciplines of knowledge and the way scholars in those disciplines understand their structure. But as Atkin and House point out, there were significant political and educational antecedents to these issues:

> Before the mid-1950s . . . there was a lively education debate, and it was a curriculum debate. It centered on the decades-old battle between professors in liberal arts colleges and professors in schools of education. This heated internecine conflict over who trains teachers and what they should learn had been in progress at least since the late 1800s. (Atkin & House, 1981, p. 6)

The liberal arts professors representing the specific subject matters of the school curriculum regarded the education professors, particularly the progressive educators with an experiential perspective, as too general and fuzzy-headed. The education professors accused the subject-matter professors of being too narrow (Foshay, 1970). Atkin and House contend that World War II had a profound influence on this debate.

> . . . World War II and, particularly, the development of the atom bomb, greatly strengthened both the self-confidence of university-based academic scholars and their political power. The development of the practical application of

atomic energy was seen as a triumph of theoretical, intellectual effort. Furthermore it was considered university-based and an achievement of professors.
The fruits of research were seen by the American people, as never before, as
having an impact on daily life. The United States had been increasingly enam-
ored of technology during the preceding decades, but the developments were
seen as a result of inventiveness and industry, rather than of science and theoretical inquiry. Edison and Ford had been the popular embodiments of American progress in the decades before World War II.

   With the Allied victory over Germany and Japan, Einstein became a cultural hero. This quintessential professor—pipe-smoking, unkempt, apparently
unworldly—had developed as an act of mind the basis for defeating the Axis
power. People like him had worked intensely during the war to translate theory to an awesome weapon that had saved the world from enslavement. Professors captured the respect of the American public, and academic life was
seen, for the first time perhaps, as crucial to our national survival. . . . There
was a boost to professors and importance of a university education which had
never been seen before and, many people think, is unlikely to be seen again.
(Atkin & House, 1981, p. 6)

Because of these events and because of the international political climate of the
time, education at all levels was regarded as crucial to the achievement of
national goals. The most direct beneficiary of these developments was the university professor. Probably for the first time, university-based scholars in mathematics and science were seen as having a legitimate influence on elementary
and secondary curriculum.

   University professors had long been lamenting the quality of precollege education in the battles over teacher education policy. They had been saying for
50 years that students were arriving at the university without necessary preparation. The information high school graduates possessed was insufficient, in-
accurate or unimportant—sometimes all three. What the education system
needed was more involvement by university professors in the creation of curriculum for the schools; more involvement, that is, by professors in the academic disciplines that constituted the high school curriculum. (Atkin & House,
1981, pp. 6–7)

It was in this climate that Max Beberman at the University of Illinois formed a
group of mathematicians and engineers at his university for the purpose of improving the high school mathematics curriculum. The group, formed in 1951
and called the University of Illinois Committee on School Mathematics
(UICSM), "analyzed secondary-school mathematics courses and concluded
that they seldom included concepts developed after the year 1700, and almost
never focused on the mathematical ideas professors considered important"
(Atkin & House, 1981, p. 7). Beberman himself demonstrated at the University
High School that he could successfully teach secondary school students topics
like set theory. In 1952, UICSM developed instructional materials for use by
other teachers under a grant from the Carnegie Corporation. This grant allowed
UICSM to expand, involving more mathematicians and more schools in which
it could try out the experimental materials. The "new math" was born (Atkin &
House, 1981).

FIGURE 3.4 Jerrold Zacharias.

By the mid-1950s, these developments were paralleled by developments in physics, this time spearheaded by a group of professors at MIT and Harvard under the leadership of Jerrold Zacharias (see Figure 3.4) (Zacharias & White, 1964). These scientists, after analyzing the secondary school physics curriculum, reached the same conclusions that Beberman and his colleagues had reached earlier. The physics curriculum did not include the topics that these physicists regarded as the most important. Instead, high school physics textbooks emphasized technology, in particular the physical principles underlying the operation of everyday devices like refrigerators and automobile engines.

In the Cambridge setting, Zacharias, himself involved in defense work during World War II and emboldened by successes to be achieved by well-mobilized minds, attracted a group of outstanding physicists to work on high school curriculum. Several of these physicists also had been involved in weapons development just a few years earlier.

By 1956, the 6-year-old National Science Foundation, which in its charter had been given responsibility for improving the state of American science education as well as science, began to fund Zacharias' Physical Science Study Committee (PSSC). The verve, motivation, optimism, and esprit of PSSC seemed to many observers to be reminiscent of the organization that developed the atom bomb, and by this time Americans were convinced that great minds and plenty of money could do almost anything, even change the secondary school curriculum.

It probably is no coincidence that these early nationally oriented attempts to change the curriculum were in the fields of mathematics and science. It was these subjects that were associated with success in the war effort. It was these fields that represented increasingly for the American people an unqualified good. UICSM and PSSC received considerable publicity in the nation's education press, and there were feature stories in magazines such as *Time*. The tenor of the publicity, as might be imagined, was that the outstanding scholars associated with these new projects were in the process of remedying extraordinary deficiencies in the existing education system. Indeed, they were about to "reform" the curriculum. The clear inference for the public was that schools had been mismanaged, the curriculum was antiquated, and all this was, in an almost criminal fashion, depriving youngsters and society of a rightful education. The education "establishment" was seen increasingly by the public as it had been seen for decades by academics, as self-serving, unresponsive, and probably a bit dull-witted. (Atkin & House, 1981, pp. 7–8)

On October 4, 1957, these developments took on a sudden urgency with the dramatic launching of Sputnik I by the Soviet Union:

> The defense of the United States suddenly was seen as threatened. A sense of crisis permeated the nation. Professors testified in the Congress, and their testimony was believed. They said that our national well-being depended, in part, on high-quality precollege science education. (p. 8)

It was in this context that scientists like Zacharias had been attempting to update the physics curriculum. They quickly realized that the "knowledge explosion" had created too much subject matter to allow them simply to add modern physics to the existing curriculum. They found that they needed to establish priorities. Zacharias's solution was twofold: (1) teach only the most fundamental concepts in physics; (2) teach students how to derive the rest of physics knowledge from those concepts. In a sense, children could learn a lot "while keeping very little in mind" (Bruner, 1971, p. 20). Although this notion began with physics, it quickly spread to other sciences.

These efforts provided the basis for a conference in 1959 at Woods Hole, Massachusetts, sponsored by the National Science Foundation and other foundations. Jerome Bruner's (1960) report on that conference, entitled *The Process of Education*, proposed a theoretically reasonable solution to the ongoing debate between the subject-matter specialists and education generalists based on the work of Zacharias, Beberman, and others attending the conference. This report provided the principles upon which a structure-of-the-disciplines perspective was based. First, Bruner proposed that subject matter is dynamic, something evolving, instead of a given. Second, he proposed that each discipline has its own way of conducting inquiry. There is not one scientific method, but many. Third, he proposed that the purpose of education should be to develop in children's minds several different "modes of inquiry." These proposals struck a compromise between the education professors and those in the academic disciplines. After all, both groups were, and always had been, interested in fostering understanding (Foshay, 1970). Bruner's proposal was a reasonable resolution of the dilemma and spread rapidly. In the words of Bruner (1971, pp. 19–22):

> Let me reconstruct the period in which *The Process of Education* came into being. The year 1959 was a time of great concern over the intellectual aimlessness of our schools. Great strides had been made in many fields of knowledge, and these advances were not being reflected in what was taught in our schools. A huge gap had grown between what might be called the head and the tail of the academic procession. There was great fear, particularly that we were not producing enough scientists and engineers.
>
> It was the period, you will recall, shortly after Sputnik. The great problem faced by some of my colleagues in Cambridge, Massachusetts, at the time was that modern physics and mathematics were not represented in the curriculum, yet many of the decisions that society had to make were premised on being able to understand modern science. Something had to be done to assure that the ordinary decision maker within the society would have a sound basis for decision. The task was to get started on the teaching of science and, later, other subjects. . . .
>
> The prevailing notion was that if you understood the structure of knowledge, that understanding would then permit you to go ahead on your own; you did not need to encounter everything in nature in order to know nature, but by understanding some deep principles, you could extrapolate to the particulars as needed. Knowing was a canny strategy whereby you could know a great deal about a lot of things while keeping very little in mind.
>
> This view essentially opened the possibility that those who understood a field well—the practitioners of the field—could work with teachers to produce new curricula. For the first time in the modern age, the acme of scholarship, even in our great research institutes and universities, was to convert knowledge into pedagogy, to turn it back to aid the learning of the young. It was a brave idea and a noble one, for all its pitfalls. . . .
>
> The rational structuralism of Woods Hole had its internal counterpoise in intuitionism—the espousal of good guessing, of courage to make leaps, to go a long way on a little. It was mind at its best, being active, extrapolative, innovative, going from something firmly held to areas which were not so firmly known in order to have a basis for test. . . .
>
> During the early sixties, in various projects, it was discovered again and again how difficult it was to get to the limit of children's competence when the teaching was good. It was Socrates and the slave boy constantly being replayed. No wonder then that we concluded that any subject could be taught in some honest form to any child at any stage in his development. This did not necessarily mean that it could be taught in its final form, but it did mean that basically there was a courteous translation that could reduce ideas to a form that young students could grasp. *Not* to provide such translation was discourteous to them. The pursuit of this ideal was probably the most important outcome of the great period of curriculum building in the sixties.

> With all of this there went a spirit and attitude toward students. The learner was not one kind of person, the scientist or historian another kind. The school-boy learning physics did so as a physicist rather than as a consumer of some facts wrapped in what came to be called at Woods Hole a "middle language." A middle language talks *about* the subject rather than talking the subject. . . .

The metaphor of the student as neophyte scientist nicely captures the essence of this perspective. Once we understand that this metaphor provided the foundation for the perspective, the emphasis on students' active participation in scientific inquiry, the dominant role of university scientists, and the importance of providing students with the fundamental concepts of the disciplines all make perfect sense.

BEHAVIORAL

The dominance of scientists and mathematicians in curriculum development during the 1950s and early 1960s did not go unnoticed by behavioral psychologists. They were concerned that all the knowledge they had gained during the previous fifty years about how children learn was being ignored. Furthermore, with all the federal dollars being committed to curriculum development since Sputnik, they wanted a piece of the action. They argued that the strictly disciplines-based curricula were failing to teach science and mathematics effectively, that there was much more to curriculum development than providing materials that reflected the structure of the disciplines. According to these psychologists, curriculum development needed to focus not on content, but on what students should be able to do—i.e., the behaviors they learn—as a consequence of instruction. Further, educators need to take into account how students acquire these behaviors—i.e., the conditions of learning—as they plan instruction. In order to understand these criticisms and proposals, we must first consider the development of these views.

The roots of behavioral views, like most other views, can be traced back to Greek philosophers, particularly Aristotle. In an important work on memory and recollection, Aristotle argued that imagery is the basis for memory, that the associations a person makes between images are the basis for recollection, and that the principles of comparison, contrast, and contiguity are the basis for all associations. That is, the differences and similarities between images, as well as when they occur, account for the ways in which we relate our images, and those relationships in turn determine what we remember at any given time. Many of Aristotle's ideas found expression in the classical empiricism of John Locke (1913) in the seventeenth and David Hume (1957, 1967) in the eighteenth century. This view of knowledge was based on the assumption that all knowledge is rooted in sense impressions, i.e., the effects that seeing, hearing, touching, tasting, and smelling things in the world have on our minds. These sense impressions form the building blocks of experience, much as atoms form the building blocks of the physical world—as Sir Isaac Newton proposed at about this same time. These "atoms" of experience are then connected by associa-

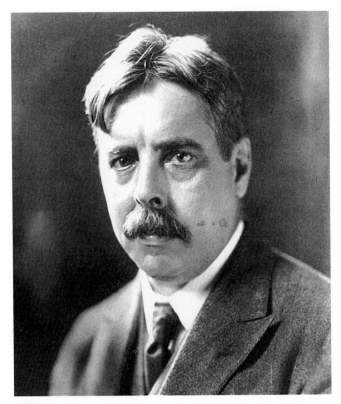

FIGURE 3.5 Edward Thorndike.

tions into complex ideas. However, as Hume (1957) so succinctly put it, no matter how complex the ideas, "there is nothing in the mind which was not first in the senses."

The founder of behavioral psychology is often considered to be Edward Thorndike (see Figure 3.5). His highly influential work near the beginning of the twentieth century in the areas of mental measurement, the laws of learning, the psychology of arithmetic, and transfer of training also established him as the founder of educational psychology. In addition, his exhaustive works on behavioral objectives in arithmetic contributed to his influence on the curriculum field during its formative years in the beginning of the twentieth century. It was Thorndike's preeminence and his promise of a behaviorally based science of education that led to the parallel emergence and common behavioral roots of educational psychology and curriculum as fields of professional study.

While Thorndike provided the necessary scientific basis, Franklin Bobbitt provided the necessary technology for a behaviorally based theory of curriculum. His two major works, *The Curriculum* (1918) and *How to Make a Curriculum* (1924), established behavioral analysis, termed "life-activity analysis," and specific objectives derived from the analysis as the principal methods of curriculum development. As long as one could assume that preparation for current life activities also prepares people to live in tomorrow's world, Bobbitt's methods seemed reasonable. Furthermore, basing curriculum on actual life activities, rather than on traditional subject matter, seemed to be consistent with the progressive movement sweeping the nation at the time. However, once educators realized that they were living in a rapidly changing world, and that life-activity analysis could lead educators to develop curricula that reinforced the existing social structure and were doomed to technological obsolescence, they began to regard Bobbitt's methods as too conservative. But Bobbitt's technology for developing curricula based on activity analysis left a legacy. After Bobbitt many educators believed that curriculum development is a process best left to experts, i.e., those with specialized knowledge. This belief transformed the field to one based on a technical production framework (see Chapter One).

Ralph Tyler continued the technical production and objectives orientation of curriculum into the 1930s, 1940s, and 1950s. In his seminal book, *Basic Principles of Curriculum and Instruction* (1949), he presented a method for analyzing each curriculum objective into its substantive, i.e., content, dimension and its behavioral dimension.[5] Tyler's notion of the behavioral aspect of an objective served as the basis for Benjamin Bloom's (1956) highly influential work on a taxonomy (a classification) of objectives. Bloom's taxonomy (see Chapter Four) systematized the behavioral dimension and, in doing so, reinforced the belief that objectives are fundamentally expressions of the behaviors that educators want learned—as opposed to the content teachers want to teach or the experiences educators want students to have.

While Bobbitt provided educators with the technology to identify important objectives, Robert Mager and Fred Keller provided the technologies necessary for expressing those objectives in clear, unambiguous terms; their work gave teachers a blueprint they could use to redesign their courses according to behavioristic principles. Mager's little book *Preparing Instructional Objectives* (1962) has done more to influence educator's beliefs about objectives—and in particular, their proper form—than any other work. Likewise, Keller's (1968) approach to teaching, termed Personalized System of Instruction (PSI), has arguably done more to change college instruction than any other single innovation. In this approach, a course is broken down into a step-by-step series of behaviors, each of which must be "mastered" before the student is allowed to move on. By uncritically transferring their extensive experience in industrial training to public education, Mager and Keller were able to stipulate the requirements for well-formed objectives and for effective course organization, respectively. The major requirement for Magerian objectives is a verb that expresses observable behaviors. As we shall explore in greater depth in Chapter Five, Mager's insistence on observable behaviors and his stipulation of a simple procedure for writing this type of objective, and Keller's requirements for content sequence and for student progress through that sequence, have provided educators with straightforward, if not reductionistic, technologies for implementing B. F. Skinner's (1968) behavioristic psychology of learning.

CONSTRUCTIVIST

In primary and secondary education, as in the universities, a challenge to the behavioral orientation that dominated psychology came from constructivists. Ironically, the foundations of modern constructivist views can also be traced to Greek philosophy, but in this case to Plato. Although some of Plato's theory now seems strange, his views had a strong influence on antecedents of constructivism. Plato believed that a person's knowledge and ideas are innate, or inborn; all that a teacher needs to do is help the person recall them. Therefore, according to Plato learning is recollection, and recollection is the search for and discovery of innate ideas followed by the construction of new concepts from those ideas. Plato's rendition of Socratic dialogues has remained, for many educators, the prototype of great teaching. Socrates seemed capable of teaching complex, abstract ideas without appearing to tell his students anything. As implausible as Plato's view of innate ideas might seem to us now, it has been very influential and formed the basis for many modern ideas of learning as discovery.

In spite of Plato's influence, the predominant views about learning and knowledge through the nineteenth century were empiricist ones, according to which all knowledge derives from sensations and the associations made between them. Modern constructivist views, though rooted in Platonic idealism formulated more than 2,000 years earlier, may, therefore, be understood as a response to nineteenth-century empiricism. By arguing that the empiricist account of knowledge is fundamentally flawed, Immanuel Kant in the nineteenth century established the foundation for the constructivist perspective. Sensations and associations, he argued, are insufficient as an account of knowledge. Kant then asked the fundamental cognitive question: "What goes on in the mind that allows us to form knowledge?" His answer was that empiricists failed to take into account the structure of the mind. The mind, he said, has categories that structure perceptions. Experience does not consist of raw sensations, but of sensations structured by the mind.

In part because some of the methods used by some constructivists to study the mind proved to be unreliable (particularly the method known as introspection), their work was discredited and ignored for almost a century.

For example, the work of the Swiss psychologist Jean Piaget went largely unnoticed for thirty years until the 1950s. Piaget (see Figure 3.6), as he sought to understand the development of intelligence, was particularly interested in children's beliefs about space, e.g., volume; time; natural phenomena, e.g., the sun; and moral questions (Piaget, 1929). By providing detailed accounts of how these beliefs develop and how young children's thinking differs from that of adults, Piaget provided educators with an in-depth understanding of children's minds and convinced many educators that they must wait until the child is cognitively "ready," before teaching abstract concepts. Furthermore, his notion that the mind both "assimilates" new ideas into an existing structure and also "accommodates" new ideas by reorganizing this structure has formed the basis for modern constructivism.

FIGURE 3.6 Jean Piaget.

While Piaget was showing educators the cognitive limitations on abstract thinking in young children, Noam Chomsky (1968) was portraying the incredible accomplishment that young children manage to complete within two to three years, namely, language acquisition. He developed a mode of analyzing the structure of language, showing that language is far more complex than previously believed, and that behaviorist accounts of language development are incapable of explaining these complexities. He argued that innate structures (a "language acquisition device") are necessary for explaining how someone learns such a complex language in so short a period of time. In his argument he made an important and highly influential distinction between competence (which he defined as the existence of mental structures, such as understanding of grammatical rules) and performance (in other words, observable behaviors, such as utterances). The study of the relationship between knowledge and performance continues to be of fundamental concern to cognitive psychologists studying such topics as problem solving, language, decision making, and even teaching.

Although the work of Piaget, Chomsky, and many others has provided the basis for modern constructivist views of education, little direct attention had been given to problems of learning per se until David Ausubel's (1968) work on "meaningful learning." Although Ausubel approached the problem from a different perspective, he joined the behavioral psychologists in criticizing the proponents of the disciplines-based curricula, particularly for their use of "discovery learning" and for their failure to distinguish between the "logical structure" of the disciplines and the "psychological structure" of the learner (Ausubel, 1964). His work and that of "schema" theorists like Richard Anderson (1977) after him established the view that "the single most important determinant of learning is what the learner already knows; ascertain that and teach him accordingly" (Ausubel, 1968).

Much of the recent work in this field has been aimed at discovering what it is that learners already know, i.e., their existing concepts and beliefs; how that knowledge affects their performance on school-related tasks such as comprehension and problem solving; and how to teach learners to perform difficult tasks and to understand abstract ideas (Bereiter & Scardamalia, 1992). As you will learn in Chapter Five, this range of concerns has produced a variety of approaches to curriculum, all of which can be constructivist oriented, including those based on child development,[6] concept learning,[7] multiple intelligences,[8] and the thinking process.[9] More recently, the notion of the "thinking curriculum" attempts to resolve conflicts among these different views by

> offering a perspective on learning that is thinking- and meaning-centered, yet insists on a central place for knowledge and instruction. Cognitive scientists today share with Piagetians a constructivist view of learning, asserting that people are not recorders of information (as in the traditional perspective) but builders of knowledge structures. To know something is not just to have received information but also to have interpreted it and related it to other knowledge. To be skilled is not just to know how to perform some action (as in the behavioral perspective) but also to know when to perform it and to adapt the performance to varied circumstances. . . . Thinking and learning merge in today's cognitive perspective, so that cognitive and instructional theory (and we might add, curriculum theory) is, at its heart, concerned with the Thinking Curriculum. (Resnick & Klopfer, 1989, pp. 3–4)[10]

Summary

To summarize the five perspectives, we can imagine asking the proponents of each one how they would advocate reforming schooling in general and curriculum in particular. Their responses might be as follows:

1. *Traditional* Schools need to return to the basics, that is, to a mastery of basic literacy and computational skills, to a knowledge of basic facts and terminology that all educated people should know, and to a set of common values that constitute good citizenship.
2. *Experiential* Schooling is too detached from the interests and problems of the students, that is, from their ordinary life experience. Make schooling more functionally related to the students' experience, that is, less contrived and artificial, and students will grow more and become better citizens.

3. *Structure of the disciplines* There is too large a gap between school subject matter and the scholarly disciplines from which they derive. Reduce that gap by engaging students of all ages in genuine inquiry using the few truly fundamental ideas of the disciplines, and students will develop both confidence in their intellectual capabilities and understanding of a wide range of phenomena.
4. *Behavioral* There is too much vague talk about objectives, and there are too many unsystematic approaches to the development of curricula. Just decide what the successful graduates should be able to do in very specific measurable terms, analyze those behaviors to identify their prerequisite skills, provide opportunities for students to practice each skill with feedback to the point of mastery, and then evaluate the students' performance. We have the technology to ensure that all students master what they need to know. We need only the determination to implement our knowledge.
5. *Constructivist* Schools emphasize rote learning too much and do not put enough emphasis on real understanding and thinking. Curricula need to allow students to construct their own knowledge based on what they already know and to use that knowledge in purposeful activities requiring decision making, problem solving, and judgments.

Perspectives not only provide vantage points that increase our educational vision but also may influence and be influenced by our views of reality. An understanding of this point is essential before you attempt to use the perspectives for curriculum analysis.

A theoretical perspective functions as a metaphor for thinking and talking about the mind, teaching, and curriculum. Traditional curricula conjure up the metaphor of the mind as a storehouse, while constructivist curricula appear to view the mind as a building site. Behavioral curricula conceive of teaching as shaping behavior, structure-of-the-disciplines curricula view teaching as the induction of novices into a community of scholars, and experiential curricula consider teaching to be working behind the scenes to facilitate and guide student-directed projects. Behavioral perspectives conceive of curricula as the specific destinations or targets toward which education is aimed, whereas traditional perspectives imagine curricula as encyclopedic repositories of ideas, skills, people's names, events, books, and values that all students should master.

Metaphors such as these are powerful. They affect the language we use to discuss education, and they make certain proposals reasonable and others unreasonable. They even help determine what we consider to be common sense. For example, the claim by behaviorists that you cannot determine your itinerary and mode of travel until you decide specifically where you want to go is used as an appeal for highly specific educational objectives.

But we must always be cautious of metaphors. Although they help us understand the unfamiliar in terms of the familiar, they also distort. The things or experiences that a metaphor equate are never really exactly the same. That is, all metaphors have inherent limitations. They can be taken too far. More important, unless we are aware of our use of metaphors and their limitations we can become captive to them and encapsulated by them (Zais, 1976). The experienced curriculum analyst is continually monitoring the use of metaphors in educational discourse, particularly in curriculum proposals.

In Chapter Twelve, we will examine in more detail the limitations of the theoretical perspectives introduced here. An understanding both of the perspectives and of their limitations will provide the basis for the reflective eclecticism discussed in Chapter One.

Curriculum Analysis Question

1. What perspective, if any, does the curriculum represent?

As you answer the question, remember that at this point you can only hypothesize about the curriculum's perspective. Don't be afraid to go out on a limb here. Subsequent chapters will enable you to test your hypothesis. If you can see no perspectives, don't hesitate to say so.

Notes

1. See, for example, writers like E. D. Hirsch, Jr. (1987), William Bennett (1988), and Allan Bloom (1987).
2. I wish to thank George Willis for his contribution to this section of the book.
3. See Cremin (1961).
4. See Aikin (1942).
5. See Bloom, Hastings, and Madaus (1971) for an elaboration of this two-dimensional analysis of objective.
6. Typically based on the work of Piaget (1929) or Kohlberg (1971).
7. Typically based on the work of Ausubel (1968) or Bruner, Goodnow, and Austin (1956).
8. See Gardner (1983, 1991).
9. For example, those derived from the work of Taba (1967) on inductive thinking, Sternberg (1985) on critical thinking, and deBono (1970) and Torrance (1965) on creative, or "lateral," thinking. Note that these psychologists would not necessarily call themselves "constructivist."
10. Interestingly, although the cognitive (or "constructivist," as we are calling it) and the behavioral psychologists may bitterly debate the way people learn, both psychologies represent technical production perspectives on curriculum. Both consider learning to be the purpose of education, although they may come to blows about what it means to learn something and how best to facilitate the process. Furthermore, both perspectives consider curriculum development to be a technical process requiring the expertise of psychologists, although they obviously each consider their own brand of psychology to be the most useful.

PART TWO

The Curriculum Proper

What purposes does the curriculum intend to accomplish? What content does it include? What assumptions do the purpose and content imply? How is the curriculum organized? These questions concern the curriculum proper. In Chapter Four these questions direct the study of the curriculum's goals, objectives, and content. In Chapter Five two approaches to a curriculum's purpose and content are explored, one focusing on behavioral outcomes, the other on thinking and conceptual development. Chapter Six examines the structure of a curriculum's objectives, content, and media. Chapter Seven analyzes three approaches to curriculum organization and explores them in depth, enabling you to see how curriculum organization embodies fundamental beliefs about learning and knowledge.

CHAPTER 4

Curriculum Purpose and Content

Basic Concepts

Jim Woodward is a sixth-grade social studies teacher in the Thauteville School District. The district's Board of Education has recently decided that, in response to the growing public criticism of education, Thauteville schools would focus their efforts on "improving the ability of students to think critically and to solve problems effectively" (from District Mission Statement, adopted by the Thauteville Board of Education, 1990).

This action by the board came just weeks after the local newspaper published a report of statewide testing showing that Thauteville students across the grades scored above the state mean in basic computational skills; reading skills; spelling and punctuation; and recall of geographical facts, scientific terminology and formulas, and historical names, dates, and events. However, Thauteville students did relatively poorly on tests asking students to write a paragraph that develops an argument for or against a position on an issue, to solve problems using their knowledge of mathematics and science, and to analyze a current issue in the news in terms of their historical, geographical, economic, or cultural knowledge.

The Social Studies Department in Thauteville Middle School is in the process of selecting new textbooks for Grades 6 through 8. Jim is on the textbook selection committee and wants to help choose books that are consistent with the board's decision. The committee has narrowed the selection to 10 books for Grade 6. As Jim prepares for the next round of deliberations, many thoughts go through his mind:

1. *What does "thinking critically and solving problems effectively" mean for social studies?*
2. *How to sort out, articulate, and weigh the wide assortment of aims, goals, and objectives that are being thrown at the teachers—including the board's new goal, other board goals like increasing attendance and reducing the dropout rate, goals issued by the State Education Department, the objectives of the Social Studies Curriculum (Grades K through 6 and 7 through 12), the statewide competency tests, and the objectives expressed in each of the textbooks he examines.*
3. *What are the differences between the textbooks? More specifically, which textbooks are more consistent with an approach that emphasizes memorization of historical,*

geographical, economic, or cultural facts and terminology and which are more consistent with an approach that emphasizes the use of information and concepts to interpret current events?

This chapter will enable you to analyze a curriculum's aims, goals, objectives, and content. If you were in Jim's place, this chapter would help you to prepare for the meeting and perhaps even to take a leadership role in the Social Studies Department.

TRAINING AND EDUCATIONAL CONTEXTS FOR CURRICULUM

In everyday language some of the basic terms used to discuss the purpose and content of education are used loosely. Terms like "education" and "training" are used interchangeably. "Purpose" is usually defined as "an intended or desired result," and the terms "goal" and "objective" are often considered to be synonyms. However, when we use these terms in curriculum discourse, we need to be more precise.

First we consider the distinction between training and education as contexts for curriculum.

Although used interchangeably, the two terms "training" and "education" refer to fundamentally different contexts. *Training* refers to contexts in which we can predict with some confidence the specific situations in which people will use what they learn. For example, if we want to prepare students to be automotive mechanics, and we know precisely the kinds of tasks automotive mechanics need to perform, we can develop curricula to train students for these tasks. In this context, targeting the curriculum directly at the tasks the graduates will perform is the most efficient approach to job preparation.

Education, on the other hand, refers to contexts in which we cannot predict with any specificity or certainty the situations in which people will use what they learn. For example, if we assume that social studies is intended to prepare students for their civic responsibilities, but that we do not know precisely how they will use their social studies knowledge, we must develop curricula that educate these students broadly. Some educators believe that building curricula around fundamental principles and concepts—a "content" approach—serves this purpose. Others believe that teaching students how to solve problems, formulate problems, and locate resources—a "process" approach—is the preferred approach to preparing students for changing times. Regardless of the approach used, the assumption when formulating curricula for educational contexts is that most of the situations for which we prepare students are unpredictable.

Broudy's analysis of the uses of knowledge leads to a similar distinction. He argues that if we were to consider knowledge useful only to the extent that we use it in the same way that we learn it, then much of the knowledge we acquire in school would be useless. Knowledge of literature, the fine arts, music, and history, among others, is used "associatively" and "interpretively" (Broudy, Smith, & Burnett, 1964) in the sense that these subjects supply images and conceptual frameworks that enrich experience and help us to find meaning in it. It is this sense of their utility that makes these subjects appropriate for educational, rather than training, contexts. Vocational skills, arithmetic computation, and typing, on the other hand, are among the forms of knowledge used "replicatively" and "applicatively." When students use the knowledge gained from these experiences, they use it in a form and context closely resembling the situation in which they learned it. This similarity between learning and use is what makes it appropriate to say that the teaching of these subjects and topics takes place in training contexts rather than educational contexts.

What follows from this distinction is that we can develop curricula for either training or educational contexts, that schools provide both educational and training contexts, and that neither context is inherently more valuable. The question this distinction raises is: How much of schooling and what proportion of each subject should we conceive of as education, and how much should we conceive of as training? For example, should science instruction be aimed at training scientists or cultivating scientific literacy? Should vocational preparation stress fundamental principles, i.e., education, or job-related skills, i.e., training? The former helps workers avoid extensive retraining as technology changes. The latter provides workers with immediately marketable skills.

You will be asked to determine which aspects of a particular curriculum are aimed at training and which at education, and to determine the appropriateness of the curriculum with regard to this distinction. In addition, we will see in Chapter Five that certain curriculum features (e.g., objectives) designed for one context can be inappropriate for the other. Thus, the distinction between training and education is important to keep in mind as you read the rest of this book.

AIMS, GOALS, AND OBJECTIVES

Frequently, we hear people speaking of their "educational objectives" or "purposes" without clarifying their terms. In such cases, it is difficult to know whether they mean broad educational aims of the state or school district, or more specific objectives of an individual teacher. In fact, there is no consensus on the meaning of such terms as "aims," "goals," and "objectives." Therefore, we need to stipulate definitions of some of these basic terms for the purposes of this text. In so doing, we seek to make distinctions between different sorts of purposes or objectives that have an educational significance. Later we will use these terms as conceptual tools for analyzing curricula. Figure 4.1 depicts the following discussion schematically.

Societal Goal

Improving equality of opportunity, increasing America's competitive edge, fostering world peace, decreasing unemployment, reducing crime, and protecting the environment are but a sample of goals that citizens might want to accomplish through their country's political, economic, and social institutions. The school is one of the society's most significant institutions and is, therefore,

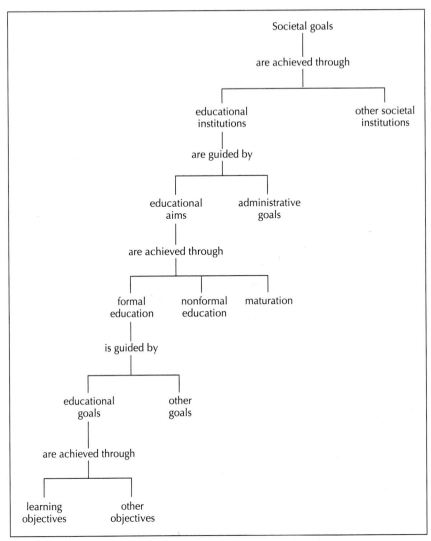

FIGURE 4.1 Aims, goals, and objectives.

expected to contribute to the accomplishment of these goals. Strictly speaking, societal goals are not primarily educational aims or goals, because they do not refer to outcomes achievable through learning; however, almost any societal goal has some educational dimension. For example, schools might attempt to help decrease unemployment by offering vocational education programs with the goal of providing young people with knowledge and skills for careers in high-technology occupations (an educational goal). During the progressive movement between the 1890s and the 1930s, the schools assumed an increasing responsibility for achieving societal goals, thus making societal and educational goals more congruent and mutually supportive.

Administrative Goal

Schools and colleges are organizations and, as such, are concerned not just with the education of their students, but also with the maintenance and improvement of the organization. Typically, many board-of-education goals tend to be of this sort. Accomplishing goals such as limiting budget increases to 10 percent, hiring more minority teachers, lengthening the school year, adding a new science laboratory, and repairing the high school's roof may indirectly improve the quality of education but are not educational objectives themselves.

In this chapter's lead-off scenario, "increasing attendance and reducing the dropout rate" are administrative goals. We call them administrative goals to distinguish them from educational aims and goals.

In contrast with societal and administrative goals, which, strictly speaking, are not *educational* goals,[1] the next three terms all refer to the intended consequences of the educational process. However, they differ in an important respect. They represent decreasing degrees of remoteness from the actual events of teaching and learning. *Educational aims* are more remote from events of teaching and learning than *educational goals*, which, in turn, are more remote than *learning objectives*. The more remote an intended consequence is, the more general and long-term it tends to be. As a result, the consequences that educational aims describe tend to be produced by a wider range of experiences than those described by curriculum objectives. Although the more remote consequences tend to be more difficult to evaluate, they also tend to be more profound (Zais, 1976, pp. 305–306).

Educational Aim

The stated aims of education "describe expected life outcomes based on some value schema either consciously or unconsciously chosen" (Broudy, 1971, p.13). For example, the aim of developing a respect for people of different cultural backgrounds is based on the value of cultural diversity. The achievement of an educational aim is a long-term affair and may occur only after the completion of schooling; it may result not only from schooling but also from a variety of influences, including maturation, the home, and mass media. Lists of educational aims have been periodically issued by philosophers, commissions, and professional societies. Two of the most famous are those included in Herbert Spencer's (1861) prescription for "what knowledge is of most worth" and the Seven Cardinal Principles of the Commission on the Reorganization of Secondary Education (1918). Four related categories of educational aims are conventionally cited, although the particular emphasis depends upon the value schema of the writer:

1. *Personal development* includes "self-cultivation" (Broudy, 1961) or "self-actualization" (Maslow, 1959) and personal living.
2. *Socialization* includes citizenship and interpersonal relations.
3. *Economic productivity* includes both vocational and consumer aspects.
4. *Further learning* includes command of basic skills and other requirements for continuous and independent learning (Johnson, 1977).

All four categories include both educational and training dimensions. For example, personal development includes both developing an appreciation for music (education) and developing proficiency in playing particular musical instruments (training). Socialization includes both the understanding of the history of one's country as a context for interpreting current political issues (education) and learning how to operate a voting machine (training). Economic productivity includes both understanding basic economic concepts (education) and acquiring job skills (training). Further learning includes both acquisition of basic concepts from the academic disciplines (education) and learning to use computers for automated library searches (training).

As societal values have changed throughout history, the intended purpose of an education has followed suit. In ancient Greece, the Spartans, proud of their athletic prowess, fighting skills, and sense of civic responsibility, based their educational system on these aims. In contrast, the Athenians valued physical, moral, intellectual, and aesthetic development, employing the *trivium* (grammar, rhetoric, and logic) and *quadrivium* (arithmetic, geometry, astronomy, and music) to achieve the latter two aims. During the Middle Ages, religious and moral development were the primary aims; consequently, catechism, psalmody, and the study of religious writings constituted the curriculum. The Renaissance brought a shift from religious aims back to intellectual, aesthetic, moral, and physical development—what were called "manly arts"—adding the teaching of proper manners, which had become important to the educated upper class as courtly life developed. During the Colonial Period (seventeenth century) in America, religious salvation again became the primary aim, and Greek and Latin were taught as the languages of religious writings.

Spencer's (1861) rationale for his answer to the question "What knowledge is of most worth?" marked a departure from the traditional educational aims by representing a more utilitarian set of values and associated educational aims. Spencer contended that self-preservation, procuring necessities of life, rearing children, social and political relations, and appreciation of culture should be the primary aims, and that, if they were, many useless studies would be discarded. Of course, what is "useful" or "useless" depends on one's educational aims.

As the progressive movement continued, this utilitarian view of education was elaborated, as evidenced by the many commission reports published during the first half of the twentieth century. The most famous was that of the Committee on the Reorganization of Secondary Education (1918), who formulated the so-called Seven Cardinal Principles. This report was followed by recommendations from Bobbitt (1924), the Department of Superintendence (AASA, 1928), and the Educational Policy Commission (Educational Policies Committee, 1938, 1947) (*The Purposes of Education in American Democracy* and *Ten Imperative Needs of Youth*). As Table 4.1 indicates, the similarities of all of these are striking.

Compare these comprehensive listings of aims with the narrow view proposed at a White House Conference in 1961 as the central purpose of education, namely, the cultivation of the ability to think. This dramatic shift from a view

TABLE 4.1 A Comparison of Progressive Educational Aims

1918	1924	1928	1938	1947
Health	Health Keeping mentally fit	Self	Self-realization	Good health and fitness
Leisure time	Leisure occupations Religious activities	Nature God		Good use of leisure time; appreciation of literature, art, music, and nature; understanding of the influence of science on human life
Home membership	Parental responsibilities		Human relationships	Understanding of the significance of the family
Citizenship	Citizenship	Society	Civic responsibility	Understanding of rights and duties of the democratic citizen; developing respect for others
Ethical relationships	General social contacts			
Vocation	Vocational activities Unspecialized practical activities		Economic efficiency	Developing salable skills; knowing how to purchase and use goods and services intelligently
Fundamental processes	Language activities			Developing ability to think rationally

of education as the primary agency for social improvement to a view focusing on one intellectual aim may seem remarkable. However, the period between 1949 and 1961 was marked by a fundamental reexamination of the educational system in the light of pressing national needs. The Cold War between the United States and the Soviet Union began and escalated, and military superiority became both countries' preoccupation. The launching of Sputnik by the Soviets was perceived by most Americans as a symbol of America's fall from a position of dominance in military technology and represented an imminent threat to U.S. security. The schools were identified as one of the primary tools for regaining superiority, and this task was seen as achievable only if the schools focused on the development of the mind. After all, according to popular belief, World War II was won as a result of the accomplishments of physicists like Albert Einstein, the prototype of the intellectual genius. Thus, as national priorities shifted from social reform to national defense, educational aims shifted from preparation for life to the development of the intellect.

The years from the late 1960s through the early 1970s were marked by a return to a liberal social agenda with aims intended to increase equality of educational opportunity, provide an education "relevant" to children's lives, and increase awareness of ecological crises.

The 1980s and 1990s marked a return to a narrow view of educational aims. Under the banner of educational "excellence" and "standards," schools returned to an overwhelming preoccupation with traditional educational aims; the focus on basic skills was modified only by the addition of computer literacy as an aim.[2] Clearly, the conservative political environment of this decade was reflected in educational aims. These shifts from broad sets of aims encompassing social reform to narrower ones reflect the cyclical nature of educational reform.

The new millenium continues this narrowing of aims with the renewed emphasis on standards and standardized testing.

Educational Goal

In order for schools to implement an educational aim, it is first translated into goals reflecting the sorts of accomplishments that can be attributed to schools and colleges (Zais, 1976). These *educational goals* are described in terms of the characteristics that are supposed to result from learning over the years and across the subject matters of schooling. They do not in themselves express desired learnings, but instead describe the characteristics of the well-educated person. For example, a school or college may expect that its graduates develop the following characteristics as a result of its educational program:

1. Facility in using the English language
2. Familiarity with another language
3. Proficiency in solving problems and thinking critically
4. Sense of self-respect and insight into own uniqueness, including interests and capabilities
5. Habits conducive to good health, physical fitness, and personal safety
6. Capacity for creative expression and aesthetic judgment
7. Self-discipline
8. Appreciation of own cultural heritage balanced with a respect for cultural diversity
9. Ability to fulfill obligations of a citizen of a democracy
10. Concern for protecting public health, property, and safety
11. Ability to make informed decisions concerning the environment
12. Ability to assume responsibility for own learning, and interest in continuing learning
13. Awareness of career options and training opportunities

Of course this list is not exhaustive and leaves out many important goals, such as ability to use mechanical tools and apparatus, family living skills, and job-entry skills and work habits, to name just a few others. Presumably, every curriculum of a school or a school system would attempt to contribute to the accomplishment of one or more of the school's educational goals. If the state itself has set forth educational goals, then each school and school system within that state would be expected to show how its curricula lead to the attainment of the state goals. Clearly, the distinction between an educational aim and a goal is not sharp, and there is a continuum between the two categories. For example, Thauteville's Board of Education (in this chapter's lead-off scenario) wanted its students "to think critically and to solve problems effectively." This statement is probably best considered a general educational goal. However, an argument could be made that these sorts of outcomes result from many influences besides schools and that the statement is therefore best considered an educational aim. There is no definitive answer to this question of categorization, since the distinction relies on matters of degree rather than of kind.

Learning Objective

Learning objectives are the intended educational consequences of particular courses or units of study. They may vary in specificity from objectives of single lessons, i.e., *lesson objectives,* to objectives of an entire course, i.e., *course objectives.*

As we noted earlier, there is no consensus in the field on terminology. A statement of an intention that someone learn something may be called an "intended learning outcome" (Johnson, 1967; Goodlad & Richter, 1966) or a "learning objective." Just remember that whenever and however we are able to express what we want students to learn, we are dealing with learning objectives. As we will see in Chapter Five, though, how learning objectives can and should be expressed has been a matter of significant debate among psychologists. Table 4.2 summarizes the various levels of educational purposes presented thus far.

TABLE 4.2 Levels of Educational Purposes

Societal goals What citizens or policymakers want their country's political, economic, social, and educational institutions to accomplish.

Administrative goals What leaders of organizations want to accomplish that allows for the maintenance and improvement of the organization.

Educational aims What citizens or policymakers want society's educational institutions to accomplish; generally long-term and the result of many influences, only one of which is the school; generally expressed in terms of characteristics of people who have been well educated.

Educational goals What citizens or policymakers want formal educational institutions— i.e., schools and colleges—to accomplish expressed in terms of characteristics of people who have been well-educated.

Learning objectives Whatever people are intended to learn as a consequence of being students in educational institutions.

Just as our overview of the history of educational aims showed us that changes in educational aims reflect changes in societal values, history also shows that changes in educational aims reflect changes in educational goals and learning objectives. After all, aims serve as justification for educational goals and educational goals for learning objectives. For example, during the seventeenth century, when the primary educational aim was religious salvation, achievable through Bible study, being literate in Greek and Latin (an educational goal) was necessary for students to have access to classical religious texts. With this justification, the Latin curriculum emphasized the objective of learning to translate classical texts. English grammar was taught, in part, as an aid to learning Latin! Later the justification for learning Latin changed to the aim of acquiring mental discipline, and the emphasis in the Latin curriculum shifted from translation and classical texts to learning Latin grammar. Currently, Latin instruction is experiencing a resurgence justified by some people as a way to prepare for college—or at least for the Scholastic Aptitude Tests (SATs). This justification leads to a curriculum emphasizing vocabulary. A similar analysis of the relation between educational aims, educational goals, and learning objectives could be done for the study of reading, science, mathematics, and history.[3]

Since categories of learning objectives reflect the way one conceptualizes such notions as knowledge and learning, the range of learning objectives is as wide as the range of conceptions of knowledge and learning. When educational psychologists write about objectives, they have tended to use terms like "cognitive," "affective," and "psychomotor" (Bloom, 1956) in the past, or, more recently, terms like "motor skills," "verbal information," "cognitive strategies," "intellectual skills," and "attitudes" (Gagne, 1977). When philosophers write about objectives, they tend to use terms like "know that," "know how" (Ryle, 1949), and "know with" (Broudy, 1977). These differences reflect the psychologists' claim on the term "learning" and the philosophers' claim on the term "knowing." Obviously, there is much to be gained from both bodies of literature.

The Taxonomy   The first volume of the *Taxonomy of Educational Objectives* was edited by the psychologist Benjamin Bloom and published in 1956; it proposed three "domains" of objectives and provided details on one of them. Bloom and his colleagues termed the three domains that were to make up their completed taxonomy the cognitive, the affective, and the psychomotor. The cognitive domain is the focus of the 1956 volume and includes "those objectives which deal with the recall or recognition of knowledge and the development of intellectual abilities and skills" (Bloom, 1956, p. 7). Six major classes of cognitive objectives are described; they are listed in Table 4.3 in presumed order of increasing complexity.

There has been considerable criticism of this classification on the grounds that it is not, in fact, hierarchical—in other words, that one can learn a "higher-level" skill without first learning the corresponding "lower-level" skill—and that the concept of knowledge is trivialized into mere rote recall and recognition. Critics argue that knowledge represents far more than rote learning;

TABLE 4.3 The Cognitive Domain*

1.00	*Knowledge*	"Recall or recognition of ideas, material or phenomena" (p. 62).
2.00	*Comprehension*	"Understanding the literal message contained in a communication" (p. 89).
3.00	*Application*	Knowing how and when to use an abstraction in a new situation or problem.
4.00	*Analysis*	Breaking down "material into its constituent parts" and detecting "relationships of the parts and of the way they are organized" (p. 144).
5.00	*Synthesis*	"Putting together of elements and parts so as to form a whole" (p. 162).
6.00	*Evaluation*	"Making of judgments about the value, for some purpose, of ideas, works, solutions, methods, material, etc." (p. 185).

*Page references are to Bloom (1956).

knowledge is perhaps the ultimate purpose of all education. Nevertheless, in spite of all its weaknesses, the taxonomy of the cognitive domain has forcefully made an important point: Much of our teaching and testing is aimed at low-level objectives. There is far more to education than recall and recognition of information. In a sense, the taxonomy has served as a vocabulary for the criticism of fact-oriented curricula.

The affective domain was the subject of the second volume of the taxonomy, which has been less widely used and accepted than the one detailing the cognitive domain. The second volume, published in 1964 and edited by David Krathwohl and others, concerns interests, attitudes, values, and appreciations. It is organized into five classes in increasing levels of internalization, from just listening to an idea (Level 1), to responding to it (Level 2), to developing values and commitment to the idea (Level 3), to developing a value system based on the idea (Level 4), to being characterized by a value or value complex (Level 5).

The criticism of the taxonomy of the affective domain has been as strong as that of the cognitive domain. Critics argue that classifying objectives into separate cognitive and affective domains distorts education. Thinking and feeling cannot be reasonably separated, they say. Further, critics argue that rather than providing a taxonomy based on kinds of affective learning outcomes, as the volume describing the cognitive domain does for cognitive learning outcomes, the volume describing the affective domain provides a taxonomy based on the degree of internalization of some cognitive learning. That is, it describes degrees rather than kinds of learning, never actually clarifying the relations between affective outcomes like attitudes, appreciations, interests, and desires. Nevertheless, the mere presence of a systematic description of an affective domain has forced educators to consider student interests and attitudes as possible objectives of education.

The group of psychologists that developed the first two volumes of taxonomies never completed their proposed trilogy by publishing a taxonomy of the psychomotor domain. However, several other individuals have proposed their own during the past twenty years. Anita Harrow (1972) eventually published a taxonomy that has since been accepted as the third volume of the set.

The taxonomies are not the only classifications of learning objectives. Among the other classifications that have been published, two that have had great influence on the way people conceive of learning objectives are from the work of Robert Gagne and Gilbert Ryle.

Gagne's Categories.   Robert Gagne, a psychologist, proposed a scheme that consists of five major categories of learning outcomes: intellectual skills, cognitive strategies, verbal information, motor skills, and attitudes. Intellectual skills include making discriminations, classifying objects and ideas, and using rules. Cognitive strategies involve "regulating one's own internal process of attending, learning, remembering, and thinking," particularly in solving problems (Gagne, 1977, p. 35). "Verbal information" refer to the storage in memory of "names, facts or ideas" (p. 181). Motor skills consist of the "coordination of muscular movements" (p. 205). "Attitudes" refer to "internal states that influence the individual's choices of action" (p. 231). As with the three major parts of Bloom's taxonomy, there is no assumed order of the major categories. However, within particular categories, Gagne claims that there are "learning hierarchies" (p. 142). In such cases he argues for the importance of acquiring the "prerequisite" or "subordinate" capabilities before proceeding to the "target skills"(p. 143).

The major strength of Gagne's scheme is its eclectic nature. Although its treatment of certain categories of learning, particularly attitudes, may seem simplistic to some educators, it does attempt to integrate both cognitive and behavioral analyses of learning into one comprehensive framework. It also provides a vocabulary for distinguishing between some of the curriculum emphases. Fact-oriented curricula focus on verbal information. Conceptual curricula expand this focus to include intellectual skills. Behavioral curricula reject the focus on verbal information. The strict behaviorist favors motor skills, while the less strict includes intellectual and cognitive strategies.

Ryle's Two Types of Knowledge.   Before the reader begins to assume uncritically that the analysis of learning objectives is the exclusive province of psychologists, we should mention an important treatise published by the philosopher Gilbert Ryle about fifty years ago. In *The Concept of Mind* (1949), Ryle argued that there are two major types of knowledge one can acquire, "knowing that" and "knowing how." "Knowing that" refers to "propositional knowledge," what we typically call "subject matter." Ryle includes knowledge of facts, e.g., knowing that Montpelier is the capital of Vermont; concepts, e.g., knowing that integers are positive or negative whole numbers; and principles, e.g., knowing that the price of a product is determined by both the supply of the product and the consumer demand for it. "Knowing how" refers to performance capabilities, what we might call "skills." Knowing how to sew, write a persuasive essay, and solve quadratic equations are all examples of Ryle's know-hows. Ryle's basic distinction has led to Johnson's (1977) distinction between "cognitions" and "performance capabilities" and Posner and Rudnitsky's (1994) distinction between "understandings" and "skills." Know-thats are characteristic of not only fact-oriented curricula but also conceptual curricula. Know-hows are clearly more characteristic of skill-oriented as well as experiential curricula.

These two types of knowledge, Ryle persuasively argues, are distinct, and one type cannot be reduced to the other. Knowing a procedure is a know-that if we mean knowing that first one does this step, and then one does that step—in other words, if we mean understanding the procedure. It is a know-how if we mean being able to perform the procedure. Know-hows require practice. Telling someone how to ride a bike is no substitute for practice in riding it if the intended outcome is the skill.

Likewise, know-thats cannot be reduced to know-hows. Just because someone is able to recite Newton's three laws of motion does not mean that person knows them in the sense that most people mean when they use the word "know." Scheffler (1965) refines the concept of know-thats[4] by arguing that three conditions are necessary for a claim that someone "knows a proposition": (1) the person must believe the proposition; (2) the proposition must be true (if not, we have knowledge in a "weak sense"); and (3) the person must have good reasons for the belief. In other words, knowledge is justified, true belief (for the "strong sense" of knowledge). Simply being able to recite a proposition like Newton's first law of motion (i.e., a know-how) does not necessarily mean that one really knows the proposition (i.e., a know-that). In addition, one might know a proposition without being able to recite it on demand. Therefore, proof of a person's propositional knowledge is always tenuous. In contrast to know-thats, evaluation of know-hows is not so problematic. Of course, the possibility does exist that one could know how to do something but be unable to do it in a given situation, because of emotional stress or physical injury, for example. However, when we see a person ride a bike, we have absolute proof that the person knows how to do it.

If schooling were justified solely on the basis of people's acquisition and explicit use of know-thats and know-hows, it would be considered a colossal failure. Much of what students learn in schools, they never use explicitly, and they quickly forget. Clearly, schools must teach such subjects as social studies, science, literature, and geometry for other reasons. One such reason is that learning content in these subjects and others allows people to understand a wide range of situations they are likely to face. What they have studied in these cases need not be made explicit or fully conscious in order to be used (Broudy, 1977). In the words of philosopher Michael Polanyi (1966), much of our knowledge is "tacit." Broudy, then, claims that along with knowing how and knowing that, there is another, equally significant outcome of schooling, namely, "knowing with":

> Knowing with furnishes a context within which a particular situation is perceived, interpreted, and judged. Contexts can function without being at the center of consciousness, without being recalled verbatim, and without serving

as hypothetical deductive premises for action. . . . Context is a form of tacit knowing. . . . For example, when we studied theorems of Euclid in school we kept them at the focus of our attention. Many years later they constituted a geometrical context for situations to which they were relevant. . . . When listening to talk about putting space capsules into orbit . . . we may no longer know certain mathematical truths or how to prove them, but we think *with* these truths as context for our understanding the space talk. (Broudy, 1977, pp.12-13)

Broudy's notion of knowing *with*, proposed in order to take into account tacit or contextual knowing, adds a needed dimension to discussions of objectives. Without this notion it would be difficult to justify the teaching of poetry or, for that matter, most of the humanities. Nevertheless, how to express knowing-with objectives without vague generalities remains a serious challenge.

Although there is a temptation to try to relate these various categorization schemes for objectives to one another, the danger of distorting ideas far outweighs the possible benefits. For example, Gagne's "attitudes" seem analogous to Bloom's "affective domain," until one realizes that Gagne proposes a cognitive, an affective, and a behavioral component of any attitude. Similarly, Bloom's notion of "knowledge" (Level 1.00) may seem related to Ryle's "know-thats." However, as Scheffler (1965) has pointed out, being able to recall knowledge is neither equivalent to, nor even necessary for, acquiring knowledge. Actually, Bloom's notion of "knowledge" as recall may be more appropriately considered one type of "know-how," i.e., knowing how to recall ideas stored in memory. Table 4.4 summarizes the classifications of learning objectives we've just discussed.

CONTENT

We now turn to the topic of content, what many people consider to be the heart of any curriculum. We will treat content as a curriculum topic separate from educational purpose. After all, we could teach the same content for many different purposes, and we could pursue any objective with a range of different

TABLE 4.4 Three Classifications of Learning Objectives

Bloom (1956) and Krathwohl (1964)	Gagne (1977)	Ryle (1978) and Broudy (1977)
Cognitive	Verbal information	Know that
	Intellectual skills	
	Cognitive strategies	Know how
Psychomotor	Motor skills	
Affective	Attitudes	
		Know with

content. However, in a sense content is one dimension of a learning objective. First of all, know-thats consist of content in the form of propositions the teacher might want students to learn. Furthermore, any learning objective, even a know-how, or skill, has an aspect of content: The verb of the objective expresses the behavior, and the object of the verb expresses the content. For example, one learns to interpret (the behavior) poetry (the content). I have identified two ways of thinking about content that are useful for curriculum analysis. The first of these two approaches is promoted by behavioral psychologists, according to whom content is merely a dimension of learning objectives. The second approach, derived from the work of cognitive psychologists in their study of teaching and teacher education, is more pedagogical in tone.

Content: A Behavioral Psychological View

Odd as it may seem, nearly all thinking of psychologists about learning objectives has historically focused on the type of objective, with little attention given to the substance or content of objectives, to the "stuff" teachers teach. One exception has been the work on "tables of specification."

Building on the ideas of Tyler (1949), Bloom, Hastings, and Madaus (1971) showed how to examine both the behavior and content dimensions of learning objectives with a single instrument useful for curriculum analysis and evaluation. The idea is quite simple. The analyst determines the types of objective according to whatever classification scheme seems appropriate, although some variation on Bloom's taxonomy is most typical. Then the analyst consults a content specialist for a content outline of the curriculum. These two dimensions of the curriculum, i.e., the behavioral and content dimensions, can then be combined into a behavior-content matrix known as a table of specifications. Each cell of the table represents a combination of a particular behavior and a particular topic, and therefore a possible learning objective.

Table 4.5 is an example of a table of specifications for a literature curriculum; it was prepared by Alan Purves (1971). Purves analyzed a wide array of documents describing the literature curriculum in U.S. secondary schools, derived categories of content and behaviors from those documents, and determined the relative emphasis on each behavior-content cell as expressed in the documents. This table, according to Purves, represents a view of the total U.S. literature curriculum in 1967; it also serves as an illustration of what a table of specifications for a particular curriculum might look like. After preparing this master table, Purves analyzed several specific curricula in order to compare them with each other and with the master table. For example, Table 4.6 depicts Purves' comparison of two literature curricula, representing two of the most frequently used approaches to teaching literature: the thematic curriculum used most typically in eleventh-grade American literature courses, and the genre curriculum used most typically with tenth-grade students.

If you want to compare curricula in your analysis or to determine what parts of the total picture in a particular subject-matter domain your curriculum emphasizes, you will find the handbook produced by Bloom et al. (1971) invaluable.

TABLE 4.5 A Table of Specifications for a Literature Curriculum

	Knowledge	Application						Response	Expressed Response										Participation		
Behavior →	Know (A)	Apply knowledge of specific literary texts (B)	Apply biographical information (C)	Apply literary, cultural, social, political, and intellectual history (D)	Apply literary terms (E)	Apply critical systems (F)	Apply cultural information (G)	Respond (H)	Recreate (I)	Express one's engagement with (J)	Analyze the parts (K)	Analyze the relationships, the organization, or the whole (L)	Express one's interpretation (M)	Express one's evaluation (N)	Express a pattern of preference (O)	Express a pattern of response (P)	Express a variety of responses (Q)	Be willing to respond (R)	Take satisfaction in responding (S)	Accept the importance (T)
CONTENT / Literary Works																				
1. Epic and narrative poetry (precontemporary)*	1	1	1	1	2	0	0	1	0	1	2	2	2	1	0	0	0	0	0	1
2. Epic and narrative poetry (contemporary)	0	0	0	0	0	0	0	0	0	0	0	0	0	0	0	0	0	0	0	0
3. Lyric poetry (precontemporary)	1	1	1	1	2	0	0	1	1	1	2	2	3	1	0	0	0	0	0	0
4. Lyric poetry (contemporary)	1	1	0	0	0	0	0	0	0	0	0	0	1	0	0	0	0	0	0	1

(continued)

	5. Poetic drama (precontemporary)	1	1	1	1	0	0	1	0	3	1	2	3	3	3	3	2	0	1	1	1	2
	6. Poetic drama (contemporary)	0	0	0	0	0	—	0	0	0	0	0	0	0	0	0	0	—	—	—	—	0
	7. Prose drama (precontemporary)	0	0	0	1	0	0	1	0	1	1	1	1	1	1	0	0	0	0	0	0	1
	8. Prose drama (contemporary)	1	0	0	1	0	0	1	1	1	1	1	2	1	2	0	0	0	0	0	0	1
	9. Novel (precontemporary)	1	1	1	1	1	0	1	0	1	1	1	3	2	3	0	0	0	0	0	0	1
	10. Novel (contemporary)	1	0	0	0	0	0	1	0	1	0	1	0	0	2	0	0	0	0	0	0	0
	11. Short fiction (precontemporary)	1	1	1	1	0	0	1	0	1	0	1	1	1	0	0	0	0	0	0	0	1
	12. Short fiction (contemporary)	1	1	1	1	0	0	1	0	1	0	1	1	1	2	1	0	0	0	0	0	1
	13. Nonfiction prose (precontemporary)	1	0	0	0	0	0	1	0	1	0	1	0	0	1	0	0	0	0	0	0	0
	14. Nonfiction prose (contemporary)	0	0	0	0	0	0	1	0	1	0	1	0	0	1	0	0	—	0	0	0	0
	15. Belles lettres (precontemporary)	1	1	1	0	0	0	1	0	1	0	1	0	0	1	0	0	0	0	0	0	1
	16. Belles lettres (contemporary)	0	0	0	0	0	0	0	0	0	0	0	0	0	1	0	0	0	0	0	0	0
	17. Any literary work	2	1	2	3	1	1	3	3	3	3	3	3	3	3*	1	0	1	2	3	3	1
	18. Movies and television	1	0	—	—	—	—	—	0	0	—	0	—	—	0	0	—	0	0	0	0	0
	19. Other mass media	1	1	—	—	—	—	—	0	0	—	0	—	—	0	—	—	—	0	0	0	0
Contextual Information	20. Biography of authors	1	0	—	—	—	—	—	—	—	—	—	—	—	—	—	—	—	—	—	—	—
	21. Literary, cultural, social, political, and intellectual history	2	1	—	—	—	—	—	—	—	—	—	—	—	—	—	—	—	—	—	0	0
Literary Theory	22. Literary terms	2	0	—	—	—	—	—	—	—	—	—	—	—	—	—	—	—	—	—	—	0
	23. Critical systems	0	—	—	—	—	—	—	—	—	—	—	—	—	—	—	—	—	—	—	—	—
Cultural Information	24. Cultural information and folklore	2	—	—	—	—	—	—	—	—	0	0	0	0	0	—	—	—	—	—	—	0

The figures in the cells represent the emphasis in all the curriculum statements taken as a whole.

3*...extremely heavily emphasized
3....heavily emphasized
2....major emphasis
1....minor emphasis
0....mentioned but not emphasized
—....not mentioned

*The division between precontemporary and contemporary literature is now the First World War (c. 1915).

TABLE 4.6 A Comparison of Two Approaches to Teaching Literature: The Carnegie Curriculum

	A	B	C	D	E	F	G	H	I	J	K	L	M	N	O	P	Q	R	S	T
1	—	—																		
2	—																			
3	—																			
4	—																			
5	—																			
6	—																			
7	—																			
8	1	3		2	1	0					1	2	3							
9	1	3		2	1	0					1	2	3							
10	1	3		2	1	0					1	2	3							
11	—																			
12	—																			
13	1	3		2	1	0					1	2	3							
14	—																			
15	—																			
16	—																			
17	—																			
18	—																			
19	—																			
20	1	1																		
21	2	3																		
22	2																			
23	1																			
24	—																			

(continued)

TABLE 4.6 A Comparison of Two Approaches to Teaching Literature: The G I N N Program

	A	B	C	D	E	F	G	H	I	J	K	L	M	N	O	P	Q	R	S	T
1	1	0			3						3	3	2			2				
2	1	0			3						3	3	2			2				
3	1	0			3						3	3	2			2				
4	1	0			3						3	3	2			2				
5	1	0			3						3	3	2			2				
6	1	0			3						3	3	2			2				
7	1	0			3						3	3	2			2				
8	1	0			3						3	3	2			2				
9	1	0			3						3	3	2			2				
10	1	0			3						3	3	2			2				
11	1	0			3						3	3	2			2				
12	1	0			3						3	3	2			2				
13	1	0			3						3	3	2			2				
14	1	0			3						3	3	2			2				
15	1	0			3						3	3	2			2				
16	1	0			3						3	3	2			2				
17																				
18																				
19																				
20																				
21																				
22	3																			
23	2																			
24																				

Content: A Pedagogical View

If we conceive of curricula as materials to guide teaching, then we can view them pedagogically, that is, as embodiments of knowledge about what to teach and how best to teach it to students. Concerns about content can then focus on two aspects of the curriculum, namely the conception of the subject matter and the forms of representation.

First of all, any discipline of knowledge can be organized in a variety of ways (Schwab, 1964). For example, biology has been portrayed in curricula as a science of molecules that explains living phenomena in terms of the principles of their constituent parts, as a science of ecological systems that explains the activities of individual units by virtue of the larger systems of which they are a part, or as a science of biological organisms, from whose familiar structures, functions, and interactions one weaves a theory of adaptation (Shulman, 1986, p. 9).

Thus, any curriculum represents a particular, and probably deliberate, conception of the subject matter, whether it be science or music, a foreign language or driver education. The conception of the subject matter chosen for the curriculum results in an emphasis on certain aspects and an approach to the subject matter that distinguishes one curriculum from another. A history curriculum that conceives of the subject matter as historiography might emphasize student interpretation of primary sources such as the *Congressional Record* and eyewitness accounts of historical events. In contrast a curriculum that conceives of history as biography might emphasize the words and deeds of great men and women. A physical education curriculum conceiving of the subject matter as sports might emphasize the rules and skills of sports, as well as participation in competitive team sports. However, a curriculum that conceives of physical education as the development of knowledge, skills, and attitudes that lead to physical health and fitness might, for example, emphasize certain sciences, such as physiology, kinesiology, and nutrition, as well as conditioning programs. A science curriculum that conceives of science as those activities in which scientists engage might emphasize observing, measuring, hypothesizing, and other so-called science processes. On the other hand, a science curriculum that conceives of science as the fundamental concepts that have formed the basis for modern science might emphasize those concepts by weaving them throughout the curriculum. By identifying a curriculum's conception of the subject matter, we find out one reason why the curriculum has developed a particular emphasis and also find out how students may think about the subject matter after exposure to the curriculum.

The second aspect of content goes beyond "the subject matter per se to the dimension of subject matter for teaching" (Shulman, 1986, p. 9). This aspect of content concerns the forms of representing the important ideas in the subject matter, "the most powerful analogies, illustrations, examples, explanations, and demonstrations—in a word, the ways of representing and formulating the subject that make it comprehensible to others" (p. 9). These forms of representation are important to identify, because they have important implications both for what content is taught and for how well it is taught. For example, many mathematics curricula teach that numbers are discrete entities through their use of set theory represented in Venn diagrams. On the other hand, some math curricula teach that numbers are continuous phenomena by representing them with number lines. To note that a science curriculum draws an analogy between electric circuits and plumbing systems or between the structure of atoms and solar systems is to identify possible sources of student misconceptions. A social studies curriculum that relies on reading, memorizing, completing, and constructing maps to teach history may lead to improved geographical knowledge, but does little to develop an understanding of the philosophical ideas that have influenced political movements. By determining the dominant forms of content representation in the curriculum, you identify possible blind spots and possible misconceptions that may result.

Content: A Multicultural View

From the perspective of multiculturalists the purpose of education is to accommodate the diversity of the student population. The history of eudcation, especially the last hundred years, has been shaped in large part by mass immigrations of people to the U.S. from many parts of the world. The newest waves of American immigrants are primarily Asian and Hispanic. In 1965 there were only one million Asian Americans; in 2000 there were more than ten million. The Hispanic population grew by 58% during the 1990s. The history of the United States is a history of people from diverse backgrounds coming together. The history of multicultural education is a history of theories and strategies designed to deal with that diversity in the schools.

One of the first attempts by American educators to cope with the diverse population of students was exemplified by a school in Carlisle, Pennsylvania. Founded in 1879 on rigid assimilationist principles, teachers tried to "civilize" Indians by forcing them to adopt (i.e., assimilate) white European ways (Sutton and Broken Nose, 1996, cited in Tatum, 1999, p. 147). Children were taken from their parents, brought to live at the school, and forced to speak only English, to dress as Europeans, and to work hours every day at physically laborious tasks. The school was abandoned after fifty years, after many Native American students became isolated from their tribes, finding no welcome and few jobs in white communities.

By the early part of the twentieth century, tracking evolved from the assimilationist model to a model that would designate placement within public schools for all U.S. students. Educators like Ellwood Cubberly thought all students could be educated; it was only a matter of developing an appropriate education for the different classes, to "adapt the instruction given to the new needs and conditions of society" (Cubberly, 1919, cited in Oakes, 1992, p. 579). The newly arrived Eastern European immigrant children were eventually channeled into vocational and agricultural tracks, while the children of the country's more affluent continued in their more academic spheres. Some have argued that the schools continue to tailor instruction to meet the needs of U.S. industry, preparing children from different economic classes to fill jobs similar to those of their parents (Bowles and Gintis, 1976).

Current models of multicultural education echo those of the preceding centuries, although the ethnic backgrounds of the students may differ. E.D. Hirsch (see page 48) represents a traditionalist perspective on multicultural curriculum. His model exemplifies a way to deal with diversity by, in effect, ignoring it. He proposes a similar core curriculum and way of teaching for every student, regardless of background. In *Cultural Literacy* (Boston: Houghton Mifflin Company, 1987) he discusses the importance to children and to the nation of having all children learn a core curriculum rather than the "diversity and pluralism [which] now reign without challenge" (Hirsch, 1987, p. 161). Without this core curriculum based on information about our cultural heritage, he says, American culture, always large and heterogeneous, and increasingly lacking a common acculturative curriculum, is perhaps getting fragmented enough to lose its coherence as a culture" (Hirsch, 1987, p. 167). His subsequent books list in detail information our children should be taught in each grade—ranging from Aesop's Fables and Shakespeare to the Constitution, with little recognition of the cultures of the most recent American immigrants.

The Carnegie Foundation also calls for all students to be taught the same information, the goal being that minority students become part of mainstream culture. Carnegie staff, however, differs from Hirsch in acknowledging different learning styles and consequently suggests teaching methods that address those styles. The report states: "Different approaches to learning are required, but all students, regardless of background, should be given the tools and encouragement they need to be socially and economically empowered" (Carnegie Foundation, 1988, cited in Fillmore and Meyer, 1992, p. 631). The Foundation furthermore suggests ways to encourage parents to become more involved with the schools and their children's educations.

In opposition to traditional perspective are those who emphasize the inclusion of views that represent our diversity. This usually means including the views and experiences of minority students. Most who say they espouse multicultural education would agree with Fillmore and Meyer who state "One effort of multicultural education is to display to students—all students, not just minority students—that although cultures and cultural life patterns vary greatly, beneath the obvious diversity is a humanity that is shared by all " (Fillmore and Meyer, 1992, p. 651).

How this ideal is translated in the classroom, however, differs widely. To some, multicultural education means the addition of the names of such authors as James Baldwin, Langston Hughes, and Maya Angelou to English class reading lists. Elementary school staff might celebrate the food, customs, and holidays of minority groups. Some talk about multicultural education as a subject of interest only to minority students.

James Banks, while focusing primarily on bringing differing perspectives into the classrooms, extends the basically additive methods of those discussed to this point. Instead of calling for adding information about cultures, Banks calls for revision of the entire curriculum toward what he terms "multiethnic education." He wants "to provide all students with the skills, attitudes, and knowledge they need to function with their ethnic cultures and the mainstream culture" (Banks, 1988, pp. 35-36). School curricula and staff must reflect the country's ethnic diversity, that minority students must be allowed to look at how they have been victimized, and that multi-cultural education is for all students, not just students of color. For Banks, then, multiethnic education is for every student. He suggests that the experiences of minority students permeate every aspect of a school. Staff should reflect the diverse population and have regular workshops on multiethnic education. Cafeteria menus should draw on foods from every ethnic group in the school. Resources reflecting diverse perspectives should be available to students in every class they take. Teaching and assessments of learning should take into account differing learning styles and cultures because as Banks points out "students who are members of minority groups, especially those who are poor, often have values, behavioral patterns, cognitive styles, expectations, and other cultural components that differ from those of the school's culture" (Banks, 1988, p. 276). Most important, perhaps, is that all students according to Banks "should look at events and situations from the perspectives of mainstream groups and also from the perspectives of people who are members of ethnic minority groups" (Banks, 1988, p. 276).

Banks, however, stops short of finding ways to make changes beyond those in school settings. His methods do not address ways to change the larger societal issues of racism, sexism, and economic inequality (Banks 1988). Others such as Paulo Freire (1973), Kyle Fiore, Nan Elsasser (1988), Christine Sleeter and Carl Grant (1988) push for student research into social issues and for action as part of curriculum. These theorists believe that for all students to succeed, students and teachers must address the social and economic inequalities that lead to different educational opportunities. Sleeter and Grant, in advocating education that they call "multicultural and social reconstructionist" suggest students conduct research on such issues as job opportunities, decision making opportunities in government, and availability of types of housing (Sleeter and Grant, 1988, p. 213). The thrust of the curricula they advocate incorporates student action. If students find out, for example, why businesses don't locate in poorer neighborhoods, Sleeter and Grant suggest students "study ways of attracting business" (Sleeter and Grant, 1988, p. 213). Fiore and Elsasser developed a curriculum for women to encourage them to look critically at their marriages and at their economic situations. Theoretically based on the Freire's ideas of teaching students to question and think critically about their lives, Fiore and Elsasser encouraged women in their classes to look at and find ways to move beyond the oppressive situations they often face.

Standards

Within all this discussion of curriculum purpose and content, where does the current emphasis on standards fit? First, it is important to remember that standards outline content to be learned. "To paraphrase a famous question, these standards specify what students should know and when they should know it" (National Council for the Social Studies, 1994). The standards, however, are more than a listing of content for students to know. While embedded in most standards documents are implicit and explicit understandings of content, standards typically strike a balance (or attempt to strike a balance) between content and process. Some examples illustrate the point:

NCTE (NATIONAL COUNCIL OF TEACHERS OF ENGLISH) STANDARD 3:

Students apply a wide range of strategies to comprehend, interpret, evaluate, and appreciate texts. They draw on their prior experience, their interactions with other readers and writers, their knowledge of word meaning and of other texts, their word identification strategies, and their understanding of textual features (e.g., sound-letter correspondence, sentence structure, context, graphics).

NCTE STANDARD 7:

Students conduct research on issues and interests by generating ideas and questions, and by posing problems. They gather, evaluate, and synthesize data from a variety of sources (e.g., print and non-print texts, artifacts, people) to communicate their discoveries in ways that suit their purpose and audience.

NCTM (NATIONAL COUNCIL OF TEACHERS OF MATHEMATICS):

The Content Standards—Number and Operations, Algebra, Geometry, Measurement, and Data Analysis and Probability—explicitly describe the content that students should learn. The Process Standards—Problem Solving, Reasoning and Proof, Communication, Connections, and Representation—highlight ways of acquiring and using content knowledge.

NCSS (NATIONAL COUNCIL FOR SOCIAL STUDIES):

Social studies programs should include experiences that provide for the study of culture and cultural diversity, so that the learner can:

a. analyze and explain the ways groups, societies, and cultures address human needs and concerns;

b. predict how data and experiences may be interpreted by people from diverse cultural perspectives and frames of reference;

c. apply an understanding of culture as an integrated whole that explains the functions and interactions of language, literature, the arts, traditions, beliefs and values, and behavior patterns;

d. compare and analyze societal patterns for preserving and transmitting culture while adapting to environmental or social change;

e. demonstrate the value of cultural diversity, as well as cohesion, within and across groups;

f. interpret patterns of behavior reflecting values and attitudes that contribute or pose obstacles to cross-cultural understanding;

g. construct reasoned judgments about specific cultural responses to persistent human issues;

h. explain and apply ideas, theories, and modes of inquiry drawn from anthropology and sociology in the examination of persistent issues and social problems.

Most standards also emphasize helping students to understand how the discipline functions, including how new knowledge and understanding are generated in the discipline. Standards across all disciplinary areas encourage immersing students into the activities of the disciplines, that is, the standards expect the students to be able to use knowledge of the discipline to ends beyond the classroom.

- The National Council of Teachers or English Standards expect students to "conduct research on issues and interests by generating ideas and questions, and by posing problems. They gather, evaluate, and synthesize data from a variety of sources (e.g., print and non-print texts, artifacts, people) to communicate their discoveries in ways that suit their purpose and audience" (National Council of Teachers of English & the International Reading Association, 1996).
- The National Science Education Standards sets out four goals for school science that all address the use and the experience of science, i.e., students are able to "use appropriate scientific processes and principles in making personal decisions" (National Research Council, 1996).
- The foreign language standards encourage students to work with texts written by and for native speakers and use the language in non-school contexts (American Council on the Teaching of Foreign Languages, the American Association of Teachers of French, the American Association of Teachers of German, and the American Association of Teachers of Spanish and Portuguese, 1999).
- Most of the individual standards in The National Educational Technology Standards begin, "Students use . . .", i.e., "Students use telecommunications to collaborate, publish, and interact with peers, experts, and other audiences" (International Society for Technology in Education, 2000).

Most standards documents also address issues of how content is taught, though typically this is not narrowly defined. Standards ". . . are not prescriptions for particular curriculum or instruction" (National Council of Teachers of English & the International Reading Association, 1996), but standards push curriculum (and educational practice more broadly) in new directions. The NCTM standards go so far as to include a CD-ROM and website with interactive "e-examples" that allow students and teachers to work with educational technologies. (See *standards.nctm.org/document/eexamples/index.htm*). The standards documents also typically include vignettes of what standards-based teaching look like. Clearly, standards are about more than *what* to teach.

Generally, approaches to content, processes and teaching differ from what has traditionally occurred in classrooms in substantial ways. Current standards documents are more than descriptions of facts to know, but highlight also the processes and skills associated with the disciplines and the fundamental natures of the disciplines. See Figure 4.2

As standards have gained a prominent place in most subject areas, publishers of curriculum material now produce curriculum that are "aligned with the standards." Alignment here means that the objectives of the curriculum are derived from the standards for the discipline. Although standards are often thought of as curriculum, standards themselves are facts, skills, and processes that students are expected to learn; they are not typically (and typically do not include) materials for students to use in the learning process. Standards are

Changing Emphases	
The National Science Education Standards evision change throughout the system. The science teaching standards encompass the following changes in emphases:	
LESS EMPHASIS ON	MORE EMPHASIS ON
Treating all students alike and responding to the group as a whole	Understanding and responding to individual student's interests, strenghts, experiences, and needs
Rigidly following curriculum	Selecting and adapting curriculum
Focusing on student acquisition of information	Focusing on student understanding and use of scientific knowledge, ideas, and inquiry processes
Presenting scientific knowledge through lecture, text, and demonstration	Guiding students in active and extended scientific inquiry
Asking for recitation of acquired knowledge	Providing opportunities for scientific discussion and debate among students
Testing students for factual information at the end of the unit or chapter	Continuosly assessing student understanding
Maintaining responsibility and authority	Sharing responsibility for learning with students
Supporting competition	Supporting a classroom community with cooperation, shared responsibility, and respect
Working alone	Working with other teachers to enhance the science program

FIGURE 4.2   Changing Emphases in Science Teaching.
(National Research Council, 1996, p. 113)

sometimes (depending largely on subject-area) stated as measurable, behavioral objectives. Generally the standards place a greater priority on higher level thinking in both the curriculum and teaching practices than did the existing curricula. Standards attempt to target understanding and application simultaneously. They address all four categories of educational aims (see page 76). Standards are often stated in terms of what students should be able to do:

Data Analysis and Probability Standard for Grades 9–12
Instructional programs from pre-kindergarten through grade 12 should enable all students to—
• Formulate questions that can be addressed with data and collect, organize, and display relevant data to answer them
• Select and use appropriate statistical methods to analyze data
• Develop and evaluate inferences and predictions that are based on data
• Understand and apply basic concepts of probability
(National Council of Teachers of Mathematics, 2000)

As the above example requires application, it might be thought of as a set of behavioral objectives. These particular objectives, however, require fairly complex behaviors that constitute the practice of the discipline of probability. Likewise in other areas of the NCTM standards and in standards of other subjects, the target of standards is the complex work of the discipline, not just learning a definition or procedure.

Questions you will want to ask as you review curriculum include the following: "Does the curriculum facilitate student understanding of the content and processes espoused in the standards?","How will I and my students be held accountable to the standards?", and "Are state and national standards in alignment?"

TECHNOLOGY AND CONTENT

Technology offers the possibility of approaching and organizing content in new ways and creates opportunity to teach content not otherwise possible. Arguably, the most important technologies in the history of education (so far) are the blackboard and the mass-produced textbook. The blackboard allowed a large communal display at the front of the classroom permitting the teacher to display large amounts of information and to allow students to work problems at the front of the room. Textbooks standardized the curriculum in an unprecedented way (Pausch, 2002).

Changes at this scale have not yet come to fruition as a result of modern educational technologies, but such changes may be looming. In 1994, the Internet was available in only 3% of public school classrooms. By 2001, that figure had risen to 87% for individual classrooms with access somewhere in the building in more than 99.5% of public secondary schools (National Center for Education Statistics, 2002)! What changes will come from this technology infusion are largely speculative, but some changes have already taken place as a result of the profusion of electronic educational technologies.

The National Education Technology Standards (see Figure 4.3) lay out one framework for what students should come to understand and be able to do using technology. Each of the six standards has implications for how content and technology are related within a curriculum. Looking through the standards, how does each expectation in the standard relate technology to content organization and coverage?

Technology can change how content is covered in at least the following ways:
1. By creating new disciplinary areas, including computer science and video production.
2. By reconfiguring disciplinary course content, i.e., mechanical drawing courses have largely been replaced by computer-aided drafting/computer-aided manufacturing (CAD/CAM) courses. Many vocational programs are technology intensive and the technology, and therefore the curriculum, is constantly changing.

3. By offering tools that provide new ways to process information. This includes but is hardly limited to the use of word processors, spreadsheets, and graphing calculators.
4. By offering tools that provide new ways to share information, most importantly, the Internet. Courses might be structured around data-sharing in science[5] or may be offered in a completely online format (an estimated 40,000 to 50,000 students were enrolled in at least one online class in the 2001-2002 school year (Clark, 2001)). See *www.class com/* for several examples of online courses.
5. By improving teacher productivity, for example through speeding paperwork tasks.

Technology Foundation Standards for Students

1. Basic operations and concepts
   - Students demonstrate a sound understanding of the nature and operation of technology systems.
   - Students are proficient in the use of technology.
2. Social, ethical, and human issues
   - Students understand the ethical, cultural, and societal issues related to technology.
   - Students practice responsible use of technology systems, information, and software.
   - Students develop positive attitudes toward technology uses that support lifelong learning, collaboration, personal pursuits, and productivity.
3. Technology productivity tools
   - Students use technology tools to enhance learning, increase productivity, and promote creativity.
   - Students use productivity tools to collaborate in constructing technology-enchanced models, prepare publications, and produce other creative works.
4. Techonology communication tools
   - Students use telecommunications to collaborate, pubish, and interact with peers, experts, and other audiences.
   - Students use a variety of media and formats to communicate information and ideas effectively to multiple audiences.
5. Technology research tools
   - Students use technology to locate, evaluate, and collect information from a variety of sources.
   - Students use technology tools to process data and report results.
   - Students evaluate and select new information resources and technological innovations based on the appropriateness for specific tasks.
6. Technology problem-solving and decision-making tools
   - Students use technology resources for solving problems and making informed decisions.
   - Students employ technology in the development of strategies for solving problems in the real world.

FIGURE 4.3   The National Education Technology Standards for Students
(International Society for Technology in Education, 2000)

FIVE PERSPECTIVES ON PURPOSE AND CONTENT

After all this discussion about ways of categorizing purposes and content, we still have not answered the fundamental curriculum question: "What should be the purpose and content of education?" As you might suspect after reading Chapter Three, the answer to this important question depends on one's perspective. Using some of the terminology and concepts in this chapter, we are now in a position to compare and contrast differing perspectives on education. Each perspective discussed in Chapter Three represents a clear sense of what counts as a legitimate purpose, a body of content for a curriculum, and a conception of that content.

Traditional

For proponents of a traditional perspective, the purpose of education is to transmit the cultural heritage. Therefore, the content of the curriculum is selected from that cultural heritage and represents what educators believe to be the most timeless, established, and accepted facts, concepts, principles, laws, values, and skills known to humankind. Table 4.7 provides an example of a traditionalist plan for education in Grades K through 8 in the United States.

This perspective leads to an emphasis on (1) familiarity with terms and names (e.g., the definition of a sonnet and the names of the U.S. Presidents) necessary for communicating with other educated members of society, (2) competence in a set of basic skills (e.g., reading, writing, and computation) necessary for productive membership in the society, and (3) acceptance of a set of fundamental values (e.g., honesty and respect for authority) necessary for the society to function smoothly. For example, in science a traditional perspective leads to a conception of the subject matter as a cumulative body of scientific knowledge that the curriculum assumes to be true and that the student is expected to acquire. In addition to an emphasis on facts and scientific vocabulary as advocated by Hirsch, many traditionalists would add the "attributes and skills" necessary for learning the "scientific method" (Bennett, 1988, p. 40).[6]

Experiential

According to the experiential perspective, development is the primary purpose of education (Hamilton, 1980). But any specific development must be in a direction that leads to the individual's continuing, general development (Dewey, 1938, p. 36), particularly those areas of development Sizer (1973) termed "agency." Agency is "the personal style, assurance, and self-control that allow [the individual] to act in both socially acceptable and personally meaningful ways" (Sizer, 1973). Thus, experiential education aims to "increase the competence of youth in such areas as planning, finding and making use of appropriate resources; persistence at a task; coping with new ideas, conflicting opinions, and people who are different; taking responsibility for others' welfare; and carrying

TABLE 4.7 A Traditional Plan for Education, Grades K-8.

Subject	Kindergarten through Grade 3	Grades 4 through 6	Grades 7 and 8
ENGLISH	INTRODUCTION TO READING AND WRITING (phonics, silent and oral reading, basic rules of grammar and spelling, vocabulary, writing and penmanship, elementary composition, and library skills)	INTRODUCTION TO CRITICAL READING (children's literature; independent reading and book reports; more advanced grammar, spelling, and vocabulary; and composition skills)	Grade 7: SURVEY OF ELEMENTARY GRAMMAR AND COMPOSITION Grade 8: SURVEY OF ELEMENTARY LITERARY ANALYSIS
SOCIAL STUDIES	INTRODUCTION TO HISTORY, GEOGRAPHY, AND CIVICS (significant Americans: explorers; native Americans; American holidays, customs, and symbols; citizenship; and landscape, climate, and mapwork)	Grade 4: U.S. HISTORY TO CIVIL WAR Grade 5: U.S. HISTORY SINCE 1865 Grade 6: WORLD HISTORY TO THE MIDDLE AGES	Grade 7: WORLD HISTORY FROM THE MIDDLE AGES TO 1990 Grade 8: WORLD GEOGRAPHY and U.S. CONSTITUTIONAL GOVERNMENT
MATHEMATICS	INTRODUCTION TO MATHEMATICS (numbers; basic operations; fractions and decimals; rounding; geometric shapes; measurement of length, area, and volume; bar graphs; and estimation and elementary statistics)	INTERMEDIATE ARITHMETIC AND GEOMETRY (number theory: negative numbers, percentages, and exponents: line graphs: the Pythagorean theorem and basic probability)	*Two from among the following one-year courses:* GENERAL MATH, PRE-ALGEBRA, and ALGEBRA
SCIENCE	INTRODUCTION TO SCIENCE (plants and animals, the food chain, the solar system, rocks and minerals, weather, magnets, energy and motion, properties of matter, and simple experiments)	Grade 4: EARTH SCIENCE AND OTHER TOPICS Grade 5: LIFE SCIENCE AND OTHER TOPICS Grade 6: PHYSICAL SCIENCE AND OTHER TOPICS	Grade 7: BIOLOGY Grade 8: CHEMISTRY AND PHYSICS
FOREIGN LANGUAGE	(OPTIONAL)	INTRODUCTION TO FOREIGN LANGUAGE (basic vocabulary, grammar, reading, writing, conversation, and cultural material)	FORMAL LANGUAGE STUDY *Two years strongly recommended*
FINE ARTS	MUSIC AND VISUAL ART (songs, recordings, musical sounds and instruments, painting, craftmaking, and visual effects)	MUSIC AND VISUAL ART (great composers, musical styles and forms, elementary music theory, great painters, and interpretation of art and creative projects)	MUSIC APPRECIATION and ART APPRECIATION *One semester of each required*
PHYSICAL EDUCATION/ HEALTH	PHYSICAL EDUCATION AND HEALTH (body control; fitness; sports, games, and exercises; sportsmanship; safety; hygiene; nutrition; and drug prevention education)	PHYSICAL EDUCATION AND HEALTH (team and individual sports, first aid, drug prevention education, and appropriate sex education)	PHYSICAL EDUCATION AND HEALTH (strategy in team sports, gymnastics, aerobics, self-assessment for health, drug prevention education, and appropriate sex education)

Source: Bennett, 1988.

out commitments to others" (Hamilton, 1980, p. 191). These specific competencies, while contributing to the happiness and productivity of youth and adults, are considered by the experiential educator indicators of the ultimate aim, development, rather than as goals for their own sake (Hamilton, 1980, p. 191). Similarly, according to this perspective, no subject matter has more inherent value for facilitating development than any other, without regard for the needs and capacities of the student (Dewey, 1938, p. 46).

To an experiential educator subject matter derives from ordinary life experiences (Dewey, 1938). For Dewey, education should begin with subject matter that grows out of experiences children have already had. But relating subject matter to previous experiences is only the first step; the next step is even more crucial. It requires "the educator to select those things within the range of existing experience that have the promise and potentiality of presenting new problems which by stimulating new ways of observation and judgment will expand the area of further experience" (Dewey, 1938, p. 75). As experience is expanded, it also becomes more organized, ultimately approximating the organization "in which subject matter is presented to the skilled, mature person" (p. 74). History, for example, to the experiential educator is the study of the past as "a *means* of understanding the present" (p. 78, italics in original), rather than as a means of transmitting our cultural heritage. Science begins with the scientific principles underlying "everyday social applications" (p. 80). By understanding technologies the student eventually comes to understand the problems these technologies cause.

In this chapter's lead-off scenario, Jim is faced with social studies textbooks based on these first two perspectives, the traditional and the experiential. He will have to decide which ones are more likely to help students learn to think critically. Which of the two perspectives do you believe is more committed to this goal?

Structure of the Disciplines

According to the structure-of-the-disciplines perspective, the primary purpose of education is the development of the intellect (King & Brownell, 1965) and the disciplines of knowledge constitute the content best suited to this purpose.[7] Each discipline of knowledge has a distinctive structure, and acquiring this plurality of structures is given the highest priority in schools. Subject matter should represent domains of disciplined, systematic inquiry with curriculum for each subject based on (1) certain fundamental ideas that function as tacit assumptions or premises guiding inquiry (e.g., accepted theories) and (2) certain ways of answering questions and conducting inquiry (e.g., what counts as evidence). Modern biology, for example, is based in part on an acceptance of evolutionary theory and of the biochemical basis of life. Biologists use these ideas to frame their research questions. A structure-of-the-disciplines curriculum emphasizes the fundamental ideas of the discipline and allows the student to engage in inquiry that approximates the way scholars conduct their own research.

Behavioral

According to the behavioral perspective, the content of the curriculum comprises a set of skills described by statements specifying observable and measurable behaviors, termed "behavioral" or "performance" objectives. The behavioral perspective claims to be neutral with regard to purpose. Let the educator determine the purposes to which behavioral principles will be applied. However, the perspective clearly is not neutral. Only purposes that can be described in terms of terminal behaviors are legitimate. Since the content of this perspective consists of skills or other formulations of content that can be translated into observable behaviors, other aspects of content, such as facts and concepts, are either translated into behaviors or are considered only vehicles for teaching and learning the behaviors.

From this perspective any subject matter can be reduced to a set of discrete behaviors—termed "skills," "competencies," or "processes"—that can be expressed as observable, measurable behaviors. Mastering these behaviors constitutes learning the subject matter. In vocational training programs, for example, curriculum development requires a job, or task, analysis. The person conducting the analysis either observes workers performing job-related tasks or surveys workers or their supervisors on these tasks. The analysis results in the identification of a set of "terminal behaviors" that constitute what the competent worker can do. These terminal behaviors are in turn analyzed to identify the "enabling behaviors" that are prerequisites for successful performance of the terminal behaviors. In mathematics education a behavioral perspective requires the identification of the mathematical skills that constitute mathematical competence. In science education this perspective requires one to conceive of science as the things scientists do. These "processes" of science include such things as measuring, observing, categorizing, and predicting, which, for the strict behaviorist, constitute the body of science. With these processes receiving the emphasis, the facts, concepts, and principles of science, i.e., its traditional content, assumes primarily an instrumental role as the vehicle for teaching the basic science processes.[8] Writing too has been conceived of as a set of discrete skills, resulting in a curriculum consisting of exercises to develop these separate writing skills. We will examine this perspective in greater detail in Chapter Five.

Constructivist

Like the structure-of-the-disciplines perspective, constructivist perspectives consider the development of the mind to be the central purpose of education. A Constructivist perspective focuses on the development of construction of meaning to accomplish this purpose.

Proponents of constructivist perspective believe that subject matter (1) is a body of knowledge about which to think—e.g., the content of a course focusing on current social issues; (2) is itself a form of thinking, reasoning, or problem solving—e.g., computer education, physics, or math may be taught as problem solving; (3) may also constitute the tools of thought—e.g., writing may be taught as a means of reflective thinking. For example, Hull conceives of writing as a complex cognitive process embedded in a social context. Writing is more than a stringing together of separate skills; it is an activity in which various cognitive processes—planning, transcribing text, and rewriting—happen recursively and in no particular order. . . . [Writing is] a complex problem-solving activity involving the individual in complex cognitive and linguistic processes such as organizing, structuring, and revising. (Resnick & Klopfer, 1989, pp. 14-15)

For Hull such a conception of writing implies a curriculum providing (1) "authentic tasks" that require "extended, purposeful problem-solving activity," that is writing for a real purpose, not as an exercise; (2) social interaction and support that encourage writers "to stretch beyond their current capacity," as peers help each other build on one another's ideas (in a process Hull calls "scaffolding"); (3) a means by which teachers can interpret a writer's difficulties in terms of the history and logic of the performance (Hull, 1989, p. 15), based on the assumption that whatever students write they write for a reason.

In Chapter Five we will examine the constructivist perspective more closely, comparing it with the behavioral perspective.

Curriculum Analysis Questions

Chapter Four has provided a technical vocabulary for discussing any curriculum's purposes and content. The curriculum analysis questions that follow will give you the opportunity to use this vocabulary as a tool for understanding your curriculum's purposes and content better.

The first question addresses an important aspect of the underlying purpose of the curriculum.

1. What aspects of the curriculum are intended for training, and what aspects are intended for educational contexts? It would be unfair to expect the curriculum to use these terms or to make this distinction explicit. It is your task as the analyst to infer this distinction.

The second question is intended to help you identify statements of purpose and to sort them out into different levels.

2. At what level, if at all, does the curriculum express its purposes? Look for expressions of societal goals, administrative objectives, educational aims, educational goals, and learning objectives. As with the previous question, don't expect to find this terminology used. Try to sort out the curriculum's statements into these types of statements.

The third question attempts to help you decide the priorities of the curriculum. These may not be explicit, and, therefore, may require a bit of reading between the lines.

3. What educational goals and educational aims are emphasized, and what are their relative priorities?

The fourth question moves from general purposes to more specific purposes, particularly learning objectives. The intent in this question is for you to see if any of the categorizations of learning objectives helps you to extend your understanding of your curriculum.

4. What types of learning objectives are included in the curriculum? What types are emphasized? What types are deemphasized or excluded—i.e., what is the null

curriculum? Use whatever categorization seems appropriate for your analysis. If you want to make comparisons between curricula, construct a table of specifications for each curriculum. This is a useful analysis procedure, even if you don't want to compare curricula. Does the curriculum emphasize process (e.g., skills, procedures, or methods) or content (e.g., facts, terminology, principles)?

The fifth question focuses on content. The intent is to give you a way to examine the subject matter and the way the curriculum attempts to make that subject matter understandable to the student. In particular, this question refers to the section titled "Content: A Pedagogical View."

5. What are the primary ways in which the curriculum represents that subject matter to the student? In answering this question, first try to identify the curriculum's conception of the subject matter.

6. Does your curriculum embody a view of multicultural education in its content? Would you consider it an assimilationist, multiethnic, or social reconstructionist view?

As you complete (or before you complete) your curriculum analysis, you will need to do some level of analysis of relevant standards. Every teacher should have some sense of what experts in their field have to say about what all students should know and be able to do in and with the discipline. That is precisely what the standards are intended to portray.

7. How is it determined if students have met the standards? What are the consequences for students, teachers, and schools if it is determined that students have not met standards? Does it matter if you adhere to the standards?

8. Is the curriculum aligned with the standards? Does the curriculum facilitate student understanding of the content and processes espoused in the standards? Are the portrayals of the nature/structure of the discipline congruent between the curriculum and the standards? Are the balances of depth and breadth of the curriculum and the standards congruent? Are the standards cited for each topic/acitivity?

At the end of the chapter, beginning on page 91, a section is devoted to showing that each of the five perspectives represents a package of conceptions of appropriate purposes and curriculum content and that each package is different in some fundamental ways. These perspectives are not a set of pigeonholes into which you must fit the curriculum you are analyzing. If your curriculum clearly presents one particular perspective on purpose and content, however, then this section can be very helpful in suggesting answers to this question. If your curriculum is more typical and does not clearly present a particular perspective, then try to answer this question without invoking the five perspectives, since they are likely to get in your way of describing the conception of purpose and content. In order to determine the curriculum's conception of the subject matter, try to answer this question: What would a student successfully completing your curriculum think of the subject matter? For example, according to the curriculum, what is English or social studies or whatever the subject matter of your particular curriculum? For example, is English a series of heroic epics, a set of grammatical rules, or lists of vocabulary words? Is social studies a chronology of past events, stories of great men and women, or analyses of current events? Next try to identify the dominant forms used to represent the subject matter. For example, does the curriculum rely on films, maps, stories, physical models, diagrams, problem sets, or simulations (to name just a few possibilities)?

NOTES

1. Though aims, goals, and objectives differ for training and educational contexts, we will use the term "educational" in a generic sense to reduce the complexity of an already vast array of terms.
2. See, for example, the NCEE (1983) report.
3. A "curriculum objective" is a broad category of purposes that are specific to a particular curriculum. This category might include such purposes as the key problems a curriculum intends students to solve, i.e., "problem-solving objectives"; the intended educational experiences students are expected to have, i.e., "expressive objectives" (Eisner, 1994); the specific performances students are expected to demonstrate, i.e., "performance objectives"; and learning outcomes students are intended to achieve, i.e., "learning objectives."
4. What Scheffler (1965) terms "propositional knowledge."
5. See *http://www.globe.gov* for one example.
6. In the humanities, this perspective might require that all students read a set of Great Books or study a core curriculum. See Bennett (1984).
7. See also Phenix (1964).
8. See Chapter Seven for the analysis of an elementary science curriculum of this sort.

CHAPTER 5

Curriculum Purpose and Content

Conflicting Perspectives

All the kindergarten, first-grade, and second-grade teachers in the Reed-Enwright School District are meeting with the District Curriculum Coordinator at a Superintendent's Conference Day to discuss and possibly decide what to do about a serious problem the district faces. Reed-Enwright has been cited by the state for its high percentage of third-graders falling below the mean on the state's Basic Reading Competency Test (BRCT).

The superintendent, Dr. Eleanor Spagnola, maintains that the primary reason for the poor test performance is the fact that a relatively large number of children in the district come from economically disadvantaged homes. Reed-Enwright, she points out, is a poor district with the highest unemployment in the state. She cites a high correlation between family income and reading scores to support her argument. According to Dr. Spagnola, poor children begin school at a significant disadvantage. If the district is to improve reading scores, it will have to help these children overcome their disadvantage.

Opinions differ on how to address the problem. The curriculum coordinator is a former reading specialist. He agrees with the superintendent and contends that the best way to improve test scores is to teach children the skills tested on the BRCT. One of the first-grade teachers, Phil Schmidt, vehemently disagrees, pointing out that reading cannot be broken down into discrete skills, that reading skills must be taught while children read material that matters to them, and that even disadvantaged children bring to school a rich background of experiences to use as a basis for reading instruction.

As a faculty member present at the meeting, you try to understand this debate. What assumptions underlie each position? What is the problem? What approach to the problem is best? This chapter will help you to understand the debate over the reading program at Reed-Enwright, and to answer these and other questions on some common approaches to formulating the purpose and content of curricula.

FOCUS: TWO APPROACHES TO PURPOSE AND CONTENT

Having examined in the previous chapter both the purposes of education and the conceptions of subject matter as a whole and from each perspective, we turn to an in-depth treatment of two conflicting perspectives on the purpose and content of curriculum. This dialectical treatment of the topic will allow us to highlight some of the key assumptions in curriculum discourse about formulating objectives and about the nature of content in the curriculum.

Proponents of two perspectives, the constructivist and behavioral, have engaged in an ongoing debate about the purpose and content of the curriculum. Both agree that the purpose of education is to promote learning, and psychologists in both groups, because they have expertise in understanding this process, believe that they are uniquely qualified to develop curricula. By examining this issue from these two particular perspectives, we will explore in greater detail how different views of purpose and content are based on implicit notions about what learning is and how it takes place, how teachers facilitate learning, what kinds of objectives are necessary for expressing intentions for learning outcomes, and what kinds of curricula follow from these objectives. That is, we will see how these two perspectives illuminate issues regarding the definition and process of learning, the instructional process, the nature of objectives, and the concept of curriculum. With this understanding, you will be in a better position to examine the purpose and content of your curriculum and to determine the kinds of psychological assumptions underlying it. Before we leave the topic, we will also try to investigate the inherent tunnel vision of these two perspectives and how it limits any analysis of the topic conducted by proponents of either perspective.

BEHAVIORAL

According to a strict behavioral perspective, learning is a change in behavior.[1] Since, according to this perspective, learning is a fundamentally similar process in all species of animals, experiments with laboratory animals such as rats and pigeons have relevance to the study of human learning. These experiments have shown the significance of the environment in shaping behavior. The focus on environmental conditions, such as stimuli and reinforcements, has led to a lack of attention to internal aspects of humans, such as instincts, intrinsic motivation, and innate capacities and ideas. The learner is, for all practical purposes, a blank slate (a *tabula rasa*) on which the environment writes.

As Joyce and Weil (1986, p. 313) point out, "the key ideas in behavior theory are based on the stimulus-response-reinforcement paradigm in which human behavior is thought to be under the control of the external environment." Behavior is a response or complex set of responses to a stimulus, i.e., to conditions, events, or changes in the environment (Taber, Glaser, & Schaefer, 1967).

Behavioral changes are determined by the consequences of a person's responses to stimuli. Anything in a person's environment that increases the frequency of a behavior is termed a "reinforcer." The more immediately the reinforcer is delivered, the more effect it will have. But immediacy is not the only factor that affects frequency of behaviors. The frequency and schedule of reinforcement are also important. Although continuous reinforcement, i.e., reinforcement after every desired response, produces rapid learning of responses, more irregular reinforcements produce greater retention of learned responses (Joyce & Weil, 1986, p. 315).

The view of objectives that follows from this concept of learning is best represented by the work of Robert Mager. As Mager (1962, p. 3) has said, "an objective is an intent communicated by a statement describing a proposed change in a learner. . . . It is a description of a pattern of behavior (performance) we want the learner to be able to demonstrate." According to this perspective, in order to be complete an objective must include a description of the following (Mager, 1962):

1. The overall behavior
2. The important conditions under which the behavior is to occur: i.e., givens, restrictions, or both
3. The criterion of acceptable performance

Similar prescriptions can be found in writings of many other writers on objectives. With regard to the basic argument, they are in agreement:

> It is necessary . . . to describe . . . objectives in terms of measurable learner behaviors—that is, in terms of what the learner can do or how he will act at the conclusion of instruction. Objectives stated in this way will leave little doubt about what the teacher's intentions are. (Popham & Baker, 1970, pp. 20–21)

Or as Robert Mager has stated:

> A meaningfully stated objective, then, is one that succeeds in communicating your intent. . . . Though it is all right to include such words as "understand" and "appreciate" in a statement of objective, the statement is not explicit enough to be useful until it indicates how you intend to sample "understanding" and "appreciating." Until you describe what the learner will be DOING when demonstrating that he "understands" or "appreciates," you have described very little at all. . . . Thus, the most important characteristic of a useful objective is that it *identifies the kind of performance* that will be accepted as evidence that the learner has achieved the objective. (Mager, 1962, pp. 10–13)

The argument for behavioral objectives has been compelling to many educators over the years, in spite of the serious objections raised by its critics (see Eisner, 1994). One reason the dispute has continued for so many years is that there are underlying differences in what people expect students to do with their knowledge after they leave school. In the beginning of Chapter Four you read about the difference between training and education contexts. Let us examine the behavioral objectives argument with that distinction in mind. If we believe that students are in school to be trained, that is, to use their knowledge replicatively and applicatively, then behavioral objectives make great sense. For example, we might want to train automotive mechanics to adjust disk brakes. The overall behavior we want students to learn can be described in observable and measurable terms, i.e., "to adjust disk brakes." The conditions under which the behavior is to occur can also be specified and are not arbitrary. These are the conditions that exist on the job, including the tools with which the student/mechanic needs to work. Similarly, the criteria that should be used to judge the students' success and the standards that should be applied are neither arbitrary nor problematic. The criteria are those that employers use on the job. For example, if the flat-rate manual says the job should take 20 minutes, then the employer can use that figure for billing customers. Notice that what makes the choice of behavior, conditions, and criteria nonarbitrary is the predictablity of the situation in which the student will ultimately use what he or she has learned in school, that is, the assumption that this is a training context.

However, when we shift to an educational context, the whole situation changes. When students learn the causes of the Civil War, they are doing so for educational purposes, that is, for unspecified kinds of use in unpredictable situations. In this case we can predict that a teacher, school, or testing agency might ask questions about the Civil War. But notice that in this use situation, the choices of behaviors, conditions, and criteria are all arbitrary. Should the behavior be "reciting the causes of the Civil War," "selecting the causes from a list of possible causes," or some other type of test item? Should the criterion be three out of four correct, all correct, or some other criterion? The conditions under which the behavior is to occur are the test conditions, rather than the conditions of use in life outside of school, and are therefore also arbitrary.

It thus appears that when a curriculum is intended for a training context, behavioral objectives make sense. When the curriculum is intended for an educational context, behavioral objectives take on an arbitrary and dysfunctional character. So the central curriculum questions become: How does the curriculum developer expect the learners to use the subject matter? Can the curriculum developer predict how learners will use it, and will they use it in the way they learned it? Or is it impossible to specify exactly how the learners will use the subject matter after school, and will they use it in ways different from the way they learned it? We contrast two reading curricula that differ in the way they view the process of reading and the way to teach reading effectively, a contrast that results from different answers to these questions.

A behavioral perspective provides a distinctive concept of objectives.[2] Objectives must be stated "appropriately" for their primary function of guiding evaluation. This preoccupation with evaluation has led to objectives that must be expressed as know-hows ("the learner will be able to"), are presented in lists of succinct sentences, employ verbs expressing only observable and measurable behaviors, and include objects describing highly specific content. As a consequence of these requirements, behavioral objectives express knowthats or know-withs only by transforming them into know-hows. For example, learning a concept ("dog") becomes nothing more than being able to point out instances that are examples of the concept ("collie") and distinguish them from nonexamples ("wolf").

As you might expect, a particular perspective on learning leads to a particular perspective on teaching. Traditionally, responsibility for learning rests on the students; the behavioral view places the responsibility on the teachers, since they presumably control the instructional environment. According to this view, if the student does not learn, then something is wrong with the teaching methods, and the teacher can and should be held accountable for this problem.

Teachers attempt to influence behavior, i.e., cause learning, with various stimuli. They demonstrate (or "model") behavior or provide other opportunities for students to observe the desired response. There may also be an attempt to guide the students with various signals or cues as they attempt to demonstrate the behavior. Teachers also try to influence learning by managing the consequences of behaviors. They reinforce behaviors selectively and as immediately as possible, using grades and praise. Reinforcement serves not only as feedback to the students on the adequacy of their responses, but also as a source of extrinsic motivation—i.e., motivation derived from their environment, rather than from inside the student as in intrinsic curiosity. In its most basic outline teaching requires the presentation of a stimulus; the modeling of responses if possible; the provision of opportunities for practicing the desired responses to the stimulus—first guided, then unguided practice—and the reinforcement of appropriate responses as immediately as possible (Joyce & Weil, 1986, p. 316). Variations on this theme are termed "direct instruction," "explicit teaching," "effective teaching," and "mastery teaching."[3] For example, if the teacher is teaching the addition of fractions, the following steps might be employed:

1. Presentation of an addition-of-fractions problem (the stimulus)
2. Demonstration of the correct method for solving the problem (modeling)
3. Getting students to practice using this method on similar problems, first as seatwork, then as homework (providing opportunities for practice)
4. Rewarding students who get the correct answers (reinforcement)
5. Repeating Steps 1 through 4 for those who do not get the correct answers

This basic model is employed in several current "research-based" approaches to teacher education. For example, Madelaine Hunter (1994) uses this basic behavioral model for in-service teacher education. Table 5.1 presents Hunter's model for the "design of effective lessons."

In all behavioral models teachers are supposed to have a set of clear and specific objectives toward which they aim their teaching. Teaching then consists of explaining and demonstrating the intended behavior clearly and giving students practice with feedback to help them acquire proficiency in performance.

The view of curriculum that follows from a behavioral perspective rests on the following principles (Sockett, 1976, p. 16):

1. A curriculum consists of a set of "terminal objectives" stated in observable and measurable, i.e., operational, form.

TABLE 5.1   The Seven Elements in Hunter's Design of Effective Lessons

1. *Anticipatory set* The teacher gets students' attention and may also gather diagnostic data.

2. *Objective and purpose* The teacher states what students will learn and how it will be useful.

3. *Input* The teacher provides opportunities for students to acquire new information necessary for students to achieve the objective. This requires a prior task analysis of the learning objective.

4. *Modeling* The teacher provides opportunities for students to see what they are supposed to learn.

5. *Checking for understanding* The teacher ascertains that students understand what they are supposed to do and have the prerequisite skills for doing it.

6. *Guided practice* Students practice their new knowledge or skill under the direct supervision of the teacher. Mistakes are corrected.

7. *Independent practice* After the teacher is reasonably confident that the students will not make serious errors, the teacher assigns independent practice exercises.

Source: Hunter, 1984, pp. 175–176.

2. The purpose of instruction is to change behavior. The change is from "entry behavior" to the "terminal behavior" specified in the behavioral objective.
3. Both the content taught and the method by which it is taught are means to the terminal objectives.

As Sockett points out, some authors hold all three of these views, others only one or two of them. The three principles taken together constitute what Sockett terms the model of "rational curriculum planning by behavioral objectives" (Sockett, 1976, p. 17). It represents a radical and behavioristic extension of the linear technical production perspective we examined in Chapter One. (See Table 1.4.)

You will recall that the assumptions of the technical production perspective are as follows:

1. *Production orientation* The purpose of schooling is to promote learning.
2. *Linearity of planning* Intended learning outcomes serve as the appropriate starting point for planning.
3. *Means-ends reasoning* Curriculum planning is an enterprise in which the planner develops the means necessary to produce the desired learning outcomes.
4. *Objective basis* Planning can, and therefore should, be conducted objectively and on scientific bases.
5. *Role of the technical expert* Decisions on issues of instructional content and method are technical decisions and are best left to people with technical expertise.

The model of "rational planning by behavioral objectives" (Sockett, 1976, p. 16) accepts all five of these assumptions and adds the following qualifications:

6. *Behavioral requirement* Learning in assumption 1 above is defined as a change in behavior.
7. *Specific knowledge base* The objective or scientific basis of planning in assumption 4 is the psychology of learning developed and promoted by behavioral psychologists.
8. *Type of expertise* The technical expertise relevant to developing learning objectives in assumption 5 derives from the study of behavioral psychology; the expert is the person trained by the behavioral psychologists.

A model presented by Popham and Baker represents this view in a popular and straightforward version. As its promoters concede, the model emphasizes the decision making of the teacher prior to and after instruction, rather than the teaching procedures themselves:

> First, the objectives of instruction are specified in terms of learner behavior. Second, the student is pre-assessed as to his current status with respect to those instructional objectives. Third, instructional activities that should bring about the intended objectives are designed. And fourth, the student's attainment of the objectives is evaluated. (Popham & Baker, 1970, p. 13)

Clearly, behavioral objectives are the centerpiece of this model. As its promoters argue:

> The first step in a systematic approach to instruction is unquestionably the specification of objectives in operational terms. . . . The more clearheaded the teacher is about what he is attempting to accomplish with his learners, the more easily he can accomplish it and the more readily he can judge whether he has accomplished it. (Popham & Baker, 1970, pp. 43–44)

The Case of Distar: A Behaviorally Oriented Curriculum

Distar (Kim, Berger, & Kratochvil, 1972) is a program designed for educationally disadvantaged young children intended to teach them the skills they lack. It is perfect for someone looking at reading from the view supported by the superintendent, Dr. Spagnola, and her curriculum corrdinator in the Reed-Enwright School District (see the chapter's lead-off scenario). Siegfried Engelmann developed the program with Carl Bereiter, and later Wesley Becker. These men developed similar programs in language, reading, and arithmetic that came to be known as the Engelmann-Becker materials, until they were marketed by the commercial publisher Science Research Associates under the name Distar Instructional System (see Figure 5.1). The basic approach is still available in a home-schooling reading program (Engelmann, Haddox, and Bruner, 1983). In this analysis we focus only on the reading program, although most of what you will study also applies to the other two programs. All three programs employ similar teaching techniques and assumptions about teaching.

FIGURE 5.1 A teacher using Distar materials.

Distar is based on a set of beliefs about children and teaching. First, according to Distar, the major difference between advantaged and disadvantaged children is the skills they possess. Second, the necessary basic skills are the same for all children. Third, children learn what they are taught. Fourth, all children can learn these skills with an appropriate instructional program. Fifth, such a program begins with a series of behavioral objectives stated as tasks for which it is clear whether the child has mastered the desired learning (Kim et al., 1972, p. 27). Sixth, development of a curriculum designed to achieve these objectives requires a thorough task analysis, careful ordering of the task components, prescribing teaching routines to teach explicitly each component in small groups using reinforcement techniques, and frequent testing both to provide feedback to the children and for assessment.

The reading program teaches those skills necessary "to look at a word, sound it out, and to say it, followed by the development of reading comprehension and advanced reading skills" (Kim et al., 1972, p. 3). These skills include reading sounds from symbols, spelling by sounds, blending sounds, and rhyming. The teacher employs precise techniques for explicitly teaching these skills to avoid confusion and offers cues to the child in order to ensure the child's success.

Instruction is characterized by distinctive teacher behaviors, student behaviors, and text characteristics. Teacher behaviors include the continual use of prescribed hand signals like finger snaps and hand claps, voice inflections, continual questioning, and eye contact, as well as drill and correction procedures for any errors or hesitancies by any children. Student behaviors include "energetic and vigorous" (Kim et al., 1972, p. 15) choral responses by the children, as well as seatwork activities following the small-group instruction. Text characteristics include the use of textual cues like markers and arrows and the use of small type for silent letters in the early stages of the program.

The program prescribes a reward system to reinforce appropriate behavior. This reward system includes liberal and immediate use of praise for correct responses and hard work, although occasionally the program employs more tangible rewards in the form of candies, raisins, colored stars, and handshakes. Interestingly, one of the distinguishing characteristics of Distar is the frequent use of "Take-Homes," which are considered rewards for hard work, rather than as the oppressive burden that homework becomes later in the upper grades.

Now, in what sense is Distar behavioral? First and foremost is the focus on behaviors. The whole development process begins with objectives that are observable and measurable. Everything that follows, including the task analysis, the development of specific teaching presentations, and the teacher's behavior, derive from the objectives (Kim et al., 1972, p. 27).

Second, the program is intended to teach skills explicitly. The developers identified these skills as the sole difference between educationally disadvantaged children and their more advantaged counterparts. Individual differences in school performance are never attributed to differences in innate abilities; differences in IQ mean that some children have not been taught certain skills. In this sense, the curriculum is highly optimistic regarding who can learn to read.

Third, these skills are taught in highly controlled settings, at least initially, without consideration for the context in which they are used or the background experiences that the children bring to the classroom. This decontextualization of skills derives from the initial questions that led Bereiter and Engelmann to develop the program: What do these children lack that they need to learn? How can it be taught to them most efficiently (Kim et al., 1972, p. 21)? These questions imply a view of children as merely suffering from deficiencies, rather than as having a wealth of cultural experiences and knowledge on which the teacher can draw and to which the teacher must relate the new skills and knowledge.

Fourth, the instructional process is based on behavioristic reinforcement principles, including the complete reliance on extrinsic rather than intrinsic motivation, the use of tasks with graduated levels of difficulty, the principle of teaching only one skill per task (Kim et al., 1972, p. 29), and the use of immediate feedback and correction.

Fifth, the developers of Distar employed a linear, means-ends, technical production model. Once the objectives were established, the most efficient means were selected for achieving the objectives. The program was dominated by experts from its original inception through its development. Even classroom implementation was prescribed by the experts with no input from the teachers. The program provides a complete script for the teacher, eliminating the need for teacher training. The teacher is given what she is to say, how she is to signal the children to respond, when she is to praise, and how she is to handle incorrect answers (Kim et al., 1972, p. 5).

CONSTRUCTIVIST

Whereas a behavioral perspective on learning focuses on behavior and performance per se, a constructivist perspective focuses on the acquisition of internal mental structures and processes, sometimes termed "schemata" and "cognitive operations," respectively, that are necessary for successful performance (Shuell, 1986). As the field of psychology, and in particular educational psychology, has undergone a revolution from behavioral to constructivist views during the past two decades, the interest of psychologists has shifted from rote learning (e.g., recall of nonsense words and syllables) to meaningful learning (e.g., reading comprehension, mathematical and science problem solving, and story composition) and to other tasks that require understanding and sense making.

A constructivist perspective can be seen as a response to a behavioral perspective. It rejects the overriding interest in learning and behavior. Constructivist psychologists are as interested in such phenomena as thinking, reasoning, mental development, decision making, memory, and perception as they are in learning per se. Furthermore, as can be seen from this list, constructivists reject the behavioral perspective's aversion to mentalistic operations like thinking. This interest in thinking leads them to conclude that understanding human learning requires the study of human beings and not other animals. Finally, a constructivist rejects the blank-slate assumption that we can trace back to Aristotle and the nineteenth-century classical empiricists. Constructivist views derive directly from the ideas of the philosopher Immanuel Kant, who claimed that people may be born with certain capacities or "structures" for acquiring language, concepts, and skills (Keil, 1981). These innate structures develop as the individual develops. Furthermore, knowledge and beliefs the individuals acquire affect the way they perceive and think about subsequent ideas, objects, and events. Thus, people do not passively receive information from their senses; rather, they actively construct ideas and generate meaning from sensory input by interpreting the input on the basis of existing ideas and previous experience.

The most active and influential view in educational research and curriculum development was summarized by Resnick as follows:

> First, learners construct understanding. They do not simply mirror what they are told or what they read. Learners look for meaning and will try to find regularity and order in the events of the world, even in the absence of complete information. This means that naive theories will always be constructed as part of the learning process.

Second, to understand something is to know relationships. Human knowledge is stored in clusters and organized into schemata that people use both to interpret familiar situations and to reason about new ones. Bits of information isolated from these structures are forgotten or become inaccessible to memory.

Third, all learning depends on prior knowledge. Learners try to link new information to what they already know in order to interpret the new material in terms of established schemata. (Resnick, 1983, pp. 472–473)

More recently Resnick (Resnick & Klopfer, 1989) has added principles of motivation and social interaction to her perspective, though still based on the assumption that knowledge is central to thinking:

Good thinkers and problem solvers differ from poorer ones not so much in the particular skills they possess as in their tendency to use them. . . . The habit or disposition to use the skills and strategies, and the knowledge of when they appl(y), [need] to be developed as well. (pp. 6–7)

The social setting provides occasions for modeling effective thinking strategies, . . . opening normally hidden mental activities to students' inspection. (p. 8)

Social settings may also provide opportunities for students to work cooperatively to solve problems that no student could have solved alone. Furthermore, working together may encourage mutual criticism, help students refine their work, and give them encouragement to engage in thinking and support as they do it. That is, "through participation in communities, students would come to expect thinking all the time, to view themselves as capable, even obligated, to engage in critical analysis and problem solving" (Resnick & Klopfer, 1989, p. 9). Clearly, with this new emphasis on collaborative work, the distinctions between the constructivist and the experiential perspectives are beginning to blur.

In contrast with behavioral psychologists, constructivists make a fundamental distinction between a person's performance on tasks (e.g., the answer students give on a test) and the psychological processes and structures necessary for that performance (e.g., understanding of the subject matter and ability to take tests).[4] A constructivist approach to objectives focuses on internal thought processes and cognitive structures, rather than on performance. Therefore, proponents of this perspective believe that objectives should refer to changes in students that are not directly observable. These internal changes are described using devices such as schematic diagrams depicting the interrelationships of acquired concepts, called "concept maps" or "semantic networks" (see Figure 5.2); flowcharts of cognitive processes (see Figure 5.3); and lists of cognitive operations or concepts (see Figure 5.4). Objectives are framed in these ways rather than using lists of behavioral objectives.

Although there is a wide array of approaches to teaching that could legitimately be termed "constructivist," two are worth noting here, because of the way they compare and contrast with the behavioral instructional model. One model derives from a concern by cognitively oriented educators with the misconceptions that students bring to the classroom. This model can be described as a *conceptual change approach* to teaching; it is summarized in Table 5.2.[5]

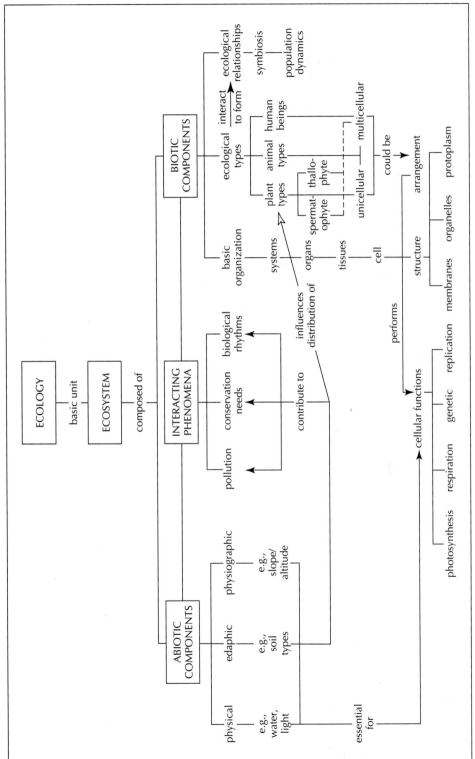

FIGURE 5.2   A concept map for a curriculum in ecology.

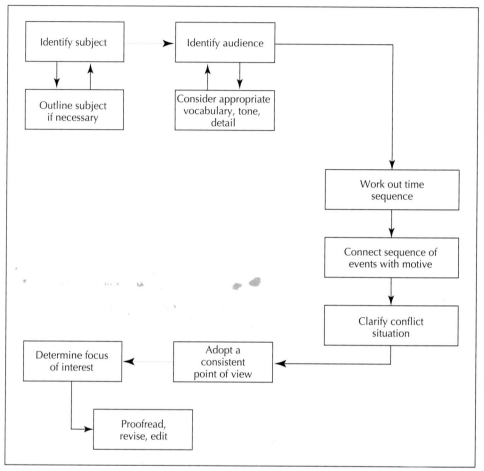

FIGURE 5.3   A flowchart for a curriculum in narrative writing.

Of the five components listed in Table 5.2, the second, third, and fourth distinguish this model from the behavioral model discussed earlier. Whereas the behavioral perspective assumes that the major task facing the teacher is providing clear communication, along with practice and feedback opportunities, this constructivist approach assumes that making explicit and challenging the students' existing conceptions are the major tasks facing the teacher.

A second model derived from the constructivist perspective views teaching and learning as most productive in the form of a "cognitive apprenticeship," in which "students participate in disciplined and productive work, just as youth once served as apprentices to master craftsmen." According to Resnick and Klopfer (1989), this model places three requirements on the curriculum and teaching:

The student should be able to design a simple experiment given a hypothesis.

a. Identify the variables of the hypothesis.
   (I) Determine which variables are presumed causes (independent) and which are effects (dependent).

b. Operationalize the variables in measurable terms.

c. Understand the idea of control and the need to vary variables one at a time (in a way that each variable's influence can be independently determined—thus one at a time or orthogonally).

d. Form the set of all possible combinations of variables.

e. Analyze the measured effect of independent variables on dependent variables in order to reach a decision about hypothesis.

FIGURE 5.4 A list of cognitive operations for an inquiry-oriented science curriculum.

Socratic Method

1. "Real" tasks, like challenging and engaging problems to solve, difficult and engrossing texts to interpret, or persuasive but flawed arguments to analyze. They would be "real" because they would provide intrinsic motivation, e.g., challenge or curiosity, rather than extrinsic motivation, e.g., earning a grade.
2. "Contextualized practice," rather than exercises on component skills "lifted out of the contexts in which they are used" (p. 10). The tasks may be shortened or simplified, but they would remain whole.

TABLE 5.2 A Conceptual Change Approach to Teaching

1. *Introduction* The teacher provides advance organizers, review, and motivating experiences.

2. *Focus* Students witness an event and a problem is posed. The teacher provides opportunities for students to make their own ideas and explanations of the events explicit.

3. *Challenge and development* Conflict is introduced through presentation of a discrepant event and/or Socratic questioning. Students reflect on their own thinking. New ideas, e.g., new analogies, that resolve discrepancies are introduced.

4. *Application* Students solve problems using the new ideas and discuss and debate their merits.

5. *Summary* Teacher and/or students summarize findings and link them to other lessons.

Source: These five components are Margaret McCasland's synthesis of Neale et al. (in press), Driver et al. (1985), Driver and Oldham (1986), and Osborne and Freyberg (1985).

3. Sufficient "opportunity to observe others doing the kind of work they are expected to do" (p. 10). Since the purpose of this requirement is to provide standards and guidance for performance, special attention must be given to ways of making the usually hidden, actual processes of thinking overt for the student to observe.

Notice that although this approach to teaching resembles Hunter's design of effective lessons, with its emphasis on modeling, a cognitive apprenticeship differs in two important respects. First, the "behaviors" it wants the teacher to model are fundamentally covert, typically tacit, mental processes, which the teacher must make explicit. Second, the "behaviors" are modeled in the context in which they are actually used, rather than decontextualized.

In contrast to a behaviorally based curriculum, which emphasizes student mastery of a set of behavioral objectives, a constructivist curriculum focuses its attention on helping students to think more effectively and to make sense of the world. Curriculum development efforts are aimed at encouraging students to develop understandings of the world that are sensible and useful to them (Osborne & Freyberg, 1985).

The Case of Reading Recovery: A Constructivist Curriculum[6]

Like Distar, Reading Recovery (Pinnell, DeFord, & Lyons, 1989; Pinnell, 1991) is a reading program designed for students in early primary school who are at risk of educational failure. However, in comparison to Distar, Reading Recovery focuses more on the teachers' professional growth than on a specific set of materials and is more individualized, focused more on reading strategies than on discrete skills, and based more on the child's strengths than on perceived deficiencies. This curriculum is well suited for someone like Phil Schmidt in the chapter's lead-off scenario.

> Reading Recovery supports the development of reading strategies by helping the children use what they already know. Some "remedial" models focus on drilling children on the very items that confuse them. In contrast, the Reading Recovery teacher assesses each child's strengths in great detail and builds on those strengths in daily, individual lessons. [In so doing] they learn specific strategies for applying their own knowledge." (p. 3)

Reading Recovery was developed by Marie Clay (1985) in New Zealand for use with six-year-old children in their second year of school who, for whatever reason, had not yet caught on to reading and writing. (See Figure 5.5.) Because of its initial successes, the program was adopted nationally in New Zealand in 1979. Reading Recovery was first introduced in the United States in 1984 when Clay, who has since returned to New Zealand, established a training program at Ohio State University. It is being used in five countries including nationwide in New Zealand (since 1979), 22 U.S. states, and 2 Canadian provinces. Ohio (since 1987) and Illinois are committed to statewide implementation (Pinnell, 1989).

FIGURE 5.5   Marie Clay—the founder of Reading Recovery.

Since New Zealand has a strong introductory language arts program, very similar to "whole language" approaches in this country,[7] most students are independent readers and writers by the age of six, albeit at a beginning level. In New Zealand, Reading Recovery has targeted the bottom 10 percent of first-grade students, based on teacher judgment and on a Diagnostic Survey of Reading developed by Clay. In the United States the percentage of children who compose the target population varies from system to system depending on the relative need and the availability of trained personnel. Within a period of 12 to 18 weeks of daily thirty-minute one-on-one sessions with a specially trained Reading Recovery teacher, nearly all children "develop a self-improving system for continued growth in reading" (Pinnell et al., p. 2) that enables them to sustain their success without any further need for additional help. An added bonus is that they also increase their abilities as writers.[8]

The program is intended to be used as early as possible, serving as a "first net" *before* children are labeled or—more important—see themselves as incompetent students. In this sense, the program is preventative rather than remedial.

The idea is to provide intensive and focused intervention while the child is in the process of learning the early strategies of reading.

Reading Recovery is not just a reading program. It is best described as a "system intervention" which "requires the long-term commitment of an entire school system" to a "carefully designed set of interlocking principles and actions" in order for the program to produce sustained results (Pinnell et al., p. 5). The program has elements similar to those of other programs, but the *combination* of these elements in a single program is unique:

1. Each child has an individual program.
2. The teaching methods are based on what research has shown to be beneficial for most children acquiring literacy skills.
3. Only tasks that are meaningful to the child are used, so that the child can detect errors when the message does not make sense.
4. The child is encouraged to work independently of the teacher on what he or she knows at the outset—i.e., during the first week. On new tasks the teacher and child work as partners for successful completion of literacy tasks.
5. Task difficulty is constantly being increased to keep the child in the "zone of proximal development" (Vygotsky, 1962, 1978), that is, where the work is feasible, but stretches the child into new territory. The teacher selects books of interest to each child falling within this zone.
6. Throughout the program, the child is carefully and constantly evaluated by a fully trained teacher, so that the teacher can design an appropriate program and assess when the child is ready to return full time to the regular classroom (Clay, 1985).

While the program emphasizes the differences between individual children, the lessons all follow a standard structure. The basic format of a lesson includes the following phases: (1) The child rereads several small, familiar books strengthening the child's fluency, while the teacher may make a few corrections selectively. (2) The teacher carefully analyzes the kinds of errors the child is making in order to tailor the program accordingly. (3) The child composes a story or a brief message to a parent, a sibling, a friend, or anyone of the child's choice, and then writes the message or story with the teacher's support. (4) The teacher introduces a new book, and the child reads it.

The program is based on the premise that children are active learners. Although the teacher selects the materials and activities that can help each particular child develop effective reading strategies, the children "bring their own meaning to the books they read." Although the teacher provides "choices and support," each child "must do the work and solve the problems."

Reading Recovery focuses on helping children "develop the kinds of strategies that good readers use" (Pinnell et al., p. 2) and enabling them to become independent readers. These strategies include "self-monitoring, cross-checking, predicting and confirming." Children learn "to use multiple sources of information while reading and writing" and "to 'orchestrate' strategies while attending to the meaning of text" (Pinnell et al., p. 3). There is little emphasis placed on memorizing any specific lists of words.

Unlike Distar the program is not based on a particular set of materials, either texts or workbooks. Reading Recovery teachers often use what are termed "trade books" (books sold in bookstores and available in libraries) rather than textbooks (termed "basals"), although several companies are now producing more literary texts appropriate for use in Reading Recovery. Teachers select from a list of several hundred "short and interesting story books . . . those that suit the child's interests, that have appealing language and stories, and that are at a relatively easy level for the child to read. Thus, at every level of text difficulty, children read fluently and for meaning and enjoyment" (p. 4).

Reading Recovery shares with Distar a belief that nearly all children can learn to read independently and that some children need to have explicit instruction in reading; however, the proponents of Reading Recovery believe that children should develop an understanding of letter-sound relationships as a *result* of reading and writing, rather than learn discrete letter-sound relationships as a *prerequisite* to reading and writing. According to Reading Recovery's developers, one-to-one relationships between letters and sounds should not be taught, since there are many sounds for each letter, and sometimes more than one letter per sound. Letter-sound relationships need to be learned flexibly to handle the complexity of the English language.

The child's motivation in Reading Recovery is based on the early experiences of success in reading and writing, on the appeal of reading personally interesting works, and on the child's ownership of the writing process. Each of these represents intrinsic rewards. Each gives children an important message about themselves as successful students and about the value of reading and writing for fun, for acquiring interesting information, and for communication. Reading Recovery also builds confidence as children "realize that what they already know and can do has value in the reading-writing process" (Pinnell et al., p. 3).

Reading Recovery can be considered a constructivist curriculum for several reasons: It is theoretically related to the work of constructivist psychologists, such as Vygotsky (Clay, 1985); it emphasizes both the teaching of concepts about reading and the teaching of reading for meaning; and its lesson format is based on constructivist pedagogical assumptions. These assumptions include the following: (1) reading is a process taking place inside the reader's mind, where readers actively construct understandings; (2) children are taught how to solve problems using specific strategies (Pinnell et al., p. 3); (3) the relationships between written and oral language are key to both the reading and writing processes, and these relationships can be taught; (4) the child's prior experiences and knowledge are an appropriate basis for further instruction, thus building on strengths that the child has already developed.

While a one-on-one tutorial program is necessarily less social than a classroom-based program, Reading Recovery does emphasize the social dimension of learning. Not only is the tutorial relationship between teacher and child fundamentally a social relationship, but also reading and writing are conceived as processes requiring the construction of shared meanings. Furthermore, social concepts of literacy such as authorship and audience are constantly employed.

LIMITATIONS OF THE TWO PERSPECTIVES

The literature on objectives from these two perspectives constitutes an ongoing debate between them. Each responds to the perceived inadequacies of the other.[9] Although proponents of both perspectives have made substantial contributions to the formulation of objectives, proponents of both perspectives also fail to see the limitations of the way they have framed the problem at the outset. This framework now limits the scope and quality of their debate. It is as though they were having a conversation that outsiders, on overhearing it, might recognize as important but find incomplete in its scope, perhaps a bit myopic. And outsiders, in this case, include practicing teachers.

One of the major problems with the debate is that it has been monopolized by psychologists, as though concerns about learning and learners were the only considerations in determining the purpose and content of the curriculum. What has ensued from this monopoly has been the technicization of the curriculum literature on objectives. Discussion of the purposes and content of education has become the province of educational psychologists. Behavioral psychologists have been preoccupied with the question of how to state those purposes. Constructivists have been concerned with the same issue, but have added content-related issues to the discussion. But as psychologists they have limited the scope of these discussions to issues of knowledge acquisition and skill development, even though they have begun to recognize the social dimensions of these issues. By formulating the problems of purpose and content as problems of learning, the discussion has excluded from the debate many educational philosophers, scholars in the disciplines, and journalists, particularly educational critics—not to mention elected officials, teachers and their unions, and parents.

Among the issues that go unaddressed by educators formulating the purposes of education and selecting its content are the following:

1. Whose knowledge is considered legitimate and whose interests benefit from these decisions? Consider, for example, the competing interests of the educational psychologists themselves, the subject matter departments, the administrators, the college-bound students, the testing industry, college admissions departments, and the textbook industry, among others.
2. What is the influence of these groups on the purposes school pursue and the content they teach? Consider in particular the null curriculum.
3. To what extent can the purposes pursued and content taught in schools help students become more aware of and understand their own social conditions and the means by which they can "act collectively to build political structures that can change the status quo"? (Giroux, 1983, p. 353)

These questions represent only a sample of the kinds of questions that a technical view of education misses.

The point here is not that any discussion of curriculum purpose and content must consider these issues. Rather, the point is that the psychologically based literature on purpose and content objectives forms only a part of the possible curriculum discourse on this topic. In particular, it is the technical part of the discourse. Let us examine this limitation more closely.

HEGEMONIC FUNCTION OF OBJECTIVES

According to critical theorists,[10] the major problem with technical discussions of objectives is that they divert us from an examination of hegemony. The concept of *hegemony* is used by critical theorists to denote the domination of one class or group by another. In this view, the dominating group, the oppressor, either consciously, as in a conspiracy, or without conscious awareness, attempts to legitimize its interests at the expense of those of the oppressed. Furthermore, the oppressor attempts at least to maintain, if not to increase, its power over the oppressed.[11] For these theorists, objectives are a hegemonic device in both direct and indirect ways.

The Official Curriculum   As an explicit expression of one group's (e.g., a school board's) educational intent for another group (e.g., pupils) objectives become an effective and direct means for controlling people, or at least what they study. When the dominant group is not only older and presumably wiser, but also of a different social class, ethnic group, race, or gender than the dominated group, then the objectives may be serving directly in a hegemonic role, particularly when coupled with accountability measures such as tests. For example, objectives that embody racial, ethnic, social, or sex stereotypes may be hegemonic in this direct sense, serving as a means to reinforce a social order that serves the interests of those in power. Teaching that certain careers are for women and others are primarily for men is an obvious case. Another case in which objectives might function hegemonically has to do with the teaching of history. History curriculum objectives might reflect a version of history that serves the interests of the dominant group. For example, the facts that the students are required to memorize might serve to glorify the events that led to the dominant group's rise to power, whereas the facts that are never mentioned might represent the violence done to other groups during the dominant group's ascendence.

The Hidden Curriculum   Objectives may also act more indirectly by diverting attention from the hegemonic forces of the school as an institution. When we focus our attention on the objectives of the official curriculum, we can lose sight of the fact that the school's hidden curriculum may have a more profound and durable impact on students than the official curriculum. I know that schools I went to taught me a number of powerful lessons through their hidden curriculum: that individual competition is the fairest and most effective way to run an institution like a school; that whether I succeeded or failed in school, I got what I deserved—that is, that school is basically meritocratic;

that males are inherently better at science and math than females; that punctuality, neatness, and effort are often more important than achievement; that following instructions, i.e., compliance, is often more important than learning; and that intellectual skills like the ability to manipulate symbols are more important than other characteristics like business acumen, leadership, and creativity. It wasn't until I had experiences after and outside of school that I realized both the impact of these unofficial lessons and their limited validity. I realized that these lessons of the hidden curriculum created or reinforced myths that are still difficult for me to forget. I even occasionally find myself operating as though these myths are true. Perhaps you have had similar experiences. Students may remember that they are not suited for a career in medicine long after they forget the parts of an amoeba. They may remember the distinction between work and play, the importance of being neat, orderly, and on time, and the inevitability of having to do meaningless tasks long after they forget the names and dates that constitute much of social studies. This hidden curriculum becomes even more hegemonic in its effect when different groups of children, segregated by "ability" or geography into socially, economically, or racially homogeneous schools or tracks, receive different hidden curricula preparing them for different positions in the social order.[12] By focusing the public and professional debate on the official curriculum, criticism of the school's hidden curriculum may be avoided.[13]

The Null Curriculum   Objectives may function hegemonically in other indirect ways. The curriculum implicitly legitimizes the content that the objectives embody, while it delegitimizes the null curriculum (see Chapter One). When the legitimized content is drawn from the culture of the dominant group—i.e., the school authorities—and the culture of the pupils and their parents is delegitimized, then the objectives and the curriculum that includes them may be acting hegemonically. For example, the call for multicultural education is based on the assumption that there is not one "American" culture for the schools to transmit. Although it was acceptable earlier in this century to attempt to "Americanize" the large immigrant population, such attempts are now considered hegemonic by many people. To many people a more pluralistic approach to education seems warranted. New York State's "curriculum of inclusion" is one significant attempt to expand the content considered legitimate by school authorities. Debates in many states on bilingual education also exemplify this issue.

Critical theorists[14] maintain that the curriculum serves important, though ideologically problematic, functions. For one thing, it supports the status of those with power, influence, and wealth in the existing political, social, and economic order. One way the curriculum serves this conservative function is with a hidden curriculum that convinces people that inequities are inevitable or self-inflicted and therefore are not the fault of those in control. It also serves a conservative function with an official curriculum that equips one class of students with knowledge and skills for professional and executive careers and another class of students for blue-collar and unskilled jobs. Thus, according to these writers, the explicit and implicit curriculum serves to reduce people's sense of political efficacy and increase their political acquiescence. These writers introduce an ideological dimension to curriculum analysis and may even provide an opportunity to engage in an ideological analysis of a seemingly neutral curriculum.

Curriculum Analysis Questions

Examine the purposes and content of your curriculum, trying to identify the epistemological, psychological, and sociopolitical assumptions that underlie it. The following series of questions is intended to help you do this analysis.

1. What conceptions of learning, objectives, curriculum, and teaching underlie the curriculum materials you are analyzing? Are any of these conceptions consistent with either the behavioral or the cognitive perspective? Again, keep in mind that it is unlikely that your curriculum, much less its objectives, represents a pure case of any one perspective—and that it is even less likely that it represents a clear case of one of the two perspectives on which we focused in this chapter. Therefore, you are faced with the task of unpacking the curriculum's underlying concepts of learning, objectives, curriculum, and instruction from whatever evidence in the curriculum you can find.

With few but important exceptions, curricula cannot be neatly categorized as behavioral or constructivist. Many—though certainly not all—curricula do, however, manifest elements of one or both perspectives. Perhaps the objectives are expressed in behavioral terms, but they represent concepts and principles, rather than skills. Or the curriculum focuses on structural features of the subject matter, but the instructional methods utilize behavior modification techniques[15]

Curriculum analysis entails the examination of various components of the curriculum materials to identify underlying assumptions, then an attempt to reconcile apparent contradictions, and finally a search for implications of the uncovered assumptions. Question 1 reflects this approach. Notice the tentativeness with which we approach analysis. Analysis requires turning materials over and over, looking this way at them and then looking that way at them, each time seeing something different, sometimes contradicting, sometimes supporting an earlier hypothesis.

2. What aspects of a hidden curriculum are likely to accompany the conceptions and perspectives underlying the curriculum?
3. To what extent is the curriculum likely to play a hegemonic role in its purposes or content?

Question 2 deals with the hidden curriculum. Conceptions of learning, objectives, curriculum, and instruction may lead to particular implicit messages to students about their roles as students; how they learn; the potential meaningfulness of the subject matter; the necessity to do busy work neatly, promptly, and willingly; their own capacity to create or discover new knowledge; the authority of the teacher, textbook writers, and experts in the subject matter; the potential utility of the subject matter; and the value of cooperation and competition with fellow students. The curriculum is likely to send these messages to students through the dominant types of teaching method it employs, its use of stereotypes, and the focus of its approach to evaluation and testing.

Question 3 asks you to try to determine whether the curriculum plays any other hegemonic role. For example: Is it intended for only one class of students? Is it designed in such a way that certain students are more likely to succeed in it than others? Does it delegitimize the culture of certain students? In its null curriculum does it exclude certain important aspects of the subject matter? For example, U.S. history books make little mention of the role religion has played.

NOTES

1. A more moderate interpretation of this perspective recognizes the distinction between one's intended learning outcomes and ways one can evaluate the attainment of these outcomes, but still requires that any objective be expressed in operational form in order to be meaningful. See, for example, Skinner (1968).
2. See Strike (1974) for a comprehensive analysis of the "expressive potential" of behavioral objectives.
3. See, for example, Rosenshine (1983) and Hunter (1984).
4. This follows Chomsky's (1957) distinction between competence and performance.
5. Note that not all the components need to be in every lesson, or in this sequence.
6. I wish to thank Margaret McCasland for her contribution to this section of the book.
7. See Chapter Nine for a description of whole language.
8. Clay has found that only 1 to 2 percent of New Zealand students are unable to benefit from either the regular classroom techniques or Reading Recovery and therefore need special help in reading and writing beyond first grade—a statistic that challenges many assumptions about innate ability, learning disabilities, and environmental deficiencies (Clay, 1975).
9. See, for example, Mager (1962), Popham and Baker (1970), Strike and Posner (1976), and Greeno (1976).
10. See, for example, Apple (1981).
11. See, for example, Freire (1970).
12. See, for example, Anyon (1983).
13. See Giroux and Purpel (1983) for a fine collection of works about this topic.
14. See, for example, Beyer and Apple (1988).
15. Distar is an example of this approach.

CHAPTER 6

Curriculum Organization
Basic Concepts

The Sheridan School District Curriculum Committee has been in operation for five years. During that time this 15-member joint committee of the faculty, school board, and administration has approved, and sent for adoption to the board, curricula in almost all the subject areas. It has a lot to be proud of. However, there are some members of this committee who are dissatisfied. Alice Huey, a board member; Sam Diamond, a librarian; Henry Capraro, a fourth-grade teacher; and Lee Bosco, a high school English teacher, have been pushing the committee to examine the relationships between subjects. They argue that the curriculum has become increasingly fragmented and compartmentalized. Students see no relation between the study of health and science, practical arts and science, science and math, English and social studies, or art and music, to mention just a few pairs of closely related subjects. Furthermore, they contend that there is little or no articulation between the elementary and the middle school or between the middle and the high school curriculum in any of the subjects.

Most others on the committee disagree. They contend that the connections are in the curriculum and that the "good" students are able to see them. Besides, they point out that each subject area has its own "structure" that must be respected.

The superintendent, Dr. Rachel Ehrenberg, a member of the committee, has suggested that the matter is serious enough to warrant a study by a subcommittee of the Curriculum Committee. The committee votes to establish the subcommittee, and Sam Diamond is chosen to chair it.

At its first meeting the Subcommittee on Curriculum Organization decides to analyze existing curriculum documents of the district in order to answer the following questions:

1. *To what extent do courses appear to be collections of discrete, unrelated topics rather than forming coherent wholes?*
2. *Are there any concepts, skills, or themes that curricula in different subjects have in common? What are the possibilities for interdisciplinary studies in the district?*
3. *To what extent does the curriculum of one educational level build on the curriculum of the previous level?*

This chapter introduces the basic concepts of curriculum organization that would help Sam and his subcommittee to discuss these and other questions.

BASIC TERMS

Virtually every curriculum model[1] includes some consideration of the organization of content, objectives, or experiences as a crucial component. However, this apparent agreement on the importance of curriculum organization obscures underlying conflicts. In this chapter we attempt to clarify basic terms and patterns of organization necessary to sort out fundamentally different approaches to curriculum organization. The purpose for making these distinctions explicit is to enable you to unpack the organization of any curriculum and to raise questions regarding the sensibility of that organization. The curriculum analysis section at the end of the chapter applies these terms and patterns to the curriculum you have selected.

We begin with several important terms: curriculum organization, macro and micro levels, and vertical and horizontal dimensions of organization.

Curriculum Organization

The word "organize" means "to form as or into a whole consisting of interdependent or coordinated parts" (Random House, 1984, p. 937). The "parts" in this case are elements of the curriculum. Therefore, the term "curriculum organization" can have a wide range of meanings, depending on which definition of the term "curriculum" is being used and what kinds of elements are to be organized.[2] Obviously, if you were asked to analyze a curriculum's organization, you would first have to determine these two things.

Macro and Micro Levels of Organization

The term "curriculum organization" is also used at different levels of specificity. The broadest level refers to the relations between educational levels, such as elementary and secondary education, or between educational programs, such as vocational and general programs. The most specific level refers to relations between particular concepts, facts, or skills within lessons. We might term these two ends of the specificity continuum the *macro level* and *micro level* of organization, respectively. Of course, there are many levels of specificity between these two extremes. Thus, we must remember that "macro" and "micro" are relative, rather than absolute, terms. However, typically when we talk about "micro levels" of curriculum organization, we are referring to the organization of a course or unit. Likewise, we typically reserve the term "macro level" for the organization of courses to form programs.

Vertical and Horizontal Dimensions

"Curriculum organization" denotes a systematic arrangement of curriculum elements. At least two dimensions of organization are significant. If we think of educational events as occurring along a time line, then we can describe them as occurring either within the same time frame or subsequent to one another.

The former dimension concerns what is taught in conjunction with a particular topic or course. The latter dimension concerns what follows a particular topic or course. It is conventional in curricula to place the time line arbitrarily on a vertical axis. Then the aspect of curriculum organization that describes the correlation or integration of content taught concurrently is termed *horizontal organization.* The aspect of curriculum organization that describes the sequencing of content is termed *vertical organization.* A scope and sequence chart (see Figure 6.1) displays both the vertical, i.e., the sequence, and the horizontal, i.e., the scope, dimensions of a curriculum. Using this terminology, issues of horizontal curriculum organization would include the meaning and value of interdisciplinary studies; the integration of subjects (e.g., American history and English become American studies); the coordination (termed "correlation") in the scheduling of topics in different subjects so that they complement one another (e.g., symmetry in math, biology, and art); the need for corequisites (e.g., a student must take a calculus course while studying physics); and the value of providing more coherence and personal or social relevance of content through project- or problem-oriented curricula. Likewise, issues of vertical curriculum organization would include the need for prerequisites, ways of providing continuity in the curriculum (Tyler, 1949), making sure content builds on previously taught content, and ways of sequencing skills or concepts for effective learning. Since the vertical/horizontal distinction is independent of the macromicro continuum, many of these issues can be discussed at different levels. For example, we can discuss the need for pre- or corequisite courses, a macro-level issue, or pre- and corequisite skills, a micro-level issue. The vertical/horizontal aspect of curriculum does not represent a choice between two different dimensions of organization. Rather, most curricula display some organization along each of these two dimensions.

BASIC STRUCTURES

Although curricula can be organized in a seemingly endless variety of ways, there is a limited set of basic structures. The variety results from variations on and combinations of these basic structures.

Content Structures

Depending upon the degree of vertical and horizontal organization, content can assume different configurations. At one extreme is a curriculum in which all content is discrete, unrelated to, or at least independent of, all other content. In such a case, order does not matter at all. The *Sesame Street* curriculum is constructed in this way, since there is no way to ensure that the child sees any particular previous or subsequent program. Therefore, each program must be self-sufficient. We might term this type of configuration "discrete." At the other extreme is a curriculum in which each concept or skill requires the mastery of the immediately previous concept or skill. Mastery learning strategies (Bloom,

A K-6 LIFE SCIENCE
SCOPE AND SEQUENCE CHART

Kindergarten	First Grade	Second Grade	Third Grade	Fourth Grade	Fifth Grade	Sixth Grade
Concepts	Concepts	Concepts	Concepts	Concepts	Concepts	Concepts
Green plants grow; animals grow and move.	Living things have young, grow, and die; nonliving things do not.	Plants and animals are grouped according to characteristics they have in common.	Living things get energy from food: energy flows through a food chain.	Adaptations help species survive.	Plants and animals use and store energy from food: the energy in food can be traced back to green plants—and the sun.	All living things respire, combining food and oxygen, releasing carbon dioxide, water, and energy.
People and other animals use their senses.	Seeds are spread and can grow. Different plants have different kinds and numbers of seeds.	How plants grow changes with the seasons.	All communities depend on green plants and the sun.	Only members of the same species can mate and reproduce.	Nonliving materials cycle: decomposers break down materials from living things.	Only green plants can photosynthesize, using light energy, carbon dioxide, and water and producing food and oxygen; all life depends on this process.
Kinds of plants and animals can be sorted into groups.	People use plants for food, clothes, and houses.	How animals look and what they do may change with the seasons.	Seeds can make new plants; pieces of some plants make more of the original plant.	Plants are adapted to grow toward what they need.	Competition for food, light, and water changes with the increase or decrease of populations.	Adaptations come from changes in populations over time, often in response to changing environments.
Each plant and animal lives one life, starting young and growing older.	Young plants and animals come from adults of the same kind and grow to look like them.	Plants need light, water, and air; plants make food.	Seasons change because the amount of the sun's energy we get changes.	Most plants reproduce by flowers; flowers develop into fruits.	Living and nonliving parts of an ecosystem interact; changes in one part of an ecosystem can change another part.	Conservation of green plants and the ecosystem supporting them is essential for all life.

FIGURE 6.1 Scope and sequence chart, life science, Grades Kindergarten through 6.

1971) and the Keller Plan, also known as Personalized Systems of Instruction (Keller, 1968), require this type of "linear" configuration.

Saxon's math and reading curricula exemplify this approach. The Saxon curricula are based on the belief "that the most effective way for students to learn is through a gentle development of concepts and the practice of those concepts extended over a considerable period of time." Saxon calls these methods *incremental development* and *continual practice and review.*

> At its simplest, incremental development is the introduction of topics in easily understandable pieces (increments), permitting the assimilation of one facet of a concept before the next facet is introduced. Both facets are then practiced together until another is introduced.

> The incrementalization of topics is combined with continual review, wherein all previously learned material is reviewed in every lesson for the entire year. Topics are never dropped but are instead increased in complexity and practiced every day, providing the time required for concepts to become totally familiar.

> As concepts become familiar and the requisite skills become automated, learning becomes a game at which students can succeed and through which they find satisfaction and self-worth. More importantly, the automation of fundamental skills frees students' minds to consider the concepts on a more abstract level. Genuine learning is demonstrated not only through the understanding of a concept but also through the ability to apply that concept to new situations.

Between these extremes is a configuration in which multiple unrelated concepts or skills, rather than single concepts or skills as in the linear configuration, are necessary for learning subsequent concepts or skills. When a whole curriculum is organized this way, it assumes a pyramidal, or "hierarchical," structure (Briggs, 1968). Gagne's elementary science curriculum, known as *Science: A Process Approach* (S:APA) and developed under the aegis of the American Association for the Advancement of Science (AAAS, 1967), represents an elaborate hierarchically organized curriculum. We will discuss this curriculum in depth in Chapter Seven.

One other important configuration between the extremes is the "spiral" curriculum popularized by Jerome Bruner (1960). Bruner, adapting Piaget's ideas on cognitive development, argued that concepts are internalized or "represented" in different modes by children at different ages and, therefore, must be taught in different ways at different educational levels. Initially, children represent concepts through actions; Bruner calls this the "enactive" mode. Therefore, according to Bruner, we should teach concepts to very young children through role plays, games, and other active methods. Subsequently, children can represent concepts as images; Bruner calls this the "iconic" mode and says that they can then be taught using drawings and models. Later, children can represent concepts as abstract symbols—the "symbolic" mode—and we can teach them using such symbols as words and mathematical formulas. This theory led Bruner to be optimistic about teaching concepts in some form to children of any age and to argue the futility of teaching any concept once and for all. Instead, he suggested that we begin to teach important concepts in a form for which the child is ready and that we return to concepts repeatedly at higher and higher levels of sophistication and abstraction. This spiral pattern of content forms the basis for the organization of M:ACOS.

Figure 6.2 summarizes these configurations of content structure. The letters signify different learning outcomes.

Media Structures

"Curriculum organization" may refer to more than the ways in which content is arranged. When writers do not try to make a clear distinction between curriculum and instruction, "curriculum organization" may refer to the ways in which instructional activities, methods, and materials—"media" in the broadest sense—relate to particular objectives. Again, it is useful to examine extreme cases.

A "parallel" structure is based on the assumption that each medium (here "method") of instruction is optimally suited for teaching certain objectives to any student. Thus, each method teaches a set of objectives without explicitly relating it to objectives taught by other methods. For example, the chemistry text and laboratory guide might represent essentially separate courses with no attempt to make connections for the student. The Chemical Bond Approach Project (CBA) was just such a course. Since the text and laboratory guide were designed to parallel and reinforce each other, but were not deliberately built into an integrated sequence, the teacher was left considerable freedom to work back and forth between the two as he or she saw fit (Goodlad, 1964, p. 31).

A "convergent" structure is based on the assumption that there is no one way to achieve an objective and that students differ in their ability to learn from any one medium. All significant learning occurs as a consequence of many contributing educational experiences. Therefore, overlapping instructional activities and methods are necessary for achieving significant objectives with a group of diverse students. M:ACOS exemplifies this media structure. For example, felt-board simulations, role plays, films, readings, and class discussions are all used to teach the concept of adaptation, each providing a different mode of representing the concept.

A "divergent" structure is based on the assumption that any activity leads to a diverse set of learning outcomes. Educational experiences are rich to the extent that they have the potential to lead in a number of different directions. Instruction should be designed to capitalize on the richness of each activity. Most project- or problem-centered curricula select a focus of study and activity, be it the publication of a magazine like *Foxfire*, the analysis of a school's discipline problems, or the building of a school playground. They use these foci for teaching a wide variety of "lessons," from specific skills, such as proofreading; to concepts, such as the meaning of cooperation and community; to attitudes, such as a sense of responsibility for the welfare of others.

Between these extremes is a "mixed" curriculum that capitalizes on the strengths of each activity and method to teach certain content but regularly focuses all the activities on a common objective. The curriculum also employs activities that teach multiple objectives whenever possible.

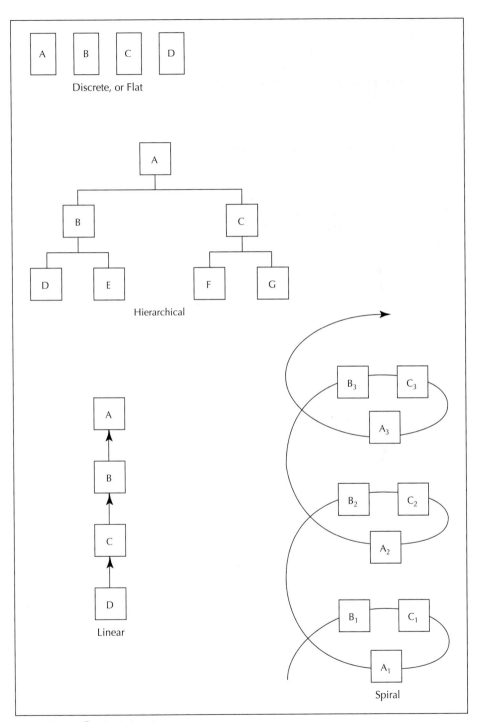

FIGURE 6.2   Content structures.
(Adapted from Heimer, 1969).

Figure 6.3 summarizes the major media structures. The letters signify learning objectives and the numbers signify media.

TYPICAL MACRO-LEVEL CURRICULUM ORGANIZATIONS

The macro-level organization of the U.S. primary and secondary curriculum is so familiar that we tend to take it for granted, accepting it unquestioningly. Let us consider some typical organizations, in order to think about curriculum organization in terms with which we are familiar. The elementary schools are dominated by reading and other "language arts," including spelling and writing. Mathematics, principally arithmetic, rounds out the traditional "basic skills" of the elementary grades. Science, social studies, and health are given widely varying amounts of time, typically increasing in the upper elementary

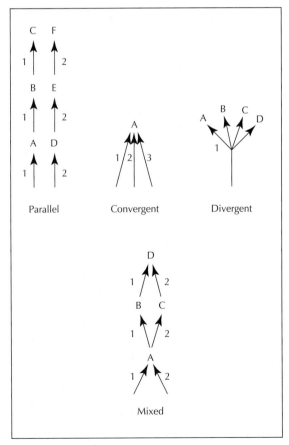

FIGURE 6.3   Media structures.

grades, but remaining minor subjects compared to the basic skills. In the secondary school, the English curriculum again combines grammar, spelling, writing, reading, and literature study. English is the dominant subject, with most states requiring it for every student in every grade. As in the elementary grades history, government, geography, and social sciences are taught in conjunction under the rubric of social studies. However, at the secondary level, particularly in the upper grades, this subject is a close second to English in priority, most states requiring students to study it at least three of their four high school years, i.e., Grades 9 through 12. Physical education, as in the elementary grades, is required of everyone in every grade but is not typically regarded as an academic subject on a par with the other subjects. Mathematics and science complete the secondary school's "big five," the subjects required of all students in virtually all states during at least half of their secondary school years (Grades 6 or 7 through 12). As a continuation of the upper elementary grades, health as a subject is required of all students through the lower secondary grades (usually Grades 6 through 9). Other subjects, including foreign languages, music, art, computer skills, and occupational subjects including business, are highly variable from school to school and from student to student, typically gaining significance as electives, rather than as required subjects, which are termed "constants."

This outline of the public school curriculum is so familiar to most of us that it may seem like a waste of time even to delineate it. Until we realize that each of these features of the U.S. public school curriculum is a relatively recent invention, the curriculum appears absolute and timeless. For example, even the basic skills are a relatively recent innovation. Schools prior to the nineteenth century were primarily guided by a religious purpose, with a resulting emphasis on the Bible. Reading was important only so that one could read the untranslated word of God. Since the Bible, at least the New Testament, was originally written in Latin, this language was the only one a person needed to learn to read. Arithmetic, termed "ciphering," arrived in the nineteenth century, as the schools addressed the needs of a growing commercial class. Clearly then, the main features of the school's macro-level curriculum can be seen as a response to the changing purposes of the school as a societal institution.

The same is true of the macro-level organization of individual subjects. Mathematics typically begins with arithmetic, covering addition, subtraction, multiplication, division, and fractions, followed by either general and business mathematics or a sequence of elementary algebra, geometry, intermediate algebra, trigonometry, and, for those who get that far, calculus. In the secondary schools, science begins with general or physical science, usually in Grade 7 or 8; this is followed by earth science, biology, chemistry, and physics—again, for those who get that far. Elementary school social studies usually proceeds up the grades from a study of the family, the school and neighborhood, and the community, to the study of the state, the nation, the Western Hemisphere, and finally, other parts of the world. Secondary school, and occasionally upper elementary, social studies treats history in chronological order, from Greek and Roman times through the medieval to the modern periods.

For most of us these typical organizations are taken for granted. Only when we are confronted with alternative organizations do we realize that these organizations are not absolute but are the result of deliberate choices. For example, New York State's decision to follow the precedent set by European schools years ago by reorganizing secondary school mathematics was based on this sort of realization. In the past 10 years, New York has integrated algebra, geometry, and trigonometry previously studied in Grades 9 through 11, adding logic, statistics, and probability to a spiral curriculum simply called Course I, II, and III, or integrated mathematics.

For a century, earth science, previously called "physical geography," consisted of separate studies of the earth's land, including topography and geology; water, including oceanography; air, including climatology and meteorology; and, in the later version, life forms, including paleontology, and also astronomy. Figures 6.4 and 6.5 present the tables of contents of two earth science textbooks published eighty years apart. Figure 6.6 presents the table of contents from an earth science text published about ten years after the one shown in Figure 6.5. Notice that the organization is no longer based on the same principles as the organization of the earlier ones. Rather than using the four "spheres," the atmosphere, hydrosphere, geosphere, and biosphere, as the primary basis, the newer book uses concepts like cycles, materials, energy, space, and time as the organizational basis. Similar shifts could be seen if we contrasted different biology, physics, and chemistry texts, different physical education curricula representing the current shift from a sports orientation to life skills, and texts and curricula for other subjects that have undergone significant organizational changes.

The point is that curriculum organization is a cultural construction and is, therefore, subject to change. Curriculum study should result in an increased awareness of this fact and of the organizational alternatives available. A bit of skepticism regarding current practice in curriculum organization is preferable to blind acceptance.

ORGANIZATIONAL PRINCIPLES

One way to develop this awareness is to examine the kinds of organizational principles that have been employed. An organizational principle states the basis or reason for organizing a curriculum in a particular way. Without these principles, describing curriculum organization only in terms of the basic structures presented earlier in this chapter is like describing a family as a triad, omitting the idea that the family includes a mother-child, a father-child, and a father-mother relationship.

We have seen that curriculum organization includes both a vertical and a horizontal dimension. Organizational principles, like other aspects of curriculum organization, apply to both the vertical and the horizontal dimensions. A principle of vertical organization describes the reason for ordering or sequencing curriculum elements in a particular manner. For example, a chronological approach to organizing a history curriculum uses time as the sequencing principle.

FIGURE 6.4   Table of contents for a nineteenth-century physical geography textbook. *From: D.M. Warren,* Elementary Treatise on Physical Geography. *Philadelphia: Conperthwait, 1873.*

UNIT I THE EARTH AND ITS LAND FORMS

UNIT II THE EARTH AND THE UNIVERSE

UNIT III THE EARTH AND ITS ATMOSPHERE

UNIT IV THE EARTH AND ITS OCEANS

UNIT V THE EARTH AND ITS CLIMATES

FIGURE 6.5 Table of contents of a 1950s earth science textbook.
From S. N. Namowitz and D. B. Stone, Earth Science: The World We Live In. *New York: O. Van Nostrand, 1953.*

Contents

FIGURE 6.6   Table of contents of an earth science textbook that originated in the 1960s. *From American Geological Institute,* Investigating the Earth, *4th ed. Boston: Houghton Mifflin, 1987.*

A principle of horizontal organization describes why the curriculum presents certain elements in conjunction, or why the curriculum is organized around a particular element. For example, a thematic approach to organizing a history curriculum might use concepts such as industrialization and nationalism as the basis for organization.

There are many organizational principles. In order to present these principles to you in a manageable form, some sort of categorization scheme is helpful. A simple basis for categorizing organizational principles is Schwab's four commonplaces: (1) the subject matter, (2) the learner and the learning process, (3) the teacher and the teaching process, and (4) the milieu in which education takes place (see Chapter Two). Figure 6.7 presents Schwab's commonplaces in schematic form.

Most curricula are organized on the basis of principles related to only one of the four commonplaces. At the macro level that commonplace has tended to be the subject matter, resulting in what we might call the "separate subjects" organization. While the subjects have expanded and, in some cases, fused, the assumption that the school curriculum should be organized around separate subjects has gone largely unchallenged. For example, while reading, writing, and spelling in the elementary grades are now thought of and taught collectively as language arts, they are still usually taught separately from mathematics, science, social studies, health, and the other subjects.

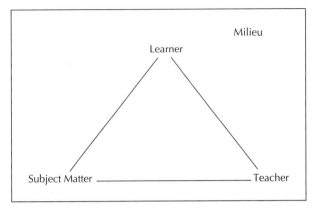

FIGURE 6.7   Schwab's four commonplaces.

Even at the micro level the separate subjects dominate. General science is typically simply a collection of units, one in biology, termed "life sciences," and one in physical sciences, which includes physics and chemistry. However, two exceptions are worth noting. In social studies there has been a tension between the subject matter (e.g., history and geography) and the milieu (e.g., current events) as a basis of organization. Another exception is the subject of health, which uses the subject matters of nutrition and human biology, the social problems associated with sexuality, and the developmental problems of students as bases for curriculum organization.

There have been concerted efforts to organize the entire curriculum or portions of it around one or more commonplaces other than subject matter. Whatever successes have been achieved have been either short-lived or limited in scope. We will discuss several examples of these alternatives in the sections that follow. Note, however, that they are exceptions to the rule and have never been widely accepted as the basis for mass education in this country.

In fairness to the curriculum developers, it is difficult to design a systematic arrangement of courses at the macro level or of concepts, fact, and skills at the micro level, much less to take all four commonplaces into consideration while doing so. Our purpose, therefore, is not to find fault, but to discover the principles that the developer employs and the perhaps unexamined assumptions that underlie them. It is this sort of analysis that will allow us to identify alternatives, to determine the limitations of each when applied to real curricula, and to decide on necessary adaptations that address the limitations.

In order to perform this sort of analysis of curriculum organization, we need to examine in some detail the principles related to each of the four commonplaces.

Subject Matter

Organizational principles based on the subject matter are diverse; however, they all base curriculum organization on the way the subject matter itself seems to be organized. A fundamental epistemological distinction between the *world* as it exists and the language and *concepts* we use to think or talk about the world—i.e., between the empirical and the conceptual—allows us to sort out these principles into "world-related" and "concept-related" principles.

World-related principles derive from observable relationships between events, people, and objects as they exist or occur in the world. Examples of curricula based on such principles are a chronologically sequenced history curriculum; a geography curriculum organized according to the location of cities, states, countries, and continents; and a comparative anatomy curriculum in which content is grouped according to species that, in turn, are sequenced according to their physical complexity.

While world-related principles presumably reflect the organization of the empirical world, concept-related principles reflect the organization of the conceptual world. When one decides to use a concept-related principle of organization, one assumes that curriculum organization should be consistent with the way ideas themselves relate to one another. Examples of pedagogy based on such principles are the teaching of sound and light as cases of wave motion in physics (class membership), the sequencing of geometry theorems as a series of logical derivations (propositional relations), the inclusion of set theory in early elementary grades and its subsequent refinement in later grades (conceptual sophistication), and the requirement of a calculus course before taking some advanced physics courses (logical prerequisite).

Inquiry-related principles are similar to concept-related principles but reflect the processes by which knowledge is derived, rather than the way knowledge as a product is organized. Different views of the logic of inquiry yield differing organizational principles. A view that considers discovery to be a matter of generalizing over numerous instances, i.e., induction, might provide minimally guided experiences with objects or ideas before attempting to have the student generalize a rule. For example, students may "mess around" with bulbs, wire, and batteries before the teacher asks them to form hypotheses about circuits. On the other hand, a view that considers discovery to be a matter of testing bold conjectures will seek to elicit hypotheses—e.g., about the factors that contribute to the development of cities—and then turn to a process of evidence collection—e.g., analysis of the characteristics of major U.S. cities. Curricula organized on the basis of some notion of the scientific method or some problem-solving method are also of this type.

Learners and Learning

Most psychologists, although they might disagree about the particular approach to curriculum organization, would agree that the nature and structure of the subject matter is not as relevant as are findings about the characteristics of learners and the way they learn.

Characteristics of learners relevant to curriculum organization include their interests, problems, needs, abilities, previous experiences, preconceptions, and developmental levels. These characteristics can be used to give the curriculum a starting point, a focus, or a basis for ordering content. For example, student interest in sports can be used as a way to introduce a topic—a physics teacher asks why a spinning baseball curves—or as the focus of a course in sports journalism. Or student conceptions about heat and temperature can be used as the point of departure for a science unit intended to produce conceptual change.[3] Or elementary social studies can be taught with a changing focus based on the child's expanding world, shifting from the family to the neighborhood, the community, the state, the nation, the world, as the child progresses from year to year.

Psychological findings about the learning process relevant to curriculum organization include the significance of prerequisite skills (Gagne, 1965, 1970); factors affecting task difficulty, e.g., reading level; information processing requirements of tasks (Posner, 1979; Resnick, 1975, 1976); the need to provide opportunities for practice of procedures and skills (Rosenshine & Stevens, 1986); and the processes by which people internalize beliefs (Krathwohl, 1964). For example, a reading program might be sequenced with least difficult and prerequisite skills taught first: e.g., long vowel sounds before short ones and phonemes before blends. Or questions like "which" and "what" questions, which require the least depth of information processing, might be employed before questions requiring greater depth of processing, like "why" questions.

More recently, the work of Gardner points to the multiple "intelligences" with which people are able to solve problems or to make things of value. Using biological as well as cultural research, he formulated a list of seven intelligences. (Gardner, 1983, 1991) Each of these seven intelligences comprises a basis for organizing the curriculum:

> Logical-Mathematical Intelligence enables one to detect patterns, reason deductively, and think logically. This intelligence is most often associated with scientific and mathematical thinking.

> Linguistic Intelligence gives one a mastery of language. This intelligence includes the ability to effectively manipulate language to express oneself rhetorically or poetically. It also allows one to use language as a means to remember information.

> Spatial Intelligence gives one the ability to manipulate and create mental images in order to solve problems.

> Musical Intelligence encompasses the capability to recognize and compose musical pitches, tones, and rhythms.

> Bodily-Kinesthetic Intelligence enables one to use one's mental abilities to coordinate one's own bodily movements. This intelligence challenges the popular belief that mental and physical activity are unrelated.

> Interpersonal Intelligence encompasses the ability to understand the feelings and intentions of others.

> Intrapersonal Intelligence enables one to understand one's own feelings and motivation.

These last two intelligences constitute Golman's "emotional intelligence. (Golman, 1995)

Philosophers too have promoted learner-centered organizational principles. During the progressive movement in the United States,[4] some progressive educators took learner-centeredness to the extreme, organizing the entire school curriculum around the students' "immediate felt needs and interests" that the teacher identified as "genuine," rather than merely "whims" or "fancies" (Zais, 1976, p. 409). In order to identify these needs and interests, teachers engaged in cooperative planning with students, rather than preplanning the entire curriculum. Furthermore, rather than focus on learning content, the curriculum focused on the problems students encountered as they pursued their interests. Subject matter was employed as a means to solve these problems, rather than as an end in itself. Horizontal organization was provided by identifying themes to organize student interests. For example, Dewey's Laboratory School used as themes four "human impulses": the social impulse, the constructive impulse, the impulse to investigate and experiment, and the expressive and artistic impulse (Zais, 1976, p. 411). Another laboratory school used "centers of interest," namely, home life, the natural world, the local community, and food, to organize student interests. Vertical organization was more problematic. Some progressive educators attempted to use child development research[5] as a basis for sequencing student needs and interests. Others simply tried to identify age-specific needs and interests. However, the range of interests of children at any age, and the extent to which these interests depend on the child's local environment, resulted in the lack of any viable solution to the vertical organization problem. Nevertheless, learner-centered principles have been playing, and will likely continue to play, a significant role in curriculum organization, particularly as a response to the excesses of subject-matter-dominated approaches.

Teachers and Teaching

Many organizational decisions are based on factors related to teachers' characteristics and the tasks teachers face, though they are rarely made explicit in official curricula. Teachers' interests and strengths can determine curricular focus, emphasis, or starting point. For example, a history teacher with special expertise and interest in military history might organize the study of the Civil War around major battles.

The tasks involved in teaching large groups of youths, against their will, and in crowded conditions, act as a strong influence on curriculum organization. As we will discuss further in Chapter Eight, these tasks include covering some prescribed subject matter and skills; getting students to master that subject matter and those skills; engendering some degree of positive affect toward school, teacher, or curriculum; and managing the group so that it can work toward some common goals (Westbury, 1973). Furthermore, teachers accomplish these four tasks while dealing with a system of accountability, both of students and of teachers (Doyle, 1983). These tasks, and the conditions under which teachers must accomplish them, lead teachers to employ pragmatic organizational principles such as the following:

1. In the elementary grades, teach the basic skills in the morning when the children are fresh and willing to comply, leaving science, health, and social studies for the afternoon (if time permits!).
2. Change activities as often as is necessary in order to maintain students' attention.
3. Keep students busy and active; that is, maintain a fast-paced classroom.
4. Because students perceive work that is unfamiliar as ambiguous, and therefore risky, they tend to transform unfamiliar into familiar tasks. Therefore, begin teaching with familiar tasks until students develop trust and self-confidence.
5. Don't linger on any topic too long.
6. Keep topics discrete enough to develop a sense of productivity in the class and to provide stopping points for periodic testing.[6]

Milieu

The social, economic, political, physical, and organizational contexts in which education occurs may all affect curriculum organization, although these contexts tend to function more like influences on, rather than principles of, organization.

Social   Social perspectives have periodically dominated curriculum work. Each of these efforts has required new focal points around which to organize the school curriculum. These efforts range from Stratemeyer, Forkner, McKim, and Passow's (1957) proposals to organize the curriculum around "persistent life situations" to the efforts of political activists in the 1960s to organize curricula around topics of social "relevance," like war, poverty, and political oppression. Much of this work can be traced back to Herbert Spencer's (1861) essay and the Commission on the Reorganization of Secondary Education (NEA, 1918), mentioned in Chapter Four. In Spencer's influential writings, he contended that the knowledge "of the most worth" prepares people to function effectively in five basic areas: direct self-preservation; indirect self-preservation, e.g., securing food; parenthood; citizenship; and leisure activities. In the 1918 Commission's Seven Cardinal Principles (NEA, 1918), health, command of fundamental processes, worthy home membership, vocation, citizenship, worthy use of leisure time, and ethical character were identified as the areas of living around which to organize the curriculum.

Economic   Likewise, economic pressures during times of unemployment such as the Depression, periods of shift in the economy such as the long period of industrialization, and challenges from abroad—e.g., the trade competition between the United States and Japan—have generated periodic calls for reform in curriculum organization. In addition to these economically based, large-scale educational movements, the student's prospective economic roles can provide specific curricular initiatives. Aspects of a person's consumptive (i.e., as a consumer) and productive (i.e., as a worker) economic roles can form the basis for changes in curriculum organization. For example, consumer mathematics, business education, career education, computer education, and vocational training all attempt to use the economic realities of life after school as a basis for curriculum organization.

Political A political perspective on schooling suggests that the curriculum organization serves some people's interests at the expense of others': that is, some people stand to benefit and others to suffer from it. The sorting function of school, particularly in tracked or selective programs, influences the sequencing of courses and topics within courses. For example, in pre-medical programs difficult courses such as calculus and physics may be scheduled early in order to separate the "high-ability" from the "low-ability" students. The curricular focus of some courses may be influenced by the desire to increase the prestige of the subject matter, thereby also increasing the prestige of its teachers. For example, esoteric terminology, written tests, and abstract treatment (Young, 1971) may be used to change a formerly practical subject matter such as industrial arts into one that is more theoretical ("technology education").

Organizational The fact that the curriculum must fit into the organization of an institution exerts a strong influence on the curriculum's organization. In particular, the departmental structure of schools increases the compartmentalization of knowledge; the stronger the departments, the stronger the compartmentalization. The assignment of specific responsibilities to particular departments—e.g., only the English department holds students accountable for their writing—further compartmentalizes the curriculum.

Scheduling limitations can affect coordination of instruction in different subjects.[7] For example, a specially coordinated American studies curriculum combining history and English is more likely to be developed and implemented if the teachers have time to jointly plan the program and if students can fit the special sections of both courses into their schedules.

Physical The physical facilities and the materials available also affect curriculum organization. Availability or absence of special facilities can influence choice of curriculum focus. For example, the availability of an outdoor education facility might lead to an environmental approach to some of a school's science courses. Building a science lab in an elementary school is likely to result in the reduction of interdisciplinary efforts in many classrooms and in emphasis on science as a separate subject. Such a move is also likely to lead to a more hands-on approach to science.

Geographical location, characteristics of the school site, climate, and seasons all can affect sequencing and emphasis. For example, a physical education curriculum would typically include activities according to the season when they can most easily be taught.

Availability of materials can have substantive effects on curriculum organization. Replacement of all basal readers with books of children's literature and books in content areas might potentially lead to the elimination of reading as a separate subject and the implementation of a whole language approach.[8]

Obviously, such a change would have to be accompanied by staff development programs on whole language.

A curriculum analysis requires an examination of both the principles employed in the curriculum's organization and the influences that contribute to organizational decisions.

Perspectives on Organizing Principles

How does the above discussion of organizational principles relate to the discussion of the five perspectives presented in Chapter Three? One would expect each perspective to employ certain principles more than others. Let us briefly examine each perspective to see which principles it emphasizes.

Traditional   The focus of the traditional curriculum is on content, particularly those facts that every educated person should know; basic skills; and traditional values. The facts are typically grouped into topics that form the organizing elements of the curriculum. Content sequence is typically based on the organization of the subject matter itself, with world-related sequencing principles predominant. The core knowledge approach of Hirsch is a popular example of this principle (Hirsch, 1993). For example, as mentioned in Chapter Four (see Table 4.7), one elementary curriculum proposal that comes from a self-proclaimed traditional educator, former Secretary of Education William Bennett, organizes the macro-level curriculum around subjects: English, social studies, mathematics, science, foreign language, fine arts, and physical education and health. At the micro level of individual subjects, Bennett proposes a primary grade curriculum organized around biographies of famous men and women, stories such as legends and folk tales, symbols and rituals such as the flag and the Pledge of Allegiance, songs, skills such as penmanship, and facts learned by rote such as the multiplication tables. In the intermediate grades (Grades 4 through 6) the focus shifts to works of literature and to subject-matter topics, such as grammar in English, the Civil War in social studies, perpendicular lines in mathematics, and food groups and nutrition in science. The micro-level curriculum also manifests clear subject-matter-based subdivisions. For example, Bennett argues for grammar, spelling, reading, composition, vocabulary, penmanship, and literary analysis in English; geometry, arithmetic, statistics, measurement, and graphs in mathematics; history, geography, and government in social studies; earth science, life science, and physical science. These subdivisions become the major curriculum categories explicit after the third grade. From the seventh grade onward, these categories are subdivided further. For example, physical science becomes chemistry and physics; history becomes U.S. and world history.

Structure of the Disciplines   Curricula designed to teach the structure of disciplines derive their organization from that structure itself. The central concepts in the disciplines serve as the organizing elements of the curriculum, with concept- and inquiry-related sequences most typical. Disciplines-based curricula take as their starting point for curriculum development the most fundamental ideas of the disciplines, deriving the more specific content from and organizing that content around these more basic ideas. Because of this characteristic, we term these curricula "top-down." In the next chapter we examine this approach to curriculum organization in greater depth.

Experiential   In experiential curricula, the experiences students have as they engage in purposeful activities, typically in the form of projects, serve as the organizing elements of the curriculum. Content is most typically sequenced according to the way it will be used in dealing with everyday problems, needs, and issues. According to Dewey (1938), the curriculum should be organized around only those "situations" (p. 42) that provide continuing growth of the individual. In order to act as a "moving force" (p. 38), these situations must represent an "interaction" or interplay between "objective and internal conditions" (p. 42), that is, between the students' physical and social environment on the one hand, and the interests, needs, and previous experiences of the student on the other hand. For this reason, these situations cannot be fully planned by the curriculum developer or teacher, but must be planned cooperatively by the teacher and the students. We will analyze this perspective in greater depth in the next chapter.

Behavioral   As might be expected, behavioral curricula are organized around behaviors, described by written behavioral objectives. Like developers of structure-of-the-disciplines curricula, developers of behavioral curricula take as their starting point for curriculum development the general, then deriving the particular from the general. However, the similarity between the two approaches ends there. From a behavioral perspective the general, from which the particular derives, consists of the terminal behaviors toward which the curriculum is designed to lead, rather than general ideas. And teaching a behavioral curriculum entails building student skills up from the most elementary, prerequisite ones to the terminal ones, rather than trying to teach the most fundamental ideas in increasing degrees of sophistication, as in the structure-of-the-disciplines approach. For this reason we term the behavioral approach to curriculum organization "bottom-up," and in the next chapter we contrast it with the structure of the discipline's "top-down" approach.

Constructivist   Proponents of a constructivist perspective organize curricula around whatever cognitive elements they emphasize. Those who emphasize cognitive assimilation organize content around superordinate concepts that subsume other, more specific content. If the cognitive theory stresses that individuals use different modes to represent these concepts—e.g., visual, verbal, graphic, and kinesthetic—then the curriculum might be organized around these modes. Those favoring a perspective concerned with accommodation would likely organize a curriculum around misconceptions and the discrepant events designed to facilitate conceptual change. Proponents of a thinking-skills approach would likely choose the steps or elements of thinking as they conceive them.

Technology and Curriculum Organization

Technology can play a pivotal role in the organization of a curriculum. A course might be completely focused on a particular technology or family of technologies (i.e., computer science, CAD/CAM design, video production) or it might have a particular technology play an important but not central role in student and teacher work (i.e., word processors, spreadsheets, or graphing calculators). It is not feasible to fully delineate all the ways in which educational technologies might influence curriculum organization in the space of a few pages, but looking at examples of how web-based materials have influenced curricula can be instructive.[9] We will take a brief look at an environmental science program and mention other kinds of electronic curricular resources.

In chapter Four, the *Global Learning and Observations to Benefit the Enironment* (GLOBE, 1995) program was mentioned as a program around which a school class might engage technology in a variety of ways. GLOBE is a program where Kindergarten through 12th grade students collect and share data over the Internet. GLOBE data is then (selectively) used by scientists in their research. The GLOBE web site, *www.GLOBE.gov,* is impressive in scope and is a good place to begin looking at how the Internet might relate to curriculum change. From the site, students in GLOBE-affiliated classrooms can upload data to share with other students and scientists around the world. Likewise, they can download data for analysis and find software for data analysis. There is web-based software that can generate and animate graphs and maps of student data and the international data set. Students can also view videos that show how to follow specific protocols for the different activities, however in order for a school to fully participate in the program at least one teacher needs to complete the weeklong workshop on the program and use equipment that meets the programs specifications for accuracy.[10] Anyone with a web connection can access the data, but schools cannot add to the data set until teacher training has been completed.

The GLOBE program employs a range of technologies beyond the Internet including Global Positioning System (GPS) units, pH pens, digital cameras, and software for graphing and animating data including Geographical Information System (GIS),[11] software that can create and animate maps. This sophisticated use of technology allows for the easy sharing of quality data among students from around the world—teachers have been trained in GLOBE protocols around the world, and even though a minority of trained teachers continue data input, the data set and number of participants is still quite large and publicly available.

While the use of data sharing seems most relevant for science classes, the potential for sharing of information through the web is much broader. Foreign language students may exchange e-mail with students around the world and read websites in virtually any language with daily news and much, much more. Likewise, social studies can engage in electronic conversations with others around the world and easily keep current on events almost anywhere in the world. Students and teachers may also find a wide array of reproductions of original historical, scientific, and artistic documents. See the Smithsonian Institution's web site for one such site *(www.smithsonian.org/).*

Textbook publishers themselves have extensive websites in support of their curricula. A look at one major publisher's site, Holt, Rinehart & Winston *(www.hrw.com),* shows a range of web-based materials related to their curricula. Some of these materials are listed in Table 6.1. Likewise, the subject-specific professional organizations have curricular resources that generally correspond to each discipline's national standards. Companies and organizations that once provided films and videotapes to schools are increasingly moving to providing video streaming via high-speed web connections. This not only changes the speed with which videos may be procured but also changes how they may be used—the simplicity of showing short clips is vastly increased. See *www.unitedstreaming.com/* for one example. Another example that shows different mathematics curricula in practice is The Modeling Middle School Mathematics Project at *mmmproject.org/.*

This array of largely web-based curricular materials raises important questions related to the social and political contexts of the curriculum. What are the implications of web-based tutoring, for example, for students who do not have good access to the Internet at home, when most of their fellow students do have such access? Likewise, it raises important questions about the most fundamental aspects of curriculum organization. By its nature a book presents information in a linear fashion. By its nature the Internet, the World Wide Web, is a web of interconnections. What might this mean for curriculum organization?

TABLE 6.1 Examples of web-based materials available from textbook publisher Holt, Rinehart & Winston *(www.hrw.com).*

- Full text of books,
- Electronic "tutoring"
    - Online homework and tutorial (multiple, choice, true/false matching, fill-in-the-blank, drag the correct label in world languages courses to the correct picture (i.e., a fancier matching question)
    - Interactive Shockwave animations (i.e., manipulable ray diagrams in optics)
- Assessment exercises
- Connections to resources for current events
- Lesson plans correlated to state standards
- Collections of links to websites
- Ordering information with many sample activities for ONE-STOP PLANNER CD-ROM WITH TEST GENERATOR for Macintosh and Windows
- Audio of book text in English and Spanish
- Parent guides (i. e., homework with explanations)
- State guides (standardized test mock-ups, of which the first five states I tried had the same test!)

EPISTEMOLOGICAL DIMENSIONS: THE STRUCTURE OF KNOWLEDGE

When I first tried to analyze the organization of particular curricula, I naively assumed that a developer would attempt to organize a curriculum in a coherent way—even, perhaps, according to some grand scheme representing the way knowledge is organized. My assumption was based on my understanding that philosophers and educators have long searched for coherent ways of organizing knowledge. Such classifications, if developed, might offer a logical basis for organizing not only macro curricula, but even entire educational institutions. Great thinkers like Aristotle, René Descartes, and Auguste Comte have proposed ways of classifying and describing the various subject matters of knowledge. For example, Aristotle organized all studies according to the purpose that each serves and the nature of the subject matter with which it deals. He divided knowledge into just three classes: the theoretical, the practical, and the productive. The theoretical—in descending order, theology or metaphysics, mathematics, and physics—is worth *knowing* for its own sake and consists of subject matter that is unalterable by human beings. The practical—ethics and politics, the latter including economics and rhetoric—is aimed at *doing* and concerns matters of deliberate choice of conduct. The productive—the arts and engineering—concerns *making* things and giving life to forms. The modern-day distinction between the academic and the vocational curriculum is suggestive of this ancient classification.

Descartes (1931) developed a coherent system of knowledge founded on a small set of metaphysical principles, from which he believed that one could derive all knowledge using mathematical, deductive principles: "Philosophy as a whole is like a tree whose roots are metaphysics, whose trunk is physics, and whose branches, which issue from this trunk, are all the other sciences" (p. 211).

Comte classified each body of knowledge according to the complexity of substances it studies. Comte's hierarchy began with physics at the bottom, because it studies the simplest substances, i.e., atoms, followed by chemistry, which studies combinations of and interactions amongst atoms, followed by biology, which studies organization of and interactions amongst chemicals, and, finally, sociology, which studies organizations of one class of living thing (Schwab, 1964).

Modern colleges, faced with decisions regarding basic graduation requirements, typically try to classify curriculum content in the hope of developing categories from which students should choose their core courses, also termed "distribution requirements." The categories colleges develop usually represent the natural sciences, the social sciences, and the humanities, including the arts. Mathematics is either considered a separate requirement or included in the natural sciences. Similarly, writing is either considered a separate requirement or included in the humanities. History is usually considered part of the humanities but occasionally a social sciences discipline. To make matters more complex, disciplines emerge that cross disciplines, such as biochemistry, and even cross major divisions, such as philosophy of science.

In contrast with these sincere though unsuccessful attempts to build coherent, unambiguous, and logical systems of content, content organization in primary and secondary schools is more aptly described as a hodgepodge. School subjects bear varying degrees of resemblance to the disciplines of knowledge from which their content ultimately derives. Mathematics, the sciences, and foreign languages as school subjects are closely related to their parent disciplines, and occasionally scholars from the parent disciplines even participate in the writing of school texts and the training of teachers. English, at the secondary level, and language arts, at the elementary level, include elements of the scholarly discipline of literature, although content areas that exist only in school curricula, such as reading and spelling, dominate these subjects, particularly in the lower grades. Grammar, a body of content that bears only a superficial resemblance to its analogue in the discipline of linguistics, also remains a significant source of content for English. Little music theory is taught in most primary and secondary music classes; these generally emphasize the performance aspects of music. History, geography, political science, economics, and anthropology are included in social studies, although the proportion of the subject derived from each discipline and the consistency between the disciplinary knowledge and the school knowledge has varied greatly, as changing political and cultural forces have influenced the curriculum.[12] In Chapter Seven we will discuss characteristics of disciplines and the requirements for organizing curricula according to the structure of disciplines.

Although much of the primary and secondary curriculum derives from disciplines of knowledge, some does not. Occupational subjects derive from analyses of the tasks performed in the occupations, rather than from any intellectual discipline. Many physical education programs serve as opportunities for students to let off steam or as a "farm system" for the interscholastic sports program, rather than for the development of lifelong skills and an understanding of topics like conditioning and prevention of injuries.

One way to graphically represent the structure of knowledge embodied by a curriculum is to construct a "concept map" of the curriculum.[13] Figures 6.8, 6.9, and 6.10 show concept maps assumed to reflect the structure of entire disciplines.

Although conceptions of the structure of knowledge have influenced curriculum organization, clearly there are other influences as well. The failure of philosophers to produce a grand scheme of knowledge that could serve as a basis for organizing the macro curriculum, the typical hodgepodge of principles underlying the primary and secondary curricula as well as the college curriculum, and the typically weak relationship between disciplines of knowledge and school subjects all point to the need to consider other dimensions of curriculum organization.

POLITICAL AND SOCIOLOGICAL DIMENSIONS

Susan Malloy (a pseudonym), one of my former students, was the director of a college's Learning and Study Skills Center. She developed a course based on current cognitive psychological research. The course was intended to teach students how they learn, read, and process information. The rationale for the

① The central idea of economics is the scarcity concept, namely, that every society faces a conflict between unlimited wants and limited resources.

② Out of the scarcity concept a family of ideas emerge. Because of scarcity, human beings have tried to develop methods to produce more in less time, or more with less material and in shorter time. Various types of specialization were discovered in order to overcome the conflict between unlimited wants and limited resources. We specialize geographically, occupationally, and technologically.

③ Because of specialization, we are interdependent; interdependence necessitates a monetary system and a transportation system.

④ People had to discover an allocating mechanism, and this is the market, where through the interaction of buyers and sellers price changes occur. Prices determine the pattern of production, the method of production, income distribution, and the level of spending and saving, which, in turn, decide the level of total economic activity.

⑤ The market decision is modified by public policies, carried out by the government, to assure welfare objectives. These welfare objectives are determined in the United States through the political interaction of 200 million people that generates thousands of welfare objectives that can be reduced to five: attempts to accelerate growth, to promote stability, to assure economic security, to promote economic freedom, and to promote economic justice.

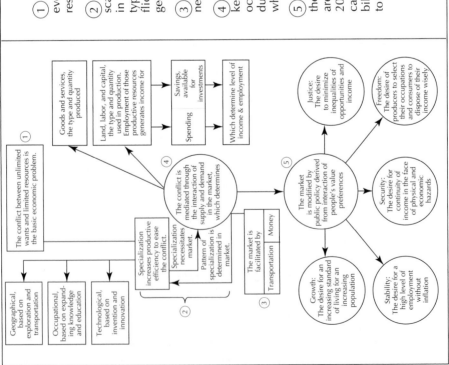

FIGURE 6.8 Fundamental ideas of economics.

Adapted from Lawrence Senesh, New Paths in Social Science Curriculum Design. Chicago: Science Research Associates, Inc., 1973, pp. 10–15.

1. Members of society have many wants, which they hope to satisfy.

2. Some of these wants will be satisfied through the economic, family, educational, and religious systems. Wants that cannot be satisfied by any of these systems are channeled to the political system.

3. As the people's wants enter the political system for satisfaction, they become demands. These demands are screened.

4. The screening process operates through formal or informal organizations. These organizations act as gatekeepers. Some of the demands vanish. Others become issues debated in the political community, a group who share a desire to work together as a unit in the political solution of problems.

5. The issues are molded by cleavages in the political community and by the authorities who translate these demands into binding decisions.

6. The binding decisions affect the social systems and the participants in them, generating positive or negative support.

7. The support may be directed toward the political community; toward the regime, a political system that incorporates a particular set of values and norms and a particular structure of authority; and/or toward the authorities, the particular persons who occupy positions of political power within the structure of authority.

8. The binding decisions generate new wants, which appear again at the gate of the political system asking for recognition.

9. The source of the support for the political community, regime, and authorities may originate from the social systems in the forms of education, patriotism, and other mechanisms.

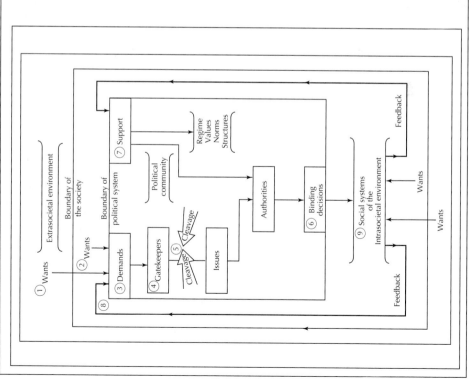

FIGURE 6.9   Fundamental ideas of political science.
Developed with Professor David Easton of the University of Chicago.

① Human societies exhibit patterned social behavior that can be described and explained.

② Much of the human behavior is guided by shared values that people voluntarily follow.

③ Also, much human behavior is guided by a set of norms and beliefs that people follow under the threat of punishment or promise of reward.

④ One important part of the social system is organizations. People work together in organizations to achieve specific goals.

⑤ Another important part of the social system is groups. People come together informally—some to strengthen their common values, some to strengthen their emotional identification.

⑥ Organizations and groups have many positions that people fill. Positions are more formal in organizations than in groups.

⑦ The unique way a person fills a position is her role. People play roles differently depending on other people's expectations and on their own attitudes, personalities, and life experiences.

⑧ Another important part of the social system is social aggregates. Social aggregates consist of people who have many socially significant characteristics in common and therefore have the possibility of developing organizations for social action.

⑨ Two types of forces tend to shape organizations and social aggregates. Some forces lead to stability and regularity, such as recognition of complementarity, isolation of one organization from another, compromise, and submission. Other forces lead to tension and strain, such as uneven distribution of values and power that may result in human rights revolutions.

⑩ Values, norms, beliefs, organizations, groups, positions, roles, and social aggregates influence human behavior and the makeup of the social system resulting in support or modification.

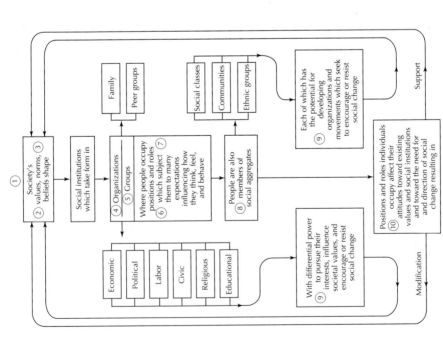

FIGURE 6.10 Fundamental ideas of sociology.
Developed with Professor Robert Perrucci of Purdue University.

course was based on the assumption that if they understood their own cognitive processes better, they would be able to become more effective as students. Susan approached the college's curriculum committee for approval of her new course. She was shocked when members of the committee decided that she could offer the course only for no academic credit. The grounds for their decision included the following:

1. The course purported to be a psychology course, but she was not a member of the Psychology Department, nor did she have a doctorate in psychology.
2. The course was clearly a "remedial" course, and students could not earn academic credit for remedial courses. (In fact, the course was not designed exclusively for students with academic difficulties.)

Susan was unprepared for the committee's ruling because she had assumed that the curriculum decisions would be based on criteria related to the technical adequacy of the course, psychological validity of the content, and needs of students. She had not considered the political and sociological dimensions.

What we need to help us understand the political and sociological dimensions of curriculum organization is a set of concepts intended specifically for this purpose. Young (1971) and Bernstein (1971) introduce the concepts of *specialization, openness, stratification,* and *status* in order to describe what some sociologists term the "social organization of knowledge" (Young, 1971). "Specialization," or narrowness, of a subject is the degree to which the scope of the curriculum is restricted. For example, a social studies curriculum becomes increasingly specialized as it becomes transformed from global studies to American history to Colonial history. Typically, specialization increases as the age of the students increases and as their programs become more vocationally oriented. Debates about how early specialization should occur and which students should specialize in what subjects have been perennial. The United States delays specialization in its schools more than almost any other industrialized country, and yet supporters of liberal arts education and general education believe that even the United States tends to overspecialize.

"Openness" (or "closedness") refers to the degree to which knowledge areas are related.[14] Openness of subjects suggests the likelihood that interdisciplinary studies are likely to occur. For example, American studies is likely to develop to the extent that social studies and English are seen as related, or open. Attempts to integrate closed subjects typically run aground. Although there may be significant advantages to the students from teaching mathematics and science in a more integrated manner, attempts to integrate them have been largely unsuccessful. This failure has been due, in part, to the tendency by mathematics and science educators to view their subjects as separate. Subjects are not only bodies of knowledge, but also identities of teachers. For example, in social settings a person might be introduced as "a math teacher," not just a teacher. Thus, integration of subjects threatens to change a person's identity.

"Stratification" describes the degree to which value is assigned differentially to different kinds of knowledge. When knowledge is highly stratified, it is quite clear what counts as legitimate knowledge, what does not, and what the basis is for selecting and excluding curricular content. Highly academic curricula that include subjects like science, Latin, and mathematics are more highly stratified than more practical curricula consisting of home economics, physical education, vocational education, and industrial arts. Stratification is significant because it defines the sharpness of the distinction between the teacher on the one hand and the student and parent on the other hand. Curricula are less likely to be open for negotiation with laypeople like parents, and students are less likely to be given choice of topics in highly stratified subjects. The more highly stratified the curriculum, the sharper is the difference likely to be between being an expert and a layperson. This difference may lead to sharper differences in their roles and power.

To the degree that different subjects are assigned different social value, and, therefore, are stratified, they will be accorded different levels of status. Young (1971) contends that high-status subjects are assessed formally using written presentations; taught to the "ablest" students; taught to homogeneous ability groups; characterized by individual and competitive, rather than group and cooperative, work settings; and are abstract and unrelated to the everyday experience of the student. In some cases higher status is also associated with less openness and increased specialization.

"Status" is difficult to determine in a definitive way, and any definition invites suggestions of exceptions and inconsistencies. However, generally speaking, indicators of status include whether or not academic credit is assigned to the subject; whether a subject is required or an elective, and the number of years of it required; the number of days per week each student attends class in the subject; and the academic standing of the students who take the subject. Some subjects, like mathematics, are clearly high status using Young's indicators; others, like driver education, are clearly low status. Status of other subjects, like computer education, is less clear. Clearly, Susan Malloy's difficulties with her college's curriculum committee stemmed in part from issues related to her status and the status of a course such as the one she proposed.

The concepts of stratification and status are especially useful for understanding why teachers may resist certain curriculum changes and embrace other changes, if those changes entail any shifts in their relative status. For example, the concepts help to explain the trend toward identifying "industrial arts," formerly "shop," more closely with science and technology and for increasing the reliance on assessment of written rather than practical student work. The concepts also help to explain why teachers launching interdisciplinary efforts like American studies, which might threaten teachers' identities and status, tend to focus their efforts on the highest-ability students.

Likewise, these concepts are important for analyzing the social and political dimensions of the curriculum you have chosen for analysis. If your curriculum is designed to prepare people for an occupation, the concepts may also prove useful for anticipating changes in occupations and in their preparation programs. Members of occupations may strive to increase their relative prestige, an increase that typically leads to increases in pay, power, and influence, by increasing the status of their curricula; for example, they may want to increase the use of written tests, selectivity for entrance, and specialization of their knowledge. Many occupations to which women historically have been limited are cases in point. Consider, for example, nursing and elementary school teaching. Once viewed as possessing no special knowledge but perhaps a bit more patience than other people, elementary teachers and nurses had little prestige compared with their male counterparts in other occupations involving the care of other people, such as doctors and high school and college teachers. By learning new technologies, e.g., computers; developing specializations, e.g., psychiatric nurses and reading specialists; increasing the difficulty of entering the occupation, e.g., by increasing the length of preparation programs; developing esoteric terminology, e.g., a nomenclature for learning disabilities; and increasing the research base of the occupation, e.g., research on effective teaching, these occupations are attempting to increase their prestige. All of these occupational changes are clearly reflected in the curricula of their preparation programs.

The concepts of stratification and status are also useful for understanding tracking in schools.

Tracking as a Response to Diversity[15]

The development of tracking illustrates one way educators chose to deal with social, economic, and political pressures on public schools. In the second half of the nineteenth century may immigrants saw education as a key to their children's futures. At the same time industrialists in a growing economy needed a manageable labor force. Schools become overcrowded and classes unruly. Influential education theorists saw tracking as the answer. The schools could provide different kinds of education for children of different social, economic, and ethnic backgrounds. With some minor changes in both structure and rationale that fundamental concept of tracking has continued to this day.

Today, as at the turn of the twentieth century, poor and minority students are most likely to be placed in the least intellectually demanding academic tracks (Gamoran, 1989). Even in the elementary years poor and minority students are more likely to be placed in groups designated for those with lower abilities. This continues through the middle school as they are placed in remedial programs and, as Jeannie Oakes states, "they have little access to the topics and skills that would prepare them for higher level academics in high school" (Oakes, 1988, p. 113). Oakes concludes that "Students placed in low ability groups in elementary school are likely to continue in these tracks in middle school and junior high; in senior high they typically are found in non-college-preparatory tracks"(Oakes, 1988, p. 116).

In studies of high school math and science classes, for example, the Educational Testing Service showed higher percentages of white students in higher levels classes and higher percentages of Blacks and Hispanics in lower level classes (Meier, Stewart, and England, cited in Oakes and Lipton, 1999, pp. 297-298). Tracking in the United States, then, has resulted in fewer educational opportunities for those placed in less challenging classes.

The tracking system had adversely affected non-Asian minority students to such an extent that in 1967, Washington D.C. Judge Wright declared: "The track system amounts to an unlawful discrimination against those students whose educational opportunities are being limited on the erroneous assumption that they are capable of no more. . . Even in concept, the track system is undemocratic and discriminatory" (HOBSON V. HANSEN, 1967, cited in Oakes, 1985, p. 184). Wright based his decision, according to Oakes, on several factors: inappropriate tests given to students to assign them to classes, lack of remedial education for students in lower tracks, the new impossibility of student movement from one track to the next, and the negative label placed on lower track students (Oakes, 1985).

Ironically, one of the reasons tracking persists to the extent it does may be a result of one section of Judge Wright's ruling. He stated that some type of educational support must be provided to students who have not been given access to the mainstream educational system. "Any system of ability grouping which, through failure to include and implement the concept of compensatory education for the disadvantaged child or otherwise fails in fact to bring the great majority of children into the mainstream of public education denies the children excluded equal opportunity and thus encounters the constitutional bar" (HOBSON V. HANSEN, 1967, cited in Oakes,1985, p. 184). Today, students tracked into lower-level courses are placed in remedial classes as well. This placement skirts Wright's objections to tracking, although, as Oakes found, it has not resulted in movement from lower to higher tracks.

Perhaps the damage to students is so extensive because being placed in lower tracks means having access to only certain types of knowledge. Studies consistently reveal a focus on basic skills and discipline (i.e., lower status knowledge) in classes designated as lower track with higher order thinking reserved for those students in more academically-oriented classes. This difference, too, can be found from the elementary years through high school. In reading, for example, groups that teachers think of as low ability often focus on decoding and phonics drills with worksheets. In groups with more sophisticated readers, teachers focus more on discussion, allow more independent reading, and interrupt students less often (Oakes, 1992).

Oakes found that high school teachers presented math and science differently depending on whether they defined students as having high or low ability. "Students in upper level classes," she states, "focused primarily on mathematical concepts; low level classes focused almost exclusively on computational skills and math facts" (Oakes, 1988, p. 117). Note the relevance of Young's concept of low and high status knowledge from the previous section.

The difference in the way material was presented may be due to teachers' perceptions of how much time must be devoted to controlling or disciplining students. Nel Keddie (1971) found that students designated as lower ability asked questions about such things as the meaning of concepts and that students in the upper level classes were more accepting of some of the basic concepts in a given field (even when they might not understand them fully). As a result, teachers thought of the lower track students as more disruptive, needing more control and more discretely focused skill and fact-based instruction (Keddie, 1971). Oakes, too, found that teachers of lower track students spent much more time on discipline and control than did teachers of higher track classes (Oakes, 1985).

Being consistently in lower level classes, of course, influences post-secondary school or career choices. The consequences for non-Asian minorities are most severe, even for those going into vocational education—an example of tracking within the more general all-school tracking system. Oakes notes that Blacks and Hispanics are most often enrolled "in programs that train for the lowest-level occupations" (Oakes, 1992, p. 590).

This is an especially dismal picture when so much research shows that all students learn more in higher-level courses (Oakes, 1985) and when there are so many classroom alternatives to tracking. Teachers could develop strategies reflecting Howard Gardner's theory of multiple intelligences, might structure collaborative groups, might provide time for lessons on specific topics for small groups within a class. Nancie Atwell illustrates a multitude of ways to structure language arts classes that meet the writing needs of all students. Shirley Brice Heath shows how to build curricula based on the strengths of students from different ethnic and social backgrounds.

Curriculum Analysis Questions

The ultimate purpose of presenting the basic concepts in curriculum organization has been to enable the reader to identify the patterns of organization of a curriculum. Once identified, these patterns can be examined in order to unpack the curriculum's underlying assumptions.

1. What provision, if any, is made for macro-level vertical and/or horizontal organization?

Look for any attempts to provide for coordination between subjects, i.e., horizontal organization, or to sequence courses from one year to the next so that content follows a progression, i.e., vertical organization. Does the curriculum mention any content taught in other subjects? For example, a health curriculum might mention biology concepts; a science curriculum, while discussing rates, might mention a mathematics course covering ratios and proportions; a British history curriculum might mention the works of Shakespeare. Or does the curriculum mention what the students are expected to know when they arrive on the first day—e.g., a familiarity with the basic mathematical operations—or what future courses the curriculum is designed to prepare students for, e.g., how French I prepares students for French II?

2. At a more micro level, what basic configurations are found in the content organization?

Look for evidence of discrete, vertical, hierarchical, or spiral configurations. If none of these configurations is found, consider whether the curriculum provides only discrete elements.

3. How are various media and technologies employed to deliver curriculum?
4. What organizational principles does the curriculum employ? Does or can technology play a role in the curriculum organization?

5. What are the social and political implications of technology in curriculum organization?
6. Does the curriculum organization increase or decrease the likelihood that tracking will be used?

NOTES

1. See discussion in Chapter One.
2. When "curriculum" means a course of study, then curriculum organization might refer to the sequence of courses taken by students, including both pre- and corequisites. We might call this sequence the students' "course structure." When "curriculum" means the content actually taught to students, then curriculum organization might refer to the way instructional content is clustered into topics and the way topics are sequenced. We might call this sense of curriculum organization "content structure." When "curriculum" means the knowledge from the scholarly disciplines, then curriculum organization might refer to the "structure of knowledge" in a particular discipline like physics. When "curriculum" refers to instructional media by which the objectives or content are delivered to the students, curriculum organization might refer to the "media structure." The media structure would describe the ways different instructional media complement each other in helping the teacher teach the content and reach the objectives. When "curriculum" refers to what was learned by students, then curriculum organization might refer to the way students' knowledge is organized in their minds. We might call this psychological sense of organization "cognitive structure." Finally, when "curriculum" means students' actual educational experiences, then curriculum organization might refer to the interrelationships students perceive in those experiences.
3. See, for example, Driver (1983).
4. See Chapter Three.
5. See, for example, Piaget's work (1929).
6. See Doyle (1986, 1992) and Jackson (1968) for a more complete analysis of the way teaching tasks influence curriculum.
7. Scheduling limitations also affect delivery methods within subjects. For example, forty-minute periods for all subjects severely limit the kinds of tasks around which teachers can organize their instruction and homogenize the subjects they teach. Such scheduling patterns can lead to a hurried, choppy, and monotonous school atmosphere. Scheduling affects students not only directly but also indirectly.
8. See, for example, Goodman (1986).
9. We will not look in any detail, for example, at the role of the word processor or the graphing calculator here though these technologies have influenced curricula substantially. Likewise, we will not investigate the place of student publishing or the potential of Geographic Information Systems for teaching. There are a great many more emerging technologies with tremendous potential for changing curriculum and assessment, far too numerous to even list here.
10. While the GLOBE program has technology as a key focus, it is important to investigate the full range of program expectations for any such curricular program. GLOBE strongly encourages schools to record observations daily and to meet or maintain rigorous standards. While this is one aspect of science it is time and labor intensive and requires trade-offs for large scale implementation. What do you give up to have students collecting data daily? How do you assure quality for data?

11. GIS is a class of software with great potential for influencing curriculum. See *www.esri.com* for examples from the largest producers of GIS software.

12. See, for example, FitzGerald (1979).

13. See Posner and Rudnitsky (1994) and Novak and Gowin (1984) for explications of concept maps and procedures for constructing them.

14. Bernstein (1971) refers to this characteristic as "classification."

15. Nancy Zimmit was a major contributor to this section.

CHAPTER 7

Curriculum Organization

Conflicting Perspectives

For many years the Sequent-Hall School District has taught health in all elementary and middle school grades, as well as requiring one-half year at the high school level to meet graduation requirements. However, there has never been a Kindergarten through Grade 9 or even a Kindergarten through Grade 6 health curriculum. Each teacher just did his or her own thing.

The new Assistant Superintendent for Curriculum, Tony Pirelli, has been on the job for one year and has called a group of elementary teachers and all middle and high school health teachers to a meeting to discuss the feasibility of a comprehensive health education curriculum. At the meeting one of the elementary teachers suggests an analysis of the existing health curriculum in operation. Mr. Pirelli points out that such an analysis would require the examination of the texts and other instructional materials currently in use in each of the Sequent-Hall classrooms in which health education is taught. Further, he suggests that the teachers decide on some framework for analyzing the curriculum and reporting the findings of the study.

Various frameworks are suggested. One of the teachers, Mr. Berkey, suggests that the district first needs to identify the skills possessed by a person with good health habits. Once identified, these skills could be used to derive all the prerequisite skills necessary to develop these habits. These prerequisite skills could then be used by the group as a comprehensive curriculum on which to chart each of the skills taught by each teacher in the district. Another teacher, Ms. Schuck, argues that first the major concepts in health education need to be identified and mapped schematically along with subordinate health concepts in order to show their interrelationships. Then the group could determine which of these concepts each teacher covers and where the gaps and overlaps exist. Another teacher, Ms. Kent, contends that neither of the two suggested approaches takes into account the way she teaches health, as a series of projects, each project designed to serve as a vehicle for learning a multitude of skills and concepts. The group grinds to a standstill, not knowing which direction to go.

1. What are the implications of each point of view?
2. Which makes more sense?
3. What should the group do now?

This chapter will help you to answer questions of this sort and to evaluate different approaches to curriculum organization.

FOCUS: THREE APPROACHES TO ORGANIZATION

One important expression of an educational perspective is the organization of a curriculum. As we saw in Chapter Six, different perspectives organize curricula around different elements and sequence curricula according to different principles. In this chapter we present in depth three major perspectives on curriculum organization, derived from a structure-of-the-disciplines, a behavioral, and an experiential perspective on education.

One logical conclusion you might reach after reading Chapter Six is that the world of curriculum organization is highly complex. It is a world populated by thousands—maybe even millions—of curricula, both at the micro and macro levels, representing permutations and combinations of different structural patterns, media structures, and organizational principles functioning both horizontally and vertically. In Chapter Six, we began to see that the five perspectives presented in Chapter Three can help you understand this world a little bit better. We now continue this approach by examining in more detail three contrasting patterns, termed the "top-down," the "bottom-up," and the "project" approaches, in order to make further sense of this world and to begin to unpack the assumptions underlying any curriculum's organization.

TOP-DOWN APPROACH

Simply stated, a top-down view is based on the assumption that the curriculum should be organized around fundamental concepts, themes, or principles, and that from an understanding of these fundamental concepts the student develops the ability to derive particular facts and applications. These concepts may derive from particular disciplines of knowledge, e.g., an anthropological concept of language, or they may derive from interdisciplinary studies, as do concepts like rate of change, system, interaction, equilibrium, and interface.

The former view is similar to the view expressed by Ms. Schuck in this chapter's lead-off scenario. The most historically significant expression of this view was articulated in the structure-of-the-disciplines perspective, which we examined in depth in Chapter Three. In order to understand this perspective as an approach to curriculum organization, we need to develop a way of describing its epistemological foundation, to use ideas from Chapter Six to unpack its organizational principles and content structure, and, finally, to identify its major claims about curriculum organization.

Epistemological Foundation

Epistemology concerns how we come to know things, the organization of that knowledge, and the grounds for changes in knowledge. A top-down approach to curriculum organization is based on a view of knowledge that assumes that we can deductively derive all knowledge from a small set of general, abstract ideas. We might consider these ideas to be basic truths. In mathematics, these fundamental ideas would be basic axioms; in science, they might be overarching themes, theories, or laws; in other disciplines, they might be central concepts. For example, we might try to develop a history curriculum from the concepts of nationalism, revolution, modernization, and migration. According to a top-down view, also termed a "hypothetical-deductive approach," from these fundamental ideas it is possible to deduce theoretical claims of lesser scope and, ultimately, empirical claims about the world and how it actually works. In science, the truth of the fundamental ideas depends on whether predictions about the world derived from those ideas turn out to be accurate. For example, a law in Newtonian physics states that in any interaction of matter, mass and energy are conserved; this law provides an accurate description of actual physical interactions. In mathematics, the fundamental ideas are accepted as axioms, self-evident to anyone who understands them. For example, in Euclidean geometry, one such axiom is that parallel lines never meet. Interestingly, these fundamental ideas in classical physics and mathematics have been reinterpreted on the basis of more recent developments in Einsteinian physics and non-Euclidean geometry, respectively. Thus, disciplines undergo radical conceptual changes (or "revolutions" according to Kuhn, 1970) when their fundamental ideas are overthrown.

According to a hypothetical-deductive approach, what proves the worth of a theory is its ability to withstand serious attempts to falsify it. According to this view, scientific method is a matter of proposing bold hypotheses about the world against a background set of theories and concepts in a discipline, deductively elaborating the empirical consequences of these hypotheses, and then trying to falsify them by collecting relevant data (Strike & Posner, 1976). Those hypotheses that the scientist is unable to falsify support the theories and concepts from which they derived.

This hypothetical-deductive view is best represented in the work of the philosopher Karl Popper (1959). More recent developments in philosophy of science, beginning with the work of Thomas Kuhn (1970), raise important issues about the process by which the basic assumptions and hypotheses of science change. These philosophers question why even great scientists do not simply abandon their theories in the face of falsifying evidence. While the philosophers' answers to this question vary, they agree that Popper's logical analysis (i.e., the hypothetical-deductive view) of the scientific method does not describe the way science actually works. They further agree that any analysis of scientific method must be based, at least in part, on an examination of what scientists actually do and to what particular beliefs about the world they are committed. The curricula that I am calling "top-down" (Strike & Posner, 1976) appear to rely on Popper's views, particularly his emphasis on fundamental concepts and theories in a discipline; on the importance of predicting, i.e., deducing, the outcomes of experiments based on these ideas; on the importance of attempting to falsify rather than to verify scientific theory; and on the responsibility to question one's fundamental ideas when data are inconsistent with one's theory. At the same time, however, they seem also to grapple with the problems of conceptual change raised by Kuhn and other recent philosophers of science: in particular, the way scientists persevere in (or is it stubbornly adhere to?) a theory in the face of falsifying evidence.

While Popper's ideas seem to offer the most coherent epistemological framework for top-down curricula, Joseph Schwab's (1962, 1964) analyses of the structure of disciplines have been the most explicitly influential for curriculum development, perhaps because Schwab himself applied his analyses to a major curriculum development project, the Biological Sciences Curriculum Study (1968), that served as a prototype for others. According to Schwab (1962, 1964), any discipline has both "substantive" and "syntactical" structures. The substantive structures are formed by the basic concepts, principles, or themes that organize the more specific facts in the discipline. In biology, for example, concepts like ecosystem, homeostasis, and natural selection serve this role. The substantive structures are essentially the fundamental ideas of the discipline that form the context within which scientists formulate their research questions—the questions that direct their inquiry. The syntactical structure of a discipline is the way scholars in a discipline establish truth and validity. How scientists justify their conclusions, what counts as evidence for a claim, and what kinds of inferences are legitimate are all aspects of a discipline's syntactical structure. These aspects provide the rules for settling disputes between competing knowledge claims. Schwab called these rules the syntactical structure because they determine what someone can legitimately claim, and, thus, function as a syntax (or set of rules) of inquiry in the discipline. According to Schwab, a discipline is a body of subject matter with a coherent set of substantive and syntactical structures. In Chapter Six we discussed some of the difficulties faced in using disciplines as a basis for analyzing school subjects. Even though many have tried, no philosophers have yet established a clear, unambiguous definition of a discipline.[1] Human knowledge simply cannot be neatly compartmentalized. How to set boundary conditions for a discipline, how to decide whether a subfield is a separate or a subdiscipline, and what we mean by interdisciplinary, multidisciplinary, and cross-disciplinary curriculum efforts are just three of the problems that remain unresolved.[2]

Organizational Principles

Based on a hypothetical-deductive view, top-down curricula sought to identify the fundamental ideas that, in Schwab's terms, form the substantive structure of disciplines, typically termed "overarching themes." For example, the Biological Sciences Curriculum Study (BSCS, 1968) identified nine major themes:

1. Change of organisms through time as evolution
2. Genetic continuity
3. Complementarity of structure and function
4. Complementarity of the organism and its environment
5. Regulation and homeostasis
6. The biological basis of behavior

7. Diversity of type and unity of pattern
8. Science as investigation and inquiry
9. The history of biological concepts

The BSCS curriculum development team believed that these themes could provide the same basic structure for a curriculum as they believed ideas provided for biology as a discipline. The curriculum they developed taught these themes "through the use of a variety of organisms best illustrating the concept in question" (BSCS, 1968, p. viii). Once identified, these themes served as the basis for deriving the content of the curricula in a parsimonious manner. The developers did not see the need to include all the science content previously taught:

> Thus, use of micro-organisms, plants, and animals conveys the pervasiveness of these themes in all living things. . . . It is the interweaving of the themes with organisms and levels of organization that gives biology a structure as a science. . . . The BSCS program presents a balanced approach to the science of biology without presenting excessive details. (BSCS, 1968, p. viii)

In some of the new curricula, not only did the themes provide a framework for making sense of the details, but also many of the specific facts and applications of the themes could even be omitted entirely, leaving them up to the student to derive. After all, the hypothetical-deductive view held that all the claims of science could, *in principle,* be derived from the fundamental theoretical ideas.

By assuming congruence between disciplines and curricula, content could be organized in the curriculum in a way that reflected the way Popper described knowledge to be organized in scientific disciplines. This organization was, in the view of both Popper and the developers of the new curricula, based on the logical organization of concepts, with the most general, basic concepts serving as a basis for understanding more specific concepts and facts.

Content Structure

Top-down curricula display unique approaches to the problems of content structure. Since the fundamental concepts in any discipline are very profound, they tend to be expressed in abstract terms. None of these concepts can be learned once and for all. But they can be learned. Bruner, in words that became both famous and controversial, even hypothesized that "any subject can be taught effectively in some intellectually honest form to any child at any stage of development" (Bruner, 1960, p. 33). Bruner attempted this ambitious curricular feat with a content structure that was designed to revisit periodically a small set of concepts, each time at increasingly higher levels of sophistication, that is, with a spiral curriculum.[3] Recall that M:ACOS is organized around just five central concepts, each of which the child revisits in each of the six units.

During this time of competition with the Soviets for military superiority, few people listened to critics who questioned the assumption that what teachers *could* accomplish, they necessarily *should* accomplish. It seemed self-evident that if children could be taught advanced subject matter earlier, they should be.

Major Claims

Let us now try to summarize the major claims that formed the basis for these curricula, before we examine one case in some detail. Table 7.1 summarizes the major claims of the top-down approach.

The Case of PSSC Physics

The first major post-World War II curriculum reform project was the PSSC, headed by Jerrold Zacharias in the late 1950s. (See Figure 7.1.) In Chapter Three we described the historical setting of that project. Here we examine the curriculum in more depth as an example of the top-down approach to curriculum organization. Although the PSSC physics curriculum is not widely used in U.S. schools in its original, pure form, it is rare to find a high school physics text today that does not acknowledge the influence of PSSC physics.

The PSSC decided to develop a new course to fit into the existing high school curriculum—that is, to develop a course to replace the physics course normally taken by eleventh- or twelfth-graders. Furthermore, since most of the students who took physics prior to PSSC were ranked in the upper half of their classes academically, PSSC decided to gear the course for them. PSSC chose to offer a course that conceived of physics as physicists do, that is, "as an explanatory system, a system that extends from the domain inside the atom to the distant galaxies" (Finlay, 1966, p. 67). The curriculum took the form of "a unified story—one in which the successive topics are chosen and developed to lead toward an atomic picture of matter, its motions and interrelations" (p. 67). This was a structure-of-the-disciplines curriculum because "the aim was to present a view of physics that would bring a student close to the nature of modern physics and to the nature of physical inquiry" (pp. 67–68). The student was to

Table 7.1 Major Claims of the Top-Down Approach

1. *Epistemological* Each discipline is distinct and has its own structure; the structure includes a set of interrelated fundamental themes, concepts, or principles, and a mode of inquiry.

2. *Psychological* The learning process of children is similar to the inquiry process of scholars working at the frontiers of knowledge.

3. *Educational purpose* Education should consist of understanding the structure of each major discipline of knowledge.

4. *Curriculum* There should be a congruence between the disciplines and the school curriculum. Emphasis in curricula should be on studying each discipline the way scholars conduct inquiry in it, grappling with the same ideas that scholars grapple with.

5. *Curriculum development* Scholars from the disciplines should be the major actors in the process of curriculum development, because they have the relevant expertise.

FIGURE 7.1 An example of PSSC-designed laboratory equipment. A "ripple tank" (left) used to study wave motion and two images (right) produced using this equipment.

"see physics as an unfinished and continuing activity" and to realize "something of the satisfaction and challenge felt by the scientist when he reaches vantage points from which he can contemplate both charted and uncharted vistas" (p. 68).

To add modern physics to the already crowded high school physics curriculum would have been infeasible, strictly in terms of available time for covering the content. Moreover, without thoroughly rethinking the content the course would not have been able to achieve its ambitious goals of providing a unified view of physics for the student and would have left little time for allowing the student to engage in real scientific inquiry. Therefore, a decision was made to greatly reduce the amount of traditional content covered

> in favor of a deeper development of ideas that are central to a comprehension of the fundamentals of contemporary physical thought. This deeper development meant carrying key concepts to higher levels than have been ordinarily reached in secondary-school courses. Deeper development also meant a more extensive exploration of the substructure of experiment and thought that underlies the basic physical principles. (Finlay, 1966, p. 68)

These two meanings of "deeper development" were clearly aimed at helping students understand the substantive and the syntactical structures of the discipline, respectively (Schwab, 1964).

The PSSC wrote a textbook, designed laboratory experiments, made films, and commissioned the writing of supplementary paperback books to support the teachers as they worked toward these goals. In physics textbooks prior to PSSC, principles, definitions, and laws were asserted, applied to show how modern devices work, used in end-of-chapter problems for practice in application, and applied in the laboratory for illustration and confirmation. In PSSC materials, "the student is expected to wrestle with a line (or with converging lines) of inquiry, including his own laboratory investigations, that leads to basic ideas" (Finlay, 1966, p. 68). In this sense PSSC physics represents a structure-of-the-disciplines perspective.

The top-down approach of this curriculum derives from the assumptions made about how ideas in a curriculum should be organized. PSSC represents the application of Bruner's principle of structure that claimed that "by understanding some deep principles, you could extrapolate to the particulars as needed . . . whereby you could know a great deal about a lot of things while keeping very little in mind" (Bruner, 1971, pp. 19–22). PSSC assumed that a person, equipped with only the fundamental ideas of a discipline and a knowledge of the method scientists use to generate the more particular ideas, can in fact "extrapolate to the particulars as needed." We will examine the validity of this assumption shortly.

Thus, the PSSC curriculum is organized around fundamental ideas in physics. Part One concerns "matter and its setting in space and time" (Finlay, 1966, p. 70). It explores motion in terms of the relation between distance, velocity, and acceleration both in one dimension and in two dimensions (using vectors). Then Part One turns to ideas of mass and conservation of mass, investigating the size and arrangement of atoms and molecules in crystals and gases. This discussion leads to the idea of physical models as human constructions of the physical world.

Part Two concerns light. First, it examines light phenomena, for example, shadows, reflection, and refraction. Then the curriculum offers a physical model in an attempt to account for these phenomena. The model presented is the particle model: i.e., light is a stream of particles. Just when the model seems to be fairly successful in explaining light phenomena, the textbook and films show the student some phenomena that this simple model cannot explain. The curriculum turns to another model, the wave model: i.e., light is a wave, something like waves in water. This model too seems successful, until, in Part Four, the student finds that light (and even matter itself) acts both as a particle and as a wave.

Part Three again takes up the topic of motion, but this time from a dynamic point of view, that is, by considering forces. Gravitation, momentum, and energy are explored, and the law of conservation is investigated.

Part Four returns to the atomistic character of matter and the study of forces introduced in Parts One and Three, respectively. It is concerned with electrical forces and energy and begins to relate these ideas to wave properties introduced in Part Two. All these ideas are finally used in the study of the structure of matter, i.e., atoms. It is here that the wave-particle duality of matter (and light) is finally discussed.

Thus, fundamental ideas like Newton's laws of motion, properties of waves, and the law of conservation of matter and energy are developed in great depth. Technological applications of these ideas are scarce in the curriculum. PSSC assumed that students would be able to derive an explanation of the applications with these ideas firmly understood. For example, the curriculum leaves out an explanation of sound. Although sound was a significant topic in pre-PSSC texts, the PSSC text does not even include it in its index. Since sound is a wave, presumably with a thorough knowledge of waves the student would beable to derive principles of sound. Similar reasoning leads to sharply reduced coverage of such traditionally taught topics as pulleys, levers, optics, and the working of many everyday devices like automobile engines and refrigerators.

Although there have been many criticisms of the structure-of-the-disciplines perspective, here we focus on one major criticism of the organization of the curriculum, that is, of its top-down approach. This criticism is based on the assumption made about students' ability to derive the applications of fundamental ideas of the discipline on their own. While it may be possible in principle to derive most of the scientific concepts underlying modern technology from these fundamental ideas, most students cannot. Perhaps a small percentage of students have this ability. But most are not able to manipulate these concepts with sufficient facility to make the necessary derivations. Because PSSC vastly overestimated the percentage of students that possessed this ability, most students viewed the curriculum as very difficult. Some critics have even linked the drop in the percentage of high school students taking physics—from around 25 percent to 16 percent—to the use of PSSC physics in schools. Thus, the critics could claim that the characteristics of the students PSSC expected to take physics became a self-fulfilling prophecy.

BOTTOM-UP APPROACH

The problems of scientists and mathematicians in developing and implementing new curricula did not go unnoticed by educational psychologists, many of whom had been left out of the intellectually invigorating and heavily funded process of curriculum reform. When they observed the difficulty students were having with the new curricula, they concluded that these curricula ignored the psychology of learning. In particular, several psychologists argued that curricula needed to respect the "psychological" rather than the "logical" structure of knowledge. By this they meant that curriculum organization should reflect the way people learn, rather than the way knowledge is organized in disciplines. This view was expressed by both cognitive and behavioral psychologists (Ausubel, 1964; Gagne, 1965, 1970).

We will examine in detail the behavioral version of the argument. This argument we term "bottom-up," or "inductivist," in order to show how it contrasts sharply with the top-down, or hypothetical-deductive, view discussed earlier. Then we will see how the bottom-up view was applied to curriculum development as the basis for an influential elementary school curriculum.

In brief, the bottom-up view assumes that the most important determinant of learning is the possession of prerequisite skills. Curriculum development consists of working backward from the intellectual skills desired at the completion of the curriculum by asking the question "What does the learner have to be able to do in order to do this?" Successive answers to this question produce a "learning hierarchy" that includes all the objectives that all learners must master on the way to achieving the final, or terminal, objectives. Instruction then proceeds up through this learning hierarchy, from the simplest to the more complex objectives. The "learning route" described by the learning hierarchy ensures that "relevant lower-order skills are mastered before the learning of the related higher-order skill is undertaken" (Gagne, 1970, p. 240).

Epistemological Foundation[4]

The epistemological foundation of the bottom-up approach to curriculum can be traced to the eighteenth-century philosopher David Hume. According to Hume (1957, 1967), knowledge originates in experience, and in particular, sense impressions. These sense impressions produce ideas, which are simply mental copies of the sense impressions. Knowledge, in turn, consists of the association or linking of these ideas. People, according to Hume, develop knowledge by generalizing from the relations they observe between sense impressions. Higher-level generalizations are, in turn, constructed from lower-level ones. In short, according to Hume, the general is always constructed from the particular, ultimately from particular sensory experiences.

Like Hume, Gagne (1965, 1970) approached learning and knowledge atomistically; that is, he attempted to identify the simplest elements—the "atoms"—of learning. For Gagne, developing a curriculum entailed working backward from complex intellectual skills to discover increasingly more basic units, ultimately the simplest stimulus-response (S-R) bonds. Furthermore, like Hume, Gagne had a view of learning and knowledge we can describe as inductivist: that is, he held that the general is derived from the particular. According to Gagne, complex learning, even development of such capabilities as problem solving, is accomplished by successively linking together previously learned, simpler behaviors. Thus, S-R bonds link together to form verbal and motor chains (one word or action leads to another) and multiple discriminations (distinguishing one thing from another); multiple discriminations link together to form concepts (classes of things); concepts link to form principles (relationships between concepts); and the linking of principles leads to problem solving (finding new relationships).

Another important parallel between Gagne and Hume can be drawn. Hume was a philosopher writing about psychology at a time before psychology split from philosophy to form a separate discipline. Thus, he can be described as philosophizing about psychological phenomena. Gagne in a sense psychologizes philosophical topics. For example, consider the following statement: "Learning hierarchies are the best way to describe the 'structure' of any topic, course, or discipline. They describe the intellectual skills the individual needs to perform intellectual operations within that subject—to learn about it, to think about it, to solve problems in it" (Gagne, 1970, p. 245). This statement suggests that Gagne's view reduces the notion of the logical relations between concepts—an epistemological consideration—to an analysis of the most effective route by which someone learns those concepts—a psychological consideration. We will have more to say on this point later.

A second example of the way Gagne's psychological, and in this case behavioral, perspective can be viewed as affecting his analysis of a philosophical problem has to do with the concept of what science is. A perspective on science that affords, or even requires, a central role for behavioral psychologists in developing new science curricula is one that focuses on "science behaviors." Thus, if behavioral psychologists replace the disciplines of chemistry, biology, and physics with the "intellectual skills thought to be involved in 'doing science' " (Gagne, 1970, p. 261), they transform the curriculum development task from one that requires only experts in the subject matter to one that also requires experts trained in behavioral analyses.

Organizational Principles

As mentioned earlier, Gagne (1965, 1970) believed that there is only one principle needed to organize a curriculum. This principle derived from his psychological theory of learning. Thus, of Schwab's four commonplaces, the only one Gagne needed to address was the learner and the learning process. According to Gagne's theory, learning of a new skill, concept, or principle is greatly facilitated when the learner has the prerequisites of that skill, concept, or principle. For Gagne, there is little point to teaching anything new without first providing the necessary prerequisites. Therefore, it is the curriculum developers' responsibility to organize the learning objectives into a series of small enough steps—and with no gaps, i.e., missing prerequisites—that learners never falter. This view also had the effect of placing relatively more responsibility for educational success on the shoulders of curriculum developers, rather than with the learners or the teachers.

The principle of prerequisites derives directly from programmed-instruction technology, in which each step is at the most micro level of instruction, represented by perhaps one or two sentences of text and ten to twenty seconds' worth of instructional time. But the common sense nature of this principle extends to far more macro levels of curriculum organization. For example, what would be the point of asking a student to take Spanish II before taking Spanish I? The level of organization to which the principle of prerequisites was applied by Gagne was the level of individual learning objectives, one or two of which might comprise a lesson approximately one-half hour to one hour long.

Robert Glaser's (1969) approach to curriculum organization was similar to Gagne's in many respects. Glaser's background in psychological research on training methods for the armed forces became the basis for his subsequent work in education. Glaser developed a national reputation for his pioneering developments in programmed instruction. Programmed instruction is a carefully sequenced self-instruction method based on behaviorist reinforcement principles. Each step, or "frame," in the instructional process is small enough to ensure nearly error-free performance by the student. By giving immediate feedback to the student at each step, the student's behavior is gradually shaped toward the achievement of the terminal objective. Glaser's work on this technique became the basis for an individualized program in elementary school mathematics, known as Individually Prescribed Instruction (IPI). IPI was based on the premise that, given enough time, almost every student can master a basic set of objectives. We will examine IPI in more depth in Chapter Nine.

This same premise also formed the basis for a group-paced, rather than an individually paced, method developed by the psychologist Benjamin Bloom and known as "mastery learning" (1971). Bloom's approach to instruction, though not necessarily based on a behavioral perspective, nevertheless does, like those of Glaser and Gagne, require a carefully sequenced curriculum in which each objective builds on previous prerequisite ones.

Although Gagne, Glaser, and Bloom shared many of the epistemological assumptions of Hume, we focus on Gagne (1970) here in order to prepare for a case study of his science curriculum in the next section of this chapter.

Content Structure

The principle of prerequisites is, of course, only a sequencing principle: that is, it only addresses vertical structure. However, there is very likely to be more than one prerequisite. Therefore, this principle does not address the question of how to organize a set of prerequisites for any given skill, concept, or principle. The content structure that results from the application of the prerequisites principle is a hierarchy of learning objectives.

Figure 7.2 depicts a simple hierarchy in which learning objective A is the terminal objective, B and C are prerequisites of A, D and E are prerequisites of B, and F and G are prerequisites of C. Of course, this schematic version is very neat. An actual hierarchy would likely have learning objectives with many more than two prerequisites, with some of the prerequisites serving as objectives in other hierarchies.

We have said that all the curriculum developer needs to do to produce a learning hierarchy is to address the key question "What does the learner have to be able to learn to do in order to do this (a given learning objective)?" With this question, the developer works backward through the hierarchy, thus generating a learning sequence. Once this is developed, the learner proceeds from the bottom up, that is, from the simplest objectives, representing capabilities that the learner brings to the learning sequence, the so-called "entry behaviors," to the more complex objectives, ultimately reaching the terminal objectives of the sequence (Gagne, 1970).

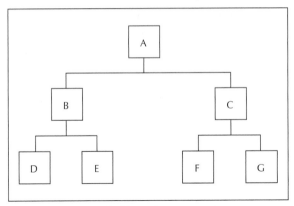

FIGURE 7.2   A simple hierarchy.

Major Claims

Before examining one bottom-up curriculum in detail, let us summarize the major claims of this perspective on curriculum organization. Table 7.2 presents the major claims of the bottom-up approach.

Note the subtle shift in responsibility for learning that occurs with the development of bottom-up, behavioral curricula. In top-down curricula the student bears most of the responsibility for understanding the major concepts, and particularly for deriving the more specific applications from the major concepts. The teacher's and curriculum developer's responsibility is to ensure that the curriculum reflects the structure of the discipline. On the other hand, bottom-up curricula are based on the assumption that student learning nearly always occurs if, and only if, the teacher and curriculum developers have sequenced the objectives properly, provided appropriate instruction, and allowed sufficient time for learning. Perhaps, even when the techniques and curricula are long forgotten or considered obsolete, this shift in responsibility for learning will remain a significant legacy of the bottom-up curriculum designers.

The Case of Science: A Process Approach

Beginning in 1962 Robert Gagne, as a member of the American Association for the Advancement of Science (AAAS) Commission on Science Education and with support from the National Science Foundation (NSF), began to develop a curriculum based on these principles of curriculum organization. The decision was made at the outset to develop a new approach to elementary school science, one focusing on what scientists do, rather than on what they know. The approach was to be a "hands-on" one: "From the start the child is an active participant in [these] scientific tasks. . . . He has the chance to work as a scientist by carrying out the kinds of tasks which scientists perform" (AAAS, 1967, p. 4).

Although this statement sounds similar to the claims of PSSC, an examination of the curriculum reveals that the similarity is superficial. AAAS decided

Table 7.2 Major Claims of the Bottom-Up Approach

1. *Epistemological* All complex or general knowledge and skills can be analyzed into more specific or simple elements. This process can be repeated until the analyst has identified all basic elements of human knowledge and skill.

2. *Psychological* People acquire complex or general knowledge and skills from simpler, more specific elements. Given proper sequencing of objectives, high-quality instruction, and sufficient time, nearly all people can learn what schools teach.

3. *Educational purpose* Education should focus on teaching intellectual skills, rather than facts, and on using techniques that allow all students to learn.

4. *Curriculum* There should be congruence between the curriculum and the most effective sequences and conditions of learning.

5. *Curriculum development* Behavioral psychologists should be major actors in the process of curriculum development, because they have the relevant expertise.

to emphasize the processes rather than the content of science. Science was thus conceived as a set of capabilities rather than a set of propositions, concepts, and ways of knowing.

> Of course, the content is there—the children examine and make explorations of solid objects, liquids, gases, plants, animals, rocks, and even moon photographs. But, with few notable exceptions, they are not asked to learn and remember particular facts and principles about these objects and phenomena. Rather, they are expected to learn such things as how to observe solid objects and their motions, how to classify liquids, how to infer internal mechanisms in plants, how to make and verify hypotheses about human behavior. (AAAS, 1967, p. 3)

According to AAAS, the processes that comprise what it means to do science include the following: observing, classifying, communicating, using numbers, measuring, using space-time relationships, predicting, and inferring. These were viewed as the processes "basic to all science" (Gagne, 1966, p. 49). Like PSSC physics, Gagne's curriculum, titled *Science: A Process Approach* (S:APA) (Figure 7.3), is not used in its original form in many classrooms today. However, like that of PSSC physics, the influence of S:APA has been profound. Acceptance by elementary teachers and science educators of the idea that science consists, at least in part, of basic scientific processes is currently widespread. It is now quite common to find curricula or state syllabi taking "science processes" or "inquiry skills" for granted and defining these aspects of a science curriculum in much the same way as did S:APA. Occasionally other "skills" are added—e.g., "making decisions," "manipulating materials," or "creating models"—but typically S:APA's eight processes are cited verbatim and without justification.

The AAAS curriculum is organized into seven parts, each roughly corresponding to one grade level (Kindergarten through Grade 6). Each part covers some aspect of at least five of the eight processes. Each part consists of a series of about twenty lessons called "exercises," each described in a separate booklet

FIGURE 7.3   A typical fifth-grade S:APA activity.

designed to guide the teacher. In addition, for each part there is a kit of class materials needed to do the science activities. There is no textbook and there are no other individual materials, written or otherwise, for the students. Thus, in contrast with many other behavioral curricula such as IPI, S:APA is not individualized either in its pace or in its activity structure; it depends entirely on group activities.

The guide for each lesson, i.e., the lesson booklet, is labeled according to the science process it teaches and its place in the sequence of lessons within that process. Thus, "Observing 4" is the fourth lesson that focuses on observation. Every lesson follows a standard format, which includes the behavioral objectives for the lesson (there are typically two or three), a sequence chart showing the hierarchical configuration of the objectives, a lesson rationale, a vocabulary list, required materials, the description of a set of activities, a "generalizing experience" designed to promote transfer, "appraisal" suggestions for determining in a general sense the success of the lesson, and a "competency measure" for determining individual performance. Figure 7.4 depicts the sequence chart for a typical S:APA lesson.

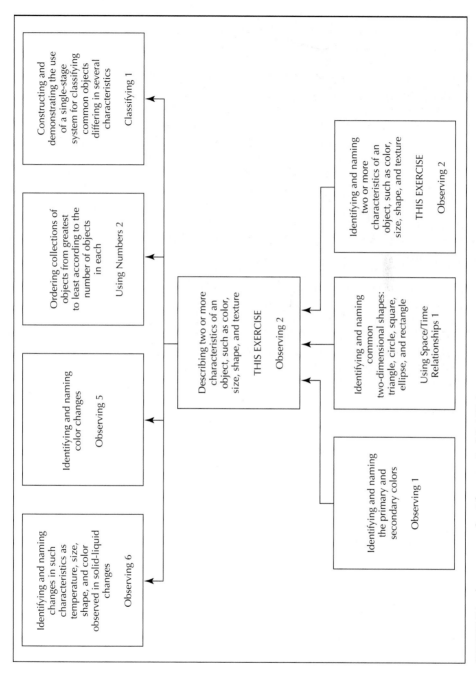

FIGURE 7.4 A sequence chart for a typical S:APA lesson.

The presence of behavioral objectives, though suggestive of a behavioral perspective, is not in itself definitive. There are, after all, many curricula that include behavioral objectives only because their audiences consider these statements to be a necessary feature of a modern curriculum. What indicates a behavioral perspective in S:APA is the conception of science as "the skills a scientist uses" (AAAS, 1967, p. 3) and the translation of these skills into the functional objectives of the curriculum. As the curriculum materials state, "The process skills are readily described in terms of component skills which correspond to observable performances or behaviors of the child. The activities of the program are structured, described, and evaluated in terms of these skills" (p. 3). S:APA is behavioral not because it includes behavioral objectives, but because it takes them seriously, organizing the whole curriculum around them.

More pertinent to our purposes in this chapter, S:APA uses a bottom-up approach to organization. It begins with a set of objectives that it expects all kindergarten children are capable of mastering, for example, "identifying and naming the primary and secondary colors" (Observing 1, AAAS, 1967, p. 1). S:APA then builds on these "subordinate skills," using them as "prerequisites" for more complex skills, such as "identifying and naming color changes" (Observing 5, AAAS, 1967, p. 1). Sets of these more complex skills are used in turn as prerequisites for other, even more complex skills, such as "identifying and naming changes in such characteristics as temperature, size, shape, and color observed in solid-liquid changes" (Observing 6, AAAS, 1967, p. 1). The teacher guide points out the centrality of the hierarchies and the cumulative nature of objectives in the curriculum.

> The hierarchies represent a sequence of instructional dependencies which have guided the ordering of exercises within each part of the program. Thus, this entire curriculum of science for the elementary school may be characterized by the sequence of stated behaviors (the objectives), one building upon another until the terminal performances for each process are reached. (AAAS, 1967, p. 10)

That is, the students proceed through this curriculum from the bottom of the hierarchy up through it, until they reach the top.

This approach to curriculum organization attempted to solve two major problems that Gagne and other psychologists saw in the top-down approach. First, S:APA addressed the problem of making science, and some topics in mathematics, accessible to a very broad range of students. By providing carefully developed sequences of objectives, S:APA offered a curriculum that leaves much less to chance, to the teacher's ingenuity, and to the students' ability to make intuitive leaps. Second, S:APA attempted to provide a more integrated approach to subject matter. As Gagne (1970) argued,

> In educational circles, the content of learning is often referred to as large categories of subject matter—English, mathematics, and so on. . . . The existence of such general "subject" categories makes it difficult to determine what human capabilities they do or should include. . . . [For example] is making an accurate description of an unfamiliar object . . . "English," or "language," or "science"? . . . These difficulties in identifying the content of learning

would be avoided if care were taken to put the emphasis where it belongs, which is on the attainments of learners . . . [which] deserve to be called *intellectual skills*. (1970, pp. 243-244) (italics in original)

Thus, S:APA breaks down some of the traditional walls between science, mathematics (as in the process of "using numbers"), and language arts (as in the process of "communicating").

Nevertheless, S:APA also created its own set of problems. First, according to critics, it misconstrued what science is. It was based on logical positivism[5] in its treatment of scientific processes as content-neutral features of scientific method. Students would see science as a set of separate, decontextualized, intellectual skills without a sense of the kinds of questions or purposes for which they are appropriate. Second, by relegating content to an instrumental role in teaching of skills, it made certain that students would not understand the substantive structure of science. As Heimer claimed,

> The connection, if any, between the (conceptual) structure of the content and the design of the associated learning hierarchy seems to be best characterized at the present as a "blur." There is most assuredly an intimate relationship between "what an individual can do" and "what an individual knows," but there is a conspicuous absence of information about this relationship in the literature. (Heimer, 1969, p. 498)[6]

Thus, we are left with the apparent dilemma of choosing between an approach that focuses so much on subject matter that it makes learning of that subject matter problematic for many students and an approach that focuses so much on the learning process that it obscures the subject matter from the learner's view. But perhaps we got ourselves into this dilemma by using a limited metaphor for thinking about curriculum. Maybe the top-down versus bottom-up metaphor is the problem.

PROJECT APPROACH[7]

So far, we have found the top-down versus bottom-up metaphor very helpful in understanding different types of curriculum organization. However, metaphors can also be dangerous; they may blind us to cases that do not fit the model. The top-down versus bottom-up metaphor has just such a blind spot, because it obscures an important type of curricular organization: the project-centered curriculum.

Proponents of the project approach organize the curriculum neither around fundamental disciplinary concepts, as in the top-down approach, nor around prerequisite skills, as in the bottom-up view. Instead, project-centered curricula are organized around student activities, which the teacher and students plan together. In brief, the project approach embodies an experiential perspective; it assumes that students learn through activities that allow "newly acquired skills [to be] applied through direct and active personal experience in order to illuminate, reinforce and internalize cognitive learning" (AEE [Association of

Experiential Education], cited in Wigginton, 1985, p. 383). Experiential projects encourage students to bring their interests, psychological needs, and previous experiences to active study of the physical and social environment. This view was expressed by Ms. Kent in this chapter's lead-off scenario.

The project approach to curriculum had its genesis in the progressive educational movement around the turn of the century. John Dewey, the leading advocate of progressivism, articulated two major strands within the movement: a new concern for children's interests and development and a belief in the power of education to improve society. These two strands came together in the progressive theory of experiential education, exemplified by the project approach to curriculum organization.[8]

Project-centered curricula emphasize "student-directed" experiences with the "real world," particularly with the social life of the community, rather than traditional subject-matter content. Through these experiences, students develop both their intellects and the attitudes and skills necessary to participate in and improve a democratic society. Perhaps most important, meaningful participation in the life of the community empowers students to take control of their lives and to make contributions to the larger good. Thus, education, as the fundamental method of social reform, shapes the individuals who will, in turn, shape society.

William Heard Kilpatrick, a Teachers College professor and Dewey disciple in the first decades of the twentieth century, took Dewey's insights and gave them a practical application in the project approach. A focal point of the project approach to curriculum is the community and the larger society surrounding the school. Issues and problems in the social world provide a source of topics for instruction, and material for student projects and activities. These activities tend to take an interdisciplinary form, because the project approach requires examination of social problems or topics as wholes, using information and skills from several disciplines. In addition, project-centered curricula often encourage students with different interests and abilities to work together in defining and studying a common problem; in this way, the students form a democratic community in miniature.

Epistemological Foundations

Dewey laid the epistemological foundation of the project approach to curriculum in two ways: (1) in his elaboration of scientific method within the context of pragmatic philosophy, and (2) with his elevation of social knowledge, "experience in which the widest groups share," to a dominant position (Dewey, 1916, p. 225).

The scientific, or "problem-solving," method, according to a Deweyan philosophy, begins with a problem. A person develops an idea in an attempt to solve some problem, tests out the idea through some action or experience in the world, and then reflects on the effects of that action. That reflection results in a new or revised idea, and the process continues in successive thought-action-reflection cycles. For Dewey, this interaction between thought and action is the heart of the scientific method, and it became the basis for the project approach. The project, like science, begins with a problem that students want to solve. Like scientists, they continually test ideas for solving the problem and reflect on their actions.

Rather than picturing abstract, general concepts and concrete, specific experiences as organized in either a bottom-up or top-down arrangement, in which one builds in a linear fashion toward the other, Dewey saw concepts in the mind and experiences in the world as having an interactive relationship—one constantly modifying the other. According to this view, good ideas are those that illuminate experience and good experiences are those that help a person test out ideas. This interactive process contributes to the growth of both knowledge and the person.

Scientific method, in Dewey's view, creates a valid pragmatic principle for reorganizing the curriculum. It "is the only authentic means at our command for getting at the significance of our everyday experiences of the world in which we live. It . . . provides a working pattern of the way in which and the conditions under which experiences are used to lead ever onward and outward" (Dewey, 1938, p. 88). The scientific method is how we come to know things; it is "the pattern and the ideal of intelligent exploration and exploitation of the possibilities inherent in experience." Thus it ought to form the organizing principle of any educational scheme (p. 86).

Dewey praises the scientific method as an organizing principle for several reasons: (1) it "attaches more importance, not less, to ideas as ideas than do other methods"; (2) it encourages students to "carefully and discriminatingly" observe consequences of an action, in order to test ideas; (3) it "demands keeping track of ideas, activities, and observed consequences" (pp. 86–87). All of these educational characteristics are not only favorable in themselves, but also useful because they foster the capacities students will need to participate effectively in democratic society.

Dewey's (1916) second epistemological contribution to curriculum organization stems from his emphasis on the social dimensions of knowledge. First, according to Dewey, education ought to address social issues and "enhance [the student's] social insight and interest," so that students will be able to contribute to and improve society (Dewey, 1916, p. 225, cited in Cremin, 1961, p. 125). Therefore, developers using the project approach organize their curriculum around knowledge about the community as discovered by students through purposeful activities in that community. Social knowledge complements the other categories of knowledge cultivated by project-centered curricula: self-knowledge, or the attitudinal changes students undergo as they progress through the activities; and knowledge as skills, which may also have vocational importance. All three types of knowledge help prepare students for citizenship and influence the structuring of projects in the curriculum.

Second, all knowledge is in a sense social. People develop knowledge within a culture, and that knowledge depends on the culture that embeds it. Therefore, it is no accident that the project approach finds students working on projects in groups, rather than in independent study arrangements. The interaction between members of groups and the collective pursuit of knowledge and goals is as important to the project approach as the task that the group is trying to accomplish.

Organizational Principles

Project-centered curricula do not follow a specific sequencing principle, since the students and teacher together must decide, as they proceed, what projects and activities to undertake. Nonetheless, the project approach does offer some general guidance in organization: the curriculum sequence should allow the students to progress through increasingly complex types of knowledge, skills, and attitudes as they work on their projects.

Most important, the project approach favors a developmental organizing principle, with students given increasing responsibility as they progress through the activities of the curriculum. This developmental approach to structuring curricula contrasts with the more traditional emphasis on logical or disciplinary organization.

Content Structure

In general, content configuration in project-centered curricula tends to be fairly flat and cyclical. Ideally, however, the project approach aims for student growth through experiential activities that return to similar content sources (e.g., social issues) repeatedly, in more and more sophisticated and developmentally advanced projects. Projects should constantly challenge students at more and more advanced intellectual and developmental levels. In this sense, the project approach may be said to have a spiral configuration of content, along developmental lines.

Major Claims

Now let us summarize the major claims of the project approach, before we move on to examine one project-centered curriculum in detail. Table 7.3 summarizes the major claims of the project-centered approach.

The Case of Foxfire

The Foxfire program is perhaps the best-known current model of a project-centered curriculum, with Foxfire-inspired projects and courses in schools all over the United States. Foxfire began in 1966, when Eliot Wigginton, a high school English teacher in Rabun Gap, Georgia, "made a desperate attempt to get the attention of his ninth- and tenth-grade English classes" by having them brainstorm ideas for a magazine (Wigginton, 1985, inside cover). Over the next twenty-five years the magazine grew into a series of best-selling books, a record company, a string band, a private press, a museum complex, and a television station—all run by high school students.

Table 7.3 Major Claims of the Project-Centered Approach

1. *Epistemological* The scientific method offers a model of the way we think, and therefore it should be used to structure educational experiences. This method consists of recurrent cycles of thought-action-reflection. The knowledge of most worth is social knowledge. An interdisciplinary, experiential, project-centered approach to learning best allows students to gain those skills, attitudes, and knowledge necessary to participate in a democratic society.

2. *Psychological* Schooling should attempt to educate the whole person. People learn by doing; they acquire new skills and attitudes through trying them out in activities that they direct and that they find relevant and meaningful.

3. *Educational purpose* Education should help students to reconstruct or reorganize their experience, so that they can contribute to the larger social experience (Dewey, 1916, pp. 89-90). Student growth and development are the central aims, rather than teaching facts, disciplinary structure, or intellectual skills except as they are necessary for student projects.

4. *Curriculum* There should be congruence between the curriculum and students' interests and developmental needs. Content should be interdisciplinary, based on "relevant" material, and provide opportunities for students to apply new learnings in "real world" activities.

5. *Curriculum development* Students and teachers in cooperation should develop curricula that are relevant to students' interests and needs. "Experts" need not be involved.

Foxfire is what Wigginton calls a "learning concept," rather than a set curriculum; and the Foxfire Learning Concept can take many forms. In its original version in Rabun Gap, Foxfire began as a magazine written, illustrated, and distributed by students about the folklore and history of their Southern Appalachian region. Students taped local "oldsters" relating stories about the community and photographed them practicing mountain crafts that had been all but forgotten by the rest of the world.

Following these interviews with community members, the pupils wrote descriptions of folk traditions as diverse as faith healing and planting by the signs of the zodiac and illustrated "how-to" articles on subjects such as toy making and building a log cabin. The resulting *Foxfire* magazine enjoyed tremendous popularity, not only with the students, who discovered pride in their roots and their own competence, but also with the local community. Soon the magazine found an enthusiastic national audience, too, as a generation of counterculturists embraced a folklore and crafts renaissance.

Foxfire's roots lie in progressive project-centered curricula and the writings of John Dewey, although Wigginton emphasizes some aspects of experiential educational philosophy, while ignoring or modifying others. Foxfire is true to its progressive roots insofar as it tries to integrate aspects (skills, knowledge, approaches) of various disciplines into the study of real world issues of practical concern to students. The Learning Concept integrates aspects of disparate subjects—English, anthropology, mathematics (e.g., designing illustrative diagrams and calculating production costs), history, science (e.g., identifying ingredients in an herbal remedy), and art—in examining real world issues such as prejudice and cultural differences, the relevance of the past, and the role of writing in real life.

Foxfire is experiential and project-centered because it emphasizes student learning through applying new skills—e.g., interviewing, writing, photograph- ing, speech making, editing, laying out copy for publication—in self-directed, socially relevant projects. In the Rabun Gap version of Foxfire, projects take the form of magazine issues, musical recordings, and museum exhibits about the folk culture of the students' own community. Wigginton, like project-method teachers in general, does point out examples of specific subject-matter content embedded in the activities, but the experiential projects, and not the discipli- nary content, organize the curriculum. Most important, Foxfire is experiential because Wigginton does not attempt to ply students with content and skills that they can then apply in a real life situation. Instead, he first gets students involved in a socially relevant project, and then gives them material as they need it in order to complete the project (Wigginton, 1985, 1989).

Although Wigginton does not explicitly teach Dewey's scientific method, he certainly uses the recurring interaction between thought and action as a basic tenet for the Learning Concept. As he states it, the

> natural ebb and flow between experience and somewhat more passive recep- tion of information and concepts, and back to experience again armed with new approaches and insights and questions, is the way we are stretched and grow mentally. It is the way we learn "on the job," and the best schooling sim- ulates and exploits the pattern. (Wigginton, 1985, pp. 208–209)

Foxfire, and project-centered curricula in general, view knowledge as falling into three basic categories: (1) knowledge about the community and real world—in Foxfire, multidisciplinary study of local folklore and traditions, plus involvement in the publishing and recording industries play this role; (2) self- knowledge, the attitudinal changes students are to undergo as they progress through the projects; (3) knowledge as skills, which, in Foxfire, range from writ- ing a business letter or operating a camera to publishing a book or making a public speech.

Wigginton lists a number of overlapping goals for the Foxfire Learning Concept. Students should learn

> a number of very specific language arts skills. They also [should gain] a rich, real historical matrix within which they can fit (and appreciate) their other his- tory courses. In addition, they should be learning some math skills, and through their photography and design, they should be coming to an apprecia- tion of the role of the arts in their lives. A whole range of career objectives [should be] fulfilled through the fact that they're actually running a business, with all that that entails. They [should acquire] some understanding of culture and what culture means, and through celebrating and criticizing their own, they [should] also [be] more receptive to interactions with other cultures. And on top of all that, they [should acquire] a good dose of self-confidence and self-

esteem, and the ability to make and weigh the consequences of decisions; and . . . as members of a team that must, of necessity, work closely with other people, they [should learn] to care about others besides themselves. (Wigginton, 1985, pp. 320–321)

Project-centered curricula in general tend to have similar goals, with priority given to student choice of projects that interest them and also fulfill various objectives in subject–matter, e.g., "specific language arts skills"; personal development, e.g., "self-confidence and self-esteem"; socialization, e.g., "learn to care about others"; further learning, e.g., placing what they learn in a "historical matrix," which can apply to "other history courses"; and economic productivity, e.g., "running a business."

Although the curriculum is conceived as a sequence of concepts and courses, these are not tied to a particular age level or grade level. Somewhat more attention is paid to the horizontal dimensions of curriculum organization, since, on the micro level, Wigginton attempts to integrate many subjects and approaches into Foxfire. On this micro level, Foxfire tries to bridge compartmentalizations within the subject matter—e.g., the divorce between the mechanics of writing, such as spelling and grammar, and the expressive aspects, and also between expository and creative composition. It also attempts to bridge disciplines, e.g., by including elements of mathematics, history, and science.

Foxfire clearly seems to follow a spiral pattern of content configuration: Foxfire courses are structured "to build on themes or skills initiated previously and [to] reinforce them and/or lead the students on to new levels of competence" (Wigginton, 1985, p. 334). Wigginton's "touchstones" lead students through four development levels: Level I, "Gaining Skills and Confidence"; Level II, "Growing, Reinforcing, Checking Bases"; Level III, "Beyond Self"; Level IV, "Independence" (Wigginton, 1975a). Each of these levels returns to the same themes and skills at ever higher levels of sophistication and complexity.

Foxfire, like project curricula in general, does not follow either a top-down or a bottom-up approach to curriculum organization. The Learning Concept does contain elements of both approaches: students behave as social scientists, as in the top-down approach, which has students "doing science the way scientists do it"; and the curriculum emphasizes the process by which students acquire knowledge, as in the content-neutral bottom-up model.

Foxfire takes the structure-of-the-disciplines (top-down) approach of M:ACOS or PSSC one step further. It does not train students to act like real researchers in the discipline; it trains them to be productive contributors themselves. Students perform real, professional research in the field: collecting, cataloguing, preserving, and documenting data; working in archives and museums; reporting research in published papers; giving lectures, workshops, and presentations. In this way, students acquire a sense of agency and empowerment. Knowledge is produced by students themselves—they become the experts both in technical skills, once they receive training, and on the topics of their articles.

But to reiterate the basic differences in approach, Foxfire does not begin with a set of overarching themes or concepts and then have students derive the empirical details, as in top-down curricula; nor do students work from "the simplest elements of learning" inductively to general concepts and high-level skills, as in bottom-up curricula. Instead, the Learning Concept is structured around activities and projects of various types. Projects rather than concepts or skills are the primary means of organizing Foxfire and all project-centered curricula.

Wigginton created Foxfire to solve specific pedagogical dilemmas: lack of student motivation and of opportunities for practical application of skills and content. Project-centered curricula in general address these problems, but in so doing they ignore the integrity of the academic disciplines. Their solution to the problems has both positive and negative ramifications. On the positive side, it allows interdisciplinary study of a topic in a way that engages student interest; on the negative side, it obscures the structure of knowledge. In addition, it does not necessarily present information or skills in a logical order, since students learn skills or content as needed to complete their project. Thus, students may focus on incidentals, miss fundamental aspects of a discipline, and attempt tasks without the necessary prerequisites.

Project curricula have been shown to be particularly successful with populations considered at risk of dropping out of school (Wehlage et al., 1989). According to Wehlage, youth drop out of school for two major reasons. First, they do not feel that they are an integral part of the school community. Alienation leads them to believe that the school is for others but not for them. This lack of "social bonding" leaves them with little stake in their school and makes them vulnerable to outside influences as economic and social pressures lure them away from school. Second, they do not become educationally engaged in the work done at school. Schoolwork seems irrelevant to their own situations and not worth their effort.

Wehlage found that many programs for youth at risk are able to provide for social bonding. Apparently it is not difficult to help a young person to experience a sense of community in a special school program. However, unless that program also provides for intellectual engagement, it tends to serve merely a custodial function, more suited to warehousing youth than to educating them. The most successful program he found at accomplishing both objectives was the Media Academy at Fremont High School in Oakland, California. This program, in which students essentially "major" in media, can be considered an electronic and print media (including radio, television, newspaper, and adverstising) version of the Foxfire Learning Concept. It follows all 11 of the Foxfire Core Practices.

Conclusion

We have examined in some detail only three different approaches to curriculum organization. It is quite likely that the curriculum you are analyzing is neither top-down, bottom-up, nor project-centered, though you might recognize some aspects of each of these approaches. The purpose of this chapter is only to present some illustrations of coherent approaches to curriculum organization and to show that any approach has both strengths and weaknesses. The strengths derive from the focus of the approach, while the weaknesses derive from its blind spots.[9] The strengths of the top-down approach are its uncompromising attempt to respect the structure of the disciplines and to respect the student as a neophyte member of the community of scholars. Its weakness is its failure to recognize the differences in ability, background knowledge, experience, learning processes, interests, and aspirations between adult scholars and young students. The strength of the bottom-up approach is its recognition that young students learn differently than adult scholars in terms of prerequisite skills. Its major weakness is its blindness to the structure of knowledge. The strength of the project-centered approach is its attempt to engage students in integrated, real world tasks. Its major weaknesses are its failure to show students the structure of knowledge and to provide them systematically with the prerequisites necessary for successful completion of tasks on their own.[10]

In other words, each approach represents a trade-off. The strengths of each approach address the weaknesses of other approaches, and vice versa. This trade-off is precisely what Schwab warned us about in his criticism of any single theory as a basis for curriculum.[11] And this inherent limitation would obtain whether the approach to curriculum organization were based on one of the three perspectives on which we focused in this chapter, on one of the other two perspectives discussed earlier, or on some other theoretical perspective that might underlie your curriculum.

Curriculum Analysis Questions

1. What epistemological assumptions, if any, underlie the curriculum's organization?

2. What psychological assumptions, if any, underlie the curriculum's organization?

3. What other assumptions, if any, related to your curriculum's organization underlie the curriculum? (See Tables 7.1, 7.2, and 7.3 for ideas.)

NOTES

1. See, for example, King and Brownell (1966) and Phenix (1964).
2. See Strike and Posner (1983).
3. This pattern came to be called the "spiral" curriculum. Actually "spiral" is a misnomer; "helical" would be a more accurate term.
4. This section is largely based on Strike and Posner (1976).
5. See Chapter Four.
6. See also Phillips and Kelly (1978) and Strike and Posner (1976).
7. I would like to thank Pamela Moss for her help on this section.
8. See Chapter Three.
9. See Chapter Twelve.
10. See Puckett's (1989) critique of Foxfire regarding this point.
11. See Chapter Twelve.

PART THREE

The Curriculum in Use

Up to this point, we have considered the curriculum in its documented form. That is, we have examined only the official curriculum and have ignored the operational curriculum (see Chapter One). But a curriculum that is never used is pointless. And a document, once implementation begins, starts to evolve into a curriculum better adapted to real schools and classrooms, though not the curriculum that its developers intended. An understanding of this process is essential for a full curriculum analysis. Furthermore, using a curriculum typically involves some evaluations, at least student evaluations, and occasionally evaluations of the curriculum itself. Part Three is intended to help you understand the process of curriculum implementation and that of curriculum evaluation. The former is discussed in Chapters Eight and Nine, and the latter in Chapters Ten and Eleven.

CHAPTER 8

Frame Factors

Basic Concepts

The writing program used in Beacon City School District has received attention from school officials from across the state. In fact, eight of the English teachers at nearby Hemingway High School are preparing to visit Beacon in order to determine the feasibility of implementing this program at Hemingway. The program is multifaceted, utilizing computer-equipped writing labs, small-group writing workshops, a school magazine similar to Foxfire, *interdepartmental writing standards for the entire school district, and close cooperation with a nearby college.*

At a planning meeting, the visiting team decides to prepare guidelines for all members of the team to use during its visit. Several members of the team have stressed the importance of checking out all aspects of the program that might affect its successful implementation at Hemingway High. As a member of the team with some background in curriculum study, Helen Levandosky has been asked to prepare a first draft of the guidelines.

This chapter contains the kind of information Helen needs to write the guidelines. As a matter of fact, this chapter is designed to prepare you to assess the feasibility of any curriculum.

An official curriculum is meaningless unless it is translated by teachers into an operational curriculum. However, in order for a teacher to take the weighty document labeled "the district's official curriculum" and breathe life into it, as a director breathes life into a screenplay, the teacher must take many factors into account. These factors include physical, cultural, temporal, economic, organizational, political-legal, and personal considerations that can make or break a curriculum. In a sense, these factors frame the curriculum, acting as both resources for and constraints on the process of curriculum implementation. Because these "frame factors" play a crucial role in curriculum implementation, the curriculum analyst must be able to determine which of them the curriculum developers have anticipated and which they have ignored. Only with such an analysis can one predict the problems that a new curriculum will face or understand why an existing curriculum has faltered or failed.

This chapter explicates five tasks to which all teachers must attend and the major kinds of frame factors that constrain these tasks. The chapter then examines the potential impact of these frame factors on curriculum implementation, concluding with questions that ask you to probe the explicit provisions made by your curriculum for these factors. Then the chapter seeks to identify the special, often unanticipated, factors that developers of curricula working from each of the five perspectives need to consider if their curricula are to be successfully implemented.

THE TASKS OF TEACHING

A curriculum is not implemented until a teacher uses it to teach students; that is, implementation must take the realities of teaching into consideration (see Doyle, 1992; Walker, 1990). The realities of teaching include coping with five tasks: coverage, mastery, management, positive affect, and evaluation (Westbury, 1973). Teachers must cover certain topics, content, skills, objectives, or whatever constitutes the stuff of the curriculum. But coverage is not sufficient. Not only must the teacher cover the breadth of the curriculum, but also the students must learn the material at least at some minimal level of mastery or depth. These two tasks present a dilemma facing every teacher, the coverage/mastery dilemma. The more the teacher emphasizes coverage, the less time the teacher can spend on any one part of the curriculum, thereby sacrificing mastery. On the other hand, the more the teacher emphasizes mastery, the less the teacher can cover. Thus, the teacher is always faced with trade-offs between breadth and depth of treatment.

As if these two tasks were not enough, the teacher is also faced with three others. First, the teacher must manage the classroom. In many cases, this task entails maintaining some semblance of order in a crowded room full of very different children, most of whom would rather be someplace else. Second, in order for teachers to accomplish this task without creating a police state and to derive some satisfaction from teaching, teachers must also develop at least a minimal degree of positive feeling on the part of the students toward the subject matter, the teacher, or the class. Third, the teacher is responsible for evaluating students, for deciding and (especially in the case of statewide standards) communicating what aspects of the curriculum are to "count" and to hold the students accountable for them.

Although some settings allow the teacher to take one or more of them for granted or to regard them as nonproblematic, the five tasks are inherent in teaching. A new curriculum will be resisted to the extent that it interferes with teachers' ability to accomplish these five tasks. If resistance is not politically viable, teachers will adapt or transform an unsuitable curriculum in such a way that they can make the curriculum fit the classroom realities. However, before examining these processes of resistance to a curriculum and adaptation of it, we need to consider the factors that constrain the teacher's ability to accomplish these five tasks.

FRAME FACTORS[1]

Frame factors function as limitations or constraints on teaching, and thus on curriculum implementation. Looking at these factors more positively, we can also regard them as the resources that make teaching possible. As an example, a new physical education curriculum emphasizing fitness may require for its implementation additional equipment, like exercise bikes and rowing machines. The inability of a school to obtain this equipment will limit implementation of the curriculum. Since there always seems to be newer, more sophisticated, or higher-quality equipment on the market, the actual equipment available to the school functions as a physical constraint on curriculum implementation. However, to the extent that there is any equipment at all available for physical education, that equipment functions as a physical resource for implementing the curriculum. The same point could be made regarding money, space, personnel, and administrative organization. All frame factors function two ways, depending on how we choose to look at them. A glass is half empty and half full at the same time.

Curriculum change occurs only to the extent that interactions between teachers, students, and subject matters change. Nevertheless, some frame factors act more directly than others on this interaction. Frame factors that directly affect this interaction, like the availability of textbooks and the content knowledge of the teacher, we term "proximal." Those factors, like budget size, that function more as boundary conditions for the more proximal factors, we term "distal" or "higher-order" frames (Kallos, 1973). This frame-within-a-frame conception is useful for distinguishing between factors. Economic factors, laws and regulations, and demands for accountability are higher-order factors, whereas factors that function more proximally are the temporal, i.e., time available; personal, e.g., teacher competence; organizational, e.g., ability grouping; and physical, e.g., space and equipment. A curriculum analyst who looks for both higher-order and proximal frame factors will be able to identify both factors that directly influence curriculum implementation and ones that have a significant though indirect effect.

Independent of the directness of their effect on teaching and learning, frame factors also vary in the degree to which we can manipulate them. Some factors, like money available for supplies and equipment, can be increased immediately by an administrative decision, though possibly requiring support of the school board and sometimes the taxpayers themselves. Other factors, like space and its configuration, require a significant period of time to modify, once the decision is made. Still others, like family backgrounds of the student population, are not manipulable. Although the diversity or homogeneity, the poverty or affluence, the urban, suburban, or rural character, and the family values of the school population may significantly affect teaching and learning, in most cases they function as an unalterable quality of the school. In a curriculum analysis it is important to determine which frame factors necessary for implementation are, in fact, modifiable and the length of time required to modify them (see Walker, 1990).

Temporal Frames

Time is the most precious resource of the teacher. As teachers we always seem to need far more time than is available. Time thus becomes the archenemy of the teacher confronting the coverage/mastery dilemma. In fact, if time were not limited, there would be no coverage/mastery dilemma in the first place. But because time is always in short supply, teachers are constantly making compromises based on priorities. With so much to cover and so little time, teachers pace their lessons, trying to strike a reasonable balance between breadth and depth—that is, between covering the required content and seeing to it that most students master that content. Therefore, an analysis of the temporal frame factors of a curriculum considers the sheer quantity of content included in the curriculum, the difficulty of the content, and the audience that is expected to master it, since these three factors affect the time necessary to teach the curriculum. In addition, temporal factors include time needed by teachers to prepare for teaching, e.g., lesson planning; to support students, e.g., meet with them after class; and to provide feedback to students, e.g., correct homework assignments.

The amount of time available is not the only temporal constraint on the curriculum. Frequency and duration of time also affect curriculum implementation. In elementary schools, teachers of subjects like physical education, art, and music (the so-called "specials" that often meet only once or twice a week) must deal with the problems caused by lack of continuity. In secondary schools, curricula that require laboratory and project work, as well as other teaching methods that are not neatly accommodated by forty- or fifty-minute periods, are often difficult to implement.

Seasonal changes function as both resources and constraints on curriculum. Holidays and seasons offer opportunities to relate curriculum content to the student's everyday world. But inclement weather can also make certain curriculum activities, like field trips and stargazing, problematic.

Institutional priority for each of the subjects is expressed not only by the total quantity of instructional time allotted but also by such factors as the time of day the class meets and willingness to tolerate interruptions during class. Thus, at the elementary level, reading and arithmetic typically not only are allotted more than one-half of the total and two-thirds of the instructional time (Goodlad, 1984), but also are usually taught in the mornings, when the children are presumably still fresh and ready to learn. Some elementary schools are prohibiting any announcements, pullouts (removal of children from the class for special instruction), or other interruptions during this part of the day.

At the secondary level, the different subjects vie for places in the students' schedules. This competition becomes more contentious at certain times, particularly when the stakes are raised. When there is pressure to increase graduation requirements, for example, as the NCEE report recommended in 1983, then elective subjects lose student enrollment. When this drop in enrollment occurs during a time of economic belt tightening, the costs of losing students might include loss of staff and even loss of the entire program. This sort of threat may well create an environment for certain kinds of curriculum changes, while inhibiting other kinds. For example, a business education department might develop curricula in business math and data processing in times when math and computer education are squeezing traditional business electives out of student schedules.

In your curriculum analysis you may be able to determine if the curriculum represents a response to these sorts of time pressures. You may also be able to assess the likelihood that the curriculum will thrive within the current environment of temporal constraints.

Physical Frames

If time is the most precious commodity in teaching, the physical space in which teachers teach and the stuff with which they teach are the most obvious and tangible commodities. The physical frame within which a curriculum functions includes the natural environment surrounding the school, e.g., nature trails; the built environment of the school and classroom, e.g., science laboratories; and the equipment and materials provided for teaching and learning e.g., not only computer and associated hardware and software, but also other technologies such as graphing calculators. Obviously, of these three types of physical frame factors, only the last one is manipulable in a short-term sense. The other two are either not manipulable at all or manipulable only by means of very significant outlays of money and disruptions in school operations. Therefore, physical frame factors generally exert a conservative influence on the curriculum, limiting curriculum change to those changes that fit into the existing physical setting.

It was an analysis of this conservative influence of the physical frame that led McKinney and Westbury (1975) "to point to the hand of the past as a generic *macro-frame* having a profound effect on the functioning of the schools at any given point in time" (p. 49). Until a school system can attract outside funds, increase local taxation, or use existing local funds for constructing or remodeling buildings and purchasing additional supplies and materials, the existing facilities limit curricular choice. The existing physical frame, regardless of the purposes for which it was intended, makes certain curricular forms likely, others unlikely, and still others impossible.

For the curriculum analysis your task is to identify any special physical requirements of your curriculum without which teachers will find it frustrating to implement. Then you can decide if most schools can meet these requirements.

Political-Legal Frames

Classrooms are not autonomous units. "The range of possible classroom events . . . is always circumscribed by prior decisions (about such matters as funding and time allocation) at higher governmental levels" (McKinney & Westbury, 1975, p. 48). State curricular requirements, state graduation requirements for students, state aid for building, state limits on taxation, state certification requirements for teachers, state and federal program documentation requirements, and federal mandates influence events in the classroom. For example, the New York State Regents Action Plan in the 1980s added a fourth year of high school social studies to the graduation requirements for all New York State students. The state has mandated that this additional year include a course on "participation in government." As might be expected, this mandate has spawned a variety of curriculum development efforts in school districts around the state attempting to develop more experiential social studies courses. Conversely, states with textbook adoption boards—Texas is an example—that decide which textbooks local school districts can choose from restrict decision making and curb initiative at the local level.

Perhaps the greatest impact on local classrooms from the state education bureaucracy comes from state-mandated testing. When the state, as a means of holding schools, teachers, and students accountable, prescribes a particular set of tests for all teachers to give to their students, the state focuses everyone's attention on those tests, often to the exclusion of everything else. Once the state decides to require those tests, the textbooks used in schools, advice from professional journals, admonitions from schools of education, the students' expressed needs and interests, parents' objections, and the teachers' better judgments all get pushed aside. As might be expected, the greater the pressure for accountability, the greater the influence of the test.

Related to state-mandated testing are standards. Standards have much to say about the nature of curriculum and the work of the teacher. The political influence of standards is dependent on how teachers and curriculum developers are held accountable to those standards. Their political clout is strengthened by dictates from state education departments (who are likewise experiencing federal pressures) that now often require *all* students to successfully complete standardized tests that are supposedly tied to standards. All of the major standards documents include attention to the idea that all students can learn the disciples in meaningful ways (as Bruner asserted, see page 59). Thus, implementation of a standards-based curriculum often means that tracking of students is diminished, eliminated, or reconfigured[2] (and thus is also tied to organizational frames).

Likewise, standards are closely linked cultural frames. This linkage is evident in debates over the inclusion of "Intelligent Design" or creationism as a counterweight to evolution in science standards, and in the ongoing "Math Wars" which pit reformers trying to facilitate teaching based on the NCTM standards against traditionalists who argue against the "fuzzy math" espoused in the standards (Colvin, 1999).

Standards tend to focus on the tasks of coverage, mastery, and evaluation, typically making explicit pleas to diminish the number of topics covered to allow for greater depth in the study of key ideas. *The National Science Education Standards* state that there should be less emphasis on covering many science topics and more emphasis on studying a few fundamental science concepts (National Research Council, 1996, p. 119).[3] This push to reduce the number of topics is common across the standards documents.

The issues for curriculum analysis are to determine how well the curriculum aligns with the standards in terms of coverage verses mastery and the inclusion of the same content and skills (and not a substantial number of additional topics and skills beyond those described in the standards). You should also evaluate the curriculum's approach to the nature (or structure) of the discipline and how students go about learning about the discipline. None of this is likely to matter much if schools and teachers are not held accountable to meeting the standards, so the evaluation aspect (see Chapter 10) is also necessary to describe in your analysis of the curriculum.

Organizational Frames

As stimulating or inhibiting as state- and national-level decisions are, these decisions are remote from the real action, namely, the action at the local level. In most cases it is the school district that makes textbook adoption decisions and develops curriculum, framed by state-level guidelines. Although these sorts of district- and state-level decisions influence classroom events, educators are increasingly focusing attention on the school building as the site for school improvement and curriculum change. Although the bureaucratic infrastructure of schools includes grade-level and department-level organizations in the elementary and secondary schools, respectively, the school as a whole is now recognized as the organizational unit that most significantly determines the extent to which a new curriculum will flourish or wither.[4] Sarah Lightfoot's (1983) series of portraits of "good" high schools and Theodore Sizer's (1985) study of American high schools are especially worth reading in this regard.

Beyond these general administrative factors, other organizational factors exert significant influence on curriculum change. Proximal factors such as class size, mainstreaming policies, ability groupings, and curriculum groupings— e.g., vocational and college-bound—exert a direct influence on the classroom by affecting the composition of the class, while distal factors such as school size are indirect influences. Whether a factor is proximal or distal does not necessarily determine its impact as a constraint or resource for curriculum change. A distal factor, while indirect in its effect, may nevertheless significantly constrain curriculum change. Consider, for example, the effect of grouping teachers according to their subject matters, i.e., departmentalization, on efforts to implement interdisciplinary, problem-centered courses.

The issue for curriculum analysis is the extent to which the curriculum you are examining requires special organizational provisions or can flourish in schools as they now are. Also, you need to study current national and state regulations, mandates, standards, and programs to identify any potential frictions with the curriculum.

Personal (or Personnel) Frames

Most schools operate with remarkably similar time constraints, buildings, equipment, and organizations. What makes each school unique is the personal characteristics of the teachers, students, administrators, custodians, and other support personnel who occupy it. Although student populations change due to shifting demographics or redistricting decisions and teachers retire, quit, or transfer, the school personnel functions as a relatively stable frame factor. It may shift over the years, but from year to year it is highly predictable.

Not only do the characteristics of the people that spend the majority of their waking hours in the school remain relatively stable, but also, more than any other factor, they directly affect curriculum change. Consider the importance of students and teachers in curriculum implementation. Characteristics of the student population are a major determinant of the success or failure of a curriculum. The extent to which students possess academic skills such as reading, mathematical, writing, library, and computer skills, interpersonal skills such as the ability to work cooperatively in small groups, and background knowledge such as familiarity with the classics in literature and with current events all can require major adjustments in the curriculum during implementation. Likewise, student interests, psychological and social needs, and career aspirations can lead to the negotiations between students and teachers that shape the operational curriculum we discussed in Chapter One. The teachers also play a highly significant role in determining the success and the direction of a curriculum change. Teachers' subject-matter knowledge, teaching and administrative skills, knowledge of the students and what they bring, dedication to teaching, willingness to extend themselves, sense of collegiality, and openness to new ideas all can play significant roles in determining the success of a new curriculum. Staff development can increase teachers' skills and knowledge but is less likely to alter fundamentally their basic attitudes.

In particular, the teachers' beliefs about such matters as the formality of their role with children, how children learn, classroom management, the nature of knowledge, the reasons for learning their subject matter, and their role in curriculum decision making determine the degree to which a new curriculum "fits" in a particular teacher's classroom.[5] In extreme cases, teachers totally reject a new curriculum that is inconsistent or accept one wholesale that is consistent with most of their beliefs. However, more typically teachers shape the new curriculum to their beliefs; that is, teachers adapt rather than adopt curricula. Any curriculum that teachers cannot readily adapt, they regard as "impractical" (Doyle & Ponder, 1977–1978).

For curriculum analysis you need to draw on your experiences both as a teacher (if you have them) and with teachers, in order to estimate the degree of consistency between the curriculum's implicit beliefs and those of the teachers that will implement it. If you have the time, interviews with teachers also can be informative.[6] The issue that you need to address is not whether teachers will accept or reject the curriculum, but how they might shape it as they attempt to make it fit their belief systems. Consider also the kinds of staff development programs that should accompany the curriculum if it is to be successfully implemented; think about what those programs should emphasize and what approaches they should employ.

Economic Frames

Curriculum change, like almost everything else, has a bottom line. This bottom line can be expressed in terms of costs and benefits. Usually, cost and benefit are defined in terms of dollar expenditures and income generated or saved; clearly, this interpretation is too narrow for our context. We need to consider other costs and benefits, involving such factors as staff and student morale; student learning; time and effort devoted to teaching, learning, and administration; community and parent relations; and the "ripple effect" of the change. For example, a change in staff morale might be characterized as a cost if morale appears to get worse or as a benefit if it appears to improve.

This broad view of costs and benefits can be used to explain a common phenomenon related to curriculum change: that is, why most curriculum changes last for three to five years before practices return to "normal." During the first year of a new curriculum—or, for that matter, any innovation—costs are relatively high in terms of time and effort, but typically they are subsidized by the state or the agency interested in making the change. Therefore, the teachers do not have to bear the full weight of the change. Perhaps more important, the benefits exceed the costs, as teachers feel rejuvenated by the change in routine and gain prestige as innovators. If more than one teacher is involved in the change, an esprit de corps may develop, reducing the loneliness that many teachers feel behind their classroom doors. As the third and fourth years progress, the luster of the new curriculum starts to dull and the reputation of the teachers as innovators begins to fade. At about this time, the governmental or private support for the change begins to decrease, as these groups determine that the "seed money" is no longer necessary. At some point between the third and fifth years, the costs begin to outstrip the benefits and the curriculum change effort starts to lose momentum and eventually dissipates (Doyle & Ponder, 1977–1978).

The importance of outside support for a curriculum change is particularly critical in districts that are not affluent. It takes a great deal of time, money, and energy to maintain any organization. Keeping a school district operating is particularly costly. Just getting through the day and the year leaves nearly everybody exhausted and the entire budget spent. "Crisis management" characterizes the way many school districts function, putting out daily "brushfires" so that the schools can continue to get by. Outside support in the form of additional staff and materials is necessary in most districts for them to consider seriously a curriculum change. Once that support is withdrawn, the costs of maintaining basic services to students tend to drain resources away from the curriculum change efforts, and the schools revert to more traditional practices (McKinney & Westbury, 1975).

A curriculum analysis includes an estimate of the probable costs and benefits associated with the curriculum change, including a determination of who will likely bear the costs and experience the benefits.

Cultural Frames

The frame factors presented so far help us understand the technical dimensions of curriculum implementation: that is, what provisions are necessary for implementing a curriculum successfully. However, an understanding of these frame factors is not sufficient to prepare us for implementing many curricula. A curriculum not only must fit into the temporal, physical, organizational, political-legal, economic, and personal frames of a school and its community but also must fit into a culture.

A curriculum depends on two different sets of cultural factors, the culture within the school and the culture of the community in which the school exists. A school itself represents a culture, that is, a set of accepted beliefs and norms governing people's conduct. For example, the "effective schools" research (Purkey & Smith, 1983) mentioned earlier identified certain aspects of the culture of elementary schools that were especially "effective," i.e., had comparatively high achievement test scores: (1) high expectations for and recognition of academic achievement; (2) a safe and orderly environment; (3) collegial relationships among staff members; (4) a sense of community; (5) parental involvement and support.

In a broader sense a curriculum represents those aspects of a group's culture that receive official sanction by the school. But which group's culture deserves this legitimization? Since our society is composed of many groups, this question can become quite contentious. Current debate about whether or not to declare English the official language of the United States, and the associated issues surrounding bilingual education, illustrate this point. Therefore, curriculum change is saturated with values and value conflicts.

That curricula can be value-laden is obvious in subjects like sex education and civics. It is less obvious that all curricula are inherently value-laden. Curricula do not have to be controversial or explicitly political to represent the result of some group's decisions to include, and thereby legitimize, one point of view and to ignore another. For example, history curricula select only what the developers consider to be the most significant events, people, and themes. Likewise, English literature curricula include the works of certain authors, while ignoring those of others. Even a mathematics curriculum, which is derived from a subject matter with the reputation of being true in an absolute sense, represents a set of tacit, culturally based decisions. Virtually all Western mathematics curricula emphasize the mathematical knowledge of academic mathematicians, while ignoring the "folk" mathematics of groups such as tailors, street market sellers, odds-makers, supermarket shoppers, and meat packers, who have developed coherent and highly accurate mathematical systems for accomplishing their everyday tasks.[7] In a different culture—for example, in a different country or era—the curriculum might well embody a different set of values.

A curriculum becomes controversial when a group of people within a community decide that the values embodied in it conflict with their own values and challenge the school's decision to include these offensive values. Even giving equal time to everybody's values does not necessarily extricate the school from these conflicts. Such a move still tacitly legitimizes values that some groups might find at best inappropriate, or at worst repugnant. For example, although some fundamentalists only want equal time for creationist accounts of life, most biologists consider the inclusion of creationism to be inappropriate for a biology curriculum.

Recognizing that curricula embody cultural values enables the curriculum analyst to anticipate potential conflicts that might accompany an attempted curriculum change. In order to predict these possible conflicts, the analyst needs to identify both the values embodied by the curriculum and the values represented within the local community. These two tasks of analysis become more difficult the closer one is to either the curriculum or the community. The job of the analyst is to find a set of tacit beliefs and to make them explicit; it requires the ability to examine what others take for granted.

Table 8.1 summarizes the wide array of frame factors that act as both resources for and constraints on the curriculum.

ILLUSORY CURRICULUM CHANGE: A WORD OF CAUTION

Frame factors are deceptive. Some are relatively easy to manipulate. Microscopes can be purchased, new textbooks can be ordered, schedules can be modularized, ability groupings can be abolished, grade levels can be combined, teachers can be assigned to teams, and walls can even be removed. But none of these changes by itself constitutes a curriculum change. It may be necessary to modify frame factors to permit curriculum change, but modifying frame factors is never sufficient. Changing the operational curriculum requires altering what actually happens as teachers, students, and subject matters interact, not just modifying the frames within which these interactions occur. A curriculum analyst is able to look beyond superficial alterations in order to determine if substantive curriculum change is likely to take place.

PERSPECTIVES ON CURRICULUM IMPLEMENTATION

When a curriculum based on a particular perspective is implemented in a classroom, certain frame factors become problematic as the teacher attempts to cover the curriculum, ensure that all students learn it, manage the classroom,

TABLE 8.1 Frame Factors

Factor	Description
Temporal	Time: quantity, frequency, duration, scheduling
Physical	Natural and built environment; materials and equipment
Political-legal	State and federal mandates, limits, requirements
Organizational	Administrative factors, including size, groupings, policies
Personal	Backgrounds, abilities, interests of students, staff, and parents
Economic	Costs and benefits broadly conceived
Cultural	Values and beliefs of school and community

and develop in students a positive affect toward the subject matter and the class.[8] Each perspective makes explicit provisions for certain frame factors. However, as we pointed out in Chapter Three, each perspective tends to ignore other factors.

Traditional

A traditional curriculum requires a classroom characterized by (1) focus on a single subject matter, (2) teacher-centered instruction employing lecture and recitation methods in whole-group settings, (3) materials emphasizing text-books and worksheets, (4) regular assessment by written tests, and (5) an emphasis on grades. That is, it requires a traditional classroom. The lecture and recitation methods and the emphasis on textbooks and worksheets allow the teacher to handle the time pressures resulting from the content/mastery dilemma (Westbury, 1973). These methods are complemented by the emphasis on textbooks and worksheets, the former providing for appropriate coverage and the latter providing the drill believed necessary for mastery of the content. These methods also allow the teacher to maintain control of the students and to avoid disruptive behavior. The evaluation methods not only add to the control of the teacher, but also provide for a system of accountability for both teachers and students. The subject matter focus fits well into the typical departmental organization of U.S. secondary schools, but less well into the early elementary grades.

In summary, this perspective allows the teacher to accomplish all five tasks of teaching at a minimal level at least, with its strengths in content coverage and management. It should come as no surprise that traditional curricula are well adapted to traditional schools and classrooms. In fact this perspective not only provides for at least minimal accomplishment of all four tasks, but also does so within the frame factors operative in most schools.

Experiential

Not so for experiential curricula. Experiential curricula place special demands on schools and teachers. Generally speaking these curricula have the following characteristics: (1) they cross subject-matter lines; (2) they rely more on the community as a resource than on textbooks and other prepared instructional materials; (3) they require student-centered classrooms emphasizing small-group, cooperative, rather than whole-group, competitive student work; (4) they are organized around ongoing tasks, e.g., projects, that take relatively long periods of time to complete; (5) they depend on a teacher who acts more as a facilitator and resource than as the person in control; and (6) they employ evaluation methods directed at the demonstration of competence in real world tasks, rather than on written tests emphasizing recall of facts and terminology.

Implementation of these curricula in typical U.S. schools and classrooms presents formidable problems. It takes more teaching and planning time, and more effort, to involve students in curricular and instructional decision making, and to go out into the community or to bring community resources into the classroom. Content coverage may be significantly reduced, which may cost students success on state-mandated tests.

Thus, although the personal rewards may be greater for both teacher and student, there are also substantial personal costs in terms of time and energy. Furthermore, accountability to external authorities can pose a significant threat to these programs.[9] In terms of the five tasks of teaching, mastery and positive affect are the strengths of this perspective, while coverage can present serious problems for it. While student involvement in projects can reduce management problems, small-group work and out-of-class trips require careful planning and close supervision to avoid management problems.

Structure of the Disciplines

A structure-of-the-disciplines curriculum is characterized as follows: it (1) is confined to a single discipline within a single subject; (2) focuses on a small set of fundamental conceptual themes; (3) requires extensive use of primary source material and manipulatives, e.g., labs; (4) utilizes written tests emphasizing problem solving; and (5) requires a teacher who models inquiry in the discipline, rather than acts as a source of information. The single-subject focus fits well into the departmental organization of U.S. secondary schools, but less well into the more self-contained structure of elementary school classrooms. The emphasis on fundamental themes and active inquiry requires in-depth treatment of topics. This requirement increases the time pressures placed on teachers as they attempt to prepare students for standardized tests. Unless these tests fit the curriculum, students are unlikely to have covered enough content to do well on the tests. The greater the state emphasis on accountability, the greater the time pressures become.

Personal factors are also critical. Teachers typically need a substantial amount of special training both in the discipline and in the inquiry methods of teaching. Students need a high degree of literacy, the ability to manipulate abstract ideas, and intrinsic motivation to drive their inquiry. Thus, these curricula are suited for the more academically oriented students and for teachers whose education has prepared them to be members of a scholarly community.

Thus, of the five tasks of teaching, mastery (i.e., depth) is given the highest priority. For high-ability students who find the approach intellectually exciting, the teacher accomplishes the task of developing a positive affect, but only for these students. For all other students, both the tasks of developing a positive affect and the task of classroom management can be highly problematic. For all students the task of covering the content is a problem to the extent that the accountability measures are not consistent with this perspective.

Behavioral

Behavioral curricula have the following requirements: (1) discrete performance objectives closely aligned with evaluation methods; (2) teacher-controlled methods utilizing explicit teaching of skills with ample opportunities for practicing the skills; (3) criterion-referenced evaluation methods; and (4) a reward system for appropriate behavior and successful performance. As with traditional curricula, the teacher-controlled methods and emphasis on test performance are well suited to traditional classrooms. In addition, the emphasis on discrete, skill-oriented activities with each activity culminating in a discrete product—e.g., the completion of a worksheet—lends a sense of productivity and purposefulness to the classroom. Students know clearly what is expected of them. Keeping students busy at tasks also makes classroom behavior more manageable.

On the other hand, criterion-referenced measurement, necessary in the behavioristic determination of mastery, is inconsistent with the tendency of schools to use evaluation for comparing individuals with each other in order to sort students out by level of academic achievement. Furthermore, the belief that IQ differences are not innate and that all children can become equally capable of learning tends to conflict with many teachers' beliefs.

This perspective enables the teacher to cope with all five tasks of teaching. Its strengths are in its emphasis on mastery of skills and classroom management. To the extent that positive affect develops as a consequence of successful performance, as Bloom (1971) claims it does, this perspective enables the teacher to accomplish this task admirably. Furthermore, to the extent that the curriculum consists of a set of discrete skills, this perspective allows the teacher to cover the breadth of those skills in an efficient manner.

Constructivist

Constructivist curricula (1) treat topics in great depth, (2) teach skills and concepts only in the context of students' background experiences and knowledge, (3) rely on intrinsic motivation, and (4) prefer clinical interviews and observation to standardized tests for evaluation. Emphasis on depth rather than breadth and on developing skills in the context of background knowledge and experience takes more time, resulting in less content coverage. To the extent that the state-mandated or standardized tests are not designed from this perspective, this reduced coverage puts students and their teachers in jeopardy. The constructivist perspective's deemphasis of written short-answer or multiple-choice tests exacerbates this concern. Further, a reliance on intrinsic motivation leaves the teacher vulnerable to disruptions from students who do not find the work intrinsically rewarding. Thus, the teacher's concerns for accountability and management are not well addressed by constructivist curricula in typical classrooms.

Perhaps the most significant feature of constructivist curricula is their emphasis on tasks that require students to think and to make sense of phenomena. Thought-and meaning-oriented curricula are inherently "vulnerable" and tend to get "pushed around" in typical classrooms (Doyle, 1986). The need to provide tasks that cannot be accomplished in rote or routine fashion results in the presentation of novel and ambiguous tasks requiring thought but also a substantial amount of risk for the student. Students respond by trying to negotiate with the teacher to lower the risk and decrease the ambiguity, constantly looking for clearer specification of what the teacher wants. These negotiations may transform a constructivist curriculum into one requiring less ambiguity and risk, but also requiring less thought and having less meaning—a curriculum more closely resembling a behavioral or a traditional curriculum (Doyle, 1986).

In short, the constructivist perspective derives its strength from its emphasis on mastery and understanding and the positive affect that results from students seeing the relationship of curriculum content to their own thoughts and activities. However, implementation of constructivist curricula may also lead to classrooms that are not as smooth-running and well ordered and to a slower-paced instruction. These two aspects of the constructivist perspective may present problems for teachers related to two of the five tasks of teaching: management and coverage.

An obvious conclusion from this analysis of the five perspectives is that the behavioral and traditional perspectives are best suited to the typical classroom. But does this conclusion mean that these two perspectives are better than the others? Not at all! It simply means that they offer the path of least resistance in most classrooms. More important, it means that if you tried to implement a curriculum based on one of the other three perspectives in a typical classroom without changing any of the frame factors, you would probably see the curriculum transformed into one that more closely resembles a behavioral or traditional curriculum. For example, attempts to implement inquiry-oriented curricula like PSSC physics have resulted in revamped textbooks but not revamped teaching methods, in spite of serious attention paid to in-service training. Let us look more closely at the problems one might encounter in trying to implement an experiential, a discipline-based, or a constructivist curriculum.

THE MEANING-ORIENTED CURRICULUM

The experiential, structure-of-the-disciplines, and constructivist curricula contrast with the other two perspectives in their focus on meaning, that is, in putting a premium on students making sense of their world and really understanding what they are doing. When considering implementation problems, this common focus is more significant than are the differences between the perspectives regarding the basis and essence of meaning. Those who espouse one perspective—the experiential—believe that the individual derives meaning by relating a particular curricular topic to individual interests, problems, needs, or everyday experiences; proponents of another—the structure-of-the-disciplines approach—believe that meaning derives from the relationship of knowledge to fundamental concepts in the discipline and to the inquiry process that produces the knowledge; those who favor the third perspective—the constructivist—hold that students acquire meaning when they relate content to their preconceptions and prior knowledge. However, all of them believe that providing students with a meaningful education is the primary goal, and that the struggle for meaning and real understanding constitutes good teaching.

The emphasis on meaning, sense making, and understanding has led to certain kinds of implementation problems. We could summarize the problems mentioned above by saying that the critical frame factors have been and continue to be the temporal, organizational, and personal. Because meaning-oriented curricula take the time to explore topics in greater depth and to show students how the topics relate to other things—e.g., to their own experiences or beliefs—these curricula are not able to cover as much ground. That is, they sacrifice some breadth for increased depth. This trade-off would not be problematic if it were not for the major political-legal factor, that is, accountability pressure exerted by the state and local communities in the form of mandatory statewide or districtwide testing. To the extent that a meaning-oriented curriculum does not fit the tests, there is likely to be pressure to transform it, rather than vice versa. There seem to be few policymakers seriously challenging the domination of the standardized test. Current reform efforts like the effective schools movement, outcomes-based education, curriculum alignment, and mastery learning only serve to support this domination.

To make matters worse, meaning-oriented curricula create increased management demands by changing instruction from teacher-centered to more student- or activity-centered and the teacher's role from transmitter of information, authority figure, or manager to facilitator, consultant, resource person, or colleague. These demands become problematic when personal frame factors leave teachers and students unprepared in terms of their own background and previous experiences. To have students assume an increased responsibility for their own education requires teachers who know how to assume new roles and manage complex activity structures and students who have had previous successful experience in working cooperatively without close adult supervision (Winschitl, 1999, Airasian and Walsh, 1997).

The lesson from this analysis should be clear: To try to implement an experiential, structure-of-the-disciplines, or constructivist curriculum (or some combination of the three) while coping with the temporal, organizational, and personal factors that frame the tasks of teaching is likely to result in disappointment or even disaster. One viable alternative to educational surrender is to look for educational opportunities that are not so highly constrained by these factors. For example, elective courses and the non-college-bound high school track tend to have less accountability pressure. Alternative schools may offer opportunities in which students have had more experience working cooperatively without close supervision. There are always certain teachers, classes, and even schools that constitute sites where change is possible within an otherwise stable, seemingly rigid system. Analysis of frame factors represents one way to identify those sites.

Furthermore, a reformer taking a more radical posture could use frame factor analysis to identify those aspects of schools that must change if fundamental curriculum change is to be feasible. The reformer might use a determination of the factors that constrain curriculum change—e.g., a change toward more meaning-oriented classrooms—as the basis for developing an agenda for school reform. For example, Theodore Sizer, after studying many U.S. high schools, concluded that significant school reform needs to address the following set of problems: inadequate amounts of time for teachers to do what they know needs to be done, passive and docile students, impersonalized and non-intellectual environment for students, the attempt to teach too many subjects, lack of student motivation and engagement in learning, poor working conditions for teachers, lack of respect for the craft of teaching, and a stifling top-down bureaucratic structure of schools. Note the difference between Sizer's (1985) characterization of the problems with schools and those identified by the NCEE (1983) in the *Nation at Risk* report.[10] Sizer developed a set of principles that he claims would, if implemented, address these problems. These nine principles form the platform that members of his Coalition of Essential Schools attempt to implement. The first four of the nine principles relate to purpose, content, and pedagogy, although each also has direct implications for frame factors (Sizer, 1985). The rest of the principles relate directly to specific frame factors: Principles 5 and 6 to the organizational, Principles 7 and 8 to the cultural, and Principle 9 to the economic.

1. The school's central purpose is to help adolescents learn to use their minds. This principle serves to focus the school's purpose in order to prevent dilution of school resources in nonessential areas.
2. In terms of the curriculum, "less is more. . . . Curriculum decisions should be guided by the aim of student mastery and achievement rather than by an effort to cover content" (p. 226). This principle attempts to address the time constraints faced by all teachers.
3. "The school's goals should be universal while the means to these goals will vary as the students themselves vary" (p. 226). This principle provides a way to deal with the diversity of students, i.e., the personal factor, while conserving resources.
4. The most appropriate metaphor for schools should be "student-as-worker" rather than "teacher-as-deliverer-of-instructional-services." This metaphor requires a pedagogy in the form of "coaching" students to "learn how to learn" (p. 226). This principle requires adequate time, a physical work space, and enough material resources to allow teacher and student to work together in this relationship.
5. "Teaching and learning should be personalized to the maximum feasible extent." To allow for personalization, pedagogical and logistical decisions should be placed in the hands of principals and teachers (p. 226).
6. A high school diploma should be awarded upon "demonstration of mastery," i.e., an "exhibition" by the student "that he can do important things" (p. 226). "As the diploma is awarded when earned, the school's program proceeds with no strict age-grading and no system of 'credits earned' by 'time spent' in class" (pp. 226–227).
7. The tone of the school should stress high expectations, trust, and decency.
8. Teachers and principals should each be committed to general education, rather than to a single subject, and also committed to multiple roles as teacher, counselor, and manager.

9. Services should be reduced in some areas so that these new commitments do not increase the school budget by more than 10 percent.

Sizer is one of the few educational reformers to seriously consider both issues of purpose, content, and organization as well as issues of resources and constraints on teaching.

FRAME FACTORS: A MULTICULTURAL VIEW [11]

The personal and cultural frames are both relevant to one of the key questions in multicultural education: how to adapt the curriculum so that it takes into account the students' cultural and ethnic backgrounds.

In 1928 Lewis Meriam, in writing about the education of American Indians, made an eloquent plea for teachers to adapt curricula to individual students:

> "Indian tribes and individual Indians within the tribes vary so greatly that a standard content and method of education, not matter how carefully they might be prepared, would be worse than futile. . . The curriculum must not be uniform and standardized. The textbooks must not be prescribed. The teacher must be free to gather material from the life of Indians about her, so that the little children may proceed from the known to the unknowns and not be plunged at once into a world where all is unknown and unfamiliar. The little desert Indian in a early grade who is required to read in English from a standard school reader about the ship that sails the sea has no mental background to understand what it is all about and the task of the teacher is rendered almost impossible. The material, particularly the early material, must come from local Indian life, or at least be within the scope of the child's experience" (Meriam, 1928, pp. 32-33).

With the increasing diversity in American schools, this advice to adapt curriculum to the needs of specific students and groups is more relevant than ever. Students from different social, economic, and cultural backgrounds, not surprisingly, learn best when teachers use strategies compatible with those backgrounds. There are several notable studies about how women and students from different minority groups learn best that could help guide the way toward classrooms where more children could be successful.

For many students the relationships with their teachers determine to a great extent how much they will learn. Janice Hale (1982) found that, because many Black students are accustomed to frequent personal interaction at home, they learn best when there is consistent interaction between teacher and students. Roland Tharp and Ronald Gallimore found that native Hawaiian children learned best in classrooms that were structured so that they could work collaboratively with one another (1988, cited in Fillmore, 1992). The researcher attributed this phenomenon to social interaction between children and adults in their homes. They found that Hawaiian children took a great deal of responsibility in managing their own daily activities.

For women, too, relationships with teachers are important to their learning. Mary Belenky found that for women's intellectual growth acceptance and encouragement were most important. The women she interviewed told her they learned best when they felt secure enough to ask questions, to reveal gaps in their knowledge, and to take risks. The teachers who are "benign" and provided "models of thinking as a human, imperfect, and attainable activity" enables them to feel secure enough to learn (Belenky, 1986, p. 217).

Accounts by individual students also highlight the importance of teacher-student relationships. Imani Perry (1988), for example, talks about how close children and adults in Black and Hispanic cultures are, frequently attending the same weekend parties. The adults earn children's respect as a result of these very close relationships. At school, if Black children don't have close relationships with their teachers, the children sometimes do not see a reason to follow their directions or respect their authority.

Ian Shen, who came as an adult to the United States from China, said that his learning to compose in English was "learning the values of Anglo-American society" (Shen, 1989, p. 460). The comment one writing teacher made, for example, to "Just write what you think" is based on the principle of "protecting and promoting individuality (and private property)" (Shen, 1989, p. 460). That principle is in direct contrast to the values of modestly and humbleness he learned in China:". . . presenting the 'self' too obviously would give people the impression of being disrespectful of the Communist Party in political writings and boastfulness in scholarly writings" (Shen, 1989, p. 460). To write successfully in English, Ian Shen felt that he had to redefine himself, to take on an American identity, while still keeping his Chinese identity to write in Chinese.

To help make minority students aware of the differences in writing from one situation to the next, Ian Shen says: "It would be helpful if [the teacher] pointed out the different cultural/ideological connotations of the word 'I,' the connotations that exist in a group-centered culture. To sharpen the contrast, it might be useful to design papers on topics like 'The Individual vs. The Group: China vs. America 'or' Different 'I's' in Different Cultures'" (Shen, 1989, p. 466).

Social and economic class, too, can impact students' success in school. More affluent parents with confidence and the required knowledge of the school system are more likely to intervene on their children's behalf. They can afford outside help or insure that their children are placed with the best teachers (Lareau, 1989, cited in Oakes, 1999).

No school curriculum can address all the needs of every American social or ethnic group. Some models, however, provide structures that allow different perspectives in the classroom. Whether they help minority students adjust to current school situations or allow students to question society's social and economic foundations, all these models are based on teachers' knowledge of and respect for students' cultures of origin.

Some support models are based on incorporating aspects of students' home cultures. In her book, *AFFIRMING DIVERSITY*, Sonia Nieto describes a program based on building strong, supportive relationships between teachers and students. Developed for primarily inner city Hispanics, it grew out of the knowledge teachers had of the importance of close family relationships in Hispanic households (Nieto, 1996).

Another model demonstrates the supports that can be helpful to students beginning a more rigorous academic program. (Advancement Via Individual Determination) AVID includes teaching students how to apply to college, helping them make connections with academically oriented students, and bridging cultural gaps between home and school (Moll and Ruiz, 2002).

Even the physical arrangements of our schools and classrooms can facilitate learning for students who might otherwise fail. In her article on teaching elementary Navajo children, Vera John describes two contrasting schools and the effects they have on the children. At one Bureau of Indian Affairs school on a rural reservation, the buildings are tall, the students' desks arranged in rows. Children and their parents approach the school "with trepidation and fear" (John-Steiner, 1972, p. 332). Children sit in their desks silently, rarely participating in any discussion.

In another school, the buildings are brush shelters and tents. All the students work around the same table; all the teachers and children use the same blackboard. The children act very differently in the second school, a physical setting more familiar to them. They cluster around each other, "touching their buddies' hair and arms or holding hands even during lessons. . . The Navajo children, who have been described as shy, are alert and vocal" (John-Steiner, 1972, pp. 333).

Some model curricula are based on children's varied knowledge and experiences. Shirley Brice Health, after studying the ways students from differing economic backgrounds used language at home, developed a curriculum to incorporate the strengths of each group. Children from one group learned to tell stories to entertain each other and adults in their community. Taking one event, they embellished, repeated words or lines, and made up elaborate variations. In school, however, they were consistently failing by the time they were in the fourth grade. They could not set a scene for a story or introduce characters, and often the point of the story was not clear to teachers. "The close personal network which [gave them] their context and the meaning at home [had] no counterpart at school" (Heath, 1990, pp. 296-297).

It would not have been enough for their teacher to teach points of grammar or punctuation; it was not simply the words or sentence structures that were problematic. It was the ways the children thought those words and sentences should be used. Their teachers asked the children to tape stories about their communities. Their stories were given to children from another group with different "ways with words." The listeners then taped questions they had. "Gradually the learning center tapes," says Health, "contained WHAT, WHO, WHY, WHEN questions . . ." (Heath, 1990, p. 292). The stories eventually incorporated the "ways with words" of both groups, allowing teachers to demonstrate some of the basics of sentence structure and logical organization. Each child contributed to the learning of all.

The issue for curriculum analysis is the extent to which your curriculum takes into account students' cultural and ethnic backgrounds. Further, it is important to examine the extent to which the curriculum attempts to help students adjust to the students' present school or question the status quo.

TECHNOLOGY AND FRAME FACTORS[12]

The presence in classrooms of electronic instructional technologies has grown tremendously in the last decade. In the year 2001, Internet connected computers were found in more than 99.5% of school and 87% of K through 12 classrooms (National Center for Education Statistics, 2002). While the breadth of this change is incredible, the greatest curriculum change from the widespread use of technology may be outside of the classroom. Web-based courses change virtually every aspect of the teacher/student/curriculum relationship. Indeed, teacher and student may never actually meet.

Technology has implications across all the frame factors. It influences the temporal frame, for example, by allowing courses to be taken at anytime of the day or night or throughout traditional school breaks. Distance learning courses can erase the boundaries of the school day and school year. In terms of the physical frame, graphing calculators are required for New York State's Mathematics Course B (typically taken in the 11th grade) and allowed for the Mathematics Course A (10th grade) Regents Examinations as of the June 2000 examinations (New York State Education Department, 1999). Graphing calculators are also used in AP Calculus courses. Examples of influences of educational technology on each of the frame factors in shown in Table 8.2.

Technology has the potential to vastly reshape the nature of home schooling. Students can take a wide array of courses in accredited programs without the need for much expertise on the part of their parents. (See *www.homeschool.com/,* for example.)

The issue for curriculum analysis is the extent to which the curriculum you are examining requires special technology or can flourish without such technologies. Do the related standards require the use of these technologies?

Curriculum Analysis Questions

The purpose of examining frame factors in a curriculum analysis is to be able to understand the resources available for and the constraints on implementation of the curriculum. In so doing, the analyst learns to determine the kind of environment in which the curriculum is most likely to thrive. In a sense the analyst learns to describe the ecological requirements for the curriculum. If these requirements are not taken into account, it is unlikely that the curriculum will find its ecological "niche." Failure to find a niche results in either outright rejection of the curriculum or a curriculum change that lacks durability. Each type of frame factor suggests a set of ecological requirements.

I. *Temporal* What are the temporal requirements of the curriculum?
  a. Does the curriculum have any special scheduling requirements?
  b. Will the time most schools will likely allocate for students to learn be adequate?
  c. Is the time teachers will need to prepare for their teaching of this curriculum realistic?

TABLE 8.2 Examples of Educational Technology Roles in Each Frame Factor

Temporal	Student work in web-based distance courses may be completely outside of the traditional school day or school year.
Physical	The educational technologies are part of the physical frame.
Political-legal	Legislative initiatives may mandate technology in classroom use. Most standards have explicit ideas about the use of technology in the classroom. See NCTM's e-examples (*standards.nctm.org/document/eexamples/index.htm*, for example).
Organizational	A school, district or department may require a specific software package be used or may offer technological support for only one operating system. Certain technologies, i.e., video production or webpage design, may create new curricular areas.
Personal (or personnel)	The computer specialist is a relatively new classification of school employee.
Economic	Technology can both save schools substantial amounts of money (by making services more efficient or by sharing of resources electronically) and cost them substantial amounts of money through purchasing and maintaining technology.
Cultural	School and community culture can strongly influence the eagerness with which schools adopt certain technologies. Concerns about, and responses to, student access to pornography or music websites varies from community to community, for example.

2. *Physical* What are the special physical requirements of the curriculum?
   a. Will the curriculum require any special outdoor or indoor facilities? Is it likely to work well in school facilities as they typically exist?
   b. Does the curriculum require any special equipment that the school is not likely to have on hand?
   c. What materials will the school have to purchase in order to implement the curriculum?

3. *Organizational* What are the organizational requirements of the curriculum? The issue for curriculum analysis is the extent to which the curriculum you are examining requires special organizational provisions or can flourish in schools as they are now. Within what school organization will the curriculum best fit? Consider age-segregated grades, subject-matter departments, and homogeneous student groupings.

4. *Political-legal* What are the political-legal requirements of the curriculum? What state or federal standards, requirements, or mandates will the curriculum satisfy?

Consider tests, licensing. Also, you might need to study the current national and state regulations, mandates, standards, and programs to identify any potential frictions with the curriculum. To what extent is the curriculum aligned to the standards?

    a. Does the nature of the discipline embodied in the curriculum correspond to that portrayed in the standards?

    b. Does the curriculum support inquiry into the discipline as portrayed in the standards? Does the curriculum support immersing students into the activities of the discipline?

    c. Does the disciplinary content of the curriculum correspond to the standards in terms of topics, skills, developmental appropriateness, and a balance of depth and breadth?

    d. How are students, teachers, and schools held accountable to the standards (for the specific state and for the specific discipline)? (See Items 4 above and 6 below.)

5. *Economic* What are the probable costs and benefits associated with the curriculum change?

    a. What will implementation of the curriculum cost in terms of materials and equipment purchases (see Item 2 above), additional staff, staff development (see Item 6 below), staff planning and preparation time (see Item 1), and administrative time?

    b. What are the potential benefits of implementing the curriculum in terms of teacher job satisfaction, student achievement and enjoyment, community support, efficiency of school operations, and teacher collegiality?

    c. Who is likely to bear the major burden of the costs, and who is likely to experience the benefits of implementing the curriculum?

    d. Is the balance between costs and benefits likely to shift over the next five years? How durable is the curriculum change likely to be?

6. *Personal* To what extent will the curriculum be consistent with and appropriate for the teachers' attitudes, beliefs, and competencies?

    a. What attitudes and beliefs about matters such as the teachers' role, the subject matter, learning and motivation, appropriate scope and methods of teacher control, and dealing with individual differences are implicit in the curriculum? Are teachers likely to share these attitudes and beliefs?

    b. What kinds of competencies and knowledge are necessary to implement the curriculum successfully? Are teachers likely to have these competencies and this knowledge?

    c. What kinds of staff development programs would be necessary to address any discrepancies noted in (a) and (b) above?

    d. What does the curriculum assume about the background, knowledge, competencies, and attitudes of the students? Are these assumptions realistic?

7. *Cultural* What values are embedded in the curriculum?

    a. What values does the curriculum implicitly represent through its general orientation to the subject, selection of content and reading material, or instructional approach?

    b. On what basis might some community groups disagree with the curriculum's content or find the curriculum offensive?

    c. How would the curriculum have to change in order to accommodate these groups? How might the curriculum developers respond to recommendations for changes such as these?

8. *Technology*   What technologies are required for implementation of the curriculum? (See Item 2 above.)

    a. Does the curriculum require technologies that the school is not likely to have (or not likely to have in sufficient supply)? What related technologies are likely already in place?

    b. Are the technologies required to meet the relevant standards? (See Item 9 below.) What do the technologies allow students and teachers to do that could not be done without the technologies? What do the technologies allow to be done more efficiently?

    c. Will the technologies require additional training for teachers? Will the technologies require additional support staff (i.e. a network technician)? (See Item 6 above.)

    d. What will the technologies cost? (See Item 5 above.)

9. *Standards*   To what extent is the curriculum aligned to the standards?

    a. Does the nature of the discipline embodied in the curriculum correspond to that portrayed in the standards?

    b. Does the curriculum support inquiry into the discipline as portrayed in the standards? Does the curriculum support immersing students into the activities of the discipline?

    c. Does the disciplinary content of the curriculum correspond to the standards in terms of topics, skills, developmental appropriateness, and a balance of depth and breadth?

    d. How are students, teachers and schools held accountable to the standards (for the specific state and for the specific discipline)? (See also #4 and #6)

10. *Technology*   What technologies are required for implementation of the curriculum? (See also #2)

    a. Does the curriculum require technologies that the school is not likely to have (or not likely to have in sufficient supply)? What related technologies are likely already in place?

    b. Are the technologies required to meet the relevant standards? (See also #9). What do the technologies allow students and teachers to do that could not be without the technologies? What do the technologies allow to be done more efficiently?

    c. Will the technologies require additional training for teachers? Will the technologies require additional support staff (i.e. a network technician)? (See also #6)

    d. What will the technologies cost (see also #5)?

11. *Multicultural*   To what extent does the curriculum take into account the students' cultural, ethnic, or social backgrounds? To what extent does it accommodate gender differences?

By the time you have answered these questions you should be in a good position to predict the kinds of problems the curriculum would face during its implementation and the kinds of modifications that might be needed to ensure durable curriculum change.

NOTES

1. This section draws extensively on Johnson (1977) and Lundgren (1972).

2. Some schools are creating classes of different durations that cover the same content and have the same final exam.

3. See the "Changing Emphases" tables at the end of each of several chapters in *The National Science Education Standards,* for more examples see National Research Council (1996).

4. This belief finds substantial support from many perspectives ranging from the more technical effective-schools model (Purkey and Smith, 1983) to more critical views (McNeil, 1986).

5. See Berlak and Berlak (1981) on teacher beliefs and Shavelson (1983) on teachers' implicit theories.

6. See Posner (1993) for his Teacher Belief Inventory to help with sample questions to use.

7. See Lave (1988) for discussions of this new area of research, termed "social cognition" and "ethnomathematics."

8. See Chapter Eight.

9. But see Wigginton's (1985) solution to the accountability problem.

10. See Chapter Two.

11. Nancy Zimmet wrote the first draft of this section.

12. Don Dugan-Hass wrote most of this section.

CHAPTER 9

Curriculum Implementation

Conflicting Approaches

The Minerva Board of Education is concerned that the school district is not equipping its students for the twenty-first century. Although the district has been buying computers over the past five years, it has not yet adopted a computer education curriculum.

Dr. Maria Gonzales, the district's Superintendent of Schools, is examining her options. She organizes a cabinet meeting of all coordinators, department heads, principals, and central office administrators to discuss the problem. Jerry Straight, the Assistant Superintendent for Instruction, suggests that the district contact the Regional Educational Research and Development Laboratory (RERDL). He knows that the computer education curriculum the laboratory developed under a federal grant has been used in many other school districts. RERDL not only will supply a computer education curriculum developed by experts and based on extensive research and field testing, but also will conduct evaluations of the curriculum once the district implements it. "Why try to reinvent the wheel in Minerva?" he asks.

Sylvia Friedman, the head of the Mathematics Department at the high school, disagrees. She argues that the district has several of its own experts on the faculty and that whatever expertise the teachers lack they could gain by reading professional literature. Further, she contends that the district does not need a highly structured computer education curriculum anyway; what Minerva needs to adopt is a set of basic beliefs about computer education with which all teachers can agree. Then the district should provide support so that each teacher can develop his own approach to computer education based on those core beliefs. Much debate follows Ms. Friedman's statements.

Dr. Gonzales forms a committee to study the problem and the implications of both Mr. Straight's and Ms. Friedman's suggestions and to make recommendations to Dr. Gonzales within two weeks.

Among other things, this chapter would prepare you to serve on a committee such as the one formed by Dr. Gonzales. It examines in some depth the views of curriculum implementation presented by Mr. Straight and Ms. Friedman.

FOCUS: TWO APPROACHES TO CURRICULUM IMPLEMENTATION

The influence of a perspective on curriculum extends beyond the official curriculum itself. A perspective also influences the process of implementation. As we saw in Chapter Eight, frame factors mediate the process by which official curricula are translated into operational curricula. In this chapter, we focus on two coherent approaches to curriculum implementation, one based on a behavioral perspective, the other based on an experiential perspective.

For at least the past one hundred years, since the progressive movement began to challenge the traditional curriculum, the field of curriculum has attracted reformers. The main approaches to curriculum reform during the progressive era were (1) the publication of policy recommendations by national commissions—e.g., the Seven Cardinal Principles; (2) the formation of model programs in "experimental" schools—these were labeled "laboratory schools" when associated with universities; and (3) the overhaul of entire school systems, e.g., Gary, Indiana, by administrators turned reformers. During the past thirty years, two new approaches to curriculum change have emerged, although, as we will see, their roots also extend back into the progressive era. The *Research, Development, and Diffusion* (RD&D) model (Jerry Straight's approach) manifests behaviorist assumptions and features. The *collaborative* model (Sylvia Friedman's approach) is most consistent with an experiential perspective.

THE RESEARCH, DEVELOPMENT, AND DIFFUSION MODEL

During the 1950s with Max Beberman's efforts at the University of Illinois to develop the new math, followed by Jerrold Zacharias's efforts at MIT to develop PSSC physics, the universities became the hotbeds of educational reform, with the university scholar as the major agent of change.[1] Not surprisingly, the dominant approach to curriculum implementation was conceived as analogous to university teaching. New forms of pedagogy were embodied in course materials for teachers and disseminated to them through publications and workshops. The goal was to update teachers on both content and method (House, 1980). The reformers viewed the entire task of curriculum reform as essentially nonproblematic.

By the mid-1960s a new conception of teaching was beginning to have an impact on curriculum change. Schoolteaching came to be viewed less as a "craft residing in tacit knowledge . . . learned by apprenticeship and seasoned by experience" (Atkin & House, 1981, p. 25) and more as a technology, which, like any industrial enterprise, could be rationalized as a series of separate tasks, guided by a set of technical materials, and evaluated by measuring the achievement of learning outcomes (Atkin & House, 1981). Teaching was becoming technicized.[2] Just as the public believed that improved technology and scientific research would put a man on the moon, technologies like behavioral objectives, competency-based teaching, and programmed instruction, together with educational research, would, according to the reformers, improve teaching practices.

This belief in the inherent benefits of technology and scientific research was applied to the process of curriculum change itself. Like teaching, the process of curriculum change could be technicized by rationalizing it into a series of separate tasks: *research* establishes the principles of teaching and learning; *development* applies these research findings to the production of materials that embody new curricula; *diffusion* systematically disseminates these new materials and curricula to teachers for their use. Most descriptions of this model of change add a fourth task, *adoption,* involving the actual use of the materials by teachers and the incorporation of the new courses into the school curriculum. This linear model, which we will label simply "RD&D," became formally institutionalized when the U.S. government funded a network of about thirty regional laboratories and research and development centers to produce the materials necessary for educational reform (Atkin & House, 1981, p. 25). The most influential version of this model is depicted in Table 9.1, the Guba-Clark model of educational change. Educational reform had become a matter of producing and implementing improved educational products. Knowledge about curriculum change, like knowledge about teaching, had shifted from tacit to explicit, and the approach had moved from haphazard and informal to systematic and planned.

Like any technical approach, the linear RD&D approach to curriculum change focuses on the technology itself, rather than on the nature of teaching in classrooms and schools. It views the teacher as a relatively passive consumer whose goals are similar to those of the curriculum developers, the experts; the RD&D approach expects teachers to be inclined to cooperate once the experts present the empirical evidence of the curriculum's benefits to the teachers. The model of curriculum change is one of industrial production, in which research and development efforts generate new products, which are then marketed and distributed to the consuming public.[3]

This approach to curriculum change, in spite of its difficulties, remains the dominant view of the educational change process at the federal level (Atkin & House, 1981, p. 26). A curriculum using this approach is distinguished by features such as the following:

1. Skills needed to implement it are assumed to be specifiable and learnable.
2. Development efforts focus on perfecting the materials through involvement by experts in the production, field testing, evaluation, and revision of the materials. Since the techniques are assumed to be replicable and the materials transferable, little opportunity is afforded the teacher for site-specific modifications.
3. Objectives are stated as though they are agreed upon by developers, teachers, and students alike. These objectives are the primary, if not sole, basis for the development of test items provided for evaluating student progress.

TABLE 9.1 Classification Schema for Processes Related to and Necessary for Change in Education

	Research	Development		Diffusion			Adoption	
		Invention	Design	Dissemination	Demonstration	Trial	Installation	Institutionalization
Objective	To advance knowledge	To formulate a new solution to an operating problem or to a class of operating problems, i.e., *to innovate*	To order and to systematize the components of the invented solution; to construct an innovation package for institutional use, i.e., *to engineer*	To create widespread awareness of the invention among practitioners, i.e., *to inform*	To afford an opportunity to examine and assess operating qualities of the invention, i.e., *to build conviction*	To build familiarity with the invention and provide a basis for assessing the quality, value, fit, and utility of the invention in a particular institution, i.e., *to test*	To fit the characteristics of the invention to the characteristics of the adopting institution, i.e., *to operationalize*	To assimilate the invention as an integral and accepted component of the system, i.e., *to establish*
Criteria	Validity (internal and external)	Face validity (appropriateness) Estimated viability Impact (relative contribution)	Institutional feasibility Generalizability Performance	Intelligibility Fidelity Pervasiveness Impact (extent to which it affects key targets)	Credibility Convenience Evidential assessment	Adaptability Feasibility Action	Effectiveness Efficiency	Continuity Valuation Support
Relation to change	Provides basis for invention	Produces the invention	Engineers and packages the invention	Informs about the invention	Builds conviction about the invention	Tries out the invention in the context of a particular situation	Operationalizes the invention for use in a specific institution	Establishes the invention as a part of an ongoing program; converts it to a "non-innovation"

Source: From Essay Six, "An Examination of Potential Change Roles in Education," by David L. Clark and Egon G. Guba, in *Rational Planning in Curriculum and Instruction.* Published by National Education Association. Copyright © 1967 National Education Association of the United States. Used by permission of the publisher.

4. Methods employed to certify its worth are predominantly psychometric, such as achievement tests and attitude surveys.
5. Curriculum implementation is assessed by determining the degree to which teaching practice meets the criteria of the developers, termed the degree of "fidelity" (Fullan & Pomfret, 1977).

This approach is similar to the one proposed by Jerry Straight in this chapter's lead-off scenario. As an approach to curriculum change, it is based on a behavioral perspective. The behavioral perspective is simply transposed from behavioral assumptions about the learner and the learning process to behavioral assumptions about teachers, who are thought of as adult learners, and the curriculum change process, in which teachers are expected to learn new behaviors. Both enterprises are aimed at changing people's behavior. Both enterprises consider people to be passive recipients of change efforts. Behind both enterprises are behavioral scientists, who are considered the experts with authority to direct the change process. Finally, both enterprises are evaluated by comparing the developers' objectives with the behavioral outcomes.

In order to see how this approach has been applied to curriculum implementation, we examine what might be considered a prototype of the RD&D approach.

The Case of Individually Prescribed Instruction (IPI)

IPI began as a research-based curriculum development effort at the University of Pittsburgh's Learning Research and Development Center (LRDC) under the leadership of Robert Glaser[4] and with the aim of applying principles of programmed instruction to the entire primary and secondary curriculum (see Chapter Seven). One of the federally supported regional laboratories, Research for Better Schools (RBS) in Philadelphia, was responsible for the implementation efforts. In Chapter Eleven we will examine the IPI approach to evaluation. In this chapter we look at IPI as a prototype of an RD&D approach to implementation.

The first of the IPI curricula was in elementary school math. It is organized around a set of behavioral objectives, carefully sequenced according to prerequisite skills; it is taught using self-instructional, self-paced materials that provide opportunities to teachers and students for modeling, practice, and feedback, and it assesses student learning with pretests and posttests for each objective in the sequence. The teacher's role in this program is to allow the system to function (Jung, 1972, p. 8) by performing evaluation, diagnosis, and prescription functions, as well as by circulating around the classroom and occasionally tutoring and counseling students.

There are two senses in which IPI represents an RD&D approach to curriculum implementation: (1) the implementation model and (2) the approach to teacher training. During the late 1960s IPI employed a model of implementation that divided the change process into separate tasks, each task engineered by experts; focused the change process on the technology itself and techniques for using it; focused development efforts on perfecting the technology; monitored the implementation in terms of fidelity; and utilized tests to determine its worth. The teacher-retraining effort produced a set of materials that reflected the same principles employed in the student materials (listed above).

In examining the implementation model, let us focus on the analysis of the entire RD&D process, the conception of the diffusion process, and the use of a system to monitor the implementation process. The original research on programmed instruction[5] was carried out by Glaser (shown in Figure 9.1) and other educational psychologists and technologists at the University of Pittsburgh in 1961 and 1962. Development work began in 1963–1964, when the LRDC began to work with one elementary school to develop an entire school program based on principles derived from programmed instruction. Subsequent work was conceived as "five distinct functional areas: (1) curriculum writing, (2) material production, (3) training, (4) field engineering, and (5) appraisal" (Jung, 1972, p. 17). Each of these functions had its own staff directed by experts, principally "professional educators and personnel trained in educational administration and the disciplines of education and psychology"

FIGURE 9.1 Robert Glaser.

(pp. 15–17). Thus, the entire RD&D process was analyzed into separate and distinct functions, each one directed by experts in that function.

The diffusion process was based on the assumption that "effective educational change comes about most rapidly through development and demonstration of full-blown programs that include the necessary material, teacher training, and environmental design to make them operational in a school setting" (Jung, 1972, p. 15). This assumption led to the establishment of one experimental school in 1963–1964, created for the LRDC to use to investigate the feasibility of converting an entire school to a system of individualized instruction (p. 13). The success of this effort led to the establishment in 1966 of a "demonstration" school in the same suburban Pittsburgh school district, intended to maintain close contact with the experimental school and to serve as a training ground for staff at five other demonstration schools within the RBS region. The next year's effort involved the training of personnel for fifteen "pilot" schools. (See Figure 9.2.) This approach to diffusion assumed that the benefits of the program would be apparent to educators if they could only see it in operation in another elementary school. Seeing it would be sufficient to cause them to want to adopt it in their own districts. This view of rational change is characteristic of the RD&D approach.

The monitoring process was based on the assumption that there is one correct way to implement the program. The RBS staff sent out a team of monitors to participating schools for monthly visits to collect data and to help resolve problems. We will examine the evaluation function of these monitors more closely in Chapter Eleven. For our present purpose, it is important only to note that these monitors attempted to help schools make certain that they were operating the program as a "true" implementation (Jung, 1972, p. 29). Teachers were not expected to adapt the program to their own situation.

The teacher-training program developed by RBS "concentrated on the development of necessary skills needed by teachers in implementing the system" (Jung, 1972, p. 28). Like the IPI student materials, the teacher-training materials contain "behavioral objectives, pre- and post-tests on the objectives, self-instructional materials and equipment . . . practice in using IPI skills and materials as routine exercises," and other activities (p. 28). The materials, which include programmed booklets and audiovisual materials, contain guidelines for using all the IPI materials and suggestions for proper procedures to use in organizing the classroom and writing student prescriptions. The training materials are individualized, though most teachers also attended a summer course conducted by RBS. The important aspect of these materials to notice, for our present purposes, is the implicit assumption that teachers share the beliefs and goals of the RD&D experts, that all they lack are the skills necessary to implement the program, and that it is feasible to teach these skills explicitly in a scientifically designed, sequenced, and validated training program. In a sense, these are the same assumptions underlying the behavioral perspective on curriculum purpose, content, and organization examined in previous chapters.

The RD&D approach has been helpful in systematizing and rationalizing the implementation process. It has even had some significant successes in

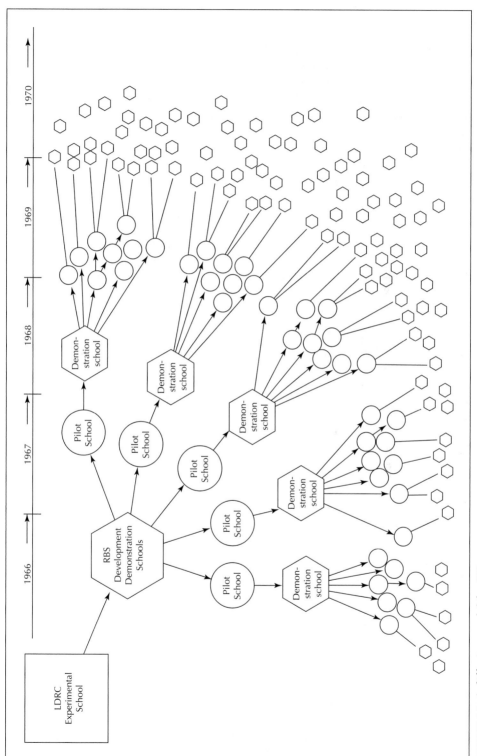

FIGURE 9.2 A diffusion model for IPI.

implementing federally supported large-scale efforts, the IPI program being one of its most notable success stories. However, the RD&D approach to implementation does little to help us understand certain problems. Why have many of the IPI schools abandoned the program in the years since its inception, in spite of success as defined by the IPI staff? Why did the vast majority of schools avoid IPI? Why did many schools that adopted IPI use it in ways that were not "true" to the program? Why were IPI programs in science and social studies far less successful than IPI mathematics? The RD&D approach would likely answer these questions by attempting to show that technical refinements were needed in either the student materials, the teacher-training materials, or both, or that teachers and administrators were not behaving rationally or professionally. Conclusions such as these would lead us to redouble our efforts or to chastise teachers, neither of which would be likely to address the underlying problems. Perhaps we need to employ a different approach to implementation. The RD&D approach assumes a compliant teacher who shares the developer's goals. We need an approach that helps us understand how local personnel try to adapt curricula to their own uses, and how local factions promote or inhibit their use. We need an approach to implementation that recognizes and legitimizes the political and cultural dimensions of curriculum change. In order to illustrate some of these points, let us examine in detail what happened in one curriculum implementation effort that ignored these dimensions of curriculum change.

The Case of M:ACOS Implementation

In Chapter Two we examined the fifth- and sixth-grade social studies curriculum developed during the 1960s under the leadership of Jerome Bruner. What we saw was a rather elegantly designed curriculum, based on Bruner's cognitive psychological research, employing a highly sophisticated multimedia approach to instruction, with content drawn from the research of world-renowned social scientists. To many curriculum students, M:ACOS was and still remains one of the best examples of curriculum development to date, in this or any other country. For example, the National Council for the Social Studies reported that a national survey of teachers in 1974 rated M:ACOS the best of all federally supported social studies projects (NCSS, 1975, p. 446), and Jerome Bruner received several awards acknowledging his leadership in the effort.

According to the admirers of M:ACOS, this reverence for the curriculum and its developers only grows deeper when we examine the implementation process. As for many other curricula developed with support from the NSF, an RD&D approach was used:

1. Academic research by experts in psychology, anthropology, and other social sciences formed the basis for the curriculum.
2. A sophisticated system of dissemination by a federally funded separate organization, Curriculum Development Associates, was employed.
3. The development effort focused on developing new materials and techniques for teaching based on these disciplines; the implementation efforts

centered on giving teachers the new social science knowledge and teaching techniques necessary to use these tools properly.

4. The implementation was based on the assumption that teachers and parents all shared the developers' goal of improving students' ability to think critically about the human condition—in other words, to think like social scientists.

In contrast to the developers of many other NSF-sponsored curricula, the developers of M:ACOS took implementation seriously. Consider, for example, staff development. Pre-service and in-service teacher education addressed the need of teachers to become knowledgeable about the anthropological and social psychological content; competent in dealing with group discussions of controversial issues related to religion, life and death, and reproduction; and comfortable in developing new roles for themselves as facilitators of open-ended inquiry. From the outset the emphasis was on quality control and on investing in teacher education. School districts desiring to adopt M:ACOS were required to send teachers to an NSF-sponsored summer institute or an approved local workshop offered by universities or school systems. The NSF not only supported the summer institutes, as they had for PSSC and other federally sponsored curricula, but also established university-based Regional Centers. These centers prepared workshop leaders for local schools, helped districts organize staff development programs, and supported colleges and universities in planning pre-service and in-service programs for teachers (CDA, 1972). Throughout the effort, teachers' knowledge of the curriculum content and appropriate teacher roles was a major research concern (House, 1979).

With such systematic and deliberate methods of research, development, and diffusion, it would seem that M:ACOS should have been a great success. On the contrary, as mentioned in Chapter Two, this curriculum found itself the target of a national uproar that shook school districts across the country, the NSF, and even the U.S. Congress. What could have gone wrong? The crisis culminated in 1975 in an attack on M:ACOS on the floor of the House of Representatives by Rep. John Conlan (R-Arizona). The attack occurred during debate on an amendment to the NSF's appropriations bill, an amendment designed to block support by the NSF not only for implementing M:ACOS but also for implementing any other NSF-sponsored curriculum, and to suspend all NSF science curriculum development projects. Although the amendment failed narrowly, this debate and the political furor surrounding M:ACOS marked the end of the federal government's involvement in curriculum development and implementation for several years.

If it seems perplexing to you that one of the most widely acclaimed curricula could have brought an end to what some observers describe as the Golden Age of curriculum development in the United States, the reason might be a cultural blind spot. Perhaps you cannot see the political problems, because your values are consistent with those of the M:ACOS developers. If this is the case, then some understanding of the M:ACOS controversy may help you anticipate political problems with your own curriculum. This discussion may help you see a curriculum as an embodiment of cultural values.

The problems started in local communities across the United States: in Florida, Arizona, New York, Oregon, Pennsylvania, Maryland, Idaho, Tennessee, California, Vermont, Texas, and Alaska (Nelkin, 1982, p. 124). In most cases the local controversies resulted in the communities dropping M:ACOS. The controversies stemmed from what one of the chief architects of M:ACOS, Peter Dow (1975), defended as an attempt to help children understand the troubled times in which they live.

> MACOS may raise troubling questions about the significance of killing, the importance of the partnership between male and female, and the moral dilemmas all societies face in caring for the very young and the very old; but these questions are always considered in the context of what they tell us, or fail to tell us, about how humankind can better understand itself and thus improve its plight. This is the overriding goal of social education. . . . (Dow, 1975, pp. 79–81)

However, the content of the curriculum became the focus of many local controversies. Recall from Chapter One that M:ACOS uses the study of animals and the Netsilik Eskimos as points of comparison and contrast for examining the human condition. For example, as they learn that salmon die before their offspring are born, children confront questions about the importance of parents in the rearing of children. The curriculum thus implicitly assumes a continuity between animals and human beings. By studying the influence of a harsh environment on the Netsilik Eskimo culture, "a society with common rules and expectations and a spiritual community of mutually held values and beliefs" (Dow, 1968, p. 5), children are expected to learn how behavior is shaped by the functional requirements of a particular situation (Nelkin, 1982, p. 50). In this context children examine aspects of the Netsilik culture that are disturbing to members of most Western cultures, including senilicide and infanticide (killing of the elderly and infants). In discussing this and other content, teachers are expected to raise questions like the following: "How does our society treat the elderly?" "What aspects of our own culture do we create in order to deal with our environment?" "How do cosmologies develop?" As Nelkin points out, M:ACOS "was clearly treading on sensitive ground, dealing with questions that are the foundation of the most dogmatic beliefs," and denying "the existence of absolute values . . ." (Nelkin, 1982, p. 51).

The type of complaint raised by parents depended on the type of community. In isolated rural communities the charge was typically "cultural relativism," "secular humanism," and "situational ethics" (Nelkin, 1982, p. 127), based on the curriculum's claim that "one kind of explanation (about the human condition) is no more human than another" (Bruner, 1964, p. 24). In urban communities parents complained about the moral implications of implicitly condoning murder, aggression, and communal living. In Bible Belt communities parents were disturbed by the religious implications of teaching evolution as fact. In university communities the interference in local schools by "those experts on the campus" was an important issue, exacerbating already strained relations between town and gown. As Nelkin points out, parents focused on whatever aspects of the curriculum signified existing local frustrations (1982, p. 126).

At the federal level, however, the major issue became whether federal bureaucrats—since the NSF was a quasi-governmental agency—and behavioral scientists like Jerome Bruner[6] should be controlling the content of social studies and thereby influencing the socialization of children. In the words of Rep. Conlan, M:ACOS not only was full of "abhorrent, vulgar, morally sick content," but also was "almost always at variance with the beliefs and values of parents and local communities," "an assault on tradition," attempting to "mold the children's social attitudes and beliefs and set them apart from the beliefs and moral values of their communities" (*Congressional Record*, 4/9/75, H2588). It was this objection to the perceived imposition of values on local communities by outside experts—i.e., federal bureaucrats and the "university elite"—that eventually resulted in criticism of the entire federal curriculum reform effort.

THE COLLABORATIVE APPROACH

Although the linear RD&D approach was widespread and well supported, its promise of scientifically based and technologically driven educational reform was never entirely fulfilled. As Hemphill (1982, p. 8, cited in Tikunoff & Ward, 1983) pointed out, "the products [of linear RD&D] have not sold themselves nor have they been eagerly sought and put into use by educators." When the materials were used, they were too often misused, according to the developers. The developers, in spite of serious efforts at in-service training, were unable to deal with teachers who inexplicably tried to "subvert" so-called teacherproof curricula. Explanations given by RD&D specialists for their lack of success included inadequate materials, poor dissemination efforts, or lack of provision for change agents, termed "linkers," needed to help teachers use the materials (Atkin & House, 1981, p. 26). But several critics pointed to the basic assumptions underlying the RD&D approach as the source of its difficulties (Tikunoff & Ward, 1983; House, 1980). These critics questioned the assumptions that there exists a consensus about the goals and problems of education upon which to base the RD&D efforts, that the teacher is a passive recipient of educational products, and that a technology of teaching is truly transferable from one situation to another. Research in staff development and teacher decision making began to support these suspicions.[7]

Another problem with the RD&D approach may have been that "the linear order—research, development, dissemination, use—seems inconsistent with how educators behave and, more importantly, with how they should behave" (Hemphill, 1982, p. 8). This separation of RD&D functions led eventually to increased specialization and professionalization within the RD&D community, which in turn led to increased isolation of the RD&D efforts from teachers. In effect, each function developed its own cadre of "experts," who became increasingly distant from classroom teachers. As a result the experts gave teachers answers and solutions to questions teachers never asked and to problems the teachers never had (Tikunoff & Ward, 1983, p. 454).

Out of the criticism of the RD&D approach grew another approach to curriculum change, a more "collaborative" approach, based on different assumptions. Rather than passive recipients of products developed by experts, teachers came to be viewed as active shapers of curriculum change to meet local needs. Rather than a linear sequence from researcher and developer to teacher (the so-called "center-to-periphery" model), curriculum reform efforts came to be seen as both influenced by, and an influence on, schools and classrooms (Atkin & House, 1981). What the RD&D approach viewed as curriculum "sabotage," these analysts described as a process of "mutual adaptation" (Berman & McLaughlin, 1978).

The reason teachers found themselves at odds with developers was that, contrary to the developers' expectations, the teachers did not necessarily share the developers' goals. Curriculum reforms in areas such as bilingual education, special education, and vocational education became arenas for an increasingly politicized curriculum. Negotiation and compromise became essential elements of curriculum change (Atkin & House, 1981). In fact, in extreme cases the differences between groups ran so deep that there were not enough shared interests and values to serve as a basis for compromise. In these cases, the teachers and developers could be considered separate subcultures with such different belief systems that misunderstanding and conflict were inevitable (Wolcott, 1977).

Collaborative approaches are intended to deal directly with these conflicts, and, thereby to avoid the mutual frustration, blame, and distrust that seem inevitably to follow from the RD&D approach (Wagner, 1988). A curriculum specifying a collaborative approach has some of the following features.[8]

1. Its developers acknowledge that although some skills needed to implement the curriculum can be specified and learned, much of the skill and knowledge of good teaching is tacit knowledge of the teaching craft, best learned by teachers working with other teachers in collegial settings such as teacher centers, rather than specified and taught by outside consultants.
2. The developers believe that development efforts are best focused at the local level on helping teachers to grow professionally by reading, observing other teachers, and discussing ideas. Based on these efforts, teachers attempt to interpret a comprehensive and integrated approach to teaching in a manner that capitalizes on their own strengths and preferred styles of teaching. Externally produced materials play a role in curriculum change, but are subordinated to the primary focus on teacher development.
3. The developers believe that curriculum change is guided by a set of beliefs about teachers and teaching, learners and learning, the subject matter and its potential meaning, and the relation of schooling to broader social and political forces—not by a set of prespecified objectives. These beliefs form a set of principles upon which to base the curriculum change effort. Rather than providing test items derived from objectives, curricula based on collaborative approaches provide benchmarks of child development to use in keeping track of student progress.

4. Evaluation methods tend to be less standardized, systematic, and formal, and derived more from classroom observations, semistructured interviews, and examination of student classwork. Rather than relying on psychometric methods, the evaluators tend to employ more ethnographic methods, yielding intensive, naturalistic descriptions of the classroom. The goal of evaluation is to understand the curriculum from the students' and teachers' points of view.

5. Curriculum implementation is seen as a process of multiple interpretations by teachers. Rather than one proper way to implement the curriculum, a collaborative approach looks for a variety of "profiles of practice" (Johnston, 1987), which, when taken as a whole, define the curriculum change.

Table 9.2 contrasts the RD&D approach with collaborative approaches. The collaborative approach to curriculum change is similar to the one proposed by Sylvia Friedman in this chapter's lead-off scenario.

A curriculum that embodies the features just listed does not deal with research, development, dissemination, and adoption as separate functions of curriculum change, each requiring specialists to direct it. Each function is conducted collaboratively with teachers, administrators, and subject-matter experts or social scientists, each playing key roles at each stage of the process. Furthermore, these functions are not conducted in a linear manner, but instead are pursued continuously throughout the change effort. There is a constant drive to seek more information, develop more materials, share these materials and new information, and experiment with new techniques, all in an effort to refine the craft of teaching.

The collaborative approach is based primarily on an experiential perspective. Earlier versions of this approach were even promoted during the progressive movement, from which the experiential perspective derives. For example,

TABLE 9.2   A Comparison of the RD&D and Collaborative Approaches to Curriculum Change

	RD&D	Collaborative
What knowledge and skills are necessary for implementing change?	Explicit taught skills	Tacit or craft knowledge
What is the focus of development efforts?	Materials production	Professional growth of teachers
What directs curriculum change?	Objectives	Teacher beliefs
What evaluation methods are used?	Psychometric	Ethnographic
What is the goal for curriculum implementation?	Fidelity of implementation	Multiple interpretations

action research (Corey, 1952) and teacher curriculum committees (Leese, Frasure, & Johnson, 1961) can be viewed as earlier forms of collaborative research (Tikunoff & Ward, 1983) and collaborative development. According to the experiential perspective, teachers, like students, should participate in decisions that affect the conditions under which they must work. Furthermore, experiential educators might add, the only route to empowering students so that they can and will think for themselves is through teacher empowerment. Both teachers and students are best viewed as people with their own sets of purposes and beliefs, who are active participants in their own development. According to this perspective, to ignore these purposes and beliefs is not only to be ineffective in influencing development, but even to cause frustration and the consequent disruptive behavior. Negotiation, compromise, and, if necessary, alternative approaches are appropriate means of educational reform. Some experiential educators take collaboration one step further by adding parents and other members of the community with central roles in both the educational process and the process of educational reform.[9]

The Case of Whole Language Implementation

Whole language is an approach to teaching literacy to elementary school children. It is based on the premise that human beings "acquire language through actually using it for a purpose, not through practicing its separate parts until some later date when the parts are assembled and the totality is finally used" (Altwerger, Edelsky, & Flores, 1987, p. 145). Therefore, according to whole language principles, "real use," rather than "practice exercises," is the best way to teach literacy (p. 145). Whole language is best viewed as a philosophy of literacy education, rather than as a technology. There are certain techniques and materials associated with whole language (e.g., "Big Books"), but these technological aspects are not central to the curriculum. The philosophy of whole language consists of principles, each of which is like a piece of a jigsaw puzzle. The pieces do not make sense in isolation, but only once they are joined together to form the full picture. Whole language teachers may differ in many of their practices, but they believe in each of the principles. There are principles related to (1) the way children acquire language; (2) the way children learn, particularly the importance of approximation, experimentation, exploration, and social interaction in learning; (3) the importance of meaning and of the individual's construction of meaning; (4) the relation between different aspects of language, particularly between written language (reading and writing) and oral language (speaking and listening); and (5) the value of observing children engaged in real language tasks in order to determine their progress.

Although whole language is not a curriculum per se, whole language classrooms (see Figure 9.3) are typically characterized by certain features:

1. Classrooms are rich in print materials.
2. Teachers utilize children's literature, rather than basal readers—i.e., books developed specifically to teach reading.

FIGURE 9.3 A whole language teacher helping children prepare their own "published books."

3. Teachers emphasize frequent writing by children for a variety of purposes, even in the very early grades, dealing with spelling and punctuation as a developmental process.
4. Children read literature in a variety of content areas and even write their own "published" books.
5. Teachers deemphasize standardized tests, relying more on observing children ("kid watching") and on "documenting growth in children's actual work" (Altwerger et al., p. 145).
6. Children discuss what they have been reading and writing.

Most of the beliefs that form the basis for whole language teaching also form the basis for the implementation of whole language. Like children learning language, teachers base their practice on prior beliefs and knowledge. Improving their practice of teaching requires successive approximations, experimentation, exploration, and social interaction. Since teachers, like children, are best viewed as members of a literate community, teachers also need opportunities to read about and to discuss professional matters. Most of all, teachers need to construct their own approach to teaching.

Thus, a collaborative approach to implementation is most consistent with the principles of whole language. A collaborative approach does not focus on a prepackaged set of materials or techniques developed externally and imposed on a school district's teachers. Instead, teachers, administrators, and outside consultants work collaboratively to produce desired curriculum changes. Since there is no general prescription for implementing whole language, perhaps the best way to describe the implementation is to tell the story of one school district's experience with this approach to literacy education. The former Director of Curriculum in the Ithaca (New York) City School District, Helena Spring, tells what happened:

The Situation. "When I came here three years ago, the language arts program was very different in each of the eight elementary schools and in each classroom. Some classrooms were using Distar, some were using a literature-based approach, and some were using traditional basals with three reading groups, worksheets, and workbooks. There was no districtwide approach to language arts. Two years before I arrived, the writing project was started. So, when I got here about fifty percent of the elementary teachers were using writing in their classrooms. I knew from my previous job that when teachers start using writing regularly in their classrooms, they become liberated from the cookbook approach to teaching and from a reliance on basals and teacher manuals. Since there are no manuals for how to teach writing, you really have to watch kids to be able to decide what to do and when to do it. In observing classrooms and talking to teachers, it was apparent that they were a very literate group of teachers. They liked to read generally and in particular to read professional literature, that is, to read about their craft. But it seemed that they were not getting that opportunity very often. So it looked as though people were ready for pulling together a consistent approach to language arts in the district."

The Conceptual Groundwork. "I began talking to teachers in the different schools, so that they could get to know me and my beliefs about teaching and curriculum. I started by presenting them with the idea of teacher as decision maker by discussing the kinds of decisions teachers make and the knowledge necessary to make those decisions. My intent was to have teachers start thinking of themselves not as cooks following somebody else's recipe but as chefs relying on their own expertise as observers of children. The decision-making model also recognizes the importance of contextual and conditional knowledge [i.e., knowing what techniques are appropriate in what situations] that teachers develop over time and that distinguishes between the mere technician and the true craftsperson. They really appreciated having their expertise and the complexity of their jobs affirmed."

Initial Awareness. "Then I started talking to them about their own personal beliefs regarding reading, writing, and literacy and having them compare those beliefs with their actual classroom practices. We talked about the difficulty in making decisions when beliefs and practices are in conflict. After that, the most important thing I could do was to reassure them that risk taking was okay, that we would like them to experiment in many areas as they were already doing in writing, to rely on their own observations in the classroom, and to talk with each other about what was going on in their classrooms. There was some anxiety by some teachers, because the approach was different: 'We were always told that we had to use the basals!' some would say. Either a manual or a district administrator had dictated what teachers did; what I was saying was that teachers themselves needed to decide what reading and writing are all about and then to form their practices based on these beliefs. For those teachers who relied heavily on basals, I began to ask them what they could do with the text to make it more productive. They could see that just because something was written in the manual, it wasn't necessarily the best thing they could do with it. We weren't trying to change their practice, but only trying to make them aware of choices they had. It's been totally amazing to me using this approach how quickly teachers have abandoned prescriptive materials and gone on their own."

Ownership.   "I think that these changes occurred so fast in part because we kept reassuring the teachers that it is okay to take risks. But the other day something else occurred to me. One of the principals asked me why we haven't written out our plan, including where we want to be in three years, what we want to look like, with objectives and time lines. I said that we could do that, but there would be a danger. The danger would be that with a specified set of objectives and time lines, then instead of teachers generating where they want to be, somebody else would be doing that. Teaching literacy is so individualistic for every teacher that if we started at the outset to put it down on paper and showed teachers what it's supposed to look like and when its supposed to look like that, then, all of a sudden, the approach to teaching and the time line is not theirs anymore. It's somebody else's. We began thinking about other districts that started whole language but are now getting resistance from the unions, something we aren't experiencing here. Maybe the difference here is that we didn't write the curriculum and time lines down but are leaving it up to individual teachers. Each teacher decides on his or her own time line in terms of what to try next."

Standardized Tests.   "During this initial period, we viewed standardized tests as an unfortunate aspect of reality. We had to reassure teachers continually that if they were going to be trying this approach, they would not be held accountable for their standardized tests scores. During that first year I would still see many teachers teaching kids the sound-symbol skills that were on the test. They would say, 'Oh, you caught me!' Then, I would ask them how they liked spending their time this way, and they would say that they hated it. However, my encouragement to them not to teach those things had limited effect, until we got rid of the subtest that was causing the most problems. When we took away that part of the test, we showed them that they have some power to affect what happens to them. That action also gave more validity to what we were telling them. In fact I went into one school to talk to the teachers about our plan to get rid of that subtest, and I got three hugs and a round of applause. You could see the tension visibly ease from them."

Outside Experts.   "After the initial awareness, addressing where the district was and where each individual teacher was, we began to share what the research had to say about literacy. Teachers would read an article and then meet either as a faculty within a school or within grade-level meetings across the district on early-dismissal days. Then we started going to conferences. We also had Peter Johnston [a faculty member and reading researcher from SUNY at Albany] come in once a month. Peter's role was that of a facilitator. He wanted us to be independent of him within one year. He insisted that we already knew what we needed to know. If we just shared our observations and talked about them, we would find that we could teach each other. He insisted that as a group we knew as much as he knew as an individual, that we already had expert knowledge amongst ourselves. He was a challenger and a questioner. He argued that there are no experts other than the teacher. Textbooks and outside consultants are not experts. There has to be a collaboration between the teacher and the student in the classroom and everyone else can only act as advisors helping to add to everyone's knowledge."

Staff Development.   "Although Peter is correct that the teachers already have at their command all they need to develop in their ability to teach literacy, there is quite a lot that we all need to learn. For example, many teachers need to learn cooperative learning techniques for dealing with heterogeneous classes as whole communities. They also need to learn more children's literature and writing techniques used by authors. But rather than asking teachers to replace what they are currently doing with a new set of skills [as in Distar, for example], we are offering teachers those things they need to know in order to give themselves and their students more choices. The more choice they can have, the more voice they can have. For example, if I know five children's books, I am not going to be able to give my students as many choices as I could if I know twenty-five books I can recommend."

Teacher Confidence.   "But the choice of how to teach is always the teachers'. Teachers need three kinds of confidence, confidence that they can teach even without manuals, confidence that children will learn to read and write by reading and writing, and confidence that children can be responsible for their own learning. Last year Peter and I visited a classroom in which the teacher was just finishing an author study unit, and the things the children had done were incredible with the books they had read. After telling the teacher how impressed I was, she said `Yeah, it's too bad that next week I have to go back to Learning Mastery [Distar].' I said 'Why?' and she said, 'Because I have to. I'm afraid they're going to miss something.' At a lunchtime seminar with Peter she brought up this conflict. He told her, 'Yes they are going to miss something.

Whatever you do they will miss and they will gain something. You have to decide what you value more. Why don't you set up a notebook and list all those things that the kids are doing during your author study and all those things they are doing when you teach Distar? Then look at the two lists and decide what's most important.' And now she is no longer using Distar."

The Present Situation.   "Each principal assesses where that school's faculty is and what it needs to do. Most of the buildings have a whole language support group that meets regularly on a voluntary basis after school. Most of the schools are using staff development money with an emphasis on purchasing professional books, rather than on outside speakers. One of the principals, for example, purchased six hundred dollars worth of professional texts. He is trying to build a community of readers amongst his faculty. Different groups will read different texts; the groups meet to discuss the texts; then they pass the texts around to other groups. He has an extended lunch period once a week for each grade level during which the teachers at that grade level get together to discuss what the kids are doing in language arts or what the teachers are reading. The focus is on literacy, both adult literacy and the children's literacy."

Next Steps.   "Now I think teachers know enough about what they are doing and what kids are doing to begin to put together ideas for program documentation. You really don't know what to document until you've been doing it long enough to know what the signs are. Now we are beginning to assemble ideas about what to put in a portfolio, what grade-level expectations to have, and what kinds of things we can communicate with parents. But I imagine that it's going to take a couple of years for us to put together a systematized documentation system for all the schools across all grade levels." (Based on a personal interview, Dec. 1, 1989.)

Summary

The collaborative approach to whole language implementation just described contrasts sharply with the IPI implementation. Rather than focus on a particular set of materials or technique, which teachers are given and expected to use in the intended manner, this implementation effort attempted to develop a collaborative relationship between teachers, administrators, and outside consultants, a relationship focused in a complementary way on both the professional development of teachers and the educational development of children. Teachers would change not by witnessing a demonstration in another school or classroom, but by experimenting in their own classrooms with ideas they have discussed with other teachers. They would need staff development, not to replace what they have always done, but to expand their professional choices and the choices they offer children in their classrooms.

Each approach has characteristic strengths and weaknesses. The RD&D approach provides for systematic and deliberate planning, carrying out, and monitoring of each RD&D function. The collaborative approach provides for teacher ownership and growth. What the RD&D approach gains in systemization, it may lose in fundamental and durable change. What the collaborative approach gains in teacher cooperation and enthusiasm, it may lose in administrative control.

Curriculum Analysis Questions

The two approaches to curriculum change that we have just examined represent opposite ends of a spectrum. Not only are there approaches that fall in between these two extremes, but also there are eclectic approaches that capitalize on the strengths of each. As extremes, the two approaches presented in this chapter may provide useful reference points for an analysis of the implementation of your curriculum.

1. What approaches to curriculum change seem to be consistent with the curriculum?

2. If your curriculum has already been implemented, what approaches characterized the change efforts?

NOTES

1. See the structure-of-the-disciplines perspective in Chapter Three.
2. See Chapters One and Twelve.
3. This shift from a university-teaching model to an industrial production model is reminiscent of the shift during the progressive movement from philosophical analyses of the teaching craft to technological analyses of curriculum making. Compare, for example, Whitehead (1929) with Bobbitt (1918).
4. See Chapter Seven.
5. See Chapter Seven.
6. See Nelkin (1982, p. 125).
7. See, for example, Griffin (1983) and Shavelson (1983).
8. Note the contrast with the features of the RD&D approach.
9. See Cremin (1961) for examples. Nelkin (1982) shows what can happen when parents are ignored during a curriculum change.

CHAPTER 10

Curriculum Evaluation

Basic Concepts

The physical education curriculum was adopted last year by the Tyler School District Board of Education. Andy Driscoll, the Assistant Superintendent, has made it a practice to begin to evaluate each curriculum within two years after it has been implemented. He plans to hire a consultant from the local college to do the evaluation. But first he wants to do two things: (1) take inventory of the evaluation instruments and data related to physical education already available within the district that could be used to evaluate the curriculum; (2) identify the concerns of faculty, administrators, students, and parents related to this curriculum that the proposed evaluation could address. In order to gather this information, Mr. Driscoll wants to design two questionnaires, one to take inventory and the other to identify concerns.

This chapter equips you with the basic concepts necessary for evaluating any curriculum. It would not equip you to serve as the evaluation consultant Mr. Driscoll wants to hire to conduct the evaluation. But it would prepare you to help Mr. Driscoll design the two questionnaires.

We have seen in Chapter Nine that all curricula are value-laden. But curricula are expressions of values in another fundamental way. Any program that consumes resources must be of value in order to warrant the allocation of resources to it, and curricula as one type of program are no exception. As a matter of fact, because they are supported by tax money and depend on a captive audience, public schools, and their curricula, are routinely expected to justify their value. Furthermore, in order to use the scarce resources of time and money afforded to schools efficiently, administrators and teachers find it necessary to determine which opportunities have the greatest relative value for each student. The process by which some individual or group makes a judgment about the value of some object, person, or process is termed evaluation.1

While evaluation is an extensive field warranting serious study in its own right, this chapter attempts to focus the study of evaluation on curriculum analysis. In so doing, we limit and direct our study to those evaluation concepts that will enable us to probe deeper into a curriculum. However, in the process of analyzing a curriculum's approach to evaluation, we will in fact cover many important evaluation concepts.

We approach the study of evaluation in two ways. First, we approach it directly, looking for any reports on evaluations in the curriculum documents themselves or, if the curriculum is prominent, in the research literature. At the same time, we are looking for any guidance the curriculum provides teachers for evaluation. Second, since most curricula have never been evaluated, we approach evaluation hypothetically by identifying a set of concerns about the curriculum that an evaluation of it could address. But before attempting to analyze a curriculum in this way, it is necessary to be familiar with a few basic terms.

BASIC TERMINOLOGY

Much of the terminology of curriculum evaluation derives from the field of psychometrics, in which psychologists attempt to assign numerical values — like IQ scores—to particular characteristics—like intelligence. Some of the terminology, however, derives from clinical psychology, in which psychologists attempt to use observation, interviews, and other techniques to develop more integrated descriptions of the person as a whole (Adams, 1964, pp. 261–262). We will not present a comprehensive glossary here; instead we will define a limited selection of terms from these two bodies of literature that you will need to know as you read this chapter.

> *Test.* A "test," as used in this book, is a set of questions with an accepted set of presumably correct answers, designed to gather information about some individual characteristics like achievement. Scoring a test usually requires the assignment of a score according to the number of correct responses given, though more complex methods are used in certain circumstances (Choppin, 1977, p. 211).
>
> *Scale.* A "scale," on the other hand, is an instrument whose questions do not typically have correct and incorrect answers. These instruments are designed to measure such characteristics as attitudes, interests, values, beliefs, and behaviors. Scales constructed as "a series of questions each with a list of alternative answers, covering various aspects of a topic" are termed "questionnaires" (Choppin, 1977, p. 229). Rather than using questions, "Likert scales" consist of a set of statements that are either favorable or unfavorable to the particular attitude under examination. Respondents simply choose where on a five-point scale (from "strongly agree" to "strongly disagree") their attitude falls (pp. 230–231). "Behavioral scales" examine behaviors rather than attitudes by asking students to report on the frequency with which they do certain things, like reading a book on a particular topic (pp. 232–233).
>
> *Standardized.* A test or scale is "standardized" to the extent that it has been administered and scored under standard, or uniform, conditions and procedures. Although psychometricians argue that even teacher-made tests should be administered and scored in this way, usually people use the term "standardized" as a synonym for "published." Teachers or administrators purchase the published tests so that they can compare their students' performance with those of other students in other settings (Sax, 1974, pp. 250–251).
>
> *Norm-referenced.* In order to make these comparisons, the standardized tests must be norm-referenced. "Norm-referencing" a test means comparing scores of individuals on a test with those of some external reference group, for example, a randomly selected group of 100 fifth-graders from across the country.

When a score on a test is reported as falling above the 25th percentile, or as representing a ninth-grade reading level, the score is norm-referenced. Of course, it is impossible to interpret these statements without knowing the characteristics of the norm group. Even with that information, scores on a norm-referenced test tell us little about what individuals can do or what they know (Sax, 1974).

Criterion-referenced. In contrast with norm-referenced tests, "criterion-referenced" tests are designed to describe specifically what objectives individuals have mastered. The individual's performance is compared to some predetermined standard rather than to the performance level of other individuals. For example, rather than describe a student's performance as being in the top 20 percent of the class, a criterion-referenced description would say that the performance reaches a level that represents mastery of the task (perhaps 90 to 100 percent correct) (Sax, 1974).

Clinical interview. A "clinical interview" is an evaluation method in which an interviewer uses questions and props (e.g., pictures, problems, devices) in order to explore the concepts, reasoning patterns, beliefs, and attitudes of students. Rather than using an interview situation to elicit answers to prearranged questions, the interviewer uses questions to get the student verbalizing his or her thoughts and then follows up each answer with a probe to explore further the student's thoughts, always encouraging the student to talk more and more freely (see Posner & Gertzog, 1982; Johnston, 1992).

Other terms needed in our treatment of curriculum evaluation will be defined in the context of the foregoing discussion about curriculum analysis.

PURPOSES AND ROLES OF EVALUATION

In analyzing a curriculum from an evaluation point of view, we first need to clarify the *purposes* of an evaluation. As we have said, one conducts an evaluation to determine the value of something. But why determine its value? What would one do with this information? Most evaluation experts contend that the main reason to conduct an evaluation of any kind in the context of a curriculum is to provide information for making decisions about either individuals or the curriculum. Figure 10.1 depicts the distinction between these two kinds of decisions and summarizes the following discussion.

Decisions about Individuals

Decisions about individuals are necessary for six purposes: *diagnosis, instructional feedback, placement, promotion, credentialing,* and *selection*. Those who must make *diagnostic* decisions require information about strengths and weaknesses and determination of areas that need special instructional attention. Diagnostic methods include (1) observations of student performance; (2) attitude, interest, and behavioral scales; and (3) standardized achievement and aptitude tests with subscores. *Instructional feedback* decisions concern adjustments students might need to make in their approach to studying a subject based on their knowledge of the progress they are making. Most teacher-made tests and

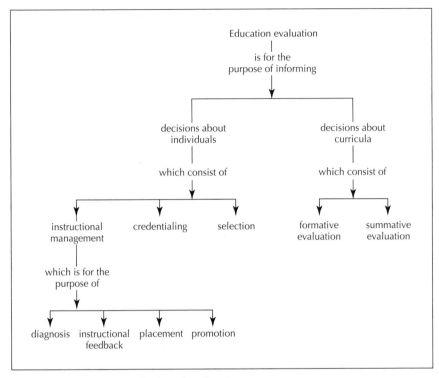

FIGURE 10.1 Purposes and roles of evaluation.

quizzes are intended, in part, to help students monitor their progress and adjust their approaches. To make *placement* decisions, information about the level of proficiency of the students in particular skills is required, in order to place them in groups that are relatively homogeneous. Similarly, decisions about *promotion* or its opposite, retention, are based on information about the proficiency and maturity of students, information necessary in order to decide whether or not to promote to the next grade level. Standardized tests, individual conferences, and teacher recommendations based on in-class observations are typically used methods for these two types of decision.[2] *Credentialing* decisions have to do with certification, licensure, and otherwise attesting to the competence of a program graduate. Typically, these decisions require attaining a predetermined passing level on a test designed by the credentialing body, typically the state or a professional organization like the American Bar Association. *Selection* decisions, such as those made by college admissions offices, typically use existing data about student achievement like grades, but may also depend on standardized tests like the Scholastic Aptitude Test.

Most curricula do not provide data regarding the students that have typically been enrolled or the performance levels attained by these students. In fact, the only attention given by most curricula to student performance on evaluation instruments is the assurance that the curriculum prepares the students for credentialing tests or for nationally normed, standardized tests.

Curriculum Decisions

Evaluation for the purpose of informing decisions about a curriculum is aptly termed "curriculum evaluation."

Since the definition of "curriculum" varies,[3] we should expect evaluation to mean many things to many people, depending upon what they think a curriculum is. If "curriculum" refers to a document such as a content outline, scope and sequence, or syllabus, then "curriculum evaluation" might mean a judgment regarding the value or worth of such a document. Is the document complete, internally consistent, and well written? Does the document represent a curriculum that has sufficient depth and breadth and is well organized, rigorous, and up to date? How can it be improved?

On the other hand, if "curriculum" refers to the experiences of the student, then "curriculum evaluation" might mean a judgment about the value of the educational experiences afforded to the students. Are the experiences educational, challenging, and engaging? Are they appropriate, wholesome, and safe for children of this particular age? Are students of different backgrounds treated equitably? How can the educational experiences be improved?

Alternatively, for a definition of "curriculum" as learning objectives, "curriculum evaluation" might refer to the actual outcomes of the educational process. For example, what concepts and skills do students learn in a particular course? How do the outcomes of this curriculum compare with those of a different curriculum, perhaps this one's predecessor? How well do the students learn what was intended? Are there any side effects? Are the students able to use what they learn? Which students seem to benefit the most and the least from the curriculum? How can the benefits to all students be maximized?

Curriculum evaluation decisions are of two types: decisions as to how to improve the curriculum require a "formative" evaluation, whereas a decision as to whether to continue to use the curriculum requires a "summative" evaluation (Scriven, 1967). Evaluation plays a formative role when it occurs during the ongoing curriculum development process. Questions of the following sort are typical: Are students getting the point? Are teachers well equipped to handle the new demands that the curriculum places on them? Is the time required to teach the curriculum realistic? Are the materials too difficult? Field testing of a curriculum constitutes one type of formative evaluation.

Evaluation plays a summative role when it enables administrators to decide whether or not a curriculum is good enough to warrant institutional support. Decisions on whether a school system should formally adopt a curriculum, or whether an external funding agency should continue to support a curriculum, are the kinds of decision that can be informed by an evaluation serving a summative role. The important difference between evaluations serving formative and summative roles is the location of the decision maker and the evaluation. In formative evaluation the decision maker is part of the curriculum development effort, and thus the evaluation is an internal process. In summative evaluation the decision maker is external to this effort and so, therefore, is the evaluation. For example, in a formative evaluation a curriculum project director might assemble a panel of historians to examine draft materials for the accuracy of facts, the biases of the writers, and the comprehensiveness of the coverage. The project director would use this information as a basis for suggesting to the project staff revisions of the materials. In a summative evaluation the same panel of historians might be assembled, but this time by an evaluator hired by the national foundation funding the project. The evaluator would use the findings of the panel as one basis for a recommendation to the foundation on future funding of the project. It is the distinction between the internal and the external evaluator, rather than the kinds of data collected, that is most significant in contrasting formative and summative evaluation.

Methods of Evaluating Individuals and Curricula

As might be expected, whether an evaluation decision is about individuals or curricula significantly affects the methods used. Methods such as questionnaires, interviews with teachers, content analyses of curriculum materials, comparisons of achievement test data for groups using different curricula, follow-up interviews of course graduates, and case studies of classrooms are typical of those used in evaluations focused on curriculum decisions. Methods such as norm- and criterion-referenced test data, clinical interviews, and family or professional conferences to identify an individual's strengths, weaknesses, problems, and concerns are typical of evaluation methods used to inform decisions about individuals.

The reason for the common confusion of these two purposes is that the same information, e.g., student test data, can be used for both kinds of decisions: about individuals and about curricula. However, failure to make this distinction can result in collecting costly but unnecessary information and missing low-cost opportunities to gather important information. For example, if the evaluation is supposed to inform decisions about a curriculum rather than about individuals—for example, if its purpose is to identify the trouble spots in the curriculum so that someone can decide how to fix them—it is not necessary to collect the same information from every student, or even to collect any information from some students. A sample of students can be used for data collection, and a wider range of information can be collected by gathering different data from different students.[4]

STANDARDIZED TESTING AS A MEANS OF MAKING DECISIONS

The widespread use of standardized tests to determine whether an individual is promoted from one grade to the next, placed in one track or another, awarded a degree, or admitted to a university can be problematic. In U.S. schools, over 114 million state-mandated, local district, or special education standardized tests are administered every year (Haney, Madaus, and Lyons in press, cited in Madaus and Kellaghan, 1992, p. 126). As a result of the Bush Administration's 2001 No Child Left Behind Act, all states, by the 2005–2006 school year, will have to assess the skills of every child, every year, in grades three through eight and once in high school in math and language arts. By the 2007–2008 school year, states will also have to assess students in science in grades three through twelve. Each assessment is to "involve multiple, up-to-date measures of academic achievement, including measures that assess higher-order thinking skills" (FairTest, 2001–2002). FairTest, a non-profit organization in Massachusetts that monitors standardized tests, has not found one test that meets this criterion.

There are definite advantages to using standardized tests. Some of what students learn can be counted; progress in some disciplines can be measured. The learning students do that can be quantified, tabulated, efficiently graded, recorded, and publicized can then be used by policy makers to support new programs. In fact, the results of standardized tests have been used to implement federal legislation such as the National Defense Education Act of 1958, the Elementary and Secondary Education Act of 1965, and the Education for All Handicapped Children Act of 1975 (Madaus and Kellaghan, 1992, p. 131).

Standardized tests also enable policy makers to initiate reforms and to control, to a great extent, the curricula in schools. As Sarah Freedman has pointed out, tests are "one of the few levers on the curriculum that [they] can control" (Freedman, 1995, cited in Kohn, 1999, p. 87). Several studies have shown a close correlation between classroom teaching and the standardized tests they know students will take (Stodolskly, 1988, cited in Madaus and Kellaghar, 1992, p. 144). Teachers are under a great deal of pressure to teach to the tests because often the stakes for their students are high. Promotion to the next grade, graduation from high school, or admission to college can be tied to scores on standardized tests.

Problems of Fairness

The potential problems with using standardized tests—especially for minorities, women, and the poor—as widely as we do in the United States lie within the advantages. The control exerted on teachers can also curtail their creativity in addressing the needs of individual students. In 19th century England, Mathew Arnold, a school inspector at the time, pointed out: "It is found possible by ingenious preparation to get children through the . . . examination in reading, writing, and ciphering, without their really knowing how to read, write and cipher" (cited in Madaus and Kellaghan, 1992, p. 122).

Standardized tests are an efficient means of grading because generally they are timed and comprised of multiple-choice questions. Multiple-choice questions reward students for choosing the correct answer and doing it quickly. Linda Bond found that 29 states used at least one test made up of only multiple-choice questions (Bond, 1996, cited in Kohn, p. 83). Unfortunately, they thereby limit the type of knowledge being tested, because there is typically little room for creativity, ambiguity, developing an idea, or reflection. In addition, for students to do well on state-mandated tests, teachers much devote considerable time to preparing students for those tests, thereby eliminating many other curricula possibilities.

Alfie Kohn, a critic of standardized tests, sees only negative results for spending class time on preparation for these tests: "Excitement about learning pulls in one direction; covering the material that will be on the test pulls in the other . . . We don't want kids to get in the habit of skimming a book, looking for facts they might be asked on a test, instead of really thinking about and responding to what they're reading" (Kohn, 1999, p. 90). In addition, Cathy Hall found that those who engaged in the most superficial thinking performed best on the SATs: "Scores were negatively correlated with a deep approach to learning" (Hall, 1995, cited in Kohn, 1999, p. 262).

Finally, because standardized tests are designed to categorize students, the questions must include items that most students will not know. Looking at how one reading achievement test was constructed, Jeannie Oakes point out that, "Only those items are kept that a substantial number of these students miss. We have no guarantee that those items that are kept are the best determinants of reading achievement per se. We know only that they best separate students along a continuum of low to high scores" (Oakes, 1985, p. 10).

Regardless of the advantages or problems with standardized tests for the general population, minority children, poor children, children of less educated parents, and women—all are groups who do less well on standardized tests than other U.S. students. During the 2000-2001 school year, minorities, except for Asians, had substantially lower SAT scores than white students. With possible scores ranging between 200 and 800, on the math section, white students scored an average of 531, Black students scored 426, Hispanics scored 465, and American Indians scored 479. On the verbal section, white students scored an average of 529, Blacks scored 433, Hispanics scored 460, and American Indians scored 481 (College Entrance Examination Board, 2002).

The poorer the students' families are, the lower their scores will be. Every $10,000 increase in income corresponds to a substantially higher SAT score. The average SAT score for students whose families earned less than $10,000 in 1998 was 873; if families earned $10,000 to $20,000, the score was 918; if $20,000 to $30,000, 972; if $30,000 to $40,000, 993 and so on up to a family income of $100,000 and above, the average score was 1130 (College Admission Test Scores by Family Income, 1998, citied in Kohn, 1999, p. 262).

In addition to income, levels of parental education also influence the scores students earn on the SATs. In 2001, the College Board found that the less education parents had, the lower from the mean score would be their children's test results. Children who had parents with no high school diploma were 95 points less than the mean score of 506 on the verbal section and 76 points less than the mean score of 514 on the math section. Children whose parents held graduate degrees scored 53 points higher on both math and verbal sections (College Board, 2001, cited in WORLD ALMANAC, 2002, p. 239). In 1998, whereas over 27% of white males and 22% of white females had completed four or more years of college, only 14% of Black males and 15% of Black females had completed four years of college; only 11% of male and 11% of female Hispanics had completed four years of college (Census Bureau, 1999, p. 169).

Gender, too, affects scores on standardized tests. For women taking the SAT IIs in physics, the scores are consistently 50 points below those of men. According to Pamela Zappardino, psychologist and executive director of FairTest (an organization that focuses on assessment reform), found that this gender gap does not vary even when family income or parental education are taken into account (American Physical Society, 1996). Zappardino found similar results with the SAT math test which, she says, usually does not accurately predict women's performance in college math classes: "I think there's a fallacy in the assumption that the SAT or GRE is actually telling us something. At best, the SAT only accounts for about 16 percent of the variance in first-year college grades. That isn't a great predictor, by anybody's yardstick. The SAT math test, for example, consistently underpredicts women's performance in college math courses" (American Physical Society, 1996, web).

The consequences of standardized test performance extend far beyond any particular grade, even beyond school years. In Massachusetts, for example, thousands of students scheduled for high school graduation in June, 2003, had not yet passed the MCAS, a standardized test required for a diploma. As of October, 2002, one in five seniors, mostly from the urban, poor communities, had not passed. FairTest estimates that "at least 10 percent of the 2003 graduating class who might otherwise have been accepted to college will instead have their way blocked by MCAS" (FairTest, 2002, web).

Responses to the Problems

Recognizing the biases and inadequacies of standardized tests, many educators are exploring the range of alternative ways to assess what students know. Many now believe that a single measure of language or mathematical ability is not an adequate assessment of a person's potential. Canadian colleges do not require students to submit SAT scores or any other standardized test results. Several U.S. schools now make submission of standardized test scores optional. Sarah Lawrence, for example, evaluates applicants on the basis of grades, class rank, extra-curricular activities, and extensive writing samples.

While the new federal law does require assessment of student performance in reading and math for students in grades three through eight, it does not require those assessments to be standardized tests. At the elementary school level, Maine and Nebraska, among other states, are developing plans to use a combination of types of assessment. In the Bangor, Maine school district, for example, students take local reading and writing tests and compile portfolios of their work in class (FairTest, 2002, web).

At the high school and university levels there are also alternative assessments. In Texas, the legislature initiated a plan in 1997 to admit the top ten percent of all graduating high school seniors to a state university. Intended to address the dropping enrollment of minority students after the Texas Supreme Court ruled against affirmative action, the plan focuses on a more comprehensive look at student performance than a single standardized test can give. University admissions officers, according to Gerald Torres and Penda Hair, look at "not only test scores but each student's complete high-school record—including class rank, the number and type of courses taken, essays, work experience, extracurricular activities, public service, and the evidence of leadership abilities" (Torres and Hair, 2002, p. B20). At the University of Texas at Austin students admitted under these guidelines have done as well as other students with SAT scores 200 to 300 points higher (Torres and Hair, 2002, p. B20).

Student portfolios can also take into account differing student backgrounds and abilities. Portfolios, says Howard Gardner, show "the development of productive and reflective skills, cultivated in long term projects" (Gardner, 1993, p. 182), in contrast to the usual standardized test that reflects mastery of information out of any context. He defines intelligence as "the ability to solve problems or fashion products that are of consequence in a particular cultural setting or community" (Gardner, 1993, p. 15). Using this definition opens a broad range of abilities—verbal, mathematical, spatial, musical, and so on—to be evaluated. To demonstrate knowledge, students of history, for example, should "be able to read the daily newspaper or weekly newsmagazine and draw on relevant historical principles both to explain what is happening and to make plausible predictions about what is likely to happen next" (Gardner, 1993, p. 190).

THE ROLE OF TECHNOLOGY IN EVALUATION

There are several important ways that technology has affected (and will affect) evaluation, primarily evaluation employing standardized testing. Technology has changed the way tests are administered and scored and the ways in which those scores are processed and publicized. It has also created new avenues for test preparation both in and out of the school setting.

Test Administration

Technology has changed the handling of test administration. For example, students can now complete tests via networked computers, as is the case for certain exams administered by the College Board. This practice has not yet had much impact at the primary or secondary level. (That is, not since the implementation of machine scored tests long ago). It is not unreasonable to assume that the use of networked computers for administering standardized tests will escalated in the next several years. Technology for managing online tests is already available. Scantron (*www.scantron.com*), the company best known for machine scoring tests now provides such technology. Another provider of sophisticated technologies to manage evaluation and assessment is Pearson Educational Technologies. (*www.pearsonedtech.com/*).

Test Preparation for Students

There is now a wider array of material marketed to prepare test takers than ever before. Much of it comes in electronic form, i.e., automatically graded practice tests available on CD-ROMs or web sites. Test publishers, both governmental and for profit, offer test preparation software. For example, the College Board offers a variety of services for takers of the SAT as do several state education departments for their own standardized tests. (New York State Regents Examinations and answer keys are available online at *www.emsc.nysed. gov/ciai/testing/hsregents.html*.) Private publishers and test preparation services (like Kaplan) also offer test preparation software for state and other standardized exams (see *www.barronseduc.com/testpreparation.html*, or *www.kaplan.com/* for example). School districts and teacher professional organizations offer online practice tests as well.

Calculator Use

The technology used by students while taking tests has changed due largely to calculators and, specifically, the graphing calculator. Graphing calculators are now required for certain Advanced Placement and state examinations.

Instantaneous Scoring

When "standardized tests" refer to tests made by curriculum publishers, then technology can provide instantaneous feedback for teachers and students in well-equipped schools. Students complete practice tests or homework assignments at the computer, which are then automatically graded by the computer, thus aiding in formative evaluation. The feedback includes not only how a particular student faired but can also include statistical analysis of entire tests or assignments or specific items within a test.

Test Generation Software

Test generation software allows teachers to pick and choose questions from databases of test questions allowing customization from a set of publisher-generated questions. While these items most commonly include multiple-choice questions, a variety of question formats are available. (See *www.eduware.com* for example.) Teachers can add to the questions either from within the test generation software of by adding their own pages to tests. Order of questions may also be randomized, making multiple versions possible. Test generation software is often included in curriculum packages or may be purchased separately, allowing teachers to use items from previous standardized state exams in place of tests provided by the textbook publisher.

Publication of Test Results

School and district results for standardized tests are now widely and easily available to anyone with an Internet-connected computer. Most state departments of education (as mandated by the "No Child Left Behind Legislation") publish school statistical data in the form of "school report cards" via the World Wide Web. Prominent in this data are standardized test results. A summary taken from the NCLB web site of what "report cards" include is shown in Figure 10.2. The wide spread availability of this data allows almost anyone to interpret (or misinterpret) the data and evaluate schools' curricula.

What are the requirements of the No Child Left Behind Act for states and school districts to publish "report cards" on school performance?

Starting with the 2002-2003 school year, state test results are reported to the public in order to hold schools accountable for improving the academic achievement of each and every one of their students. The following information must on the the report card:

- student academic achievement on statewide tests disaggregated by subgroup
- a comparison of students at basic, proficient, and advanced levels of academic achievement (These levels are determined by your state.)
- high school graduation rates (how many students drop out of school)
- the number and names of schools identified for improvement
- the professional qualifications of teachers
- the percentages of students are not tested

School districts must prepare annual reports for parents and the public on the academic achievement of all schools combined and of each individual school. The school district report cards must include the same information in the state report card. In the case of an individual school the report card must include whether it has been identified for school improvement and how its students performed on the state test compared to the school district and state as a whole.

FIGURE 10.2 What is required in school "report cards?"
(NCLB, 2001) *www.nclb.gov/next/faqs/accountability.html#4*

EVALUATION INFORMATION PROVIDED BY A CURRICULUM

The first step in analyzing your curriculum from an evaluation point of view is to try to identify any evaluation data (e.g., test scores), suggestions (e.g., questions), or instruments (e.g., scales) provided by the curriculum materials or in the research literature. If you can find any data, suggestions, or instruments specifically associated with the curriculum, try to determine the purposes and roles that evaluation information is intended to serve. Is it supposed to provide information for decisions about individual students, and if so, for what kinds of decisions? Is it supposed to provide information for decisions about the curriculum, and if so, are the decisions supposed to serve a formative or a summative role?

In searching for evaluation suggestions and instruments, look beyond the obvious sources, such as end-of-unit and end-of-year tests. Tests are only one means of gathering evaluation information. Observation checklists, cri-teria for evaluating essays, reports, and projects are occasionally suggested. Homework assignments, student projects, writing assignments, and seatwork contained in the curriculum materials can serve evaluation as well as instructional functions. Discussion questions and recommendations for student interviews and conferences can also be used to improve both instruction and evaluation.[5]

EVALUATION PLANNING AS CURRICULUM ANALYSIS

Up to this point we have examined evaluation data and strategies explicitly provided by the curriculum developers for decision making. However, we do not have to rely only on what they provide. We can devise a hypothetical curriculum evaluation ourselves as part of a curriculum analysis. Deciding what to evaluate and how provides a new angle from which to examine a curriculum. The analyst is able to view the curriculum critically and to identify the aspects of it that are crucial for its success.

What are the kinds of things you would want to evaluate regarding the curriculum? How would you know if the curriculum were a success? What is supposed to occur in classrooms, labs, or the field when the curriculum is fully implemented and taught properly? What are your concerns about the curriculum that an evaluation could help you clarify? Answers to these questions can help you determine what aspects of the curriculum you would want an evaluation to focus on.

Outcomes-Based Evaluation

Although there are many aspects of a given curriculum about which to inquire, most evaluations focus on outcomes. In this sense they are "bottom-line" or "pay-off" evaluations (Scriven, 1967). In fact, most evaluations focus on only those outcomes that reflect the curriculum's goals and objectives, what we shall term the "narrow" sense of outcomes-based evaluation. The question typically asked is "How well did the curriculum achieve what it intended to achieve?" Since different curricula have different goals and objectives, comparative outcomes-based evaluations of curricula are problematic. Curriculum "horse race" studies (Walker & Schaffarzick, 1974) comparing one curriculum with another on the basis of some achievement measure are inherently flawed, because there can be no truly neutral "yardsticks" to use in comparing curricular outcomes. Such studies merely determine which curriculum the test is more biased toward. In fact, the narrow sense of outcomes-based evaluation provides more an assessment of instructional effectiveness than one of the curriculum.

On the other hand, outcomes-based evaluations taken in the broad sense, evaluations that look beyond the official curriculum's goals and objectives, provide information on both main effects and side effects of the curriculum (Posner & Rudnitsky, 1994). "Main effects" are the major outcomes intended by the curriculum. "Side effects" are the by-products produced inadvertently by the curriculum. Side effects include biases or distortions produced by an overemphasis on one content orientation, principle of organization, teaching method, or evaluation approach. Occasionally the risk of producing undesirable side effects is so great or the possible side effects are so serious that the curriculum is too dangerous to implement. However, more typically, identification of possible side effects merely alerts teachers or administrators to pitfalls that they should try to avoid.

Whether explicitly anticipated or not, curricula have both long- and short-term outcomes. Short-term outcomes include what students remember and can do during and immediately after taking a course, teacher satisfaction with a curriculum, and community support for a curriculum, among others. Longer-term outcomes include, among other things, what students remember and can do with their knowledge well after the details of the course are forgotten, student attitudes toward the subject matter, and general support for the school generated by the curriculum. Obviously, it is long-term outcomes that ultimately matter most. Curricula that produce impressive short-term test-score results and make everyone feel good about the curriculum but leave little residue are not worth the substantial resources needed to implement them. The trouble is that long-term results are difficult to determine in a timely manner. Nevertheless, because of their significance, some effort to collect data on long-term outcomes is important to consider. Administering follow-up questionnaires to graduates of the school, monitoring the academic progress of students in a curriculum as they move from elementary to middle and to high school, studying the extent to which teachers using the curriculum engage in professional development activities, and examining the extent to which parents become involved in their children's education all can contribute to a longer-term assessment of outcomes. The more comprehensive the evaluation, the broader is the profile obtained of the curriculum.[6]

Consider the outcomes that you would want an evaluation to consider. On which educational goals and objectives[7] would you want achievement data?

What long-term benefits is the curriculum supposed to provide? To whom? What would you accept as evidence that the teachers had achieved what the curriculum had intended? On what other effects of the curriculum would you want information? Consider especially possible undesirable side effects.

Intrinsic Evaluation

Outcomes may not, and probably should not, be the only evaluation concern. Scriven distinguished between "pay-off" and "intrinsic" evaluations. He provides a useful analogy: "If you want to evaluate a tool, say an axe, you might study the design of the bit, the weight distribution, the steel alloy used, the grade of the hickory in the handle, etc., or you might just study the kind and speed of the cuts it makes in the hands of a good axman" (Scriven, 1967, p. 53).

This analogy reflects a conception of a curriculum as an instrument with features such as goals, content, and teacher-training requirements that are distinct from the curriculum's effects on students, teachers, and the community. Stake (1967) made a similar distinction between outcome evaluation data and other kinds of data he called "antecedents" and "transactions" (see Figure 10.3).

Antecedents. The term "antecedents" refers to conditions existing before students interact with teachers and subject matter. Characteristics of students and teachers, state mandates, community expectations, and available resources are all antecedents. As you have probably noted, antecedents are essentially equivalent to frame factors.[8] You can now use your analysis of frame factors from Chapter Eight to suggest your evaluation concerns regarding necessary antecedents.

Data on antecedents are particularly useful in determining whether certain claims made by the curriculum are empirically supported. For example, the curriculum might claim that it is appropriate for students with a broad range of abilities. Evaluating such a claim requires data on student ability or aptitude levels, i.e., data on an antecedent, in addition to comparative outcome data on student achievement.

Transactions. According to Stake, whenever a student interacts with a teacher, guidance counselor, coach, librarian, other students, or instructional material, a "transaction" occurs. In other words, transactions comprise the

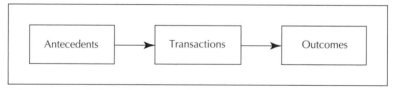

FIGURE 10.3 Stake's evaluation model.

process of education.[9] Transactions are not as distinct from one another as are antecedents and outcomes. One transaction flows smoothly into another with only arbitrary demarcations between them. Classroom discussions, individual conferences, homework problems, and seatwork are just four of the myriad examples that could be given. Data on transactions are particularly important in curriculum evaluation to explain why certain outcomes did or did not occur. For example, if certain kinds of classroom discussions are supposed to be the primary method for teaching students to analyze the validity of arguments, it would be crucial to collect some data on whether such discussions actually occurred. Time allocated to various classroom activities, type and number of questions asked and answered, and the extent to which students were engaged in the activities might be data relevant to determining whether the curriculum was ever even implemented as intended. This sort of determination would be necessary in both formative and summative evaluations.

Data on transactions also give the evaluator information on the way the curriculum has functioned, the variety of ways it has been implemented, and the possible pitfalls a teacher might face in using it. What are potential problems or rough spots in its operation? What aspects have been crucial for its success? How has the curriculum been implemented? What kinds of adaptations have been productive? What kinds have been counterproductive? What have been the trade-offs?

In Chapter Eleven, we examine the concerns that the M:ACOS developers identified as significant and at which they targeted their evaluation efforts. You might want to look at that section now to see an example of an evaluation addressed to such concerns.

PERSPECTIVES ON CURRICULUM EVALUATION

We can capture the essence of a curriculum by identifying what counts in judging the curriculum's success: that is, by identifying a curriculum's evaluation criteria. Different evaluation criteria embody different evaluation questions and methods. For example, whether students remember the major events in U.S. history is quite a different question than whether students can interpret current events in the context of U.S. history. Likewise, methods for answering these questions are very different. By identifying the evaluation questions and methods of each perspective on curriculum, we learn more about each perspective for use in curriculum analysis. Although every curriculum evaluation is concerned with the value or worth of a curriculum, what counts as valuable or worthy depends on one's perspective.

Traditional.   A traditional curriculum emphasizes recall of facts, mastery of basic skills, and inculcation of traditional values. The major evaluation questions, therefore, seek to measure whether the students have acquired the information, mastered the basic skills, and internalized the accepted values. Methods for answering these questions include comparison of standardized tests scores, answers given in classroom recitation, neatness and promptness in completing assignments, and ability and willingness to follow the teacher's directions. Evaluation is aimed at determining whether the accepted facts, skills, and values have been effectively transmitted.

Experiential.   The central purpose of experiential education is the continuing development of students through educative experiences. Evaluation questions seek to measure the broad range of both short- and long-term effects of experiential programs on students (e.g., Aikin, 1942). But, in addition to outcomes-based evaluations, experiential educators are interested in the intrinsic quality of experiences students have. Educative experiences are those that are democratic and humane, arouse students' curiosity, and strengthen their initiative (Dewey, 1938, pp. 34–38). Methods used to evaluate experiential curricula and students in experiential programs have been varied. The Eight-Year Study (Aikin, 1942) broke new ground in evaluation by providing a wide range of outcome measures, including measures of both cognitive and affective outcomes, as well as measures of personality traits. Experience-based career education (EBCE) is probably the most comprehensively evaluated program (Watkins & Corder, 1977; Biester & Kershner, 1979; Owens, 1977; Shively & Watts, 1977; Bucknam, 1976). However, nearly all these evaluations have been outcomes-based. Clearly, experiential curricula require both outcomes-based and intrinsic evaluation approaches. They require outcomes-based evaluation (in the broadest sense) to determine the effectiveness of the programs. But they also need intrinsic evaluations to determine the quality of the experiences that students have.

Behavioral.   A behavioral curriculum considers performance of skills to be the bottom line. The major evaluation question is whether students have acquired the behaviors that the curriculum targeted. Any method that objectively and quantitatively assesses behavior is appropriate, including paper-and-pencil tests, observational checklists, and practical exams. Measurement specialists dominate the design of evaluation methods, requiring that all methods achieve sufficient degrees of reliability and validity and that all curriculum evaluations be rigorously done. Criterion-referenced measures of student performance are preferred. These measures assess achievement in terms of absolute standards, rather than by comparing students with one another.[10]

Structure of the Disciplines.   A disciplinary perspective emphasizes the structure of the academic disciplines. Evaluation seeks to measure the knowledge students acquire, the nature of inquiry in which students engage, and the conceptual structure of the content taught. Questions include whether students gain insight into the conceptual structure of the discipline and whether students engage in real inquiry. Methods include giving students problems to solve, data to interpret, and experiments to design. Congruence of the curriculum with real inquiry in the disciplines is the bottom line.

Constructivist.   A constructivist perspective emphasizes students' understanding of basic concepts and development of thinking skills. Evaluation questions, therefore, seek to measure whether students acquire basic concepts meaningfully and learn to solve nonroutine problems. Methods include clinical interviews; analyses of student problem-solving efforts, including analyses of mistakes; and concept-mapping exercises. Determining what and how the individual thinks and understands is the ultimate aim of evaluation from a constructivist perspective.

Curriculum Analysis Questions

To summarize, this chapter has claimed that there are two ways in which reflecting on evaluation in the context of curriculum analysis can increase your understanding of a curriculum. The first way is by examining information provided by the curriculum developers in the form of data, suggestions, or instruments for collecting data. It is addressed in Questions 1, 2, and 3.

1. *Available Data.* What, if any, available data does the curriculum provide? What conclusions about the curriculum seem warranted based on the data provided?
2. *Standardized tests.* What standardized tests are relevant to this curriculum? How well is the curriculum aligned with the relevant standardized test?
3. *Instruments provided.* What instruments or suggestions for collecting data does the curriculum provide? Does the curriculum package include test-generation software? Are there web-based assessment and evaluation tools and/or practice evaluations provided by the publisher? If so, what are the advantages and disadvantages of these services? Are these products correlated to state and/or national standards? Do the assessment and evaluation tools reflect the same beliefs about the nature of the discipline as espoused in the standards? Are these tools equally fair for all social, economic, cultural, and ethnic groups?

The second way is by planning a hypothetical evaluation of the curriculum as a means to identify your concerns about it. It is addressed in Question 4.

4. *Concerns.* What are your concerns about the curriculum that could be clarified by evaluation data? Consider both short-term and long-term outcomes, antecedents, and transactions.

NOTES

1. See Worthen and Sanders (1973, pp. 210-215) for a comparison of definitions.
2. Of course, these latter two considerations are based on the assumption that practices like homogeneous grouping and retention are in the students' best educational interests. Some of the recent research does not support this assumption, e.g., Oakes (1985) and Goodlad (1984).
3. See Chapter One.
4. One systematic method used in this approach is termed "matrix sampling" (Sirotnik, 1974).

5. Less obvious, perhaps, is the occasional mention of classroom events that are supposed to occur and warnings about events to be avoided. By translating these informal hints into observational guidelines, the teacher has gained another important evaluation instrument.

6. See, for example, Welch and Walberg (1972).

7. See Chapter Four.

8. Antecedents include both the "input" and "context" data of Stufflebeam (1971).

9. Transactions are equivalent to Stufflebeam's (1971) "process" data.

10. See Chapter Nine.

CHAPTER 11

Curriculum Evaluation

Conflicting Perspectives

As a member of the Tyler Unified School District Curriculum Committee, Beth Savitsky, along with other members of the committee, has been examining the options for a new writing curriculum for Tyler. Of particular interest to members of the committee has been a curriculum developed by a team of teachers from Castleton, a neighboring district. But Beth has serious concerns about the value of the Castleton Writing Curriculum (CWC). Based on the evaluation data supplied by Castleton, the CWC has dramatically increased the students' scores on the State Writing Competency Test (SWCT). In fact Castleton students achieved the highest scores in the state on the SWCT, except, of course, for the two suburban districts outside the state's capital. Tyler students, in contrast, achieved among the lowest scores in the state. Obviously, the pressure on the committee to adopt the CWC has been significant.

However, Beth has serious concerns about the CWC. Do the students really learn to write or do they just receive coaching for the SWCT? Would the CWC be as appropriate for Tyler as it appears to be for Castleton? What does the curriculum look like in classrooms when it is fully implemented? To what extent has students' writing in subjects other than English and Language Arts improved? How might the curriculum be received by other teachers in the district? What are the strengths and limitations of the evaluation supplied by Castleton?

These are the kinds of questions that this chapter will help Beth address.

FOCUS: METHODS OF ASSESSMENT[1]

The study of evaluation is a critical aspect of curriculum analysis. We have already seen how basic concepts of evaluation increase our understanding of any curriculum. In this chapter, we shall extend our study of evaluation by an examination of two contrasting views. As we have found with other topics, contrasting different views brings tacit assumptions underlying current practices into sharper relief.

Dualities can always be misleading. As we have seen in previous chapters, the world simply cannot be neatly divided into pairs of opposites. And yet dualities do highlight essential differences between contrasting points of view. We have seen how fruitful it is to contrast perspectives on various curriculum topics, but also have discussed the limitations of this approach to curriculum study. In this section we use this approach in our study of curriculum evaluation by contrasting *measurement-based* with *integrated evaluation*.

MEASUREMENT-BASED EVALUATION

The dominant perspective on evaluation is a close relative of the technical production model of curriculum development. To review, this model is based on two assumptions: (1) that educational practices are justified by the learning outcomes educators seek to achieve, and (2) that these outcomes can be measured (see Chapter One).

This approach has channeled most of the effort in educational evaluation toward the development of tests to measure the schools' learning outcomes. This emphasis on measurement of outcomes linked closely to curriculum objectives has dominated educational evaluation in schools for at least the past forty years. The effect of this emphasis on measuring outcomes has been a blurring of the distinction between evaluation and psychological measurement in the work of many prominent evaluation specialists.[2]

The measurement-based approach to evaluation is consistent with an RD&D approach to curriculum change. As with an RD&D approach, "the task is to define the desired objective and achieve it" (Atkin & House, 1981, p. 26). Consensus on goals is assumed to be nonproblematic. Methods of collecting data are "narrowly focused and highly prespecified" (p. 26). Evaluation is conceived as a highly technical matter. State-level testing programs exemplify this approach. Objectives are often prespecified in behavioral terms, tests are given to evaluate achievement of these objectives, and instructional materials and teachers' activities are directed at achieving these objectives or at test performance itself.

Three different purposes of evaluation[3] have been important in the work of measurement-based evaluators: evaluation as a basis for making decisions about individuals, formative curriculum evaluation, and summative evaluation (see Figure 10.1). In each case, they have emphasized assessment that is "scientifically" based, i.e., designed according to principles of psychological measurement, objectives-driven, group- and individually administered, and norm- and criterion-referenced and standardized. Let us examine what each of these characteristics means.

By "scientifically based" most evaluation specialists mean that the instrument is constructed by "experts," termed "psychometricians," using measurement techniques that improve the reliability and validity of the tests. Such tests are presumed to be precise measures of whatever human characteristic they are supposed to measure. This presumption assures the test user that the test results are "objective" rather than "subjective." An objective evaluation instrument is reliable and unbiased and represents more than one person's observations (Johnston, 1987).

Objectives-driven evaluation means, of course, that evaluation focuses on those objectives toward which the curriculum is aimed. Without such information, the argument goes, teachers would not be able to provide appropriate instruction. How would teachers adjust their methods without knowing how well they are accomplishing their objectives? This argument is consistent with the technical-production model of curriculum.

Group-administered tests are generally preferred over individually administered tests on grounds of efficiency. Since measurement-based approaches are characterized by frequent testing, including pre- and post-unit tests, placement tests, and summative tests, testing must be conducted as efficiently as possible. Although most educators realize that individual testing yields higher-quality information, they also believe that the time constraints under which they work leave them little choice in the matter.

Norm referencing of tests, as discussed in Chapter Ten, means that determination of an individual's success on a test is based on how that individual's results compare with those of other individuals. When national or state results are available, norm referencing also means that any teacher's or school's results can be compared with the results of other teachers or other schools. Norm referencing provides a means for holding schools, teachers, and students accountable for results. Its great popularity derives from the assumption that information about relative performance levels is necessary and useful for schools, teachers, and pupils as they seek to improve their performance. Although many behaviorists prefer criterion-referenced measures, accountability pressures have maintained the predominance of norm-referenced tests.

A criterion-referenced test, as discussed in Chapter Ten, yields scores that the evaluator can interpret in reference to the instructional objective. Such a test provides information about where the student is in reference to the objective rather than in reference to the other individuals. Criterion-referenced tests are ideally suited for providing information that a teacher can use to make placement decisions and to decide whether or not a student has mastered a given unit.

According to the definition of a standardized test given in Chapter Ten, standardization of testing is necessary for any norm-referenced test, because it provides a degree of uniformity in content, format, administrative procedure, and scoring. Without standardization of these aspects of testing, we could not compare results of one testing with those of another. Furthermore, measurement specialists assume that to the degree that the context of performance is standardized the information obtained is more interpretable, because it is less "contaminated" by the particular testing situation.

The measurement-based approach has taken two principal directions. One has been followed for summative evaluation and for credentialing, selection and some instructional decisions about individuals. For these purposes, evaluation experts have required standardized, norm-referenced, group-administered tests. In summative evaluation, these evaluation efforts have typically sought to justify the expenditure of resources necessary to develop and implement a "new" curriculum by comparing the "new" curriculum with a more "traditional" one on the basis of achievement test scores.[4] On the other hand, for both formative evaluation and some instructional management decisions, evaluation experts have preferred criterion-referenced tests, based on a carefully specified set of behavioral objectives, usually individually administered, but occasionally group-administered (Lindvall & Cox, 1970).

Like the technical production curriculum model, much of measurement-based evaluation is exemplified by the work of Ralph Tyler (1942, 1949, 1958). According to Tyler, evaluation should follow seven steps:

1. Establish broad educational objectives.[5]
2. Classify objectives.[6]
3. Operationally define objectives, i.e., define them in behavioral terms.[7]
4. Identify situations in which pupils' achievement of objectives can be demonstrated.
5. Design or select measurement instruments.
6. Collect performance data.
7. Compare performance data with behaviorally stated objectives.

The influence of Tyler's approach to evaluation is evident not only in its explicit applications[8] but also in the general emphasis by educators on "alignment," or consistency, between the curriculum's objectives and the testing instruments employed.[9] This approach has been synonymous with evaluation until recently, when researchers in reading, writing, math, and science learning have begun to understand the development of literacy, subject-matter knowledge, and problem solving in greater detail.[10] This understanding has enabled them to develop methods for monitoring student outcomes based on a more dynamic, less behavioristic conception of those outcomes.

While few would claim that Tyler is a behaviorist, there is nevertheless a high degree of consistency between a behavioral perspective on curriculum and measurement-based evaluation. Both focus on the observable outcomes of instruction. Both compare these outcomes—i.e., student performance data— with behavioral objectives. And furthermore, both rely on principles of psychological testing, i.e., "psychometrics," in order to obtain these data and on statistical methods in order to analyze them.

Many people, when they think of curriculum evaluation, think of testing students using paper-and-pencil, norm-referenced, group-administered measures of achievement. This approach developed significantly during the 1960s, as new federally funded curriculum projects sought to justify the government's multimillion-dollar expenditures on curriculum development and dissemination projects. As the years advanced, so did the sophistication of the tests and the degree of reliance on them for evaluating the efforts of schools. Regular, systematic, nationwide testing by the National Assessment of Educational Progress (NAEP, 1983), as well as international comparisons of achievement test scores (IAEEA (International Association for the Evaluation of Educational Achievement), 1976), has gained wide publicity, contributing to the widespread criticism of schools. Currently most states administer tests developed in state education departments, as well as nationally normed, standardized achievement tests. Although there are good reasons to question the practice, the achievement test is now a well-accepted measure of the success of any curriculum.

As Walker and Schaffarzick (1974) pointed out twenty years ago, the value of achievement testing as a basis for evaluating curriculum is inherently limited. They showed that there is no such thing as a curriculum-neutral test. An achievement test demonstrates what content the operational curriculum includes and emphasizes. No achievement test can determine whether the curriculum was worth teaching. Rather than demonstrating the value of a curriculum, achievement testing demonstrates the degree to which the test measures what the teacher taught and vice versa—i.e., it measures alignment. Therefore, it is important to know what test evaluators use to evaluate a curriculum before concluding anything about the value of the curriculum based on the test.

While those responsible for summative evaluation and for college admissions decisions have relied almost exclusively on norm-referenced, standardized tests, educators performing formative evaluation and evaluation for instructional management have begun to turn to criterion-referenced measures. Although many elementary teachers still form reading and math groups and principals and guidance counselors still make promotion, retention, and placement decisions on the basis of global scores from norm-referenced, standardized tests, there is a growing trend toward using test items keyed to specific behavioral objectives. This trend is particularly noticeable in curricula developed as a series of behavioral objectives to be mastered, as in Bloom's mastery learning, Keller's PSI (Personalized System of Instruction), and Glaser's IPI, described in Chapters Seven and Nine. The most comprehensive documentation of this approach to evaluation can be found in Lindvall and Cox (1970).

For purposes of formative evaluation, criterion-referenced tests enable evaluators to determine whether the "logically derived ordering of objectives" (Lindvall & Cox, 1970, p. 15) is supported by empirical data. If most students master a particular objective in a sequence but do not master the succeeding objective, then the evaluators can conclude that either there is a missing step in the sequence or the objectives are out of order. Presumably the curriculum developers would then try to correct the problem.

For purposes of instructional management decisions, criterion-referenced tests enable teachers to place students correctly in the sequence and to determine when they are ready to move to the next level in the sequence. As stated by the evaluators of IPI,

> the IPI system requires each pupil to be placed in each learning continuum at the point commensurate with his performance level. The pupil then proceeds at his own rate of progress and demonstrates proficiency in each skill prescribed by his particular instructional sequence. . . . [While] the IPI program . . . allows each pupil to set his own learning pace, . . . the proficiency criteria for completion of a specified unit are identical for most pupils. . . . [Therefore] test items for measuring pupil performance must be designed to indicate whether or not specific behaviors have been mastered. . . . Each item is referenced to a particular curriculum objective. (Lindvall & Cox, 1970, pp. 15-16)

In summary, the measurement-based approach to evaluation is most closely related to a behavioral perspective. Behavioral perspectives are distinguished by their focus on behavioral outcomes of instruction. They regard these behaviors to be the learning outcomes themselves, not just indicators of learning. Therefore, from a behavioral perspective, test results represent samples of learning outcomes. From this perspective, it is technically feasible to provide test items that can conclusively show whether or not a student has mastered a unit of a curriculum. Thus, from this perspective, an absolute reliance on tests to determine when a student has mastered a curriculum is reasonable. As stated in IPI, "The tests are the basic instruments for monitoring [the student's] progress and diagnosing his exact needs. That is, they provide the basis for the continuing adjustment of his prescribed learning activities to make them more effective instruments for learning" (Lindvall & Cox, 1970, p. 21). An evaluation of a writing curriculum based solely on a test of writing skills like the SWCT (in this chapter's lead-off scenario) can be considered to be based on a behavioral perspective.

INTEGRATED EVALUATION

The problem with measurement-based evaluation, according to its critics, is its focus on trivial and contrived tasks. These tasks may not test the students' ability to use their knowledge and skills in the real world. In contrast with measurement-based evaluation, an integrated evaluation tends to be more consistent with an experiential perspective, though its proponents would likely object to any label. Like experiential education, integrated evaluation tends to be growth-oriented, student-controlled, collaborative, dynamic, contextualized, informal, flexible, and action-oriented. While few, if any, evaluations have all of these characteristics, many curricula provide for at least some of them.

Characteristics of Integrated Evaluation

Growth-Oriented. Both the experiential perspective and integrated evaluation are based on the premise that all our educational efforts, including evaluation, ought to strive for the growth and development of all students (Johnston, 1987; Hamilton, 1980). According to experiential educators and to evaluators using an integrated approach, educators have often lost sight of this goal. They have mistaken subgoals like "individual instructional tailoring, selection for special programs, and accountability" (Johnston, 1987, p. 336) for the ultimate goal of education. Mistaking subgoals for ultimate goals has led educators to practices that have not contributed to the achievement of the ultimate goal. For example, accountability has forced teachers to adopt as their goal good performance on group-administered, norm-referenced, standardized, objective tests (Johnston, 1987, p. 336). Many sound practices, such as modeling of silent reading by teachers, do not necessarily contribute to good performance on these tests. To make matters worse, some questionable practices, such as coaching for the test, do clearly improve students' test scores.

Student-Controlled.   While perspectives other than the experiential perspective might claim development of all students as their ultimate goal, no other perspective interprets this goal in terms of increasing the students' agency. As defined by Sizer (1973), "agency" is "the personal style, assurance, and self-control that allows [the student] to act in both socially acceptable and personally meaningfully ways." Giving students a measure of control over their environment by yielding a degree of decision-making responsibility (Wigginton, 1975b, p. 10) is a fundamental principle of experiential education that contributes to increasing the students' agency. Giving students the responsibility for deciding what to evaluate, as well as how to evaluate it, encourages students to "own" the evaluation and to use it as a basis for self-improvement (Graves, 1983).

Collaborative.   When we speak of collaborative evaluation, we mean that information is shared with those involved from beginning to end. The goal of the evaluation is to answer questions that both the student and the teacher or other evaluator want to answer. In this sense, integrated evaluation blurs the distinction between evaluation and learning and between the evaluator and the student, thereby encouraging reflection, thinking, and self-evaluation. It views students as "intelligent decision-makers in need of information about their own performance" (Johnston, 1987, p. 348).

Dynamic.   Although both measurement-based and integrated evaluations seek to measure student progress, they differ in the way they conceptualize that progress. An integrated evaluation seeks information on the growth of the students, on a continuous process of development, rather than on a set of discrete, static outcomes students achieve; it embodies "a shift from a snapshot metaphor to the cinematic metaphor" (Johnston, 1987, p. 342).

Contextualized.   Another principle that is consistent with both integrated evaluation and an experiential perspective is that the context of learning is paramount. To the experiential educator every detail of the school environment contributes in a cumulative way to the overall tone of the school and therefore to the experience of the student (Wigginton, 1975b, p. 8). Furthermore, every aspect of the curriculum to the fullest extent possible should be "brought to life with application in the real world for the benefit of the students involved and for the ultimate benefit of the larger society they will enter" (p. 15).

Like the experiential educator, the evaluator using an integrated approach recognizes the significance of context, particularly the contrast between the contexts of formal testing programs and those of effective learning activities. For example, the use of testing to hold a person publicly accountable makes taking the test an ego-involving task. In this context the person will likely do whatever is necessary to prevent the evaluator from finding out her weaknesses. However, for testing to be of maximum instructional use, the person tested must be willing to confront her weaknesses. Students, like accused criminals, know that they have the right to remain silent and are likely to exercise that right rather than risk having their responses used against them (Johnston, 1987). The conductor of an integrated evaluation recognizes not only that the context of testing differs from that of instruction, but also that the context of evaluation affects the nature of the procedure and the results obtained. For example, formal testing programs in reading frequently measure attainment of presumably discrete elements of the reading process. By focusing attention on these elements, the testing program encourages teachers to do likewise, resulting in programs that emphasize isolated subskills (Johnston, 1987). Some have claimed that this emphasis is responsible for the current state of reading instruction, in which an average of approximately three minutes a day is devoted to actual reading of extended discourse (Gambrell, 1984).

Informal.   An integrated orientation is less formal than measurement-based evaluation, intentionally blurring the distinctions not only between evaluation and learning but also between evaluation and teaching. What results is a more integrative view of these facets of education. Evaluations that teachers are most likely to use (1) are immediately accessible to them, (2) have purposes consistent with those of the teacher, (3) cover content similar to the content taught, and (4) provide information that the teacher personally "owns" and can relate to individual students (Dorr-Bremme, 1982; Johnston, 1987). Evaluations with these features are likely to take place in informal, one-to-one situations that arise during or in close proximity to learning activities. Group-administered, norm- or criterion-referenced, standardized tests, no matter how reliable and valid, provide information that is less timely, less closely related to the teachers' curriculum, and less easy to relate to the difficulties faced by an individual student. Integrating teaching and evaluation also implies that teachers need to know less about concepts and principles of educational measurement—e.g., how to interpret standard scores—and more about how to listen to and observe children.[11]

Flexible and Action-Oriented.   An integrated approach to evaluation is more flexible and action-oriented than a measurement-based approach. As stated above, proponents of integrated evaluation, like those who believe in experiential education, consider both short- and long-term objectives to be dynamic rather than fixed; they are constantly being revised as teachers and students collaboratively follow their progress and seize upon "teachable" moments. In the sense that information gathered is intended to be used as a basis for deciding what instructional actions are appropriate, an integrated orientation is also action-oriented. In this sense it is more akin to evaluation for decision making, as described in Chapter Ten, than to educational measurement.

Methods of Integrated Evaluation

Integrated evaluation borrows its methods from such disciplines as anthropology, psychotherapy, cognitive psychology, and sociolinguistics, rather than from behavioral psychology and psychometrics. From anthropology it borrows ethnography, a method of collecting and analyzing field notes that places the evaluator in the role of a participant observer trying to understand the meaning of the classroom environment from the perspective of its inhabitants (e.g., Erickson, 1986). From psychotherapy integrated evaluation borrows conference methods intended to encourage self-evaluation, based on the assumption that no personal change is possible without a belief in the need to change (e.g., Rogers, 1942). From cognitive psychology it borrows interview methods, including the clinical interview, designed to gain a deeper understanding of the student's thought processes. From research in sociolinguistics and social cognition it borrows methods for collecting natural samples of behavior, based on the assumption that the context of any process influences its goals, and therefore the assessment of it (e.g., Lave, 1988; Labov, 1973; Johnston, 1987; Vygotsky, 1962).

Thus, rather than emphasizing formal testing methods characteristic of measurement-based evaluation, integrated evaluation emphasizes naturalistic observations, conferences, and interviews (Johnston, 1992). Because of its recognition that context influences tasks, integrated evaluation is more likely to use natural settings as opportunities to gather evaluation information. "Kid-watching" (Goodman, 1985) has become for this approach a significant method of evaluation, but one that requires teachers to acquire new skills. In order to use observations to follow the progress of children as they acquire competence, teachers need to acquire knowledge of the processes by which this competence develops and how different contexts affect the process. "Writing conferences" (Calkins, 1986; Graves, 1983) and structured interviews (Paris & Jacobs, 1984; Posner & Gertzog, 1982) provide other ways of "getting alongside of children" (Clay, 1985; Graves, 1983; Nicholson, 1984). These approaches put the teacher in an advocacy rather than an adversarial role, in which the student's concerns are legitimate and deserving of serious attention. This relationship is similar to a professional-client relationship that emphasizes confidentiality, trust, and mutual control (Holdaway, 1979). Information *given* by students in these situations will be different from information *taken* by teachers in more formal testing situations (Johnston, 1987).

Consistent with integrated evaluation are new methods currently under development by teachers and evaluators, methods described as "authentic assessment" (Wiggins, 1989*a* and *b*; Archbald and Newman, 1988; Herman, Aschbacher, & Winters, 1992). These methods (also termed "alternative assessment") assume that the methods used to evaluate learning influence the kinds of tasks teachers present to their students. By focusing evaluation on higher-level objectives and tasks from the real world (i.e., more authentic tasks), teachers will begin to teach students to think and solve real world problems, use and integrate their knowledge and skills in real world contexts, and gain real understanding.

The concept of authentic assessment is not new. In fact, it is already well established as a successful standard in some of the less "academic" disciplines. Recitals, plays, art exhibits, and athletic contests are all assessments that students often eagerly anticipate. Preparation for these events becomes the focus of the program but is not like teaching for a test. The evaluation event is an opportunity for students to show others what they have accomplished. Unlike testing, these events are typically moments of celebration and community building.

Three major format catagories are used in authentic assessment: paper-and-pencil tasks, performances, and folios. Paper-and-pencil tasks most closely resemble traditional evaluation methods. They generally consist of a written question and a written response. What makes them authentic is the opportunity they afford for students to use their knowledge and skills in accomplishing a real world task. (See Figure 11.1.)

The boundaries between these formats are somewhat unclear; actual evaluation events typically span categories. Futhermore, the categories are not mutually exclusive but rather are nested. Performances can encompass a diversity of media, including the written word. Therefore, a paper-and-pencil task can also be a special kind of performance (and could also be a particular kind of portfolio entry). Performances may include visual and motor activities besides

---

Figure 11.1

A PAPER-AND-PENCIL TASK IN ECONOMICS.

You are the chief executive officer of an established firm. Your firm has always captured a major share of the market because of good use of technology, understanding of the natural laws of constraint, understanding of market systems, and the maintenance of high standard for your product. However, in recent months your product has become part of a new trend in public tastes. Several new firms have entered the market and have captured part of your sales. Your product's proportional share of total demand is continuing to fall. When demand returns to normal, you will control less of the market than before.

Your board of directors has given you less than a month to prepare a report that solves the problem in the short run and in the long run. In preparing the report, you should (1) define the problem, (2) prepare data to illustrate the current situation, (3) prepare data to illustrate conditions one year in the future, (4) recommend action for today, (5) recommend action for the next year, and (6) discuss where your company will be in the market six months from today and one year from today.

You must complete the following in the course of this project:

- Derive formulas for supply, demand, elasticity, and equilibrium.
- Prepare schedules for supply, demand, costs, and revenues.
- Graph all work.
- Prepare a written evaluation of the current and future situation for the market in general and for your company in particular.
- Show aggregate demand today and predict what it will be one year hence.
- Show the demand for your firm's product today and predict what it will be one year hence.
- Prepare and present your findings, predictions, and recommendations in a formal report to the board of directors.

Source: Adapted from Wiggins, 1989*b*.

writing. Performances also require practice and polishing and may take a long-term effort to produce. They also tend to emphasize integration of content and skill, collaborative group work, and student choice and design.

Folios (Mitchell, 1992) are multimedia collections of student work. They might even include records of a student's performances. What distinguishes them from mere collections is their reflective component. Students themselves select the work they want to include and actively assess and document their own progress. Teachers may guide this selection process by suggesting criteria. For example, a teacher might ask students to select the best and worst haiku poems they have written and explain why one is better than the others. Folio writing might resemble journal writing when it emphasizes students' self-reflection and aims to make students responsible for their own learning. Two types of folios, process folios and portfolios, differ in terms of what they include. Process folios document the processes of learning and creating, including earlier drafts, reflections on the process, obstacles encountered, and even dead ends. Portfolios focus on finished pieces of work. Their aim is to document and reflect on the quality and range of accomplishments rather than the process that produced them (see Figure 11.2).

Figure 11.2

GRADUATION BY PORTFOLIO AT CENTRAL PARK EAST SECONDARY SCHOOL.

As students prepare for graduation at Central Park East Secondary School (CPESS), a high school of 450 students in an East Harlem neighborhood in New York City, they work intensively to prepare portfolios of their work that will reveal their competence and performance in 14 areas. These range from science and technology to ethics and social issues, from school and community service to mathematics, literature, and history. The portfolios will be evaluated by a graduation committee composed of teachers from different subjects and grade levels, an outside examiner, and a student peer. The committee members examine the entries and hear the students' oral "defense" of their work as they determine when each student is ready to graduate.

Of the fourteen Portfolios, seven are presented orally before the Graduation Committee, four from the core subjects (asterisked below). The other seven are evaluated independently, although the student may be asked about them during the Graduation Committee hearing. While the final review is based on the individual student's accomplishments, Portfolio requirements can be based on group work.

The fourteen Portfolios include the following:

1 *Postgraduate Plan.* Each student outlines his or her current purpose for earning a diploma, since "reflecting on purposes helps to set goals." Long- and short-range career and life goals, financial concerns, living arrangements, and indicators of progress such as examinations, interviews, and letters of reference are included in this section.

2 *Autobiography.* This provides another opportunity for the student to reflect on his or her life and to plan for the future. Material included in this area may examine family history, special events or relationships, values or beliefs, in any of the variety of media—written or oral narrative, essay, art, video, drama, music, or other form selected by the student.

3 *School/Community Service and Internship.* Opportunities for working and serving others are part of student experiences each year starting in seventh grade. Students develop a formal résumé of their work experiences along with a project that demonstrates what they have learned from one or more of these experiences. Projects can include essays, videos, work samples, reference letters, and other demonstrations of their accomplishments combined with evidence of what they have learned.

4 *Ethics and Social Issues.* Students demonstrate their capacity to see multiple perspectives, weigh and use evidence, and reason about social and moral issues in any of a number of ways—by staging a debate, writing an editorial, discussing important issues raised in a novel or film, and/or creating a project that demonstrates these abilities.

5 *Fine Arts and Aesthetics.* Creative expression and creative appreciation are both evaluated. Students must create a "hands-on" exhibition of performance in any of the arts and offer evidence of knowledge or understanding in an aesthetic area by studying or critiquing a work, an artist, or a field of artistic expression.

6 *Mass Media.* Students must show that they understand how different forms of media work and how they affect people and their thinking. This understanding can be demonstrated through many types of projects or activities, ranging from essays to exhibits or media presentations, and must include a relevant bibliography.

7 *Practical Skills.* In line with CPESS's commitment to preparing students for all aspects of life, they must show evidence of working knowledge in a number of areas, ranging from health and medical care to employment, citizenship, independent living, computers and technology, and legal rights—in a variety of ways, ranging from securing a driver's license to registering to vote to demonstrating the ability to operate a computer.

8 *Geography.* A teacher-made test and a student-designed performance assessment are used to evaluate geographical knowledge and the ability to use geographical tools such as maps and globes.

9 *Second Language and/or Dual Language.* All students must demonstrate competence to work in a language other than English as a speaker, listener, reader, and writer. This requirement may be met through the New York State language proficiency exam or a College Board examination. In addition, all students must describe their personal experience with dual language issues and be prepared to discuss a key social or cultural issue associated with language use.

10 *Science and Technology.** Students must demonstrate knowledge in traditional ways—a summary of the work they have completed in high school and passage of a teacher-made or state competency test—as well as in performances that demonstrate use of scientific methodology (e.g., conducting and documenting an experiment) and awareness of how science is used in the modern world (e.g., by staging a debate or conducting research on a scientific development analyzing social costs and benefits).

11 *Mathematics.** Students must demonstrate basic skill knowledge by passing a state competency test and a teacher-made test. In addition, they must demonstrate higher-order thinking abilities by developing a project using mathematics for political, civic, or consumer purposes (e.g., social science statistics or polling, architectural blueprints) and either scientific or "pure" mathematics (e.g., using mathematics in a scientific application and/or studying a theoretical problem).

12 *Literature.** Students prepare a list of texts they have read in a wide range of genres to serve as the basis for discussion with the Graduation Committee. They also submit samples of their own essays about literary products and ideas.

13 *History.** In addition to passing a state competency test or faculty-designed test in history, students must prepare an overview of the areas of history they have studied in secondary school and a time line of major events and persons. They must also demonstrate understanding of historical work by conducting historical research using primary as well as secondary sources and developing a bibliography. Their work must draw connections between and among past and present events, weigh and use evidence, speculate on other possibilities, and evaluate how history is used or abused in current debates.

14 *Physical Challenge.* Students demonstrate and/or document their participation and proficiency in any team or individual sport or activity over the past four years. The goal is to encourage the development of lifelong health habits and attitudes of independence, interdependence, personal responsibility, and sportsmanship.

A final senior project is also required in an area of particular interest to the student, which may be one of the portfolio items explored in greater depth.

Portfolio items are evaluated for quality and demonstrated mastery using a grid which reflects major criteria: a **viewpoint** which encompasses wide knowledge and deep understanding, an ability to draw **connections** among information and ideas, appropriate use of **evidence,** an engaging **voice** and awareness of audience, use of proper **conventions,** and an understanding of the **relevance** of the topic/issue to contemporary concerns. When students have completed the portfolio, they have learned to inquire, critique, analyze, present, and defend their ideas. They have also learned to manage long-range tasks that require invention, planning, perseverance, initiative, reflection, and revision. In short, they are ready for the world outside of school.

Source: New York State Curriculum and Assessment Council 1992 *Building a Learning-Centered Curriculum for Learner-Centered Schools.* Interim report of the New York State Curriculum and Assessment Council to the Commissioner and the Regents, Albany, NY: New York State Education Department.

Use of Integrated Evaluation

Teachers have routinely performed integrated evaluations as a regular part of teaching. In addition, recent curriculum developments emphasizing meaning making by students, such as process writing (Graves, 1983), whole language (Goodman, 1986), and "constructivist" approaches to mathematics (Confrey, 1990) and science education (Eylon & Linn, 1988), employ selected aspects of integrated evaluation for formative purposes. Systematic summative evaluations of curricula exclusively employing integrated methods are extremely rare. An external agency providing funds to support a program ultimately wants to know what the bottom line is, and in education that bottom line is usually performance on some standardized test. Nevertheless, there have been some significant attempts to evaluate curricula both formatively and summatively using primarily integrated methods. Evaluation of M:ACOS is one such case.

The Case of M:ACOS

The developers of the curriculum evaluation for M:ACOS explicitly rejected behavioral psychology as a basis for evaluation.

The course has not been framed within the confines of a behavioral psychology, nor have its developers thought specifically in behaviorist terms as they prepared and tested it. Rather, the course was developed within a humanistic framework, by way of its emphasis upon the anthropological, biological and ethnographic. (Hanley et al., 1975, p. 467)

According to the M:ACOS evaluators, a behavioral perspective reduces a course to discrete behaviors. However, although such an approach is feasible, this reduction robs the course of "its special power and charm" (Hanley et al., 1975, p. 467). Instead, a more integrated approach was employed, in order to assess the success of the course and to determine areas that needed further development. The questions used to focus the assessment efforts concerned educational goals and objectives, pedagogy, and student characteristics:

1. Does M:ACOS help students learn to understand themselves and others in ways they were incapable of before, and are they able to use this new knowledge in and out of the classroom?
2. Do students gain a more accurate knowledge of specific topics by using these materials? Are they better at using evidence (including evidence from all types of media, not only written) and observing natural and social phenomena? Can they go beyond specifics to some organizing conjectures about human behavior?
3. Is there a consistent style of pedagogy embedded in M:ACOS that is identifiable by and appropriate for different types of students? Are the pedagogy and approach of the materials different from those of traditional social studies? If so, how does this pedagogy affect learning and class activities?
4. Do teachers' styles change in the course of teaching these materials?
5. How do the socioeconomic and ability variables affect the teaching and learning of this material? (Hanley et al., 1975, p. 468)

The emphasis was less on learning outcomes and more on student and teacher perceptions. As the M:ACOS evaluators contended, "In the past, evaluation has been focused too much on teacher assessments with only achievement test scores speaking for the students" (Hanley et al., 1975, p. 469).

The methods used in the M:ACOS evaluation included some tests designed to measure skills such as graphing and reading, vocabulary, attitudes, and personal preferences. However, the emphasis was on teacher and student interviews, classroom observations, and questionnaires. Periodic clinical interviews of a wide sample of students using open-ended questions, such as why they chose the answer they gave, provided explanations of the objective test performance. Interviews with teachers attempted to identify their reactions to the classroom materials, teaching styles, student responses, and staff development workshops. Classroom observations utilized checklists to gather information on classroom environment and to find out about "the interaction of curriculum, methods, students and teachers" (Hanley et al., 1975, p. 471). Questionnaires given to students helped evaluators determine student perceptions of classroom environment, student involvement and participation, success of various instructional media, what was learned from reading and homework, and student attitudes and learning styles. Open-ended questions at the end of the questionnaires helped evaluators interpret the limited-choice questions.

These methods were designed not only to find out if the curriculum achieved its goals, but also to provide insight into how it accomplished its goals and even into the process of learning itself. These methods provided information showing several notable accomplishments. Classrooms across the country consistently showed more variety of activities and materials, more small-group work and open discussion, and less reliance on teacher-dominated methods than with other curricula. This type of interactive classroom environment led the evaluators to conclude that M:ACOS was successful in establishing an environment that could lead to the accomplishment of its "social learning" (Hanley et al., 1975, pp. 472–473) goal. Student interview data also suggest that students were able to relate the lives of the Netsilik Eskimos to their own lives and even to express empathy toward the Eskimos. Furthermore, student questionnaires indicated that students did in fact find many other aspects of the curriculum relevant to their own lives.

Nevertheless, the evaluation also leaves us with significant questions regarding the success of M:ACOS. No evidence was available to determine whether the interactive classroom environments led to "learning gains, student satisfaction in learning, or attitude development" (Hanley et al., 1975, p. 473). Difficulties with concepts of natural selection, innate versus learned behaviors, and the uniquely human quality of language were evident in both tests and interviews. No data were available to determine if these conceptual difficulties could be attributed to the difficulties teachers had with the content. Neither was there sufficient evidence to determine the depth of student awareness "that what we regard as acceptable behavior is a product of our culture" (p. 474), a primary goal of the curriculum. Finally, there was insufficient data collected by the evaluators to respond to critics' charges that the curriculum materials—particularly the scenes in the films depicting the killing of children and old people and the bloody conclusion of the seal hunt—elicited emotional, and even physical, reactions for which both the children and the teachers were unprepared.[12]

IDEOLOGICAL UNDERCURRENTS

In spite of the differences between measurement-based and integrated evaluation, in some very fundamental ways they are similar. According to Apple (1977), they may both operate in ideologically conservative ways. The discussion of this contention that follows here builds directly on the discussion of hegemony in Chapter Five.

First, any enterprise is ideological if we define an ideology "as a taken-for-granted perspective held by a specific social group . . . [which] is necessarily incomplete, just as any accepted perspective is limited" (Apple, 1977, p. 475).

Using this definition, any enterprise is ideological if it maintains a conservative posture. According to Gouldner,

> What makes a theory conservative (or radical) is its posture toward the institutions of its surrounding society. A theory is conservative to the extent that it: treats these institutions as given and unchangeable in essentials; proposes remedies for them so that they work better, rather than devising alternatives to them; foresees no future that can be essentially better than the present, the conditions that already exist; and, explicitly or implicitly, counsels acceptance or resignation to what exists, rather than struggling against it. (Gouldner, 1970, p. 332)

From Apple's viewpoint evaluation is conservative to the extent that it focuses on individuals rather than on institutional structures (for example, tracking of students), and in so doing, uncritically accepts the very structures that may underlie its problems. The use of mass testing to determine the deficiencies of students with regard to evaluator-chosen performance categories, the labeling of students according to a standardized set of performance categories (like "gifted and talented," "underachievers," "slow learners," or "remedial problems") and the setting up of programs, or, as evaluations have termed them, "treatments," based on these categories all reinforce this focus.

Apple (1977) argues that a clinical viewpoint based on the concept of "deviance" manifests the conservative ideology of evaluation in an extreme form. Mercer explains that the clinical viewpoint

> is readily identified by several distinguishing characteristics. First, the investigator accepts as the focus for study those individuals who have been labeled deviant. In so doing, he adopts the values of whatever social system has defined the person as deviant and assumes that its judgments are the valid measures of deviance . . . without serious questioning.
>
> A second distinguishing characteristic of the clinical perspective is the tendency to perceive deviance as an attribute of the person . . . as a lack to be explained . . . a medical frame of reference . . . [that] sees deviance as individual pathology requiring diagnostic classification and etiological analysis for the purpose of determining proper treatment procedures and probable prognosis.
>
> Three additional characteristics of the clinical perspective are the development of a diagnostic nomenclature, the creation of diagnostic instruments, and the professionalization of the diagnostic function. (Mercer, 1968, p. 77)

Two curriculum enterprises that exemplify Mercer's analysis are special education and Chapter I programs for economically disadvantaged children. Both of these programs, as they are practiced in many U.S. schools, are based on clinical assumptions. They each employ specialists who are experts in the testing and treatment of the particular kind of "deviance." They each deal with their problem by trying to change the individual, rather than by attempting to alter the basic structure of the institution. In each case, government bureaucrats define the problem and the labels assigned to children. Finally, both programs invoke an impressive body of "scientific" research to support their practices. Reading, dropout prevention, suicide prevention, teenage pregnancy, and substance abuse programs each share some of these features and are tending to drift toward a more clinical perspective.

Curriculum Analysis Questions

1. Does the evaluation approach of your curriculum seem measurement-based? In what ways can you claim that the evaluation seems integrated? (See Table 11.1.)

2. What would a nonconservative (in Apple's and Gouldner's terms) approach to evaluation of your curriculum be like? Apple and Gouldner would be interested in the extent to which the curriculum reinforces institutional practices, e.g., tracking, testing, labeling of students, that focus attention on individuals rather than on the institution. How might you evaluate the curriculum's role in reinforcing these kinds of practices?

TABLE 11.1 Comparison of Important Characteristics of Measurement-Based and Integrated Evaluation

Measurement-based methods	"Scientific" Objectives-driven Group- or individually administered Norm- or criterion-referenced Standardized
Integrated methods	Growth-oriented Student-controlled Dynamic Contextualized Informal Flexible Action-oriented

NOTES

1. The basic ideas of this section are based on Johnston (1987).
2. See, for example, Thorndike and Hagen (1969).
3. See Chapter Ten.
4. See Walker and Schaffarzick (1974) for a review of these studies.
5. See Chapter Four.
6. See Chapter Four.
7. See Chapter Five.
8. See, for example, Metfessel and Michael (1967); Hammond (1969); Provus (1971); and Bloom, Hastings, and Madaus (1971).
9. See, for example, English and Steffy (1982) and Glatthorn (1987).
10. See, for example, Resnick and Klopfer (1989) and Larkin (1981).
11. See, for example, Y. Goodman (1985).
12. See especially Jones (1972).

PART FOUR

Curriculum Critique

You are now in a position to put together all you have learned in the previous chapters of the book in a concluding critique of the curriculum.

CHAPTER 12

Reexamination and Critique

Now where does the analysis leave us? You have looked inside the curriculum to determine its form and substance. You have even examined the assumptions on which the curriculum rests. You are now prepared to appraise the curriculum, to determine its strengths and weaknesses. More important, you are in a position to decide how you would adapt the curriculum to maximize its strengths and to minimize its weaknesses. These final points of appraisal and decision constitute what I mean by "critiquing" the curriculum.[1] We begin by revisiting the notion of reflective eclecticism, first introduced in Chapter One.

REFLECTIVE ECLECTICISM REVISITED

A theoretical perspective is indeed powerful. We have seen throughout this book that theoretical perspectives form the basis for approaches to curriculum purpose and content, organization, implementation, and evaluation. Each perspective offers a coherent view of education, explaining why many of our efforts seem fruitless, while pointing us to an approach that promises to provide a solution to the problems created by our current approaches. However, as Schwab (1970) has pointed out, curricula based on single theoretical perspectives have three inherent limitations:

> *The Failure of Scope* . . . One curriculum effort is grounded in concern only for the individual, another in concern only for groups, others in concern only for cultures, or communities, or societies, or minds, or the extant bodies of knowledge. . . . No curriculum, grounded in but one of these subjects, can possibly be adequate or defensible. (pp. 21–23)

> *The Vice of Abstraction* . . . All theories, even the best of them . . . , necessarily neglect some aspects and facets of the facts of the case. A theory (and the principle derived from it) covers and formulates the *regularities* among the things and events it subsumes. It abstracts a general or ideal case. It leaves behind the nonuniformities, the particularities, which characterize each concrete instance of the facts subsumed. . . . Yet curriculum is brought to bear, not on ideal or abstract representations, but on the real thing, on the concrete case, in all its

completeness and with all its differences from all other concrete cases on a large body of fact concerning which the theoretic abstraction is silent. (pp. 25–26)

Radical Plurality . . . Nearly all theories in all the behavioral sciences are marked by the coexistence of competing theories. . . . All the social and behavioral sciences are marked by "schools," each distinguished by a different choice of principle of enquiry, each of which selects from the intimidating complexities of the subject matter the small fraction of the whole with which it can deal. . . . The theories which arise from enquiries so directed are, then, radically incomplete, each of them incomplete to the extent that competing theories take hold of different aspects of the subject of enquiry and treat it in a different way. . . . In short, there is every reason to suppose that any one of the extant theories of behavior is a pale and incomplete representation of actual behavior. . . . It follows that such theories are not, and will not be, adequate by themselves to tell us what to do with actual human beings or how to do it. What they variously suggest and the contrary guidances they afford to choice and action must be mediated and combined by eclectic arts and must be massively supplemented, as well as mediated, by knowledge of some other kind derived from another source. . . . It is this recourse to accumulated lore, to experience of actions and their consequences, to action and reaction at the level of the concrete case, which constitutes the heart of the practical. (p. 28)

Curriculum planning can be no more based on a single theory than can other complex decisions such as choosing a spouse, buying a car, or selecting a president.

In order to repair these deficiencies of theory as a basis for curriculum planning, Schwab offers the "eclectic" as an approach to curriculum planning. Each theory brings certain features of a phenomenon into focus, helping the curriculum planner to understand better that aspect of the situation. For example, Piagetian theory helps the planner understand the student's individual cognitive development, whereas social psychology and sociology help the planner understand how children from various backgrounds interact with each other and with an authority figure. Curriculum planners trained in the "eclectic arts" not only can use theory to view phenomena but also know what aspects of the phenomenon each theory obscures or blurs. For example, theory focusing on individual cognitive development obscures the social psychology and sociology of classrooms. Finally, the eclectic arts allow the curriculum planner to use various theories in combination "without paying the full price of their incompleteness and partiality" (Schwab, 1970, p. 12).[2] These eclectic arts are as necessary for the curriculum critic as for the curriculum planner.

In order to avoid the tunnel vision associated with any theory, Schwab challenges any curriculum to address each of what he calls the four commonplaces of education, i.e., the learner, the teacher, the subject matter, and the social and institutional milieu or context.[3] According to Schwab, any curriculum that fails to take all four commonplaces into account has a fatal flaw that will eventually undermine it. These four commonplaces provide the curriculum analyst with a comprehensive map of education. Such a map enables the analyst to identify aspects of education that the curriculum has not taken fully into account.

Each of the five perspectives discussed in Chapter Three gives priority to one or two of the four commonplaces, either ignoring others or subordinating them to the ones emphasized. Those perspectives that emphasize the same commonplace differ from other perspectives in the assumptions they make about the particular commonplace.

The emphasis of the traditional perspective is on *subject matter*, and in particular on that subject matter comprising the society's cultural heritage. The structure-of-the-disciplines perspective also emphasizes subject matter, but contrasts with the traditional perspective in its assumptions about subject matter. Whereas the traditional perspective assumes subject matter to be nonproblematic, absolute, and static, the structure-of-the-disciplines perspective assumes subject matter to be evolving, tentative, and dynamic. The emphasis within the behavioral perspective is on *learning*. As psychologically based views, both the constructivist and the behavioral perspectives emphasize the *learner* and the learning process, rather than the subject matter. However, these two perspectives differ in the assumptions they make about learning. The constructivist perspective views learning as internal mental processes of assimilation, accommodation, and problem solving, while the behavioral views learning as overt changes in an individual's behaviors. The experiential perspective also emphasizes the learners, in particular their needs, interests, and purposes, not ignoring but certainly subordinating subject matter and teaching to these concerns. It is interesting that none of the perspectives emphasizes teachers, though increased teacher unionization and professionalization may foreshadow the emergence of a new perspective.[4]

Schwab's challenge to theory-driven curriculum efforts goes further. Not only must the curriculum address all four commonplaces, but also it must give equal attention to each one and not subordinate any one commonplace to another. For example, a curriculum based on examination of social problems may claim that it addresses learners, because it asks learners to select the social problems they will examine. However, in fact it is subordinating issues of learner interests, needs, abilities, and backgrounds to issues of the social milieu in which they live—not to mention the complete omission of subject-matter issues and teacher concerns.

Even when all four commonplaces receive equal attention, Schwab points out that there are dangers. From what we have said thus far, we could in principle develop a viable curriculum based on four theories, one for each commonplace—say a cognitive theory of child development, a critical theory of teacher empowerment, a philosophical theory of how scientific knowledge evolves, and a progressive theory of the school's role in community development. Ignoring the problems of how to articulate possibly inconsistent or noncomplementary theories, do we now necessarily have a viable curriculum? Possibly, Schwab might say, but it is not likely. For each theory provides only one perspective on one commonplace. A child is more than a cognitively developing human being. A child is also an emotionally fragile being, a growing personality, a member of a peer group, a family member, and a musical, athletic, or artistic talent, just to scratch the surface. We could describe teachers, subject matter, and milieu in an analogous multifaceted way.

Schwab's point is that theoretical perspectives, while they are useful intellectual tools, lead to tunnel vision. In order to avoid their inherent limitations, the curriculum analyst or critic—and, Schwab would add, the curriculum developer—must develop the "arts of the eclectic." For the curriculum analyst and critic these arts include first the ability to trace a curriculum's features to underlying perspectives. The development of this ability has been one goal of this book. Second, these arts include the ability to identify the commonplaces that the curriculum addresses and those the curriculum either ignores or subordinates. Third, these arts include the ability to determine the particular facet of each commonplace the curriculum illuminates and what facets the curriculum obscures from view. The development of these latter two abilities is the primary goal of this final chapter. With these abilities, you can begin to use theoretical perspectives as a critical tool in curriculum analysis, rather than find yourselves limited or, as Zais (1976) argues, "encapsulated" by them.

In Chapter Two you examined potential blind spots in the curriculum by identifying members of the development team. Having completed the analysis, you can now be more conclusive in your appraisal. You can revise your preliminary appraisal by reexamining the curriculum's approach to purpose and content, organization, implementation, and evaluation in the light of the four commonplaces. Which of the commonplaces receive most attention? Which, if any, are ignored? Which are subordinated to others? What are the curriculum's blind spots?

As you attempt this critique, it is important not to be fooled by superficial features of the curriculum and superficial eclecticism. Rarely will you find a curriculum derived directly and unambiguously from one or two theoretical perspectives. In fact, the examples developed in this book as case studies are the exception rather than the rule, used for illustrating certain points without clouding the picture. More typically, you will find curricula whose features you can trace to several perspectives. For example, you might notice a preoccupation with addressing student misconceptions, i.e., a constructivist approach; a focus on fundamental concepts from a discipline of knowledge as the basis for organization, i.e., a top-down approach; a provision for teachers working together as they experiment with new methods, i.e., a collaborative approach; and an emphasis on clinical interviews with students, student self-evaluation, and classroom observations, i.e., an integrated evaluation. A curriculum of this sort would lead you to conclude that there were elements of a constructivist, a structure-of-the-disciplines, and an experiential perspective. Given what we discussed in Chapter Eight regarding meaning-oriented curricula, it would be more likely to find in use in schools a combination of traditional and behavioral perspectives. For example, perhaps you will find a curriculum emphasizing both the recall of facts and the mastery of a series of discrete skills carefully sequenced on the basis of a task analysis, developed at an R&D center by experts but implemented through a one-shot in-service day initiated and directed by the school administration, and evaluated by sophisticated standardized tests.

However, in attempting to identify these sorts of elements, it is easy to confuse superficial features with underlying theoretical perspectives. In Chapter One we discussed the meaning of "technical" viewpoints and the tendency to technicize inherently value-laden decisions. The five curriculum perspectives surveyed in Chapter Three are particularly prone to being technicized. Since perspectives are highly abstract, none of them can be translated into curriculum practice without some specific means or techniques for implementing it. Therefore, each technique derives its meaning from a particular perspective. For example, as we saw in Chapters Three and Seven, discovery methods of teaching are pedagogical tools for applying a structure-of-the-disciplines perspective to classrooms. Discovery methods are intended to engage the student in a style of thought analogous to that of scholars in the disciplines, to give the student a taste of the excitement of real scholarly inquiry.[5] Although it is possible to use discovery methods without approaching curriculum from a structure-of-the-disciplines perspective, such a use of discovery methods would take on a different meaning. For example, in a traditional classroom the methods might be reduced to playing Twenty Questions with students, an I-know-it-and-you-have-to-guess-it game. Technicism focuses on the techniques of the perspective, examining only their relative effectiveness and efficiency without serious regard for their goals and underlying assumptions. A preoccupation with technique diverts attention from the theoretical assumptions from which the technique derives and by which it derives meaning.

It is possible to technicize any perspective, although some are more prone to technicism than others. The extreme case is the behavioral perspective. It focuses on developing effective behavior modification techniques. While claiming to be only a technology, it contends that its techniques are appropriate for any educational ends and are therefore value-neutral, and it regards behavioral psychologists as the experts in, and therefore the proper authorities on, educational decision making. These characteristics reveal its inherent technicism. As a curriculum analyst, you will need to be able to distinguish between curricular features that are truly rooted in particular theoretical perspectives and features that represent technicized aspects of the perspectives.

Curriculum Analysis Questions

With these warnings and your analysis in mind, you are finally in a position to critique the curriculum from a viewpoint of reflective eclecticism.

1. From this viewpoint, what are the strengths of the curriculum and what are its limitations?
2. Having identified potential limitations, consider the risks you might run if you implemented the curriculum. Of what dangers would you want to be careful?
3. In spite of these risks, the curriculum no doubt has certain strengths. How would you adapt it to maximize its benefits and strengths and to minimize its limitations and risks?

CURRICULUM STUDY REVISITED

Where does this analysis leave us? As you may recall, from the outset the analysis was chosen as a method of curriculum study (see Chapter One). We now have both a better understanding of a particular curriculum in terms of its strengths and weaknesses and also a general introduction to the field of curriculum. Having performed the analysis, are we finished with curriculum study? Not surprisingly, the answer is "No."

Although we have covered much ground, we have omitted some significant dimensions of curriculum study. While these other dimensions did not fit into a curriculum analysis project, they are nevertheless important for a thorough understanding of curriculum development. These additional dimensions include the study of curriculum deliberation, curriculum policy making, curriculum theory, current curriculum practices, curriculum research, the hidden curriculum, and curriculum reform.

There are many good references for these additional topics. Some useful general references include Decker Walker's (1990) *Fundamentals of Curriculum,* for an unusually thorough coverage of curriculum deliberation and policy making; William Schubert's (1986) general textbook, *Curriculum: Perspective, Paradigm and Possibility,* for an exceptionally thorough and readable analysis of the philosophical underpinnings of thought in this field; John Goodlad's (1984) *A Place Called School,* for the most comprehensive study of current curriculum practices; Philip Jackson's (1992) *Handbook of Research on Curriculum,* for a thorough and up-to-date review of research by the field's leading scholars; my own article in the *Journal of Curriculum and Supervision,* "Making Sense of Diversity" (1989); and Henry Giroux and David Purpel's (1983) *The Hidden Curriculum and Moral Education,* for an anthology of works on the hidden curriculum. Three influential works on curriculum reform for me have been Larry Cuban's (1990) article in *Educational Researcher* entitled "Reforming Education Again and Again and Again," Michael Sedlak et al.'s (1986) *Selling Students Short,* and Thomas Popkewitz et al.'s (1982) *Myth of Educational Reform.* In addition I would encourage you to follow up on the many references cited in this text. There is no substitute for primary sources. A textbook such as this one can serve only as a point of departure for serious curriculum study.

NOTES

1. In contrast to this view, the reader may wish to read other views of curriculum criticism, in particular Willis (1978) and Eisner (1994).
2. See also Schwab (1973).
3. Note the similarity with Tyler's (1949) three "sources."
4. In this sense Theodore Sizer's (1985) "coalition of essential schools" may be regarded as a new perspective centering on teacher empowerment.
5. See Shulman and Keislar (1966) on this topic.

Bibliography

Adams, G. S. 1964. *Measurement and evaluation in education, psychology, and guidance.* New York: Holt, Rinehart & Winston.

Ahlquist, R. 1992. Manifestations of inequality: Overcoming resistance in a multicultural foundations course. In Grant, C. A. (Ed.). *Research and multicultural education: From the margins to the mainstream.* London, Washington, DC: Falmer Press.

Aikin, W. M. 1942. *The story of the eight-year study, with conclusions and recommendations.* New York: Harper & Brothers.

Airasian, P. W. , & Walsh, M. E. 1997. Constructivist Cautions. *Phi Delta Kappan,* 78, 444–449.

Altwerger, B., Edelsky, C., & Flores, B. M. 1987. Whole language: What's new? *The Reading Teacher,* vol. 41, November, 1987, p. 145.

American Association for the Advancement of Science. 1967. *Science—A process approach: Description of the program,* Parts A–F. New York: Xerox Corp. Commission on Science Education.

American Association of School Administrators. 1928. *The development of the high school curriculum.* Department of Superintendence. Sixth yearbook. Washington, DC: American Association of School Administrators.

American Council on the Teaching of Foreign Languages, the American Association of Teachers of French, the American Association of Teachers of German, & the American Association of Teachers of Spanish and Portuguese. 1999. *National standards for foreign language education.* Retrieved October 17, 2002, *www.actfl.org/public/articles/details.cfm?id=33.*

American Institutes for Research in the Behavioral Sciences. 1972. *Product Development Reports 1-21.* Palo Alto, CA: American Institutes for Research in the Behavioral Sciences.

American Physical Society. 1996. Fighting the gender gap: Standardized tests are poor indicators of ability in physics. *www.aps.org.*

Anderson, R. C. 1977. The notion of schemata and the educational enterprise: General discussion of the conference. In R. C. Anderson, R. J. Spiro, & W. E. Montague (Eds.), *Schooling and the acquisition of knowledge.* Hillsdale, NJ: Lawrence Erlbaum.

Anyon, J. 1983. Social class and the hidden curriculum of work. In H. Giroux & D. Purpel (Eds.), *The hidden curriculum and moral education: Deception or discovery?* Berkeley, CA: McCutchan.

Apple, M. W. 1977. The process and ideology of valuing in educational settings. In A. A. Bellack & H. M. Kliebard (Eds.), *Curriculum and evaluation* (pp. 468-493). Berkeley, CA: McCutchan.

Apple, M. W. 1981. On analyzing hegemony. In H. A. Giroux, A. N. Penna, & W. F. Pinar (Eds.), *Curriculum and instruction: Alternatives in education* (pp. 109–123). Berkeley, CA: McCutchan.

Archbald, D. A., & Newman, F. M. 1988. *Beyond standardized testing: Assessing authentic academic achievement in the secondary school.* Reston, VA: National Association of Secondary School Principals.

Association of Experiential Education, cited in Wigginton, 1985, p. 383.

Atkin, J. M., & House, E. R. 1981. The federal role in curriculum development, 1950–80. *Educational Evaluation and Policy Analysis, 3,* 5–36.

Ausubel, D. P. 1964. Some psychological aspects of the structure of knowledge. In S. Elam (Ed.), *Education and the structure of knowledge* (pp. 220–262). Chicago: Rand McNally.

Ausubel, D. P. 1968. *Educational psychology: A cognitive view.* New York: Holt, Rinehart & Winston.

Ausubel, D. P., Novak, J. D., & Hanesian, H. 1978. *Educational psychology: A cognitive view.* New York: Holt, Rinehart & Winston.

Banks, J. A. 1988. *Multiethnic education: Theory and practice* (2nd ed.). Newton, MA: Allyn and Bacon.

Belenky, M. F., Clinchy, B. M., Goldberger, N. R., & Tarule, J.M. 1986. *Women's ways of knowing: The development of self, voice, and mind.* New York, NY: Basic Books.

Barnes, D. 1982. *Practical curriculum study.* London: Routledge & Kegan Paul.

Bennett, W. J. 1984. To reclaim a legacy: Text of report on humanities in education. *Chronicle of Higher Education,* Nov. 28, 1984, pp. 16–21.

Bennett, W. J. 1988. *James Madison Elementary School: A curriculum for American students.* Washington, DC: U.S. Department of Education.

Bereiter, C., & Scardamalia, M. 1992. Cognition and curriculum. In P. W. Jackson (Ed.), *Handbook of research on curriculum.* New York: Macmillan.

Berlak, A., & Berlak, H. 1981. *Dilemmas of schooling: Teaching and social change.* New York: Methuen.

Berman, P., & McLaughlin, M. W. 1978. Implementing and sustaining innovations. In *Federal programs supporting educational change,* vol. 8. Santa Monica, CA: Rand.

Bernstein, B. 1971. On the classification and framing of educational knowledge. In M. F. D. Young (Ed.), *Knowledge and control: New directions for the sociology of education.* London: Collier-Macmillan.

Bestor, A. E. 1953. *Educational wastelands: The retreat from learning in our public schools.* Urbana: University of Illinois Press.

Beyer, L. E., & Apple, M. W. 1988. *The curriculum: Problems, politics and possibilities.* Albany: State University of New York Press.

Biester, T. W., & Kershner, K. M. 1979. Longitudinal study of EBCE. Paper presented at the annual meeting of the American Educational Research Association, San Francisco.

Biological Science Curriculum Study. 1968. *Biological science: Molecules to man.* Blue Version, Rev. ed. Boston: Houghton Mifflin.

Biological Science Curriculum Study. 2002. *Biology An ecological approach* (9th ed.). Dubuque, IA: Kendall/Hunt.

Bloom, A. D. 1987. *The closing of the American mind.* New York: Simon & Schuster.

Bloom, B. S. (Ed.). 1956. *Taxonomy of educational objectives: The classification of educational goals, Handbook I: Cognitive domain.* New York: David McKay.

Bloom, B. S. 1971. Mastery learning. In J. H. Block (Ed.), *Mastery learning: Theory and practice.* New York: Holt, Rinehart & Winston.

Bloom, B. S., Hastings, J. T., & Madaus, G. F. (Eds.). 1971. *Handbook on formative and summative evaluation of student learning.* New York: McGraw-Hill.

Bobbitt, F. 1918. *The curriculum.* Boston: Houghton Mifflin.

Bobbitt, F. 1924. *How to make a curriculum.* Boston: Houghton Mifflin.

Bond, L., Roeber, E., & Connealy, S. 1996. *Trends in state student assessment programs.* Washington, D.C.: Council of Chief State School Officers, 1998.

Bowles, S., & Gintis, H. 1976. *Schooling in capitalist America.* New York, NY: Basic Books.

Brandt, R. 1994. The challenge of outcome-based education. Special issue of *Educational Leadership* (with articles by W. Spady, R. Slavin, B. J. Jones, J. A. King, E. Baker, A. Mamary), *51*(6), March.

Briggs, L. J. 1968. *Sequencing of instruction in relation to hierarchies of competence.* Pittsburgh: American Institutes for Research.

Broudy, H. S. 1961. *Paradox and promise: Essays on American life and education.* Englewood Cliffs, NJ: Prentice-Hall.

Broudy, H. S. 1971. The curriculum and democratic values. In Robert McClure (Ed.), *Curriculum: Retrospect and prospect.* Seventieth Yearbook of the National Society for the Study of Education. Chicago: University of Chicago Press.

Broudy, H. S. 1977. Types of knowledge and purposes of education. In R. C. Anderson, R. J. Spiro, & W. E. Montague (Eds.), *Schooling and the acquisition of knowledge.* Hillsdale, NJ: Lawrence Erlbaum.

Broudy, H. S., Smith, B. O., & Burnett, J. R. 1964. *Democracy and excellence in American secondary education.* Chicago: Rand McNally.

Bruner, J. S. 1960. *The process of education.* New York: Vintage.

Bruner, J. S. 1964. MACOS Position Paper. Mimeographed. Cambridge, MA: Education Development Center, p. 24, cited in Nelkin (1982), p. 50.

Bruner, J. S. 1971. The process of education revisited. *Phi Delta Kappan, 52*(1), 18–22.

Bruner, J. S., Goodnow, J. J., & Austin, G. A. 1956. *A study of thinking.* New York: Wiley.

Bucknam, R. 1976. The impact of EBCE—An evaluators' viewpoint. *Illinois Career Education Journal, 33,* 32–37.

Butler, J. E. 1993. Transforming the curriculum: Teaching about women of color. In J. A. Banks & C. A. McGee Banks (Eds.), *Multicultural education: Issues and perspectives.* Boston: Allyn and Bacon.

Calkins, L. M. 1986. *The art of teaching writing.* Portsmouth, NH: Heinemann.

Carnegie Foundation for the Advancement of Teaching. 1988. *An imperiled generation: Saving urban schools.* Princeton, NJ: Carnegie Foundation.

Center for Education Statistics. *nces.ed.gov./oubs2002/digest 2001/tables/dt134.asp.*

Chomsky, N. 1957. *Syntactic structures.* The Hague, Netherlands: Mouton.

Chomsky, N. 1968. *Language and mind.* New York: Harcourt Brace Jovanovich.

Choppin, B. H. 1977. The use of tests and scales curriculum evaluation. In A. Lewy (Ed.), *Handbook of curriculum evaluation.* Paris: UNESCO; New York: Longman.

Clark, D. L., & Guba, E. G. 1967. *Rational planning in curriculum and instruction.* Washington, DC: National Education Association.

Clark, T. 2001. *Virtual schools: Trends and issues. A study of virtual schools in the United States.* Phoenix, AZ: Distance Learning Resource Network at WestEd.

Clay, M. M. 1975. *What did I write?* Auckland, New Zealand: Heinemann.

Clay, M. M. 1985. *The early detection of reading difficulties: A diagnostic survey with recovery procedures* (2nd ed.). Exeter, NH: Heinemann.

College Board. 2001. Average SAT scores by parental education. Cited in *The world almanac and book of facts.* (New York, NY: World Almanac Books), 2002, p. 239.

College Entrance Examination Board. 2001. National report on college-bound. *Digest of education statistics*. Table 134. Washington, D.C.: National Center for Education Statistics. *nces.edu.gov./oubs2002/digest2001/tables/dt134/.asp*.

Colvin, R. L. 1999. Math wars: Tradition vs. real-world applications. *School Administrator, 56*, 26–31.

Committee on the Reorganization of Secondary Education. 1918. *Cardinal principles of secondary education*. Washington, DC: U.S. Government Printing Office.

Confrey, J. 1990. A review of the research on student conceptions in mathematics, science, and programming. In C. Cazden (Ed.), *Review of Research in Education, 16*. Washington, DC: American Educational Research Association.

Congressional Record, April 9, 1975. H2588, cited by Nelkin, p. 129.

Corey, S. M. 1952. Action research and the solution of practical problems. *Educational Leadership, 9*, 478–484.

Cremin, L. A. 1961. *The transformation of the school*. New York: Knopf.

Cremin, L. A. 1975. Curriculum-making in the United States. In W. Pinar (Ed.) *Curriculum theorizing: The Reconceptualists*. Berkeley, CA. McCutchan.

Cuban, L. 1990. Reforming education again and again and again. *Educational Researcher, 19*(1), 3–13.

Cubberly, E. P. 1919. *Public education in the united states: A study and interpretation of American educational history*. Boston, MA: Houghton Mifflin.

Curricular Options in Mathematics Programs for All Secondary Students. 2002, 11/15/02. *Curricular options in mathematics programs for all secondary students*. Retrieved November 20, 2002, *www.ithaca.edu/compass/frames.htm*.

Curriculum Development Associates. 1972. *Man: A course of study*. A booklet describing the curriculum. Washington, DC: Curriculum Development Associates.

deBono, E. 1970. *Lateral thinking: A textbook of creativity*. London: Ward Lock Educational.

DeFord, D., Lyons, C., Pinnell, G. S. 1991. *Bridges to literacy: Learning from Reading Recovery*. Portsmouth, NH: Heinemann.

Descartes, R. 1931. Principles of philosophy. In *The philosophical works of Descartes*, vol. 1. Translated by E. Haldane & G. R. T. Ross. Cambridge: The University Press.

Dewey, J. 1916. *Democracy and education*, p. 225, cited in L. A. Cremin, *The transformation of the school: Progressivism in American education 1876–1957* (New York: Vintage/Random House), 1961, p. 125.

Dewey, J. 1938. *Experience and education*. The Kappa Delta Pi Lecture Series. New York: Collier/Macmillan.

Dorr-Bremme, D. 1982. *Assessing students: Teachers' routine practices and reasoning*. CSE Report no. 194. Los Angeles, CA: Center for the Study of Evaluation.

Dow, P. 1968. In Education Development Center (Eds.), *Talks to teachers* (p. 5). Cambridge, MA: Education Development Center.

Dow, P. 1975. MACOS: The study of human behavior as one road to survival. *Phi Delta Kappan, 57*, 79–81.

Doyle, W. 1983. Academic work. *Review of Educational Research, 53*(2), 159–199.

Doyle, W. 1986. Content representation in teachers' definitions of academic work. *Journal of Curriculum Studies, 18*(4), 365–380.

Doyle, W. 1992. Curriculum and pedagogy. In P. W. Jackson (Ed.), *Handbook of research on curriculum*. New York: Macmillan.

Doyle, W., & Ponder, G. A. 1977–1978. The practicality ethic in teacher decision making. *Interchange, 8*(3), 1–12.

Driver, R. 1983. *The pupil as scientist?* Milton Keynes, UK: Open University Press.

Driver, R., Guesne, E., & Tiberghien, A. (Eds.). 1985. *Children's ideas in science*. Philadelphia: Open University Press.

Driver, R., & Oldham, V. 1986. A constructivist approach to curriculum development in science. *Studies in Science Education, 13,* 105–122.

Educational Policies Commission: 1938. *The purposes of education in American democracy.* Washington, D.C.: The National Education Association.

Educational Policies Commission. 1944. The imperative needs of youth of secondary school age. *Bulletin of the National Association of Secondary School Principals, 31,* 145.

Eisner, E. W. 1994. *The educational imagination* (3rd ed.). New York: Macmillan.

Engelman, S., Haddox, P. & Bruner, E. 1983. *Teach your child to read in 100 easy lessons.* New York: Simon and Schuster.

English, F., & Steffy, B. E. 1982. Curriculum as a strategic management tool. *Educational Leadership 39*(January), 276–278.

Erickson, F. 1986. Qualitative methods in research on teaching. In M. C. Wittrock (Ed.), *Handbook of research on teaching* (3rd ed.). New York: Macmillan.

Eylon, B., & Linn, M. C. 1988. Learning and instruction: An examination of four research perspectives in science education. *Review of Educational Research, 58*(3), 251–301.

FairTest. October 16, 2002. New report shows MCAS will block college access for thousands of students. Press Release. *www.fairtest.org.*

FairTest. Spring, 2002. Policies with promise: A look at the assessment plans for Maine and Nebraska. Press Release. *www.fairtest.org.*

FairTest. Winter, 2001-02. Provisions of the new federal law. *Fairtest examiner. www.fairtest.org.*

Fillmore, L. W, & Meyer, L. M. 1992. The curriculum and linguistic minorities. In Jackson, P. W. (Ed.), *Handbook of research on curriculum.* New York, NY: Macmillan Publishing Company.

Fillmore, L. Wong & Meyer, L. M. 1992. The curriculum and linguistic minorities. In Jackson, P. W. (Ed.), *Handbook of research on curriculum.* New York, NY: Macmillan.

Finlay, G. 1966. The Physical Science Study Committee. In W. T. Martin & D. C. Pinck (Eds.), *Curriculum improvement and innovation: A partnership of students, school teachers, and research scholars.* Cambridge, MA: Robert Bentley.

Fiore, K., & Elsasser, N. 1988. Strangers no more: A liberatory literacy curriculum. In E. R. Kintgen, B. M. Kroll, & M. Rose (Eds.), *Perspectives on literacy.* Carbondale: Southern Illinois University Press.

FitzGerald, F. 1979. *America revised: History schoolbooks in the twentieth century.* Boston: Little, Brown.

Foshay, A. W. 1970. How fare the disciplines? *Phi Delta Kappan, 51,* 349–352.

Freedman, S. W. 1993. Linking large-scale testing and classroom portfolio assessments of student writing. *Education assessment, 1,* 27–52.

Freire, P. 1970. *Pedagogy of the oppressed.* New York: Seabury.

Freire, P. 1973. *Education for critical consciousness.* New York, NY: The Seabury Press.

Fullan, M., & Pomfret, A. 1977. Research on curriculum and instruction implementation. *Review of Educational Research, 47*(2), 335–397.

Gagne, R. M. 1965. *The conditions of learning.* New York: Holt, Rinehart & Winston.

Gagne, R. M. 1966. Elementary science: A new scheme of instruction. *Science, 151*(3708), 49.

Gagne, R. M. 1970. *The conditions of learning* (2nd ed.). New York: Holt, Rinehart & Winston.

Gagne, R. M. 1977. *The conditions of learning* (3rd ed.). New York: Holt, Rinehart & Winston.

Gambrell, L. B. 1984. How much time do children spend reading during teacher-directed reading instruction? In O. Niles (Ed.), *Changing perspectives on research in reading/language processing and instruction* (pp. 193–198). Thirty-third Yearbook of the National Reading Conference: Rochester, NY.

Gamoran, A. 1998. "Rank, performance, and mobility in elemantary schools." Sociologicial Quarterly, 30 (Spring), 109–123.

Gardner, H. 1991. *The unschooled mind.* New York: Basic Books.

Gardner, H. 1983. *Frames of mind: The theory of multiple intelligences.* New York: Basic Books.

Gardner, H. 1993. *Multiple intelligences: The theory in practice.* New York, NY: Basic Books.

Giroux, H. 1983. Critical theory and rationality in citizenship education. In H. Giroux, & D. Purpel (Eds.), *The hidden curriculum and moral education.* Berkeley, CA: McCutchan.

Giroux, H., & Purpel, D. (Eds.), 1983. *The hidden curriculum and moral education.* Berkeley, CA: McCutchan.

Glaser, R. 1969. The design and programming of instruction. In H. T. James et al. (Eds.), *The school and challenge of innovation* (pp. 156–215). Supplementary paper no. 28. New York: Committee for Economic Development.

Glatthorn, A. A. 1987. *Curriculum leadership.* Glenview, IL: Scott, Foresman.

GLOBE. 1995, December 18. *Global learning and observations to benefit the environment (GLOBE).* Retrieved December 18, 2002, www.GLOBE.gov.

Golman, D. 1995. *Emotional intelligence.* New York: Bantam Books.

Goodlad, J. I. 1964. *School reform in the United States.* Los Angeles: University of California, Fund for the Advancement of Education.

Goodlad, J. I. 1984. *A place called school.* New York: McGraw-Hill.

Goodlad, J. I., & Richter, M. N., Jr. 1966. *The development of a conceptual system for dealing with problems of curriculum and instruction.* Washington, DC: Cooperative Research Program, U.S. Office of Education. ERIC ED 01 0064.

Goodman, K. 1986. *What's whole in whole language?* Portsmouth, NH: Heinemann.

Goodman, Y. 1985. Kidwatching: Observing children in the classroom. In A. Jaggar & M. Trika Smith-Burke (Eds.), *Observing the language learner.* Newark, NJ: International Reading Association/National Council of Teachers of English.

Gouldner, A. W. 1970. *The coming crisis of Western sociology.* New York: Basic Books.

Graves, D. H. 1983. *Writing: Teachers and children at work.* Exeter, NH: Heinemann.

Greeno, J. G. 1976. Cognitive objectives of instruction: Theory of knowledge for solving problems and answering questions. In D. Klahr (Ed.), *Cognition and instruction.* Hillsdale, NJ: Lawrence Erlbaum.

Griffin, G. A. 1983. Implications of research for staff development programs. *The Elementary School Journal, 83*(4), 414–426.

Grobman, H. G. 1970. *Developmental curriculum projects.* Itasca, IL: F. E. Peacock.

Hale, J. 1982. *Black children: Their roots, culture, and learning styles.* Provo, UT: Brigham Young Press.

Hall, C. W., Bolen, L. M., & Gupton, Jr., R. H. 1995. Predictive validity of the study process questionnaire for undergraduate students. *College student journal, 29,* 234–239.

Hamilton, S. 1980. Experiential learning programs for youth. *American Journal of Education, 48*(2), 179–215.

Hammond, R. 1969. Context evaluation of instruction in local school districts. *Educational Technology, 9*(1), 13–18.

Haney, W. M., G. F. Madaus, and R. Lyons, 1993 The fractured marketplace for standardized testing. Boston: Kluwer.

Hanley, J. P., Whitlo, D. K., Moss, E., & Walter, A. S. 1975. Curiosity, competence, community. In M. Golby, J. Greenwald, & R. West (Eds.), *Curriculum design* (pp. 467–480). London: Croon Helm in association with the Open University Press.

Harris, W. T. 1897. My pedagogical creed. *The School Journal, 54,* 813.

Harrow, A. 1972. *A taxonomy of the psychomotor domain.* New York: David McKay.

Heath, R. W. 1964. *The new curricula.* New York: Harper & Row.

Heath, S. B. 1983. *Ways with words: Language, life, and work in communities and classrooms.* Cambridge, NJ: Cambridge University Press.

Heimer, R. 1969. Conditions of learning in mathematics: Sequence theory development. *Review of Educational Research, 39,* 498.

Hemphill, J. K. 1982. Knowledge transformation—The D in educational research and development. San Francisco, CA: Far West Laboratory for Educational Research and Development.

Herman, J. L., Aschbacher, P. R., & Winters, L. 1992. *A practical guide to alternative assessment.* Alexandria, VA: Association for Supervision and Curriculum Development.

Hirsch, E. D. 1993. *What your sixth grader needs to know: Fundamentals of a good sixth grade education.* New York: Doubleday.

Hirsch, E. D., Jr. 1983. Cultural literacy. *The American Scholar, 52*(2), 159–169.

Hirsch, E. D., Jr. 1987. *Cultural literacy.* Boston: Houghton Mifflin.

Hobbes, T. 1962. A short tract on first principles. In R. S. Peters (Ed.), *Hobbes: Body, man and citizen.* New York: Collier.

Hoetker, J., & Ahlbrand, D. 1969. The persistence of recitation. *American Educational Research Journal, 6,* 145–167.

Holdaway, D. 1979. *The foundations of literacy.* New York: Ashton Scholastic.

House, E. R. 1979. *Three perspectives on innovation: The technological, the political and the cultural.* Washington, DC: U.S. Department of Education, Office of Educational Research and Development.

House, E. R. 1980. Technology versus craft: A ten-year perspective. *Journal of Curriculum Studies, 11*(1), 1–16.

Hull, G. A. 1989. Research on writing: Building a cognitive and social understanding of composing. In L. B. Resnick & L. E. Klopfer (Eds.), *Toward the thinking curriculum: Current cognitive research.* Yearbook of the Association for Supervision and Curriculum Development. Alexandria, VA: Association for Supervision and Curriculum Development.

Hume, D. 1957. *An inquiry concerning human understanding.* New York: Liberal Arts Press.

Hume, D. 1967. *A treatise of human nature.* Oxford, UK: Clarendon Press.

Hunter, M. 1984. Knowing, teaching, and supervising. In P. L. Hosford (Ed.), *Using what we know about teaching* (pp. 169–192). Alexandria, VA: Association for Supervision and Curriculum Development.

Hunter, M. 1994. *Enhancing teaching.* New York: Macmillan.

International Association for the Evaluation of Educational Achievement. 1976. *International studies in evaluation* (nine volumes). New York: Wiley.

International Society for Technology in Education. 2000. *National educational technology standards for students—Connecting curriculum and technology.* Retrieved November 1, 2002, cnets.iste.org/index.shtml.

Jackson, P. W. 1968. *Life in classrooms.* New York: Holt, Rinehart & Winston.

Jackson, P. W. (Ed.). 1992. *Handbook of research on curriculum.* New York: Macmillan.

Johnson, M. 1967. Definitions and models in curriculum theory. *Educational Theory, 17,* 127–140.

Johnson, M. 1977. *Intentionality in education.* Albany, NY: Center for Curriculum Research and Services.

John-Steiner, V. 1972. Styles of learning; Styles of teaching. In V. John-Steiner, C. Cazden, & D. Hynes (Eds.), *The functions of language in the classroom.* New York: Teachers College Press.

Johnston, P. H. 1987. Assessing the process and the process of assessment in the language arts. In J. Squire (Ed.), *The dynamics of language learning: Research in reading and English* (pp. 335–357). Urbana, IL: National Conference on Research in English/ERIC Clearinghouse on Reading and Communication Skills.

Johnston, P. H. 1992. *Constructive evaluation of literate activity.* New York: Longman.

Jones, R. M. 1972. *Fantasy and feeling in education.* New York: Penguin.

Joyce, B., & Weil, M. 1986. *Models of teaching* (3rd ed.). Englewood Cliffs, NJ: Prentice-Hall.

Jung, S. M. 1972. *Individually prescribed instruction—Mathematics (IPI—math).* Product Report no. 17. Palo Alto, CA: American Institutes for Research in the Behavioral Sciences.

Kallos, D. 1973. *On educational scientific research.* Lund, Sweden: University of Lund, Institute of Education.

Keddie, N., 1971. Classroom Knowledge. In Michael F. D. Young, (Ed) Knowledge and Control. New York: Collier-Macmillan.

Keil, F. 1981. Constraints on knowledge and cognitive development. *Psychological Review, 88*(2), 197–227.

Keller, F. S. 1968. "Goodby teacher . . ." *Journal of Applied Behavioral Analysis, 1,* 79-89.

Kesidou, S., & Roseman, J. E. 2002. How well do middle school science programs measure up? Findings from Project 2061's curriculum review. *Journal of Research in Science Teaching, 39,* 522–549.

Kim, Y., Berger, B. J., & Kratochvil, D. W. 1972. *Distar instructional system.* Product Development Report no. 14. Palo Alto, CA: American Institutes for Research in the Behavioral Sciences.

King, A. R., & Brownell, J. A. 1966. *The curriculum and the disciplines of knowledge.* New York: Wiley.

Kohlberg, L. 1971. States of moral development as a basis for moral education. In C. M. Beck, B. S. Crittenden, & E. V. Sullivan (Eds.), *Moral education: Interdisciplinary approaches.* New York: Newman.

Kohn, A. 1999. *The schools our children deserve.* Boston, MA: Houghton Mifflin Company.

Krathwohl, D. R. (Ed.). 1964. *Taxonomy of educational objectives, Handbook 2: Affective domain.* New York: David McKay.

Kuhn, T. S. 1970. *The structure of scientific revolutions* (2nd ed.). Chicago: University of Chicago Press.

Labov, W. 1973. *Sociolinguistic patterns.* Philadelphia: University of Pennsylvania Press.

Lareau, A. 1989. *Home advantage: Social class and parental intervention in elementary education.* London: Falmer.

Larkin, J. H. 1981. Enriching formal knowledge: A model for learning to solve textbook physics problems. In J. R. Anderson (Ed.), *Cognitive skills and their acquisition.* Hillsdale, NJ: Lawrence Erlbaum.

Lave, J. 1988. *Cognition in practice: Mind, mathematics, and culture in everyday life.* New York: Cambridge University Press.

Lee, C. C. 1985. An investigation of psychosocial variables related to academic success for rural black adolescents. *Journal of negro education, 53,* 424–434.

Leese, J., Frasure, K., & Johnson, M., Jr. 1961. *The teacher in curriculum making.* New York: Harper & Brothers.

Lightfoot, S. L. 1983. *The good high school.* New York: Basic Books.

Lindvall, C. M., & Cox, R. C. 1970. *Evaluation as a tool in curriculum development: The IPI evaluation program.* AERA monograph series on Curriculum Evaluation, vol. 5. Chicago: Rand McNally.

Locke, J. 1913. *Educational writings.* J. W. Adamson (Ed.). New York: Macmillan.

Lundgren, U. 1972. *Frame factors and the teaching process.* Stockholm: Almgrist & Wiksell.

Madaus, G. F., & Kellaghan. T. 1992. Curriculum evaluation and assessment. In P. W. Jackson (Ed.), *Handbook of research on curriculum.* New York, NY: Macmillan Publishing Company.

Mager, R. F. 1962. *Preparing instructional objectives.* Belmont, CA: Fearon.

Maslow, A. H. 1959. *New knowledge in human values.* New York: Harper.

McKinney, L., & Westbury, I. 1975. Stability and change: The public schools of Gary, Indiana, 1940–70. In W. A. Reid & D. F. Walker (Eds.), *Case studies in curriculum change.* London: Routledge & Kegan Paul.

Meier, K. J., J. J. Stewart, and R. E. England, 1990, Race, class and education: The politics of second generation discrimination (LA Folette Public Policy Series). Madison: University of Wisconsin Press.

Mercado, C., & Moll, L. C. 1997. The study of funds of knowledge. *CENTRO, Journal of the Center for Puerto Rican Studies,* 9, 26-42.

Mercer, J. R. 1968. Labeling the mentally retarded. In E. Rubington & M. S. Weinberg (Compilers), *Deviance: The interactionist perspective.* New York: Macmillan.

Meriam, L. 1928. *The problem of indian administration.* Baltimore, MD: The Johns Hopkins Press.

Metfessel, N. S., & Michael, W. B. 1967. A paradigm involving multiple criterion measures for the evaluation of the effectiveness of school programs. *Educational and Psychological Measurement, 27,* 931–943.

Mitchell, R. 1992. *Testing for learning: How new approaches to evaluation can improve American schools.* New York: Free Press.

Moll, L.C., & Gonzalez N. 1997. Teachers as social scientists. In P. M Hall (Ed.). *Race, ethnicity and multiculturalism.* New York, NY: Garland.

Moll, L. C., & Ruiz, R. 2002. The schooling of Latino children. In M. M. Suarez-Orozco & M. M. Paez (Eds.), *Latinos remaking america.* Cambridge, MA: David Rockefeller Center for Latin American Studies, Harvard University and the University of California Press.

National Assessment of Educational Progress. 1983. *The third national mathematics assessment: Results, trends, and issues.* Report no. 13–MA–01. Denver, CO: Education Commission of the States.

National Center for Education Statistics. 2002. *Internet access in U.S. public schools and classrooms: 1994 - 2001.* Retrieved December 11, 2002, *nces.ed.gov/pubs2002/internet/.*

National Commission on Excellence in Education. 1983. *A nation at risk: The imperative for educational reform.* Washington, DC: U.S. Government Printing Office.

National Commission on Excellence in Education. 1983. *A nation at risk: The imperative for educational reform : A report to the nation and the Secretary of Education, United States Department of Education.* Washington, D.C.: The Commission.

National Council for the Social Studies. 1975. The MACOS question. *Social Education,* 39(7), 446.

National Council for the Social Studies. 1994. *Expectations of excellence: Curriculum standards for social studies.* Silver Spring, Maryland: National Council for the Social Studies.

National Council of Teachers of English & the International Reading Association. 1996. *Standards for the English language arts.* Urbana, IL: National Council of Teachers of English.

National Council of Teachers of Mathematics. 2000. *Principles and standards for school mathematics.* Reston, VA: National Council of Teachers of Mathematics.

National Education Association. 1918. *Cardinal principles of secondary education.* Commission on the Reorganization of Secondary Education. Washington, DC: U.S. Government Printing Office.

National Research Council. 1996. *National science education standards*. Washington, DC.: National Academy Press.

Newman, H., & Van Moorlehem, T. 1998, January 19 - 21. Testing MEAP: A Free Press special report. *The Detroit Free Press*.

New York State Education Department. 1999. *Resource guide with core curriculum*. Albany, NY: The State Education Department.

Nelkin, D. 1982. *The creation controversy: Science or scripture in the schools*. New York: W. W. Norton.

Nicholson, T. 1984. *The process of reading*. Sydney, Australia: Horwitz-Graham.

Nieto, S. 1996. *Affirming diversity: The sociopolitical context of multicultural education* (2nd ed.). White Plains, NY: Longman.

Noddings, N. 1992. Gender and the curriculum. In P. W. Jackson (Ed.), *Handbook of research on curriculum*. New York, NY: Macmillan Publishing Company.

Novak, J. D., & Gowin, D. B. 1984. *Learning how to learn*. Cambridge, UK: Cambridge University Press.

Oakes, J. 1985. *Keeping track: How schools structure inequality*. New Haven, CT: Yale University Press.

Oakes, J., Gamoran, A., & Page, R. 1992. Curriculum differentiation: Opportunities, outcomes, and meanings. In P. W. Jackson (Ed.), *Handbook of research on curriculum*. New York, NY: Macmillan Publishing Company.

Oakes, J., and M. Lipton, 2001, Teaching to change the world. New York: McGraw-Hill.

Osborne, R., & Freyberg, P. 1985. *Learning in science: The implications of children's science*. Portsmouth, NH: Heinemann.

Owens, T. R. 1977. FY 77 Final evaluation report of the NWREL experience-based career education program. Mimeographed. Portland, OR: Northwest Regional Educational Laboratory, Education and Work Program.

Paris, S. G., & Jacobs, J. 1984. The benefits of informed instruction for children's reading awareness and comprehension skills. *Child Development, 55,* 2083–2093.

Pausch, R. 2002. A curmudgeon's vision for technology in education. In *Visions 2020: Transforming Education and Training Through Advanced Technologies*. Washington: United States Department of Commerce.

Perry, I. 1988. A black student's reflection on public and private schools. *Harvard Educational Review,* 58, 332–336.

Phenix, P. 1964. *Realms of meaning*. New York: McGraw-Hill.

Phillips, D. C., & Kelly, M. E. 1978. Hierarchical theories of development in education and psychology. *Harvard Educational Review, 45,* 351–375.

Piaget, J. 1929. *The child's conception of the world*. London: Routledge & Kegan Paul. Reprinted in 1960 by Littlefield, Adams, Totowa, NJ.

Pinnell, G. S. 1989. Reading recovery: Helping at-risk children learn to read. *Elementary School Journal, 90,* 161–183.

Pinnell, G. S., DeFord, D. E., & Lyons, C. A. 1989. *Reading recovery: Early intervention for at-risk first graders*. ERS monograph. Arlington, VA: Educational Research Service.

Polanyi, M. 1966. *The tacit dimension*. Garden City, NY: Doubleday.

Popham, W. J., & Baker, E. L. 1970. *Systematic instruction*. Englewood Cliffs, NJ: Prentice-Hall.

Popkewitz, T., Tabachnick, R., & Wehlage, G. 1982. *The myth of educational reform*. Madison: University of Wisconsin Press.

Popper, K. 1959. *The logic of scientific discovery*. New York: Science Editions.

Posner, G. J. 1979. Tools for curriculum research and development: Potential contributions of cognitive science. *Curriculum Inquiry, 8*(4), 311–340.

Posner, G. J. 1989. Making sense of diversity: The current state of curriculum research. *Journal of Curriculum and Supervision, 4*(4), 340–361.

Posner, G. J. 1993. *Field experience* (3rd ed.). New York: Longman.

Posner, G. J., & Gertzog, W. A. 1982. The clinical interview and the measurement of conceptual change. *Science Education, 66*(2), 195–209.

Posner, G. J., & Rudnitsky, A. N. 1994. *Course design: A guide to curriculum development for teachers* (4th ed.). New York: Longman.

Powell, A., Farrar, E., & Cohen, D. 1985. *The shopping mall high school.* Boston: Houghton Mifflin.

Provus, M. M. 1971. *Discrepancy evaluation for educational program improvement and assessment.* Berkeley, CA: McCutchan.

Puckett, J. L. 1989 Who wrote *Foxfire?*: A consideration of ethnohistorical method. *Journal of Research and Development in Education, 22* (3), 71–78.

Purkey, S. C., & Smith, M. S. 1983. Effective schools: A review. *The Elementary School Journal, 83*(4), 427–452.

Purves, A. 1971. Evaluation of learning literature. B. S. Bloom, J. T. Hastings, & G. F. Madaus (Eds.), *Handbook on formative and summative evaluation of student learning.* New York: McGraw-Hill.

Purves, A. 1975. The thought-fox and curriculum building. In J. Schaffarzick & D. H. Hampson (Eds.), *Strategies for curriculum development.* Berkeley, CA: McCutchan.

Random House. (1984). *Random House dictionary of the English language,* rev. ed. Jess Stein (Ed.). New York: Random House.

Ravitch, D. 1985. *The schools we deserve: Reflections on the education crisis in our lives.* New York: Basic Books.

Resnick, L. B. 1975. Science and the art of curriculum design. In J. Schaffarzick & D. H. Hampson (Eds.), *Strategies for curriculum development* (pp. 35–68). Berkeley, CA: McCutchan.

Resnick, L. B. 1976. Task analysis in instructional design: Some cases from mathematics. In D. Klahr (Ed.), *Cognition and instruction* (pp. 51–80). Hillsdale, NJ: Lawrence Erlbaum.

Resnick, L. B. 1983. Mathematics and science learning: A new conception. *Science, 29,* 177–178.

Resnick, L. B., & Klopfer, L. E. (Eds.). 1989. *Toward the thinking curriculum: Current cognitive research.* 1989 Yearbook of the Association for Supervision and Curriculum Development. Alexandria, VA: Association for Supervision and Curriculum Development.

Rickover, H. 1959. *Education and freedom.* New York: E. P. Dutton.

Rogers, C. R. 1942. *Counseling and psychotherapy.* Boston: Houghton Mifflin.

Rosenshine, B. 1983. Teaching functions in instructional programs. *The Elementary School Journal, 83,* 335–351.

Rosenshine, B., & Stevens, R. 1986. Teaching functions. In M. C. Wittrock (Ed.), *Handbook on research in teaching* (3rd ed.). New York: Macmillan.

Rousseau, J. J. 1962. Emile. In W. Boyd (Ed.), *The Emile of Jean Jacques Rousseau.* New York: Teachers College Press, Columbia University.

Ryle, G. 1949. *The concept of mind.* New York: Barnes & Noble.

Sax, G. 1974. Standardized tests in evaluation. In J. Popham (Ed.), *Evaluation in education.* Berkeley, CA: McCutchan.

Schaffarzick, J., & Hampson, D. H. (Eds.). (1975). *Strategies for curriculum development.* Berkeley, CA: McCutchan.

Scheffler, I. 1965. *The conditions of knowledge.* Chicago: Scott, Foresman.

Schmidt, W. H. 2001. *Why schools matter : A cross-national comparison of curriculum and learning.* San Francisco, Calif.: Jossey-Bass.

Schmidt, W. H., McKnight, C. C., & Raizen, S. A. 1997. *A splintered vision: An investigation of U.S. science and mathematics education*: Kluwer.

Schubert, W. H. 1986. *Curriculum: Perspective, paradigm and possibility.* New York: Macmillan.

Schwab, J. J. 1962. The concept of the structure of a discipline. *Educational Record, 43,* 197–205.

Schwab, J. J. 1964. Structure of disciplines: Meanings and significances. In G. W. Ford & L. Pugno (Eds.), *The structure of knowledge and the curriculum.* Chicago: Rand McNally.

Schwab, J. J. 1969. The practical: A language for curriculum. *School Review, 78,* 1–23.

Schwab, J. J. 1970. *The practical: A language for curriculum.* Washington, DC: National Education Association. (Revised and expanded version of Schwab, 1969.)

Schwab, J. J. 1971. The practical: Arts of eclectic. *School Review, 79,* 493–542.

Schwab, J. J. 1973. The practical 3: Translation into curriculum. *School Review, 79,* 501–522.

Scriven, M. 1967. The methodology of evaluation. In R. W. Tyler, R. M. Gagne, & M. Scriven (Eds.), *Perspectives of curriculum evaluation* (pp. 39–83). AERA Monograph Series on Curriculum Evaluation, no. 1. Chicago: Rand McNally.

Sedlak, M. W., Wheeler, C. W., Pullin, D. C., & Cusick, P. A. 1986. *Selling students short.* New York: Teachers College Press.

Senesh, L. 1973. *Our working world: New paths in social science curriculum design.* Chicago: Science Research Associates.

Shavelson, R. J. 1983. Review of research on teachers' pedagogical judgments, plans and decisions. *The Elementary School Journal, 83*(4), 392–413.

Shen, I. 1989. The classroom and the wider culture: Identity as a key to learning English composition. *College composition and communication, 10,* 459–472.

Shively, J. E., & Watts, R. 1977. Final evaluation report on 1976–77 implementation sites. Mimeographed. Charleston, WV: Experiential Education Division, Appalachia Educational Laboratory.

Shuell, T. J. 1986. Cognitive conceptions of learning. *Review of Educational Research, 56,* 411–436.

Shulman, L. S. 1986. Those who understand: Knowledge growth in teaching. *Educational Researcher, 15,* 4–14.

Shulman, L. S., & Keislar, E. R. (Eds.). (1966). *Learning by discovery: A critical appraisal.* Chicago: Rand McNally.

Sirotnik, K. A. 1974. Introduction to matrix sampling for the practitioner. In W. J. Popham (Ed.), *Evaluation in education.* Berkeley, CA: McCutchan.

Sizer, T. R. 1973. *Places for learning, places for joy: Speculations on American school reform.* Cambridge, MA: Harvard University Press.

Sizer, T. R. 1985. *Horace's compromise.* Boston: Houghton Mifflin.

Sleeter, C. E., & Grant, C. 1988. *Making choices for multicultural education: Five approaches to race, class, and gender.* Columbus, Ohio: Merrill Publishing Company.

Skinner, B. F. 1968. *The technology of teaching.* Englewood Cliffs, NJ: Prentice-Hall.

Smith, E., & Sendelbach, N. 1982. The programme, the plans, and the activities of the classroom: The demands of activity-based science. In J. Olson (Ed.), *Innovation in the science curriculum.* New York: Nichols.

Sockett, H. 1976. Approaches to curriculum planning I. In *Rationality and artistry,* Units 16, 17, and 18 of E203, Curriculum Design and Development, an Educational Studies course offered by the Open University. London: Open University Press.

Spencer, H. 1861. *Education: Intellectual, moral, and physical.* New York: Appleton.

Stake, R. E. 1967. The countenance of educational evaluation. *Teachers College Record, 68*(7), 523–540.

Sternberg, R. J. 1985. *Beyond IQ: A triarchic theory of human intelligence.* New York: Cambridge University Press.

Stodolsky, S. S. 1988. *The subject matters: Classroom activity in math and social studies.* Chicago: University of Chicago Press.

Stratemeyer, F. B., Forkner, H. L., McKim, M. G., & Passow, A. H. 1957. *Developing a curriculum for modern living.* New York: Columbia University, Teachers College, Bureau of Publications.

Strickland, D. S., & Ascher. C. 1992. Low-income African-American children and public schooling. In P. W. Jackson (Ed.), *Handbook of research on curriculum.* New York, NY: Macmillan Publishing Company.

Strike, K. A. 1974. The expressive potential of behavioral language. *American Educational Research Journal, 11,* 103–120.

Strike, K. A., & Posner, G. J. 1976. Epistemological perspectives on conceptions of curriculum organization and learning. *Review of Research in Education,* 4. Itasca, IL: F. E. Peacock.

Strike, K. A., & Posner, G. J. 1983. Types of synthesis and their criteria. In S. A. Ward & L. J. Reed (Eds.), *Knowledge structure and use: Implications for synthesis and interpretation.* Philadelphia, PA: Temple University Press.

Stufflebeam, D. L. 1971. *Educational evaluation and decision making.* Itasca, IL: F. E. Peacock.

Sutton, C. T., & Broken Nose, M. A. 1996. American Indian families: An overview. In McGoldrick, M., J. Giordano, & J. K. Pearce (Eds.), *Ethnicity and family therapy* (2nd ed). New York, NY: Guilford.

Taba, H. 1962. *Curriculum development: Theory and practice.* New York: Harcourt, Brace & World.

Taba, H. 1967. *Teacher's handbook for elementary social studies.* Reading, MA: Addison-Wesley.

Taber, J. I., Glaser, R., & Schaefer, H. H. 1967. *Learning and programmed instruction.* Reading, MA: Addison-Wesley.

Tatum, B. D. 1999. *"Why are all the black kids sitting together in the cafeteria?" and other conversations about race.* New York, NY: Basic Books.

Tharp, R., & Gillmore, R. 1988. *Rousing minds to life; Teaching learning and schooling in social context.* Cambridge: Cambridge University Press.

Thorndike, R. L., & Hagen, E. P. 1969. *Measurement and evaluation in psychology and education* (4th ed.). New York: Wiley.

Tikunoff, W. J., & Ward, B. A. 1983. Collaborative research on teaching. *The Elementary School Journal, 83* (4), 453–468.

Torrance, E. P. 1965. *Gifted children in the classroom.* New York: Macmillan.

Torres, G., & Hair, P. D. 2002. The Texas test case: Integrating America's colleges." *The chronicle of higher education,* 4, B20.

Tyler, R. 1942. General statement on evaluation. *Journal of Educational Research, 35,* 492–501.

Tyler, R. 1949. *Basic principles of curriculum and instruction.* Chicago: University of Chicago Press.

U.S. Census Bureau. 1999. Educational attainment, by race, Hispanic origin, and sex: 1960-1998. 264. U.S. *Census Bureau, Statistical Abstract of the United States.* Washington, D.C.: Department of Commerce, Bureau of the Census.

U. S. Census Bureau. October, 2000. Resident population estimates of the U.S. by race and Hispanic origin. Cited in M. M Suarez-Orozco & M. M. Paez, *Latinos remaking america.* (Cambridge, MA: David Rockefeller Center for Latin American Studies, Harvard University and the University of California Press), 2002, p. 2.

U.S. Census Bureau. October 2000. Cited in C. Ness, & R. Kim. Census reveals fast-growing diversity in U.S. *San Francisco Chronicle.* 13 March 2001, sec A.1.

Vygotsky, L. S. 1962. *Thought and language.* Translated and edited by E. Hanfmann & G. Vakar. Cambridge, MA: MIT Press.

Vygotsky, L. S. 1978. *Mind in society: The development of higher psychological processes.* Translated and edited by M. Cole, V. John-Steiner, S. Scribner, & E. Souberman. Cambridge, MA: Harvard University Press.

Wagner, T. 1998. Change as collaborative inquiry: A constructivist methodology for reinventing schools. *Phi Delta Kappan, 80,* 378–383.

Walker, D. 1971. A naturalistic model of curriculum development. *School Review, 80,* 51–69.

Walker, D. 1990. *Fundamentals of curriculum.* New York: Harcourt Brace Jovanovich.

Walker, D. F., & Schaffarzick, J. 1974. Comparing curricula. *Review of Educational Research, 44,* 83–111.

Watkins, R. W., & Corder, R. 1977. *Student outcomes and participant opinions in experience-based career education schools.* Berkeley, CA: Educational Testing Service.

Wehlage, G. G., Rutter, R. A., Smith, G.A., Lesko, N., & Fernandez, R. R. 1989. *Reducing the risk: Schools as communities of support.* New York: Falmer.

Welch, W. W., & Walberg, H. J. 1972. A national experiment in curriculum evaluation. *American Educational Research Journal, 9,* 373–383.

Westbury, I. 1973. Conventional classrooms, "open" classrooms and the technology of teaching. *Journal of Curriculum Studies, 5,* 99–121.

Whitehead, A. N. 1929. *The aims of education and other essays.* New York: Macmillan.

Wiggins, G. 1989a. Teaching to the (authentic) test. *Educational Leadership, 46*(7): 41–47.

Wiggins, G. 1989b. A true test: Toward more authentic and equitable assessment. *Phi Delta Kappan, 70*(9): 703–713.

Wigginton, E. 1975a. *Moments: The Foxfire experience.* Washington, DC: Institutional Development and Economic Affairs Service and the Foxfire Fund.

Wigginton, E. 1975b. Introduction. In E. Wigginton, *Foxfire 6* (pp. 6–24). Garden City, NY: Anchor/Doubleday.

Wigginton, E. 1985. *Sometimes a shining moment: The Foxfire experience.* Garden City, NY: Anchor/Doubleday.

Wigginton, E. 1989. Foxfire grows up. *Harvard Educational Review, 59*(1), 24–49.

Windschitl, M. 1999. The challenges of sustaining a constructivist culture. *Phi Delta Kappan, 80,* 751–755.

Willis, G. (Ed.). 1978. *Qualitative evaluation: Concepts and cases in curriculum criticism.* Berkeley, CA: McCutchan.

Wolcott, H. F. 1977. *Teachers vs. technocrats.* Eugene, OR: University of Oregon, Center for Educational Policy and Management.

Worthen, B. R., & Sanders, J. R. 1973. *Educational evaluation: Theory and practice.* Worthington, OH: C. A. Jones.

Young, M. F. D. (Ed.). 1971. *Knowledge and control: New directions for the sociology of education.* London: Collier-Macmillan.

Zacharias, J. R., & White, S. 1964. The requirements for major curriculum revision. R. W. Heath (Ed.), *The new curricula.* New York: Harper & Row.

Zais, R. S. 1976. *Curriculum: Principles and foundations.* New York: Harper & Row.

Credit

Name Index

McKinney, L., 195, 199, 288
McKnight, C. C., 4, 291
McLaughlin, M. W., 228, 282
Meier, K.J., 157
Mercado, C., 289
Mercer, J. R., 271, 289
Meriam, L., 208, 289
Metfessel, N. S., 289
Meyer, L. M., 90, 285
Michael, W. B., 289
Michell, R., 266, 289
Moll, L. C., 210, 289
Moss, E., 286

NAEP (National Assessment of Educational
   Progress), 259, 289
Namowitz, S. N., 138
National Assessment of Educational Progress
   (NAEP), 259, 289
National Center for Education Statistics, 95,
   211, 289
National Commission on Excellence in Educa-
   tion (NCEE), 37–39, 194, 289
National Council for the Social Studies (NCSS),
   91–91, 224, 289
National Council of Teachers of English
   (NCTE), 10, 92, 93
National Council of Teachers of Mathematics
   (NCTM), 92, 93, 94–95, 196, 289
National Education Association (NEA), 51,
   144, 289
National Research Council, 93, 94, 196, 289
National Science Foundation (NSF), 28, 55, 56,
   174, 225
NCEE (National Commission on Excellence in
   Education), 37–39, 194, 289
NCSS (National Council for the Social Studies),
   91–91, 224, 289
NCTE (National Council of Teachers of
   English), 10, 92, 93
NCTM (National Council of Teachers of
   Mathematics), 92, 93, 94–95, 196, 289
NEA (National Education Association), 51,
   144, 289
Nelkin, D., 226, 289
Newman, F. M., 264, 282
Newman, H., 289
Newton, I., 58, 81
New York State Education Department, 8, 211,
   268, 289
Nicholson, T., 264, 289
Nieto, S., 209–210, 289
Noddings, N., 290

Novak, J. D., 290
NSF (National Science Foundation), 28, 55, 56,
   174, 225

Oakes, J., 89, 157, 158, 159, 209, 244, 290
Oldham, V., 117, 285
Osborne, R., 117, 118, 290
Owens, T. R., 253, 290

Page, R., 290
Paris, S. G., 264, 290
Passow, A. H., 144, 292
Pausch, R., 95, 290
Pearson Educational Technologies, 247
Perrucci, R., 154
Perry, I., 209, 290
Pestolozzi, J. H., 49
Phenix, P., 290
Phillips, D. C., 290
Physical Science Study Committee (PSSC), 55
Piaget, J., 61, 62, 131, 290
Pinnell, G. S., 118, 119, 120, 121, 284, 290
Plato, 60–61
Polanyi, M., 81, 290
Pomfret, A., 220, 285
Ponder, G. A., 198, 199, 284
Popham, W. J., 16, 106, 110, 290
Popkewitz, T., 280, 290
Popper, K., 164, 165, 166, 290
Posner, G. J., 16, 81, 142, 164, 239, 250, 264,
   290, 293
Powell, A., 13, 290
Provus, M. M., 290
Puckett, J. L., 291
Pullin, D. C., 13, 292
Purkey, S. C., 200, 291
Purpel, D., 13, 280, 286
Purves, A., 40, 83, 291

Raizen, S. A., 4, 291
Random House, 128, 291
Ravitch, D., 46, 291
Resnick, L. B., 63, 101, 113–114, 114, 116, 142, 291
Richter, M. N., Jr., 16, 77, 286
Rickover, H., 39, 53, 291
Roeber, E., 283
Rogers, C. R., 264, 291
Roseman, J. E., 288
Rosenshine, B., 142, 291
Rousseau, J. J., 48–49, 291
Rudnitsky, A. N., 16, 81, 250, 290

Subject Index